The Protestant Establishment

The Protestant Establishment

ARISTOCRACY & CASTE IN AMERICA

by E. Digby Baltzell

SECKER & WARBURG / LONDON

*The author wishes to thank the following for permission to reprint material
included in this volume:*

HARPER'S MAGAZINE—for selection based on an article entitled "By Any
Other Name," *Harper's*, March 1955.

THE MACMILLAN COMPANY, THE MACMILLAN COMPANY OF
CANADA, LTD., and MRS. W. B. YEATS—for four lines from "The
Second Coming," from the COLLECTED POEMS of William Butler
Yeats. Copyright, 1924, by The Macmillan Company. Renewed 1952 by
Bertha Georgie Yeats.

THE HAROLD MATSON CO., INC.—for selection from "The Democrats'
Golden Girl" by Inez Robb, from the *Saturday Evening Post*, October 22,
1960. © Curtis Publishing Company.

NEWSWEEK—for selection from the article "Zeta Beta Kaput?," *Newsweek*
(Vol. LVII No. 13, March 27, 1961) p. 82.

SAN FRANCISCO CHRONICLE—for selection from Lucius Beebe's column, *San Francisco Chronicle*, August 1, 1960.

TIME—for selection from the article "Grosse Pointe's Cross Points" from
Time, April 25, 1960. Copyright Time Inc., 1960.

Manufactured in the United States of America

FIRST PUBLISHED IN ENGLAND 1965 BY
MARTIN SECKER & WARBURG LIMITED
14 CARLISLE STREET, SOHO SQUARE, W.1

PRINTED IN ENGLAND BY
FLETCHER & SON LTD, NORWICH

This book is dedicated to
all my undergraduate friends
at the University of Pennsylvania,
many of them grandsons of immigrants
to the urban frontier,
who, in spite of their possessing
too many Jaguars and mink-coated mothers,
have constantly renewed my faith
in the American Dream
of unlimited opportunity

The French nobility, after having lost its ancient political rights, and ceased more than any other country of feudal Europe to govern and guide the nation, had, nevertheless, not only preserved, but considerably enlarged its pecuniary immunities, and the advantages which the members of this body personally possessed; while it had become a subordinate class it still remained a privileged and closed body, less and less an aristocracy, as I have said elsewhere, but more and more a caste . . .

Alexis de Tocqueville

Preface

On a fine May morning in 1910, representatives of some seventy
nations, including nine kings, five heirs apparent, forty other imperial highnesses, seven queens and Theodore Roosevelt of the
United States, the greatest assemblage of rank and royalty the world
had ever seen, rode through the streets of London in the funeral
cortege of Edward VII, who has often been called the "Uncle of
Europe." Theodore Roosevelt, without titled rank and dressed in
civilian clothes, was hardly pleased to be walking at the very end of
the long procession of titled dignitaries dressed in their resplendent
uniforms. But his friend and one of the dead king's nephews,

Wilhelm II of Imperial Germany, mounted on a white charger and dressed in the scarlet uniform of a British field marshal, was proud to be riding at the right hand of the new king. He was also pleased to be among his relatives in a city where, for the present at least, he was quite popular. Big Ben tolled nine in the morning as the royal procession, followed by all the formal pomp of England, left the palace grounds. But on Clio's clock it was nearer sunset, for the sun of white Western world empire was symbolically setting in a dying blaze of splendor never to rise again.

Within a decade, millions of men would have laid down their lives to stem the tide of the Kaiser's armies. And the series of wars and revolutions which began on the fields of Flanders and ended with our dropping of the Bomb on Hiroshima marked the end of the Pax Britannica and the transfer of Western leadership to the United States. Whereas generations of British gentlemen had proudly, and sometimes smugly, assumed it their natural right and duty to rule the world, there is something uncharacteristic in America's assuming such leadership. But, then, we Americans have been trained to succeed rather than to lead, and all too many of us would gladly forgo the need for greatness which has been so suddenly thrust upon us.

As far as our relations with the rest of the world are concerned, we are faced with infinitely more complex problems than were our British predecessors. In the first place, we live in a crowded world community where global war and genocide are ever present, but unthinkable, possibilities. At the same time, the authority of the white race, largely built up by the Anglo-Saxon gentlemen of England between the ages of Francis Drake and Benjamin Disraeli, is now being called into question around the world. The optimistic and imperialistic ideology of the white man's burden, materially based in the Anglo-American lead in the Industrial Revolution, has now turned into a nightmare, frighteningly fed by the demon dreams of the racists in our midst. Although the decline of established authority in the modern world community is most obviously reflected in the polarization of power between the defenders of democratic capitalism on the one hand and of totalitarian communism on the other, there is, I think, a latent but far greater danger that moral authority may degenerate into complete chaos and violence if ever the world should become divided into two opposing racial camps. In other words, the central question in the second half of this century may well be whether the white Western world, led by America, will be able to retain its traditional freedoms in an overpopulated world and, at the same time, succeed in sharing the fruits of an industrial-scientific civilization with the rising races which make up the rest of mankind. In this process, white Western man must, above all, learn to share the leadership of some sort of new world community with his nonwhite peers, many of them now educated in the West, before a stable world establishment with moral authority can be re-created.

It is, in this connection, indeed appropriate that the United Nations, a struggling, still impotent, but ever hopeful attempt at creating some kind of world authority, should be located in New York City. For New York is racially and ethnically the most heterogeneous city in the world. Throughout history, of course, the elite of all nations and races have walked the streets of the great cosmopolitan centers; yet New York is historically unique in that its population is a heterogeneous one, as it were, from top to bottom. Even today its citizenry, almost half of whom are foreign-born or the children of the foreign-born, includes more Negroes than most cities in Africa, a greater concentration of Jews than at any other time or place in their long history, more Puerto Ricans than any other city outside of San Juan, more persons of Italian descent than most cities in Italy, and more sons of Ireland than Dublin. Finally, at the top of the pyramid of wealth and social prestige in the city, there is a White–Anglo-Saxon–Protestant establishment which, as this book will show, has been gradually losing its power and authority in the course of the twentieth century. New York, in short, mirrors in microcosm the problems of the world.

All over the world the people, if not always their leaders, look to

America for leadership. But America's continuing authority in the world depends on our ability to solve the problem of authority here at home. The stability of authority in any community depends to a very great extent on the maintenance of a continuity of cultural traditions. There have always been, I suppose, two kinds of people, those who have been proud of their heritage and have wanted to share it with others, and those who have been jealous of their heritage and have tried to monopolize it for themselves. A crisis in moral authority has developed in modern America largely because of the White–Anglo-Saxon–Protestant establishment's unwillingness, or inability, to share and improve its upper-class traditions by continuously absorbing talented and distinguished members of minority groups into its privileged ranks. This book will be primarily concerned with the problem of exclusion and prejudice within the white community. I have focused on the problem of anti-Semitism largely because the present position of the Jews in this country best illustrates the nature of the conflict between the social forces of caste and aristocracy, which is my central theme. The Negroes in America are, of course, faced with equally important, and far more acute, problems, but their total situation—and the test of our moral conscience posed by it—is for the moment quite different from that of the Jews, and far too complex to be dealt with here.

Gentlemanly anti-Semitism in America has, I think, been closely related to the threatened security and authority of its old-stock upper class. The gradual decline of its authority has created a moral vacuum which, in turn, has led to the development of all sorts of conspiracy theories of history. Divisiveness, suspicion and the mistrust of our neighbors has been the result. Psychologically, it seems to be tragically true that one tends to turn against one's neighbors when unable to comprehend or cope with outside threats to one's personal security. Thus a father often comes home and beats his wife or children when he is acutally frustrated by the behavior of his boss or colleagues in the office. Similarly, the Germans under Hitler turned in their frustration on the Jews, many of whom were their relatives and friends. This program of systematic and scientific anti-Semitism was made possible by the decline of established authority after World War I in Germany, which allowed the Nazi demagogues to sell the people on a conspiracy theory of history. Similarly, if to a lesser degree as yet, with the decline of authority in America all too many educated people who should know better, from the days of the Liberty League crusades to the present, have come to be convinced that the country's real enemy is in Washington rather than in Moscow (or in themselves).

In this book I hope to contribute something toward an understanding of the causes and consequences of this tragic situation. My method consists of an historical analysis of the conflicting attitudes and values of the members of the old-stock upper class in this country in the years between the generations of Theodore Roosevelt and John F. Kennedy. It is my central thesis that in order for an upper class to maintain a continuity of power and authority, especially in an opportunitarian and mobile society such as ours, its membership must, in the long run, be representative of the composition of society as a whole. Thus Theodore Roosevelt's generation, which came to maturity at the close of the optimistic nineteenth century (which had its Indian summer in the Edwardian era), was authoritatively dominated by an old-stock upper class whose members were the business, cultural and intellectual leaders of a nation which was, at the higher levels of society at least, still overwhelmingly white, Anglo-Saxon and Protestant in origins and convictions.

Since Roosevelt's day, America has become, at all levels of society, the most ethnically and racially heterogeneous nation on earth. In response to this new heterogeneity, a dialectical struggle developed within the ranks of the White–Anglo-Saxon–Protestant establishment. On the one hand, the vast majority of old-stock patricians, following the caste ideals of the Old Regime in France, concentrated on success and the protection of their privileges at the expense of power and leadership; and the Republican Party, which had protected their interests since the Civil War, gradually lost authority in the land after 1929. On the other hand, a small but growing minority of old-stock aristocrats, following the Whig tradition in England, were willing to share their privileges with distinguished members of minority groups in order to maintain their traditional power and authority within the ranks of some sort of new and heterogeneous establishment; they first became Progressives under Theodore Roosevelt, eventually supported Woodrow Wilson, and finally joined, and often led, the Democratic Party during the Great Depression; and many of their sons were inspired by the aristocratic style of the New Frontier.

Following Tocqueville's classic analysis of the decline of authority in France, I have tried to show that an authoritative leadership structure will evolve in this country only when and if a new and representative upper class and establishment are created, whose members will then be able to *discriminate* on the basis of the distinguished accomplishments of individuals rather than *classifying* men categorically on the basis of their ethnic or racial origins.

Essentially this book, both in its method and in its theoretical point of view, is a continuation of another which I completed several years ago. The earlier book was a detailed analysis of how a national and associational upper class replaced the local and communal gentry in America between the close of the Civil War and 1940. It was largely, but by no means entirely, based on a detailed analysis of the social and economic history of the City of Philadelphia. It showed how successful merchants, businessmen and bankers, often of lowly origins and crude plutocratic values themselves, produced families whose members, in each successive generation, allied themselves through education, club membership and marriage with families of older wealth and thus served to perpetuate a continuity of upper-class values and authority. On the eve of the Second World War, a small community of Philadelphia families—predominantly of English and Welsh descent, Quaker-turned-Episcopal in religion, educated at private schools and colleges like Harvard, Yale or Princeton, residents of fashionable neighborhoods, members of exclusive clubs, and listed in the Social Register—authoritatively dominated the business and cultural life of Philadelphia, as their ancestors had done since Colonial days. I deliberately concluded my analysis of upper-class institutions with the year 1940, when a rather secure establishment of Anglo-Saxon–Protestant gentlemen still ran the city. Looking to the future, however, the book ended on the following note:

> One more question remains to be raised if it cannot be answered: What is the future function of a predominantly Anglo-Saxon and Protestant upper class in an ethnically and religiously heterogeneous democracy? In many ways, this is the most important question of all. As Joseph Patrick Kennedy, Boston millionaire and American Ambassador to the Court of St. James under Roosevelt, once put it: "How long does our family have to be here before we are called Americans rather than Irish-Americans?" As has been shown throughout this volume, the American upper class has been from the beginning open to new men of talent and power and their families. By the middle of the twentieth century, however, upper-class status appears to be limited primarily to families of colonial and northern European stock and Protestant affiliations. Glancing back to the turn of the century, when a flood tide of immigrants came to these shores from southern and eastern Europe, to say nothing of the Irish Catholics who came earlier, one wonders if this American democracy has not produced somewhat of a caste situation at the upper-class level. Or are the talented and powerful descendants of these newer immigrants going to be assimilated into some future upper class way of life and social organization?[1]

I had hoped someday to explore this question further. I am therefore indebted to the Falk Foundation for providing me with a grant-in-aid which stimulated my beginning to write an article on the subject during the Christmas vacation of 1960–61. One thing led to another, including the temporarily setting aside of a partially completed essay on the contrasting social theories of Alexis de

Tocqueville and Karl Marx, and the projected article grew into this book.

I should like to thank my friends—Lawrence Bloomgarden, S. M. Lipset, Morton Keller, Michael Lalli, William Knox, Jane Piper, Dennis Leon, Seymour Leventman, David Danzig, Harry Bash, Edwin Wolf II, and especially Nathan Glazer—for their generous reading of the manuscript in various stages of completion and for their helpful suggestions. Needless to say, any errors in fact or interpretation are entirely my own. Finally, in the words of Tocqueville, whose theories of leadership have been my constant guide, "I hope to have written this book without prejudice, but I do not pretend to have written it without passion."

Villanova, Pennsylvania
July 4, 1963

It still takes some time, even in an age which has just watched its first real murder on television, to translate a raw manuscript into the printed page of a book. Soon after I had completed the final, tedious revisions on this manuscript and sent it off to my publishers for what I thought was to be the last time, John Fitzgerald Kennedy was tragically killed. Death, I suppose, transforms admiration into reverence. Yet in this final revision of the text, I have resisted any temptations to alter its original tone and have limited myself to revising the tenses of verbs when they referred to the late President and the New Frontier which he so gallantly led.

As I sat, in a state of shock and sorrow, watching the President's funeral last Monday, my mind kept going back to the funeral of Edward VII, when a sorrowful yet confident royal establishment, still assuming it ruled the world, followed the dead king's favorite charger, Kildare, through the streets of London. I thought of how far the world had traveled since that gay and formal age. At the same time, I could not help feeling that Theodore Roosevelt would have been far prouder to have taken part in the procession which was now walking from the White House to St. Matthew's Cathedral, with all the majesty of democratic dignity, behind the nervous black charger, whose absent rider symbolized so well the leadership and hopes of a new world which was so desperately trying to be born in his generation. For surely faith and hope rank higher than confidence in the hierarchy of human virtues. Thus Theodore Roosevelt was a dreamer of dreams who dared to hope that America would, in the long run, conquer the values of caste and someday send a distinguished Catholic, and eventually a Jew, to the White House. Among other things, this funeral dramatized the fact that part of his hopes have now been realized. I have written this book with the hope that when the American establishment finally rejects the caste ideas of the country-club set in favor of the ideals once dramatized at Camelot, which inspired Woodrow Wilson, the two Roosevelts, and the late John Fitzgerald Kennedy, this whole dream will surely come to be.

Thanksgiving Day, 1963

Contents

Contents

The Protestant Establishment

> If we could first know where we are, and whither we are
> tending, we could better judge what to do, and how to do it.
>
> *Abraham Lincoln*

I

The Lincoln Family:
How American Aristocrats
Are Made

The idea of Equality, a vital part of the Declaration of Independence, lies at the very heart of the American Dream and has since become the basis of the various secular religions of our time. While the socialist faiths, on the one hand, have centered on the vision of equality of conditions in a classless society, our own best traditions have stressed equality of opportunity in a hierarchical and open-class, as opposed to a classless, society. Karl Marx well understood the strengths of the Anglo-Saxon version of democracy when he wrote, in *Das Kapital*, that "the more a ruling class is able to assimilate the most prominent men of the dominated classes, the more stable and dangerous its rule."

3

I have written this book because I believe that our traditions of mobility and equal opportunity, so dangerous to the Marxian dreams of revolution, are infinitely superior to the leveling ideals of socialism. But at the same time I am convinced that these traditions are being threatened in our time by the divisive forces of racial and ethnic prejudice. Anglo-Saxonism is a debilitating denial of our Anglo-Saxon traditions. When something of value is threatened in the present, we often do well to seek inspiration in the past. And the ideal of equality of opportunity has its most inspiring example in the legendary life of Abraham Lincoln.

The American Dream and Individual Opportunity

At the time of the Declaration of Independence, there was a captain of the Virginia militia living in Rockingham County named Abraham Lincoln. These Lincolns of Virginia had come down into the Shenandoah Valley from Berks County in Pennsylvania. They were descended from Samuel Lincoln of Hingham, England, who came to America and settled in Hingham, Massachusetts, in 1637. On the advice of his close friend Daniel Boone, Abraham Lincoln sold his farm in Virginia in 1782 and took his wife and five children out to the Kentucky frontier, where, several years later, he was killed by Indians. His son, Thomas Lincoln, was an unsuccessful and wandering farmer, casual laborer and wheelwright who in his mature life was barely able to write his name. In 1806 he married Nancy Hanks, the natural child of Lucy Hanks but of unknown paternity. Whatever her natural endowments, Nancy Hanks was "absolutely illiterate" and had throughout life associated with "lowly people." On a farm of stubborn ground and in a crude cabin of logs cut from nearby timber, in Hardin County, Kentucky, in 1809, Nancy bore Thomas Lincoln a son whom they named Abraham after his grandfather. Young Abraham grew up, as legendary heroes often do, in humble and unstable circumstances. His formal schooling was sporadic and amounted to less than one year in all. Yet he was an inveterate reader of the Bible and the few classics he was able to lay his hands on, such as *Pilgrim's Progress, Robinson Crusoe, Aesop's Fables,* and Weems' *Life of Washington.* He had been mainly a drifter when he came to New Salem, a small hamlet near Springfield, Illinois, at the age of twenty-one. But in New Salem, where he held a series of low-paying jobs, he followed politics closely, read widely, and constantly studied law and the rules of grammar. Lincoln had none of the frontier vices and was too shy for women's company, yet he was usually gregarious otherwise and a leader among the young men of the town. His wide popularity brought him a brief term in the state legislature, where he was a minority Whig and vigorous opponent of the Jacksonian Democrats.

After six picturesque and formative years in New Salem, Lincoln qualified for an attorney's license and moved to Springfield, arriving in 1837 on a borrowed horse, carrying all his worldly goods in two saddle bags. In spite of his poverty and his uncouth and extremely simple frontier manners, it was not long before he became part of the best local society. His first law partner was a member of a prominent local family, an excellent lawyer, and a leading member of the Whig Party. And, like many self-made men of ability and ambition, Lincoln was soon attracted to a visiting belle of distinguished Southern ancestry, Mary Todd, who had been educated at a "finishing school" where she learned the proper social graces and to speak French with some fluency. Her father had been a captain in the War of 1812, a state senator, and was at that time president of the Bank of Kentucky, in Lexington.

Lincoln and Mary Todd were finally married, after a harried and hesitating courtship (Mary's friends considered Lincoln to be her social inferior), in Springfield, in 1842—the Reverend Charles Dresser, in canonical robes, performing the ceremony of the Protestant Episcopal Church. In rooms over the Globe Tavern, where they boarded after their marriage, their first son, Robert Todd

Lincoln, was born the next year (Lincoln had three other sons, all of whom died before maturity).

Again like many self-made men, Lincoln was a conservative in politics. A staunch party man, he gradually rose to be one of the Whig leaders in Illinois. While he never won a political office as high as governor or senator, he did serve one term in Congress. As the brilliant social life in Washington was closed to him, he lost himself in hard work and relaxed with a small circle of friends whom he charmed with his tall tales and Rabelaisian wit.

Back in Springfield after his brief stay in Washington, Lincoln concentrated on the law and rose to be one of the leading members of the bar. Though the Lincoln legend has emphasized the human-interest stories of his defense of the little man in endless small litigations, he was far more than a country lawyer. It was his excellent handling of large corporate cases which brought him in contact with leading Eastern attorneys like Edwin M. Stanton, whose snobbishness he learned to handle. At the same time that he was establishing a solid legal reputation, Lincoln continued to cultivate a political following and even sought office. After his defeat in the senatorial campaign of 1858, he challenged his good friend Stephen A. Douglas to a series of debates on the slavery issue. These debates with an outstanding member of the Democratic Party brought Lincoln national attention as a possible Presidential candidate.

As a consequence of his own accomplishments and driving, if sometimes ambivalent, ambitions, and along with his advantageous marriage and influential circle of friends, Lincoln was now a member of a solid Middle Western establishment which centered in Springfield and Chicago. On the other hand, the leaders of the Eastern Seaboard establishment were hardly ready to accept him socially, even though they made him their choice for the Presidency after hearing the famous speech which he delivered at Cooper Union, on a snowy night in February, 1860. After the success of this speech, Lincoln eventually secured the Republican nomination and went on to lead the nation during the tragic Civil War. And his

6

The Lincoln Family

Emancipation Proclamation which officially began the still-unfinished struggle for racial equality in this country, as well as the legend of his rise from degenerate parentage and poverty to the Presidency, have combined to make him *the* authentic symbol of the democratic ideal of equality of opportunity, both here and around the world.

Aristocracy, Caste and a Theory of the Establishment

Fortunately for the stability of our political institutions, the liberal idealism of the Declaration has always been balanced by the more authoritative realism of the Constitution. Similarly, it is the central thesis of this book that no nation can long endure without both the liberal democratic and the authoritative aristocratic processes. As the terms democratic and aristocratic, as well as several other key concepts which will be used throughout this book, have been variously defined by different authors, I should like in the interest of clarity to define precisely how I shall use them here.

Democracy and the Open Elite

In the first place, I shall use the term democracy to refer to that process which assures that men of ability and ambition, regardless of background, are allowed to rise into the *elite*. The elite concept has no evaluative connotations such as the "best" but refers solely to those *individuals* who have succeeded in rising to the top positions in any society. The democratic process means then that the *elite is open* and is based on the American ideal of equality of opportunity.

Aristocracy and the Open Upper Class

By an aristocracy I mean (1) a *community of upper-class families* whose members are born to positions of high prestige and assured dignity because their ancestors have been leaders (elite members) for one generation or more; (2) that these

7

families are carriers of a set of traditional values which command authority because they represent the aspirations of both the elite and the rest of the population; and (3) that this class continue to justify its authority (a) by contributing its share of contemporary leaders and (b) by continuing to assimilate, in each generation, the families of new members of the elite. As with the elite concept, I do not conceive of the aristocracy as the "best" or the "fittest" in the sense of the term "natural aristocracy" as used by Jefferson. The aristocratic process means that the upper class is open.

The Establishment and Traditional Authority

When the conditions of aristocracy (and democracy) are met, upper-class values will carry authority both within the elite and the society as a whole. The upper class, in other words, will be a ruling class or, as I should prefer to say, its leaders will form an establishment. For an establishment is essentially traditional and authoritative and not coercive or authoritarian (as is often the case with a ruling class). In a free society, while an establishment will always be dominated by upper-class members, it also must be constantly rejuvenated by new members of the elite who are in the process of acquiring upper-class status.

Caste and the Closed Upper Class

When, in any society, there is an upper class which protects its privileges and prestige but does not continue (1) to contribute leadership or (2) to assimilate new elite members, primarily because of their racial or ethnic origins, I shall refer to the process of caste. If an upper class degenerates into a caste, moreover, the traditional authority of an establishment is in grave danger of disintegrating, while society becomes a field for careerists seeking success and affluence. The caste process is the very antithesis of the aristocratic process and inevitably, in the long run if not immediately, leads to the decline of authority and a crisis in leadership.

This theory of the establishment follows the insights of Alexis de Tocqueville who, in his classic analysis of the Old Regime and the French Revolution, showed how violent revolution came to France because the nobility degenerated into a caste and refused to absorb new men of power and affluence—the bourgeoisie. The British upper class, led by the Whig establishment, absorbed the new businessmen, avoided revolution, and remained a ruling aristocracy. The French nobility retained their privileges at the expense of power and authority, while the British shared their privileges precisely in order to rule. The British, in other words, were prepared to "stoop to conquer," as Tocqueville argued in the following brilliant passage:

Wherever the feudal system established itself on the continent of Europe it ended in caste; in England alone it returned to aristocracy. It is curious to note how the English nobles, pushed by their ambition, have known how, when it appeared necessary, to mingle on familiar terms with their inferiors. . . . *Most certainly the English aristocracy was by nature more haughty than that of France and less disposed to mingle on familiar terms with the lower classes, but it was reduced to do so by the necessities of its position. It was prepared to stoop to conquer.*[1]

On the whole, we in America have followed in the British rather than the Continental tradition. And we have remained a relatively free and stable society largely because we have maintained a balance between the liberal democratic and the authoritative aristocratic processess. On the other hand, there is a crisis in American leadership in the middle of the twentieth century that is partly due, I think, to the declining authority of an establishment which is now based on an increasingly castelike White–Anglo-Saxon–Protestant (WASP) upper class. But before turning to this modern problem, I should first like to show how the aristocratic process still worked quite well in the case of the family of Abraham Lincoln, and especially how the WASP establishment authoritatively retained the

9

leadership of American society in the generation of Robert Todd Lincoln.

The WASP Establishment in the Victorian Age

While Abraham Lincoln's own career has been a well-publicized example of the democratic ideal of individual opportunity, the career of his son Robert Todd Lincoln was an equally instructive example of the less-publicized but no less important aristocratic process.[2] Abraham Lincoln himself was well aware of the importance of the aristocratic process, first when he married into an established family in the Middle West and then when he sent his son Todd to the Phillips Academy, in Exeter, New Hampshire, in order that he be educated in the style of the Eastern Seaboard upper class.

After finishing his education at Harvard College and the Law School, and after his marriage to the beautiful and fashionable daughter of Senator James Harlan, Robert Todd Lincoln went on to become one of the nation's leading corporation lawyers, a multimillionaire, and a typical Victorian aristocrat. He and his family lived at the very core of the upper class in Chicago as well as in New York and Washington. In addition to his proper education and famous family connections, his secure membership in the new, and national, associational upper class which grew up in America in the closing decades of the nineteenth century (see Chapter V for a discussion of this development) was nicely indicated by his club affiliations. An early Social Register, for example, listed his memberships in New York's patrician Union and more intellectual Century clubs, the Chicago Club in Chicago, and the Metropolitan and Chevy Chase clubs in Washington. For many years, the "Bob Lincoln Corner" at the Metropolitan was a famous gathering place for good conversation and humor.

Robert Todd Lincoln made every effort not to trade on his

father's name and sedulously avoided publicity. In one of his few speeches in memory of his father he emphasized his own faith that "in our country there are no ruling classes." Yet he was constantly in demand in a crude, plutocratic age which longed for the stable authority of tradition. Too shy and retiring to run for public office, he nevertheless served when called, in the aristocratic tradition, as a devoted and conservative Republican in the cabinets of Garfield and Arthur and as Minister to the Court of St. James under Harrison. In Chicago, where he made his home for many years, he was referred to as the "Prince of Rails" and became the nearest thing to royal authority the raw young city possessed. He was not only sought after by the fashionable, the plutocratic and the powerful in this country, many of whom, like Andrew Carnegie, he counted among his friends; he was also in demand abroad, where he was entertained by Queen Victoria and many other leaders; and of course important visitors to this country, like Lloyd George, sought him out as a symbol of the best American traditions.

Robert Todd Lincoln lived the life of a typical Victorian aristocrat in an age when his class led the nation and dominated its traditions. He was at the height of his business career as president of the George M. Pullman Company as the Victorian Age waned with the death of the Queen in 1901. In that year a British-American, White–Anglo-Saxon–Protestant (WASP) establishment, consolidated through family alliances between Mayfair and Murray Hill involving many millions of dollars, authoritatively ran the world, as their ancestors had done since Queen Elizabeth's time. It was also the year when the Protestant patrician Theodore Roosevelt entered the White House and J. P. Morgan, leading layman of the Protestant Episcopal Church and unrivaled czar of our business civilization, formed the first billion-dollar trust, the United States Steel Corporation. Morgan's close friend Bishop Henry Codman Potter, who five years earlier had blessed the most famous Anglo-American marriage of them all when Consuelo Vanderbilt brought her wealth to the House of Marlborough, was often called the "First Citizen of New York." He was probably the last Protestant clergyman to maintain a national and international decision-making position which was respected by such widely differing men of power as Samuel Gompers and Morgan. At the same time the Senate of the United States was a millionaire's club dominated by such Protestant and Republican brahmins as Henry Cabot Lodge, Boies Penrose and Nelson W. Aldrich.

But this class of Protestant patricians not only held the vast majority of positions at the very heart of the national power; it also set the styles in arts and letters, in the universities, in sports, and in the more popular culture which governs the aspirations and values of the masses. In literature, although the age of innocence and the height of the genteel tradition had passed, William Dean Howells was still dean of American letters and such writers of aristocratic tastes and temperament as Henry James, Henry Adams and Edith Wharton were still at work. Philadelphia's best brahmin physician and novelist, S. Wier Mitchell, was the leader of the city's last literary circle, which included Horace Howard Furness, Henry Charles Lea, Agnes Repplier and young Owen Wister, Porcellian friend of Roosevelt, who was hard at work on his nostalgic novel of the gentleman-cowboy of the vanishing frontier, The Virginian, a best seller the following year. In painting, Mary Cassatt, whose brother was president of the Pennsylvania Railroad and one of Philadelphia's prominent Episcopalian laymen, was not only the first American to be recognized by the French Impressionists but was also a major arbiter of taste among American collectors. John Singer Sargent, who came from an old mercantile family of Gloucester, Massachusetts, was painting the portraits of the rich, the wise and the beautiful on both sides of the Atlantic. And in a more popular vein, the ideal Anglo-Saxon male and female were symbolized in the cleft-chinned, cleft-chested and blue-blooded creations of Charles Dana Gibson (publicized by Cluett-Peabody, incorporated in 1901, on a national scale as the symbol of the all-American owner of the Arrow shirt).

At Harvard College, which in the two pre-World War I decades educated such writers as Conrad Aiken, Heywood Broun, Stuart Chase, Malcolm Cowley, E. E. Cummings, John Dos Passos, T. S. Eliot, Walter Lippmann, John Reed, Van Wyck Brooks, S. E. Morison, Charles Nordhoff, Eugene O'Neill, Wallace Stevens and John Hall Wheelock, the faculty was led by a group of devoted teachers in the social sciences and humanities who were very much a part of this establishment, in ethnic background if not always in convictions. The better-known figures included A. Lawrence Lowell, William James, Charles T. Copeland, George Lyman Kittredge, Bliss Perry, Frederick Jackson Turner, Irving Babbitt, George Santayana, Francis G. Peabody and Barrett Wendell. It was symbolic of the times that sociology at Harvard, introduced by Francis G. Peabody in 1883 with a pioneer course in social ethics, nicknamed "drink, drains, and divorce," still approached social problems in terms of Christian morality. And that Barrett Wendell, who completed his *Literary History of America* in 1900, saw himself as the defender of "American Traditions" which he felt were English and should remain so.

At Yale, an ex-Episcopalian clergyman and one of the founders of American sociology, William Graham Sumner, was preaching the Darwinian Dogma and laissez-faire economics. That his brand of sociology reinforced several generations of Yalemen's faith in themselves as well as in their wealthy fathers who had sent them there, is evident from the following summary of Sumner's scientific conclusions about the nature of society:

Competition is a law of nature. Nature is entirely neutral; she submits to him who most energetically and resolutely assails her. She grants her rewards to the fittest, therefore, without regard to other considerations of any kind. . . . Such is the system of nature. If we do not like it, and if we try to amend it, there is only one way in which we can do it. We can take from the better and give to the worse. . . . Let it be understood that we cannot go outside the al-

13

ternative: liberty, inequality, survival of the fittest; non-liberty, equality, survival of the unfittest. The former carries society forward and favours all its best members; the latter carries society downwards and favours all its worst members.[3]

The ancient College of New Jersey, which changed its rather democratic name to the more patrician-sounding Princeton in the nineties, was of course a stronghold of the establishment. Even the reforming Woodrow Wilson, who found and maintained a faculty of gentlemen at Princeton, once said that his preceptorial system depended upon the selection of men who were "companionable and clubable. . . . If their qualities as gentlemen and as scholars conflict, the former will win them the place."[4]

At the same time, the aspirations of the average American boy were being molded by proper Protestant heroes of sport. By 1901, the chivalrous exploits of Frank Merriwell of Yale made far more popular reading than Horatio Alger's sagas of dull, boot-licking bores from the Protestant hinterland who rose to wealth through fortuitous marriages with the boss's daughter. No wonder many red-blooded boys dreamed of going to Yale, made famous by Walter Camp's football teams (Camp was Sumner's brother-in-law). When Camp picked the All-American team in 1901, the sons of the WASP establishment still dominated sport: all save two West Pointers were from Ivy League schools, and five of the first eleven were from Harvard alone. The Lawn Tennis Championship of the United States was still played before a small and aristocratic crowd at Newport, Rhode Island, and was won that year by William A. Larnard, one of Roosevelt's Rough Riders at San Juan Hill and a popular clubman who finally shot himself within the patrician halls of the Knickerbocker Club.

At this point, it is well to emphasize that the aristocratic process worked quite well, and was taken for granted, throughout most of the nineteenth century, largely because the WASP upper class was still representative in an era when the vast majority of leaders, like

Abraham Lincoln, were of old-stock origins anyway. Even the few exceptions, such for example as the brilliant Jew August Belmont, were assimilated the more easily because they constituted such a small minority.

The authority of the Victorian establishment was maintained in spite of a great deal of anarchy and alienation at the lower levels of society as well as radical protest at the top. Thus the era produced vigorous and popular critics of capitalism like Henry George and Edward Bellamy, muckrakers like Ida Tarbell, Henry Demarest Lloyd and Lincoln Steffens, novelists like Frank Norris and Upton Sinclair, as well as the Social Gospel, Settlement House, and New Social Science movements, which will be treated in some detail in later chapters. The Haymarket Riot and the Pullman and Homestead strikes were among the bloodiest in our history and probably hastened the development of such radical organizations as the Populists, Grangers, Knights of Labor, General Coxey and his Army, and the Socialists. Eugene Debs became the leader of the Socialist Party in 1901. This colorful and dedicated hero of the laboring man, who had been jailed for his part in the Pullman strike, summed up the radical mood of the times in the following remarks, made upon his acceptance of the Socialist nomination for the Presidency:

Capitalism is rushing blindly to its impending doom. All signs portend the inevitable breakdown of the existing order. Deep-seated discontent has seized upon the masses. Poverty, high prices, unemployment, child slavery, wide-spread misery and haggard want in a land bursting with abundance; prostitution and insanity, suicide and crime; these in solemn numbers tell the tragic story of capitalism's saturnalia of blood and tears and shame as its end draws near.[5]

Yet in many ways radical criticism and even some violence are often symptoms of a strong, rather than a weak, establishment. The new century opened on a note of Anglo-Saxon confidence if not arrogance. Thus, the President of the Philadelphia & Reading Coal

15

Company, George F. Baer, felt perfectly secure in a world which, as he put it, "was protected and cared for by the Christian men to whom God in his infinite wisdom has given control of the property interests of this country."[6] And it was indeed no wonder that a patrician New York lawyer, John R. Dos Passos (father of the novelist, who blasted our traditions from the Left in the twenties and thirties and has been trying to rescue them as a Rightist in the fifties), should have been convinced, in 1903, that "the twentieth century is par excellence "The Anglo-Saxon Century.' . . . It is now manifest that to this great race is entrusted the civilization and christianization of the world."[7]

Caste, Alienation and the Decline of Authority

But in the years since Victoria's death, American society has been transformed. Continuous economic and political protest led to a series of reforms, including factory, labor and housing legislation, the graduated income tax, social security, and so forth, which have resulted in a new welfare capitalism within a welfare state. Today the American people enjoy the highest standard of living the world has ever known. Despite the great effort that still has to be made, there is probably less economic injustice and less class conflict than at any time since the Industrial Revolution began.

Nor, apparently, have all the measures for fostering economic equality and security diminished the opportunities for mobility and the seeking of success. In fact the postwar years have witnessed an unprecedented democratization of plutocracy. Millionaires are multiplying, and most Americans are now driven by materialistic dreams of ever greater affluence and comfort. But men on the make are rarely moralists. The radical and confident protest which marked the Victorian era, when many of the most critical intellectuals were reared within a secure establishment, has now given way to the alienated affirmations of deracinated intellectual careerists, all too often supported in bohemian affluence by foundation grants. The older breed of ideologists have been replaced by methodologists, obsessed with objectivity and a kind of statistical scholasticism. Indeed, at least as far as the internal structure of our society is concerned, we are living in a post-Marxian age.

But unfortunately success is not synonymous with leadership, and affluence without authority breeds alienation. It was only half a century ago that a small class of British gentlemen, allied with a rising class of American business brahmins, authoritatively led the world in an era of Anglo-Saxon imperialism. Today, after two world wars and the constant threat of a third, the leadership of the West has moved from Whitehall to Washington, and the sense of alienation has risen, as it were, from the factory floor to the executive suite, and now haunts the most successful of men along Madison Avenue and Wall Street, as well as in Washington. Just as Karl Marx once spoke to many sensitive people who were rightly haunted by the misery of masses of men deprived of their craft and alienated by the meaninglessness of the machine process, so Alexis de Tocqueville now appeals to more and more American leaders and intellectuals who have slowly come to sense the wisdom of his warnings of the inevitable alienation of the elite in a materialistic world where privilege is divorced from duty, authority is destroyed, and comfort becomes the only prize. "A kind of virtuous materialism," Tocqueville once wrote, "may ultimately be established in the world, which would not corrupt, but enervate, the soul and noiselessly unbend its springs of action."[8]

Walter Lippmann, long aware of the slow corruption of the American soul and the resulting paralysis of leadership, has often pointed out that this country lacks both a representative upper class and an authoritative establishment. Thus almost three decades ago, in his classic work, *A Preface to Morals*, he wrote:

Our rulers today consist of random collections of successful men and their wives. They are to be found in the inner circles of banks and corporations, in the best clubs, in the dominant cliques of trade unions, among the political churchmen, the higher manipulating bosses, the leading professional Catholics, Baptists, Methodists, Irish, Germans, Jews, and the grand panjandrums of the secret societies. They give orders. They have to be consulted. They can more or less effectively speak for, and lead some part of, the population. But none of them is seated on a certain throne, and all of them are forever concerned as to how they may keep from being toppled off. They do not know how they happen to be where they are, although they often explain what are the secrets of success. They have been educated to achieve success; few of them have been educated to exercise power. Nor do they count with any confidence upon retaining their power, nor in handing it on to their sons. They live, therefore, from day to day, and they govern by ear. Their impromptu statements of policy may be obeyed, but nobody seriously regards them as having authority.[9]

And within the past decade, social scientists have become increasingly interested in the problems of power, authority and leadership. Two of the most widely discussed books of the period were The Power Elite by C. Wright Mills and The Lonely Crowd by David Riesman.[10] These two authors had very different theories about the structure of power in modern American society: Riesman saw a highly decentralized society where power was dispersed among a series of "veto groups," while Mills had a somewhat conspiratorial view of a society dominated by an entrenched and highly concentrated "power elite" centering in the top positions of the military and corporate hierarchies and in the executive branch of the national government. Yet though their interpretations differed in many important respects, both Riesman and Mills followed Lippmann in seeing a crisis of leadership as a product of the lack of any coherent, legitimate and established upper-class authority in modern America. On the one hand, Riesman found that our elite was composed of many power groups which were more concerned with protecting their own interests than in advancing any cause of national importance: "Veto groups exist as defense groups," he wrote, "not as leadership groups." And Mills concluded his highly stimulating analysis of national power on the following note: "There is no set of men with whom members of the mass public can rightfully and gladly identify. In this fundamental sense, America is indeed without leaders. . . . Commanders of power unequalled in human history . . . have succeeded within the American system of organized irresponsibility."

The paralysis of leadership in modern America, as seen by Lippmann, Mills, Riesman and many other critics, is due in part, I think, to the failure of the aristocratic process to keep pace with an excessive individual mobility. Today, when our steadily expanding postwar economy is demanding more and more leaders of ability and education, regardless of ethnic origins, an upper class which is still based on the caste criteria of old-stock Protestant origins is simply an unrepresentative anachronism. And this anachronism has been perpetuated by the admissions policies of the nation's major upper-class clubs, both those in the city and the suburbs. For the club has become, in the course of this century, one of the most important agencies for assimilating men of talent and their families into an upper-class way of life and social organization. On a visit to this country before the First World War, Max Weber observed of our American establishment that "affiliation with a distinguished club was essential above all else. He who did not succeed in joining was no gentleman."

This had not always been so in this country, at least to the same extent. Thus Abraham Lincoln, along with countless other distinguished men of his own generation, virtually grew up with his community and reached the top levels of the local establishment because of his neighbors' respect for his native ability and distinguished accomplishments. As he had watched Springfield grow from 700 to 6,000 in population within a twenty-year period, he was able to observe from first hand knowledge, in the 1850's, that "there is no permanent class of hired laborers amongst us. Twenty-five years ago, I was a hired laborer. The hired laborer of yesterday, labors on his own account today; and will hire others to labor for him tomorrow." And Lincoln's self-made communal position did not depend on any fashionable club or associational affiliations. In fact, of the various societies, lodges and churches in Springfield at the time, he belonged only to the Whig Party and the American Colonialization Society.

In contrast to Lincoln's community-rooted position, his son's generation saw the creation of a national economy and a national mind whose direction was increasingly centered in an urban rather than rural, corporate rather than communal, leadership. And Robert Todd Lincoln was a secure member, as we have seen, of a national and associational rather than a local and communal establishment. His upper-class position was protected by his status as an alumnus of Exeter and Harvard, and his memberships in leading metropolitan clubs in New York, Chicago and Washington, the Chevy Chase in suburban Maryland, and the Ekwanok Country Club at his favorite rural-resort retreat in Vermont.

It was, then, one's club and educational affiliations, rather than family position and accomplishment alone, which placed one in a secure establishment position in the corporate and urban world which America had become by the end of the nineteenth century. But, increasingly in each decade of the twentieth century, there have been more and more distinguished Americans who, because of their ethnic origins, have been categorically ineligible for admission to this club establishment which, in Robert Todd Lincoln's generation, had still assimilated within its ranks the most distinguished men in the nation. Throughout later chapters it will be shown in more detail that, while such established educational institutions as Exeter and Harvard have continued to educate future leaders regardless of their ethnic or racial origins, most of the more distinguished clubs in America today are failing to fulfill their traditional function, largely because their admissions committees are dominated by the values of caste rather than aristocracy.

Caste and the New Immigration

This sense of caste which now prevails within the American upper class began to develop at the turn of the century in response to the flood of impoverished immigrants from Southern and Eastern Europe who came to these shores in ever increasing waves. At first these immigrants filled the lowest levels of our steadily expanding economy. As they were used to an inferior and fixed status in Europe, they were only too glad to defer to their "betters" here in America. Their children, educated in the rapidly expanding public school system, where they absorbed the American ideology of mobility, gradually improved their economic position as a whole, and a few of them, like Alfred E. Smith and Fiorello La Guardia, even rose to threaten the rule of the old-stock establishment. But though the more ambitious sons of immigrants obtained a measure of wealth and power as leaders of our urban political machines, more often than not these machines remained subservient locally to the respectable and Protestant business interests and were represented on the national political scene by such men of older stock as Mark Hanna, Nelson Aldrich or Boies Penrose. As Andrew Hacker was to put it as late as 1957: "Ed Flynn might boss the Bronx, but he would defer to Franklin D. Roosevelt (of Harvard); Carmine de Sapio rides behind Averell Harriman (of Yale); and Jake Arvey cleared the way for Adlai Stevenson (of Princeton)."[11]

Although national political leadership in America continued to be dominated by members of the traditional, WASP upper class, it is significant that Roosevelt, Harriman and Stevenson were members of the Democratic rather than the Republican party. For the two-party system is one of the important ways of both changing and then legitimizing, through votes rather than violence, the final locus of authority in our society. The stability of authority, moreover, probably depends on one or the other of our political parties remaining the majority party over considerable lengths of time. Thus, for instance, the continuing and legitimate authority of the WASP establishment was shown by the fact that its members provided the leaders and the ideals of the Republican Party which, in turn, remained the party of the majority of the American electorate from Lincoln's day to the second election of Franklin D. Roosevelt. On the other hand, it will be one of the tasks of this book to show how the WASP establishment's gradual degeneration from aristocracy to caste has been one of the causes of the decline of the Republican Party as a legitimate bearer of authority in the twentieth century: and how, in response to the castelike attitudes of an increasing number of their patrician peers who still supported the Republican Party, large numbers of men like Roosevelt, Harriman and Stevenson, who had faith in aristocratic assimilation, sought leadership careers in the Democratic Party, which today commands *political* authority because it expresses the aspirations of an electorate which is increasingly made up of the descendants of recent immigrants. But at the same time, unfortunately, one of the major reasons for the present stasis of political leadership is the fact that the heart of the WASP establishment, to say nothing of the rural Protestant voters who send the majority of representatives to the Congress, still remains in the Republican Party. And leadership of the free world in these desperately perilous times is indeed difficult when there is no real locus of authority and even the most talented and dedicated men must spend their energies in manipulating veto groups in endless internal struggles for power.

In addition to this revolution in political authority, which will be treated in more detail in later chapters, the WASP establishment's authority has also been challenged in many other areas of leadership by the rise of large numbers of minority-group members to elite positions since the close of the Second World War. In the first place, as a by-product of the New Deal's efforts to cure the economic

22

depression, the members of ethnic and racial minority groups—among the most depressed classes in the nation at the time—were drawn into the main stream of American life and started on their way to eventual middle-class respectability. The Second War, of course, when all Americans regardless of ethnicity or race fought side by side against a common enemy, also fostered an increasing sense of belonging. As an Italo-American infantryman who landed at Anzio put it: "When we marched on Rome and I was continually greeted as an 'Americano' like all my buddies, I realized for the first time that I was not a 'dago' or 'wop' Italian but a real American." But the most important break came after the war. First, many young men who would never have thought of it before were stimulated by the G.I. Bill to go to college and even to graduate school. At the same time, the unprecedented expansion of our economy has brought many new men, including a large number of these ambitious and well-educated hyphenated-Americans, into important positions of leadership.

But as there is now no recognized or representative upper class of established families which is willing or able to absorb the vast majority of them, or their children, into its ranks, they have been increasingly forced into a lonely and rootless expense-account life, centered around the most fashionable cafés of the moment. And when acceptance into a private and established world becomes unavailable, pandering to the public becomes an obsession and self-advertisement an elite vice. Today the mood of the newly affluent, so many of them engaged in a futile chase without end, is reflected in a series of recent books about status seekers, image makers, exurbanites, and organization men, as well as in the humorous style of the newest group of sophisticated, yet essentially alienated, comedians, appropriately called "sickniks." And according to those who specialize in the mores of the talented, pornography has become polite, while vulgarity and smut—which have probably declined among the embourgeoised masses—have graduated to the educated classes who now syndicate their honeymoons, send out Christmas cards displaying pictures of themselves posing for beer ads, call hundreds of their "intimate" friends by their first names, and of course are willing and anxious to Tell All, not only on the psychiatrist's couch, but anywhere at all—in the living room and café or in print and over the air.

It may be inevitable that privacy should decline in an era when established authority becomes unavailable to a rootless elite which has had to resort to the manipulation of the mass media and all sorts of social engineering to sell the public on its right to rule. But it would be wrong to assume that even the most successful do not, at the same time, long for the privacy of aristocratic authority. Thus an affluent and successful celebrity, Billy Rose, recently refused permission when *Life* magazine wanted to run a fourteen-page spread on his house, saying, "I have outgrown that sort of thing. I am trying to be a gentleman."

This book, then, is an analysis of the conflict between the *divisive* forces of *caste*, on the one hand, which seek to maintain a WASP monopoly of upper-class institutions, and the *cohesive* forces of *aristocracy* which ideally call for gradually evolving upper-class institutions that constantly assimilate new men of talent and power, regardless of ethnic or racial origins. It is an attempt to show how the aristocratic process worked fairly well in the nineteenth century, but has been in constant danger of degenerating into caste in the twentieth. It is an attempt to show why—in an era when so many distinguished figures in our political life, as well as a large proportion of the leaders in popular culture and sports, in the arts and literature, in the sciences and professions, and in the universities, are not of Anglo-Saxon–Protestant origins but are largely the descendants of recent immigrants—a closed WASP upper class is not only an anachronism but also a divisive force in American leadership. This above all is an analysis of an historical and contemporary gentlemanly racism and nativism in America, both polite and

24

impolite, deeply rooted and persistent, which has produced and perpetrated this dangerous anachronism.

Abraham Lincoln saw the intimate and logical connection between nativism and racialism, and how both of them were opposed to the American Dream as set forth in the Declaration of Independence. Like Kennedy, Lincoln was often accused of "vigorous moderateness" as he watched the racial and ethnic antagonisms that marked the decade before the Civil War. For Lincoln was not an abolitionist. Nor did he come out directly against the nativists of his own day, the Know-Nothings, whose Native American Party included among its adherents in Illinois many of his "political and personal" friends (as well as his wife, whose "weak woman's heart," as she once put it, "felt the necessity of keeping foreigners within bounds"). Yet Lincoln's position was beautifully put in a letter written to a close friend in 1854: "I now do no more than oppose the *extension* of slavery," he wrote. "I am not a Know-Nothing. That is certain. How could I be? How can anyone who abhors the oppression of negroes, be in favor of degrading classes of white people? Our progress in degeneracy appears to me to be pretty rapid. As a nation, we begin by declaring 'all men are created equal.' We now practically read it 'all men are created equal, except negroes.' When the Know-Nothings get control, it will read 'all men are created equal, except negroes, and foreigners, and Catholics.' When it comes to this I should prefer emigrating to some country where they make no pretense of loving liberty—to Russia, for instance, where despotism can be taken pure, and without the base alloy of hypocrisy."[12]

> Revolution may also arise when persons of great ability, and
> second to none in their merits, are treated dishonorably by
> those who themselves enjoy the highest honors.
>
> *Aristotle*

II

La Guardia, Weinberg and Others: Drawing the Caste Line

It was, ironically enough, the despotic and caste-creating policies of
Czarist Russia which eventually led to the most insidious and
hypocritical aspects of the racialism and nativism that have plagued
American leadership in the twentieth century. In the year 1881,
after Alexander II was assassinated and his son Alexander III became Czar, the pogrom became part of the policy of the Russian
regime. The formula was simple: "A third of the Jews in Russia
would be forced to emigrate, a third would accept baptism and the
remaining third would be systematically starved to death." On
Christmas night in that same year the streets of Warsaw were

bathed in Jewish blood in Europe's most terrible massacre since St. Bartholomew's Day, that infamous day in 1572 when the Huguenots were shot down without warning in the streets of Paris. Between 1882 and 1914 some two million immigrants were added to the American-Jewish community from the lands that lay under the scepter of the Czars. And, in Lincoln's terms, our progress in degeneracy from the American ideal was now to include the declaration that all men are created equal, except Negroes, Catholics and Jews.

In so many ways, the year 1882 was symbolic of both nineteenth-century confidence and the shape of things to come in the twentieth. As the year opened, the great and the powerful gathered for a dinner at Delmonico's restaurant in New York to honor the visiting British sociologist and Social Darwinist, Herbert Spencer, who had scientifically "proved" the Anglo-Saxon gentleman's Natural Fitness to rule the world. In that year the first American country club, whose multitude of imitators have become the bastions of Anglo-Saxon narcissism in our day, was founded at Brookline, Massachusetts. At the same time, the Anglo-Saxon's growing fears of the mongrelization of his country were written into the law of the land when the first federal statute restricting immigration was passed by the Congress. And perhaps most important of all, in that year, two of the twentieth-century's greatest natural leaders, Franklin D. Roosevelt and Fiorello La Guardia, were born. For the careers of these two men symbolized an age which arbitrarily divided its most talented leaders into first- and second-class aristocrats.

The Double Standard of Aristocracy

Roosevelt and La Guardia had remarkably parallel careers which were at the same time strikingly different, largely because of their ethnic backgrounds. Roosevelt was born of the best brahmin stock at his family's rural seat in Hyde Park, while La Guardia came into the world in the heart of the urban melting pot, of Jewish and Italian parentage, in a tenement flat in the Italian section of Greenwich Village. Both men entered politics in 1910; both went to Washington for the first time in 1917; both earned reputations for distinguished service during the First War; both had attained promising political positions by the summer of 1920, when La Guardia was stricken with almost unbearable depression as he buried his only child and beloved wife and Roosevelt came down with a severe case of poliomyelitis; both men survived their respective ordeals; and as the nation swung to the Right during the twenties, they both, in their different ways, kept alive and fought for their convictions of the justness of the American Dream of removable inequality; just a dozen years, almost to the day, after that fateful summer of 1920 when both men seemed through, the brahmin Democrat was on his way to the White House and the Republican representative of the urban melting pot on his way to City Hall.

Franklin Roosevelt—whose background as a member of the Protestant upper class was a definite advantage, in fact a prerequisite, in his struggle to attain the highest level of American leadership —was typical of the affirming aristocrat who believed in assimilating all men of talent and worth into the establishment, regardless of their ethnic origins.

In contrast to Roosevelt, La Guardia was one of this century's countless hyphenated-Americans who were forever barred from the highest social positions, as well as the highest offices, in the nation. Whereas Roosevelt, partly because of his family position and name, was eligible for both the Governorship and the Presidency, La Guardia was limited to the local leadership of the urban melting pot, his native city of New York. Indeed, this brilliant and talented leader was himself the very personification of the world which so many Protestant patricians, from Henry Adams to Madison Grant, so deplored and despised. His biographer, in a volume significantly entitled, *La Guardia: A Fighter Against His Time*, describes him as follows:

To put it sociologically, La Guardia was a marginal man who lived on the edge of many cultures, so that he was able to face in several directions at the same time. Tammany Hall may have been the first to exploit the vote-getting value of eating gefullte fish with the Jews, goulash with Hungarians, sauerbraten with Germans, spaghetti with Italians, and so on indefinitely, but this unorthodox Republican not only dined every bit as shrewdly but also spoke, according to the occasion, in Yiddish, Hungarian, German, Italian, Serbian-Croatian, or plain New York English. Half Jewish and half Italian, born in Greenwich Village yet raised in Arizona, married first to a Catholic and then to a Lutheran but himself a Mason and an Episcopalian, Fiorello La Guardia was a Mr. Brotherhood Week all by himself. And during his career he received the support of ward heelers and reformers, silk-stockings and socialists, Wall Street lawyers and trade unionists, and many other kinds of opposites. He was so many persons in one, so uniquely unparochial in that most parochial of cities, that New Yorkers of nearly every sort were able to identify themselves with him, although rarely for the same reasons. The hyphens of this many-hyphenated American were like magnets.[1]

Yet in spite of his Protestant convictions and in spite of the fact that for years he worked intimately—and filled most of the top appointive positions in his three administrations as Mayor—with Protestants and silk-stocking reformers who personally admired his ability and idealism (Newbold Morris, for example, once said that La Guardia and his old headmaster at Groton, Endicott Peabody, were the two Americans he admired most), La Guardia was always considered an outsider. And there were many experiences to reinforce a bitter but private feeling of alienation which he was fortunately able to handle because of a keen sense of humor and his ability to submerge himself in an incredible work schedule. One had to have a sense of humor (which at its best is a profound sense of the tragic) to take such an example of Anglo-Saxon ethnocentrism and insensibility as the following letter he received on the occasion of one of his milder criticisms of the then President Hoover:

It seems to me, a REPUBLICAN, that you are a little out of your class, in presuming to criticise the President. It strikes me as impudence. You should go back where you belong and advise Mussolini how to make good honest citizens in Italy. The Italians are preponderantly our murderers and boot-leggers. . . . Like a lot of other foreign spawn, you do not appreciate the country which supports and tolerates you.[2]

No doubt these remarks were beneath comment. But on another occasion he revealed his ability to handle humiliation with humor. In the early twenties, for example, there had been a good deal of public complaint to the effect that New York congressmen were nothing but foreigners representing an alien population. The New York *World* thus asked each congressman to trace his descent, to which La Guardia replied:

I have no family tree. The only member of my family who has one is my dog Yank. He is the son of Doughboy, who was the son of Siegfried, who was the son of Tannhauser, who was the son of Wotan. A distinguished family tree, to be sure—but after all he's only a son of a bitch.[3]

While in Washington during the twenties (as the first and only Italian American in Congress) La Guardia did not of course take part in the Capital social life. As he had been a gay and congenial blade among his artistic and creative friends in the Village, this was probably not entirely of his own choosing. The following comments at the end of a series of personal memoirs certainly attest to his feelings of insecurity and inferiority where social life was concerned:

Senator William M. Calder, who had represented New York in the House for many years, had befriended me when I first went to

Washington. He used to call me "Sonny" and was much concerned for my welfare and future career. . . .

Senator Calder came to me one day and said that he wanted me particularly to go to a dinner party some friends of his were giving. I told him that I never went to those things. "I know, Sonny," he said, "but this time you've got to do me a favor and come with me." Of course I accepted the invitation, and to make sure that I got there, Senator Calder called for me at my hotel in his car.

While cocktails were being served, I got into a conversation with a gentleman about Croatia and Dalmatia. I didn't like his attitude. "What do you know about Croatia and Dalmatia?" I asked belligerently. "I've lived in that part of the world for three years, and I know what I'm talking about," I told him. "I am the Serbian Ambassador here," my fellow guest replied indignantly.

Then we passed into the dining room. The lady on my left and I got into a conversation about Liberty motors for airplanes. I sounded off and told her how rotten I thought they were, and tore into General Motors in particular. I soon learned that she was related to one of the big shots of that great organization.

After dinner, when I went into the men's room, a man came in and started a conversation with us. "How do you like the party?" he asked. "Why I never saw such a bunch of nuts before," I answered. "I'm going. Want to come along?" "I can't," he said, "I'm your host."

I thought my social career was ruined forever, but soon afterwards the same host and hostess wanted to give a dinner party with me as guest of honor, on the grounds that I had been "so amusing." But not even my good friend Senator Calder could get me to submit to that one. I guess I'm still on the blacklist.[4]

Although both Lincoln and La Guardia suffered in much the same manner as lonely new Congressmen in Washington, the aristocratic process which had eventually absorbed the Lincolns into the nineteenth-century establishment had degenerated into a double standard in the generation of La Guardia. The social situation at the higher levels of American leadership was surely calculated to manufacture a large number of marginal men of great ability and affluence. And since the end of the Second World War, as more and more talented sons and grandsons of recent immigrants of non-Anglo-Saxon stock have risen to positions of power and influence, the number of marginal, second-class aristocrats has increased.

Caste and Anti-Semitism

While La Guardia's sense of social inferiority was primarily a product of his Italian-American origins, it is important to note that he was partly Jewish. And as far as Jews are concerned, once again we find the 1880's a dividing line. While sporadic and idiosyncratic anti-Semitism had been characteristic of the gentile gentleman's code since Colonial times, it was only in the 1880's, when the flood tides of immigration began to rise, that upper-class anti-Semitism gradually became rigid and institutionalized.

This new rigidity, for instance, was one of the reasons why Bernard Baruch, whom Herbert Hoover once listed among the great men of his generation, always remained just outside the central struggle for political power. And this was in spite of the fact that Baruch's roots lay deep in American history. On his mother's side, the family had been securely assimilated into the best society of South Carolina. The early family founders had been distinguished rabbis of Charleston's historic Sephardic congregation as well as wealthy planters; his mother's grandmother had danced with Lafayette upon his visit to America in 1824. His father, of German origin, was a distinguished physician who had fought in the Civil War under his hero, Robert E. Lee. After the war, the Baruchs came to New York, where young Bernard graduated from City College in the 1880's and eventually married into a mercantile family of impeccable position, of Protestant and Dutch ancestry. Baruch made a great success on Wall Street, where Morgan was his hero. But he was never accepted either on The Street or uptown in the society to which his affluence and ability as well as his handsomeness and engaging manner might have led him. Though he has always been listed in the *Social Register* and many of his and his wife's friends were of the upper-class world, the Baruchs were faced with such humiliations as their daughter's being refused admission into a dancing class which her mother had once attended. Baruch's biographer writes of his relationship to the ladies and gentlemen of the Gilded Age as follows:

The social walls were not unscalable. "We cannot fight Wall Street," was the sad cry of the Old Guard. But what of the young Baruchs? They had charm, education; the look of breeding and distinction. As for their antecedents, who could claim the heritage of old New York more than they—Annie with her Dutch strain, Baruch of the line of Isaac Rodriguez Marques? Yet prejudice made the citadel unattainable to them.

It hurt. It hurt then and rankled in Baruch fifty years later. It was not for himself that he suffered. He has said, and intimates have confirmed the fact, that in his youth he scarcely knew there was any such thing as the Social Register. But his wife knew it, and this may in part have accounted for her shyness and for her seeming more interested in her own home than anything else. They had the nicest circle of friends in New York, Baruch has said of these years. Yet, he admits that when he got into social life there was a difference; "in business there was a great prejudice. There were more difficulties when I married." There were moments when bitterness must have burned within him, when he recalled that "down South, my mother and father were the top"; or might have reflected, as did Disraeli, that his ancestors were priests in their temple of their God, when those of the Anglo-Saxons were running loose in the forests. "It hurt my wife"; he knew that, and this particular kind of discrimination was "the worst thing anyone could do. It makes a difference with children," and the children were coming along now. First was Belle, a wistful-eyed girl, named for her grandmother; then "Junior," the much-desired heir; and finally the pretty Renée. The girls were baptized in the Episcopal Church, but that made no difference. The world condemned you for what you were. . . .[5]

The "bitterness which must have burned" within the heart of young Baruch as he suffered from the snobberies of the Gilded Age was kept alive by other examples of rude, and even hysterical, anti-Semitism which he encountered later in life. And countless other natural aristocrats of similar ancestry were to suffer the same kind of humiliations. But I shall be less concerned with the Jew than with the gentile gentleman's reaction to the Jew. For my point of view follows that of Jean-Paul Sartre, who, at the end of his classic essay on the Jews, quoted the late Richard Wright: "There is no Negro problem in the United States, there is only a white problem." Sartre then added: "We may say in the same way that anti-Semitism is not a Jewish problem; it is our problem."

Anti-Semitism: A Problem of Gentile Morality

The October, 1953, issue of Fortune magazine contained two interesting articles with no apparent connection to each other. The first, entitled "Businessmen on Their Knees," was a discussion of the current revival of religion among American business leaders. Most of the illustrative material was based on the religious reawakening in and around the Pittsburgh industrial complex, where the enthusiastic Rector of Calvary Episcopal, "a sleepless fisher of men," had unusual success even among the "golf club crowd." "God loves snobs as well as other people," rightly reasoned the Rector as he took his message right into the exclusive Pittsburgh Golf Club, where he held a series of weekly meetings with executives and their wives. The article showed how many leading executives were carrying their newly found convictions into the office and onto the factory floor. For instance, one of the Rector's faithful vestrymen at Calvary, Admiral Ben Moreell, head of Jones & Laughlin and an enthusiastic "Christ Bearer" for some years, openly and persuasively discussed his convictions at his desk in "J & L's" ultramodern skyscraper on the Golden Triangle. As another example of America's activist religious revival, this article was surely reporting on an important trend at the top levels of modern industry.

Yet, upon reading the second of the two articles, I had some doubts about the actual depths of this unquestionably sincere return to religion among American business leaders. Entitled "Let's Ask Sidney Weinberg," this article was a warm and friendly outline of the business career of one of the nation's leading investment bankers, director at one time or another of some thirty-five blue-chip corporations, dollar-a-year public servant for many years, leading fund-raiser for both Roosevelt and Eisenhower, and "personal friend" of Ike (who was supposed to have offered him a Cabinet post), Henry Ford II (who is supposedly devoted to him, especially after he was responsible for blueprinting the family's transfer of stock to the Ford Foundation), Amory Houghton (brahmin president of Corning Glass, whose daughter is now married to Weinberg's son), and a host of other men who fill vital executive suites across the nation.

All in all, this fascinating saga of a Brooklyn boy who graduated from Public School 13, rose to the top on Wall Street, and then went on to serve presidents of the nation in many important capacities, was a particularly touching example of the American Dream in its Horatio Alger phase. Moreover, here was a man, according to the *Fortune* article at least, who exhibited none of the socially offensive and aggressive traits of the newly rich which are so often given as an excuse for not accepting the Jews; here was a man who has often set an example of *noblesse oblige* within the American business community; a man apparently not given to vulgar display and status seeking, who has lived, since 1923, in the original, unpretentious house he bought for his wife in Scarsdale; here was a good family man who had brought up two sons who have done well in business after good educations at Deerfield and Princeton; here was a man, as *Fortune* put it, who was "not after superficial contacts or cultivation, but was apparently more sought after than seeking."

And finally, one of the more revealing parts of the *Fortune* article consisted of a rather detailed discussion of Weinberg's frequent cruising adventures along the Maine coast with Boston's Paul Cabot (Treasurer of Harvard) and two very Proper Philadelphians, Charles Dickey (a senior partner of J. P. Morgan) and Charles Cheston. While reading of these cruises, where friendship inevitably deepens as a result of the intimacy of life on board, I could not help being reminded of the elder Morgan's well-known definition of a gentleman and real friendship: "You can do business with anyone," he once remarked at Bar Harbor, "but only sail with a gentleman."

Perhaps as a matter of conventional tact mixed with a bit of moral myopia, the *Fortune* article on Weinberg of course did not mention the fact that, even though he was a "personal friend" of so many of the leading members of the nation's business establishment, he had never been asked to join any of their top-flight clubs, such for instance as the Links in New York City, where most of the prominent men cited in the article as his intimate friends often dine and discuss shooting, boating or golf, and perhaps high policy.

All over America, membership in such men's clubs as the Links is a major requirement for eventual assimilation into the establishment. The Duquesne Club in Pittsburgh, for example, does not consider anyone of Jewish origins for membership; yet Admiral Ben Moreell, one of the leading "Christ Bearers" in the Golden Triangle according to *Fortune*, is in the habit of regularly lunching there at noon with the leading businessmen in the city, including the Bishop of the Protestant Episcopal Church, who usually sits at the Admiral's table. Thus, on finishing these two *Fortune* articles, I asked myself whether any of these business Christians had ever been struck by the possible moral ambiguity of their situation. Whatever friendship may mean at this level of leadership in American business, it apparently does not mean what it did to Mrs. Franklin D. Roosevelt, who resigned from New York's most exclusive women's club, the Colony, after her clubmates blackballed her friend Mrs. Henry Morgenthau.

Now it is important, I think, to emphasize that it is not immoral for a club not to have Jews as a group among its membership; in fact, it would be natural to have no Jews if the members of a club did not have Jewish friends and associates. The teachings of the New Testament, in contrast to so much of the Marxian moralism, say nothing about the morality or immorality of social structures per se. What the Christian religion does say is that each man is unique and to treat him otherwise is a sin. Sidney Weinberg apparently has more friends among the gentile business community than among Jews. In his *Who's Who* biography, for instance, he lists no affiliations with specifically Jewish organizations, and most of the boards on which he serves (such as that of the Presbyterian Hospital) are composed primarily of gentiles. But in spite of all this his friends are unable or unwilling to declassify him. At their club at least, he is not a unique individual but a member of a category, a category called *The Jews*. To take him into the Links Club, then, would not be to take in a personal friend, but only to take in a *Jew*. And it is this situation, with all its moral ambiguities, which will be increasingly confronted by members of the younger generation.

Caste and the Alienated Patrician

It was Solon, one of the seven wise men of Greece, who once said that the ills of world will be nearer to solution when "bystanders stand up for those who suffer wrong." There are few leaders in American industry today who do not have friends who have suffered indignities because of their Jewish origins. And most of them have remained bystanders while their friends, and even relatives, have been treated dishonorably by the collective conformity of caste which binds the admissions committees of their favorite clubs.

But no man is an island: caste may humiliate the Jew but it alienates the gentleman bystander too. And it may be highly damaging to the psychology of American leadership as a whole when those Protestant patricians who have had all the advantages, have attended the best schools and universities, and have been among the most successful of their generation, deny, and thus become alienated from, the American Dream of equal, and unlimited, opportunity.

The word "alienation" means, according to a definition in Webster's dictionary, "to become indifferent where devotion or attachment formerly existed." The attitudes of the gentlemanly bystander, indifferent to his traditions and concentrating on success and affluence at the expense of leadership, has produced far more alienation at the top levels of American society than most of us are prepared to admit. Consider, for example, the case of *Time* magazine: What are the values of its highly successful and competent editors who have been led from the beginning by gentlemen bred in the best traditions of St. Paul's and Hotchkiss, by Bones Men of Yale and Ivy Men of Princeton, and by members of the best clubs in New York and its surrounding countryside—and dominated, above all, by Henry Luce, of impeccable religious (son of a missionary), educational and club affiliations? Perhaps the following paragraph written by Edmund Wilson for the *Princeton University Library Chronicle* suggests an answer:

Time's picture of the world gives us sometimes simply the effect of schoolboy mentalities in a position to avail themselves of a gigantic research equipment; but it is almost always tinged with a peculiar kind of jeering rancor. There is a tendency to exhibit the persons whose activities are chronicled, not as more or less able or noble or amusing or intelligent human beings, who have various ways of being right or wrong, but—because they are presented by writers

who are allowed no points of view themselves—as manikins, sometimes cocky, sometimes busy, sometimes zealous, sometimes silly,
sometimes gruesome, but in most cases quite infra-human, who
make speeches before guinea-pig parliaments, issue commands and
move armies of beetles back and forth on bas-relief battle-maps, in-
dulge themselves maniacally in queer little games of sport, science,
art, beer-bottle-top collecting or what not, squeak absurd little
boasts and complaints, and pop up their absurd little faces in front
of the lenses of the Luce photographers, and add up to a general impression that the pursuits, past and present, of the human race are
rather an absurd little scandal about which you might find out some
even nastier details if you met the editors of Time over cocktails. . . .[6]

When Wilson wrote these lines, T. S. Matthews, then Managing
Editor of *Time* and former colleague of Wilson's on the *New
Republic*, read them and sent copies to Henry Luce and several of
his fellow editors "on the principle that enemies are better critics
than friends"; he received no comments from anyone. Matthews
eventually resigned from the magazine and is now an expatriate in
London. "For this is not my day in America," he wrote in his
recently published autobiography, "This day belongs to the '100
percenters,' the new-rich Texans, the Madison Avenue boys, the
professional patriots, the organization men, the hard-eyed herdsmen
of political Yahoos, the dogs that eat dogs. If they have really taken
over America, and taken it over for keeps, then I think the American
experiment has failed."[7]

But, one is bound to ask, if the class of gentleman to which
Matthews so obviously belongs have lost control of the American
experiment, may it not be partly a reflection of their own defensive
rather than affirming values, their compulsive need to succeed
rather than to lead, and, above all, their inability or unwillingness
to assimilate into their own way of life and established traditions
those natural aristocrats of different origins from theirs which the
American experiment has certainly produced in the course of the

twentieth century? In other words, perhaps it is not that the American experiment has failed, as Matthews puts it; rather, it is that the gentleman's code has failed in its aristocratic function of continuing leadership of this experiment. And nowhere, I think, has the code of the American gentlemen who have grown up with the twentieth century been more acutely and sensitively portrayed than in Matthews' highly intelligent and honest autobiography.

Matthews was born in Cincinnati in 1901, the son of an independently wealthy Episcopalian clergyman who later became Bishop of New Jersey. His mother was an heiress of the Procter and Gamble fortune, though she hated to admit it. "From my father," he writes in the opening pages of his book, "we learned to despise; from my mother, to be ashamed."[8] Like his father, Matthews was educated at St. Paul's, Princeton and Oxford, after being tutored at home and attending small schools both here and in England (the English school was for Empire children and consisted of fourteen boys on an estate of two hundred acres). After Oxford, he came back to New York and worked for the *New Republic* before going to *Time* magazine in 1929, where he rose, in the course of almost twenty-five years, from a part-time book reviewer to managing editor. Partly because of his disagreement with Henry Luce, and partly because he had never approved of Luce journalism in the first place, he eventually resigned from *Time* and now writes what suits him, at his Mayfair address in London.

From early childhood, Matthews was bred in the defensive atmosphere which is still characteristic of the American rich, and which only emphasized his sense of difference from other people in the world about him. Thus he writes of his childhood in Cincinnati: "The nursery was the heart of our world and our refuge from the rest of it. . . . The front door was not only latched but bolted . . . the parlormaid's nightly duty was to draw the curtains in all the windows that gaze on the street, and also to shut and latch the shutters. . . . The fact that we were different was never absent from our consciousness. We were ashamed of our timidity and our lack of sturdiness, but we despised the rest of the world for all that, and looked down on everybody who was not like us. And we were sure that nobody was like us."[9]

More than half of Matthews' autobiography is devoted to his childhood and family life within the bosom of the wealthy Edwardian clans of Matthews and Procter. The family seat, to which he moved at an early age, was the little village of Glendale, about fifteen miles outside of Cincinnati. His grandfather Matthews had been one of the signers of the village charter, one uncle was rector of the church, another was the apparently permanent mayor, and the "Oaks," his grandfather Procter's estate, was the largest house in the village. Matthews was of course proud of his ancestry, and aware of the caste differences within his own family tree. While the Procters were wealthier, he had always been led to believe that the Matthews were of "finer clay." "The Matthewses," he writes, "did in fact consider themselves a cut above the Procters, partly because they thought themselves better bred—their Welsh-English descent being, in their eyes, superior to the Irish-English line of the Procters—but principally for two other snobbish reasons: they had been Americans for nine generations to the Procters' three; and no Matthews, so they said, had ever been 'in trade.' "[10] Years later Matthews admitted to himself that he preferred the Procters and always had.

Religion was of course an important part of his family training. The day was opened with his father's prayers and grace was said before and after each meal. Where money was concerned, the Protestant ethic prevailed: "Conservative to the last share of stock"; the key word in the family ethos about money was "stewardship." Money was not a possession but a trust and the owner simply a trustee.

The Christian concept of "stewardship" certainly would seem to imply an obligation to use one's wealth and position in helping the less fortunate or in changing the world in some way, according to one's own convictions. But Matthews was apparently bred to con-

41

form to a conventional social position, not to a sense of power, authority and responsibility. According to his autobiography at least, he seems not to have had any compelling convictions about the terrible and turbulent events through which he lived as an adult (and wrote about as an editor of *Time*). Thus in the single half-page that he devotes to the main events of the thirties—nothing is said about the Depression, only a line or two about his attendance at New York cocktail parties to raise money for the Loyalist cause in Spain, and only a fleeting reference to the "Nazi bully-boys"— he writes: "I have lived among historical events without noticing them, as I think is commonly the case with people who are lucky enough not to get caught in them. The first Great War, the depression that ended the boom of the twenties, were hardly more to me than newspaper headlines."[11]

Matthews' alienation from historical events seems to have been at least partly the result of a lack of moral commitment. For he was alienated from his religious upbringing as he gradually came to see that there was something "ludicrous in equating a social sect like the Episcopal Church with its near-antithesis, the Christian faith." Even in the highly religious atmosphere of St. Paul's, positive commitments of any extreme sort were not quite according to the code. In a sporadic diary which Matthews kept at the school, he recorded that he had come to "the dreadful conclusion that war was indefensible, conscientious objectors right, and patriotism utterly wrong." But his private convictions almost immediately gave way to class conventions when he joined the "School Battalion" soon afterwards.

Matthews also did not seem to be able to hold on to any continuing convictions in his highly successful career as a journalist. It was a sense of stewardship and the social responsibilities of power and wealth, for example, which led Willard Straight to found the *New Republic* a short time before his death during the First War. And the convictions of his family (and his widowed wife's money) kept it alive. On the other hand, apparently because he thought it not quite right to work for something which did not "pay its own way," as he put it, Matthews eventually gave up serious journalism for a job with *Time* which he got through his Princeton and Ivy Club friend, John Stuart Martin (who has also left *Time*). "I was not proud of myself," Matthews writes of his giving up the *New Republic* for a job at *Time*. "I felt both cynical and bewildered. It was like what had happened to me ten years before, when I had been a white-hot pacifist and then, all of a sudden, found myself a volunteer in a military training camp." But he asked himself: "Was it wrong to give up the complacency of failure for the anxieties of success?" One wonders why the *New Republic* should be considered a failure just because it did not pay its own way and make a profit? Yet perhaps T. R. Roosevelt was right when he once said of the class to which he (and Matthews) belonged that their ultimate criteria of worth in life was: "Does it pay?"

Although Matthews had "wholeheartedly subscribed" to the liberalism of the *New Republic*, he never took *Time* seriously and eventually became alienated from its policies altogether. While he never reveals any strong political convictions (he is supposed to have finally broken from *Time* after a highly unfair cover story on his Princeton contemporary and friend, Adlai Stevenson, though he never mentions this in his autobiography), Matthews appears not to have gone along with Henry Luce's passionate convictions about the villainage of "the Democratic administration in general, Roosevelt and Acheson in particular." "I finally decided," he writes after some very interesting observations on the personality of Henry Luce, "that what most drew me to Luce and made me feel that we had something in common—and has kept me fond of him even when I didn't like him—was his guilty conscience."

But Matthews did have at least one hero. "Like most of the St. Paul's boys of my generation, I admired John Gilbert Winant just this side of idolatry." Winant was one of the younger masters at the school and, in his history course, he gave Matthews "a burning conviction that the United States of America was a wonderful country, the most gloriously hopeful experiment man had ever made." Yet, Matthews writes, "when he [Winant] changed his party and in effect ended his political career to follow President Franklin Roosevelt, whom he admired to the same extravagant degree that we had admired Gil, it was a *blow to my hopes but I sympathized and forgave him.*" (Italics mine.) But what were Matthews' hopes? And why did he have to *forgive* his one-time hero for following his convictions rather than a more certain path to success within the Republican Party? One has the impression that convictions, openly revealed by action, are only for radicals and reformers and forbidden by gentlemanly convention.

But, in the closing pages of this autobiography of a highly intelligent and sensitive gentleman, Matthews does reveal that he actually was alienated and expatriated from the land to which down deep in his heart he owed so much and loved so well just because he had taken young Gil Winant's convictions seriously, even though he had refused to face them in the course of his own class-limited and successful life in America. Thus he writes:

What has become of the American idea, the hope of raising a standard to which all just men could repair? Has it really petered out into a "dream," or worse, into a nervously advertised and jealously guarded "way of life"? I believe that the American experiment was intended as a conscious revolution in human affairs; that the new nation was to be not only an anthology of the best in Europe, it was to evolve a way of living, for all comers, so superior to Europe's ways that the new republic might some day become unique among the nations—a promised land that would honor its promise to any decent applicant.

What has become of that enormous invitation, and the faith it was based on? From the skeptical or European point of view the invitation and its subsequent withdrawal were alike regulated by economic demand. Once America badly needed cheap labor, and rationalized its need by declaring a limitless capacity for making new

44

American silk purses out of any old European sows' ears. The need fulfilled, the United States will now accept only a strictly limited quantity, grading its quotas by an arbitrary assessment of quality—northern and western Europeans are better stuff than southern Europeans, and Orientals almost unusable.[12]

It would be hard, I think, to find a more eloquent statement of the American Dream and its subsequent denial in Matthews' own generation. As it is so much in accord with my own thesis here, it is interesting that Matthews, in the closing pages of his book, also stresses our preoccupation in modern America with "self-protection" and the "fear of being robbed" and ends by showing how these defensive and castelike attitudes have affected our capacity to lead: "I do not believe that America . . . is the real leader of the Western world," he concludes. "It is acknowledged to be the richest and claims to be the most powerful country on earth; but I think the grimly emerging fact is that the West has no real leader."

The attitudes and values of T. S. Matthews, as revealed between almost every line of his autobiography, certainly personify the central problem now faced by the class in which he was bred. Indeed the lesson to be learned from his life is that a WASP upper class which remains content with caste defense and success—as against the aristocratic assumption of an affirming leadership—and which, at the same time, fails to honor the American promise to all "decent and talented applicants" is surely doomed to increasing alienation and eventual self-destruction. For the best in America is nothing if not an experimental dream in which freedom and equality of opportunity are the central themes. On the other hand, our present preoccupation with the so-called "American Way of Life," so nervously advertised on Madison Avenue and vigorously defended by such admittedly caste-creating organizations as the Daughters of the American Revolution, is surely calculated to deny that dream.

There she lies, the great Melting-Pot—listen: Can't you hear the roaring and the bubbling? There gapes her mouth —the harbour where a thousand mammoth feeders come from the ends of the world to pour in their human freight. Ah, what a stirring and seething? Celt and Latin, Slav and Teuton, Greek and Syrian,—black and yellow—

Jew and Gentile—

Yes, East and West, and North and South, the palm and the pine, the pole and the equator, the crescent and the cross—how the great Alchemist melts and fuses them with his purging flame! Here shall they all unite to build the Republic of Man and the Kingdom of God . . . what is the glory of Rome and Jerusalem where all nations and races came to worship and look back, compared with the glory of America, where all races and nations come to labour and look forward!

Israel Zangwill

III

The Immigrants' Progress and the Theory of the Establishment

Several years ago an Englishman, visiting America for the first time, remarked to an editor of *Harper's* magazine that nobody had prepared him for his quick discovery that this was not an Anglo-Saxon nation.[1] Although he had long been aware of our multinational, racial and religious origins in the abstract, he simply had not visualized the heterogeneity of our population in general, nor the heterogeneity of the persons of talent and ability in leadership positions. Hollywood, of course, portrays America to people all over the world. Yet the personalities of our screen stars, well-publicized representatives of the American rags-to-riches dream, had

46

done little to dissuade him of our over-all Protestant and Anglo-Saxon ancestry. A brief look at the original names of some of our more famous, pseudo-Anglo-Saxon, Hollywood heroes was indeed a revelation. A sample of the Warner Brothers stable of stars, for instance, included Doris Kapplehoff, Larry Skikne, Bernie Schwartz, Mladen Sekulovich, Marie Tomlinson Krebs, Frances Gumm, and Arthur Gelien; among the famous at 20th Century-Fox were Max Showalter, Virginia McMath, Mitzi Gerber, Balla Wegier, Claudette Chauchoin and Ethel Zimmerman; at MGM were Vito Farinola, Joseph Meibes, Tula Finklea and Spengler Arlington Brough; stars at Columbia included Dianne Laruska, Judy Tuvim, Gwyllyn Ford, Margarita Carmen Cansino, Aldo Da Re and Vincent Zoino; while Zalma Hedrick, Donna Mullenger, Sarah Fulks, Ella Geisman, Issur Danielovitch, Daniel Kaminsky, Dino Crocetti and Joseph Levitch were among the leaders at Paramount.* Just as the original names of these famous stars suggest the ethnic diversity of talent in modern America, so their assumed names attest to the Anglo-Saxon ideal which still persists in our culture. For, in spite of the fact that some forty million immigrants of diverse religious and ethnic origins came to America in the course of the nineteenth and early twentieth centuries, we were a predominantly Anglo-Saxon–Protestant people for almost the first two-thirds of our history. Thus our earliest cultural traditions—in language and literature as well as in our legal, political and religious institutions—were modeled on those of seventeenth- and eighteenth-century England. And, above all, our upper class has always been overwhelmingly Anglo-Saxon and Protestant in both origins and values. The "Sixty

* The assumed names of the stars, in the order listed above, were as follows: *Warner Brothers*: Doris Day, Lawrence Harvey, Tony Curtis, Karl Malden, Marjorie Main, Judy Garland and Tab Hunter; *20th Century-Fox*: Casey Adams, Ginger Rogers, Mitzi Gaynor, Bella Darvi, Claudette Colbert and Ethel Merman; *MGM*: Vic Damone, John Ericson, Cyd Charisse and Robert Taylor; *Columbia*: Dianne Foster, Judy Holliday, Glenn Ford, Rita Hayworth, Aldo Ray and Vince Edwards; *Paramount*: Kathryn Grayson, Donna Reed, Jane Wyman, June Allyson, Kirk Douglas, Danny Kaye, Dean Martin and Jerry Lewis.

47

Families" or the "Four Hundred," the "Rich and the Well-Born," the "Harvard Man," the "Senator," the "Diplomat," the "Social-ite," and the "Man of Distinction in the Executive Suite" are all continuing symbols of this Anglo-American ideal which the Holly-wood stars, regardless of their own ethnic origins, have tended to perpetuate. The uncomfortable paradox of American society in the twentieth century is that it has tried to combine the democratic ideal of equality of opportunity in an ethnically diverse society with the persistent and conservative traditions of an Anglo-Saxon caste ideal at the top.

The Immigrants' Progress

As we have seen, the WASP upper class remained more or less in control of the American elite throughout the first three decades of this century. This was perhaps inevitable, and, as it served to main-tain a continuity of tradition at the level of leadership, it was a healthy thing for society as a whole. In the meantime, however, new ethnic families were gradually establishing themselves on the ladder of economic, political and social mobility. By and large this was a three-generational process. The members of the first generation, long used to a subservient and fixed status in the Old Country, clung to their traditional ways, deferred to their "betters," and gradually built up rich ethnic islands in the poorer neighborhoods of our large metropolitan areas. They protected themselves from the strange and often hostile ways of the native Americans by settling along the "Irish Riviera" in South Boston, the "Chinatowns," "Lit-tle Italies," or "Ghettos" in New York's Lower East Side and many another booming industrial and commercial city; their language, their patriarchal and familistic mores, and especially their religion, remained that of their ancient ancestors. Economically, they were predominantly unskilled laborers, domestic servants or small en-trepreneurs serving the other members of their own communities.

48

These ethnic islands were, of course, located in the heart of some of the worst slums in the nation, if not in the world. In the Twentieth Congressional District of New York, which sent La Guardia to Congress, some 250,000 people of twenty-seven nationalities, each in its own enclave, were crowded into one square mile. While a vast majority of the foreign-born lived out their lives as best they could, many of their children became delinquents and some of the parents sought an explanation for their suffering in such ideologies as socialism and communism. Thus the Communist Party, although always a minority party with never more than one hundred thousand members throughout the nation, drew a major proportion of its members from foreign-language-speaking groups from the time of its founding in 1919, through the twenties, and into the early thirties. The party had an especial appeal to Finns, to Eastern Europeans who were not devout Catholics, and to Yiddish-speaking Jews.

But leveling ideologies of the socialist variety have never had a wide appeal to the vast majority of ambitious Americans. As the traditional ways to wealth and respectability in business or the professions were more or less monopolized by Protestant Americans of older stock, many of the more talented and ambitious members of minority groups found careers in urban politics, in organized crime, or, for those of the Catholic faith, in the hierarchy of the Church. Of the two largest minority groups, the Irish and the Italian, the former tended to dominate both the Church and the urban political machines which, except in the City of Philadelphia, were largely responsible for keeping the Democratic Party alive during the years of Republican rule between the Civil War and the New Deal. This dominance of the Church and politics by the Irish may have been one of the factors that led the more overambitious members of the Italian community (the vast majority of whom were solid and law-abiding citizens) into the ranks of organized crime.

The Jewish immigrants and their descendants, a smaller minority than either the Irish or the Italian, followed somewhat different

49

ways to wealth. As Daniel Bell has written in his excellent essay on crime as an American way of life:

Early Jewish wealth, that of the German Jews of the late nineteenth century, was made largely in banking and merchandising. To that extent, the dominant group in the Jewish community was outside of and independent of the urban political machine. Later Jewish wealth, among the East European immigrants, was built in the garment trades, though with some involvement with the Jewish gangster, who was typically an industrial racketeer (Arnold Rothstein, Lepke and Gurrah, etc.). Among Jewish lawyers, a small minority, such as the "Tammany Lawyer" . . . rose through politics and occasionally touched the fringes of crime. Most of the Jewish lawyers, by and large the communal leaders, climbed rapidly, however, in the opportunities that established and legitimate Jewish wealth provided.[2]

The career of Abraham Rothstein was typical of the Russian-Jewish way to wealth in the second generation. The son of David who had fled the pogroms of his native Bessarabia, Abraham Rothstein was born on Henry Street, in the heart of the East Side ghetto. He always lived strictly according to the Law and the Decalogue, and, when it came time for marriage, a schadchen arranged it with an appropriate maid from San Francisco who came from the same Bessarabian stock. In accord with custom, the couple never met before their wedding day.

Abraham Rothstein made his way in the garment industry. And having achieved wealth and position in the Jewish community, he was given, in 1919, a dinner to honor his having settled a major labor dispute. He had been chosen as arbitrator because both sides completely trusted him, and among those gathered in his honor were Governor Alfred E. Smith and Justice Louis D. Brandeis. Abraham's talk after dinner was brief:

My father bequeathed me a way of life. He taught me, above all, to love God and to honor Him. Secondly, he taught me to honor all men and love them as brothers. He told me whatever I received I received from God and that no man can honor God more greatly than by sharing his possessions with others. This I have tried to do.[3]

This was the man of whom were told countless stories of charity, years of public service, rectitude and selflessness, and whom Alfred E. Smith called "Abe the Just." But he was also the father of Arnold Rothstein, industrial racketeer and gambler, allegedly the fixer of the 1919 World Series, and, as Lloyd Morris once wrote, "the Morgan of the underworld, its banker and master of strategy." Born into a family of comfortable means, in the same year as La Guardia and Roosevelt, and raised in a decent neighborhood uptown, Arnold Rothstein nevertheless went on to a career of gambling and crime. Just as Morgan had organized the business world into trusts and saved it from competitive anarchy, within the letter of the law and a generation earlier, so Rothstein organized illegal industrial rackets and gambling in his own generation. He was murdered in a lonely hotel room on Sunday, November 4, 1928, just two days before Jimmy Walker defeated Fiorello La Guardia, Herbert Hoover defeated the Irish-Catholic Alfred E. Smith, and Franklin D. Roosevelt defeated his Jewish opponent Albert Ottinger (had he lived, Rothstein would have collected $570,000 on his bets as a result of Hoover's and Roosevelt's victories).

While the second and third generations of hyphenated-Americans supplied outstanding leaders in urban politics, the Church and in organized crime, there were at the same time many men who came to the fore in the fields of business, entertainment, and in the arts and sciences. Yet even though they supplied an invigorating talent to the leadership of the nation as a whole, hyphenated-Americans, regardless of occupation or accomplishment, remained more or less isolated from the Protestant establishment. They were too often stereotyped as members of a class of non-Anglo-Saxon immigrants who filled the urban slums of the nation.

But the position of the newer immigrants as a whole was gradually improving. Before the First World War, for example, the center of gravity of the newer immigrants was in the first generation ethnic islands. Between the two wars, however, their sons and grandsons gradually improved their economic positions. As further immigration was cut off in the twenties, by the end of the thirties the center of gravity moved to the second generation. Although the majority were still members of the laboring classes, many had moved up a notch (this was reflected by the increase during the twenties of advertisements for white-collar jobs stating that "no Catholics or Jews need apply"). As this second generation now knew the language, had been educated in the public schools, and had assimilated American values of democracy, self-respect and equal opportunity, they were ready to move into the main stream of American life. And they found support in the Democratic Party, which, in the 1930's, moved out from local machine politics and onto the national stage under the leadership of Franklin D. Roosevelt.

While the New Deal served to bridge the gap between the immigrants and their children and the main stream of American life and leadership, the Second War and the postwar boom hastened the process. By the middle of the 1950's, the descendants of immigrants to the urban slums were increasingly affluent, college educated and members of the great middle class. The center of gravity was now in the third generation.

The Third Generation
and the Triple Melting Pot

Just what kind of Americans are these members of the third generation? In their attempt to answer this question, social scientists have developed the theory of the "triple melting pot."[4] According to this theory, ethnic and nationality groups are being Americanized, in the third and fourth generation, within three main religious communities—Catholic, Protestant and Jewish. Religious pluralism is replacing the ethnic pluralism of the earlier era. The process is somewhat as follows: prosperity in the expanding postwar economy has allowed large numbers to move out of their traditional ethnic neighborhoods and occupations. This has meant suburban residence, attendance at suburban schools along with older-stock neighbors, and the consequent need for new means of self-identification (especially for children). And this has produced a rapid increase in church and synagogue affiliation. Thus the Jewishness (ethnic) of the urban ghettos, and even in the areas of second settlement like the Bronx or along the upper West Side, is now being translated into the new Judaism of the synagogue-centered suburbia (Nathan Glazer estimates that whereas 75 per cent of the children in the Bronx during the thirties were receiving no Jewish training, in the suburbs of the fifties, almost 75 per cent report attendance at Sunday Schools).[5] And similarly, the one suburban Catholic church has replaced the Irish, Polish and Italian churches and institutions which characterized the downtown neighborhoods. In short, the Italian, Polish, Russian or Irish American of the urban, first- and second-generation minorities, has now given way to the Protestant-, Catholic- and Jewish-American sense of self-identity in our postwar suburban era. While the American electorate, for instance, would not elect an obviously Irish American to the White House in 1928, they were apparently less prejudiced about the dangers of a Catholic American being sent there in 1960.

The Jewish Melting Pot and the Class Structure

Within each of the three religious communities which make up the triple melting pot there are, of course, several class levels. And mobility within these class systems is one of the major instruments of assimilation. Just as the middle-class Baptist or Methodist is likely to join a suburban Presbyterian church in the course of his rise to a

53

position of elite affluence, and then move on to an Episcopal church in order to assimilate into the upper class, so the Orthodox East European Jew rises out of the ghetto and joins a Conservative synagogue uptown or out in a largely Jewish suburb, and perhaps eventually finds a Reform congregation even more congenial to his tastes as he moves into a predominately German-Jewish upper-class community. In one of the classic novels of Jewish life in America at the turn of the century, Abraham Cahan's *Rise of David Levinsky*, for instance, the hero, just twenty-five years after his arrival in this country, reflects on his participation in this process as follows:

> I was born and reared in the lowest depths of poverty and I arrived in America—in 1885—with four cents in my pocket. I am now worth more than two million dollars and recognized as one of the two or three leading men in the cloak-and-suit trade in the United States. . . .
> Most of the people at my hotel are German-American Jews. I know other Jews of this class. I contribute to their charity institutions. Though an atheist, I belong to one of their synagogues. . . . I am a member of that synagogue chiefly because it is a fashionable synagogue. I often convict myself of currying favor with the German Jews. But then German-American Jews curry favor with Portuguese-American Jews, just as we all curry favor with Gentiles and as American Gentiles curry favor with the aristocracy of Europe.[6]

There are, of course, highly complex class systems within every Catholic community in America, marked by Polish, Italian and Irish parishes, neighborhoods and associations, and led by the Church hierarchy and perhaps a few first families like the Fitzgeralds, Kennedys and Curleys of Boston. This chapter, however, will concentrate on the nature of the rather highly organized and rigid class system which developed within the Jewish community after the Civil War. The Jewish class system, in fact, has gone through three historical periods, depending on the size and composition of the Jewish community itself, and on the reactions of the gentile community.[7]

The first Jews in America arrived at New Amsterdam from the Dutch West Indies, in 1654, and a slow flow continued throughout the Colonial period. By the time of our first census, in 1790, some two thousand Jews were spread throughout the colonies. They were mostly merchants who had come from the West Indies and England and consequently were not marked off as a visible community. There were no rabbis in America during this period when, in fact, only five per cent of the population as a whole (in contrast to some 70 per cent today) were church-affiliated. Even where there was a sense of community, as in the Sephardic congregations in Newport or Philadelphia, the small number of Jewish merchants spent most of their time with non-Jews, which fostered intermarriage and assimilation (there was a shortage of Jewish females at this time). This was especially true at the highest levels of society, where Jews were part of the merchant establishment. This, then, was the classic period of aristocratic assimilation, and even today there are leading families within the old-stock and Protestant upper class, some of whose ancestors were prominent Jews during the Colonial period. This process of assimilation continued into the early part of the nineteenth century, when immigration was at a low point because of war and depression in this country and because of the Napoleonic conflicts in Europe.

But immigration picked up after 1820. And an increasing number of Jews came to America during the 1840's and 1850's, along with other immigrants from Germany. Although many of them were considered German rather than Jewish and therefore were assimilated immediately, the American-Jewish community had grown to some 150,000 persons by the time of the Civil War. In contrast to the merchants from the West Indies and England who predominated in the Colonial period, most of the new immigrants from Germany were peddlers seeking opportunities to rise in the world. Fortunately, these pre-Civil War decades were marked by the opening of the West and the rapid growth of small-town America. Thus many Jews became pioneers, first-family founders, and leading citizens in small towns all over the nation, often within one generation of their landing. The integration of the Jews in San Francisco in the years immediately following the discovery of gold in 1849 was more or less characteristic of many other American cities in this second, and predominately German, period of immigration.

Perhaps the most important demographic factors affecting the position of the Jews during this second period was their relatively small number and wide dispersion throughout the land. As of 1880, there were Jewish communities in all states, in 173 towns and cities, with no concentration in any particular part of the country (Jews made up about 3 per cent of the population of New York City in 1880, as against 30 per cent in 1920 and almost 40 per cent today).

These numerous German-Jewish communities centered around the synagogue and the family. Though members were of all classes, they were for the most part middle-class entrepreneurs. Those who became prominent in civic and business affairs formed an elite; they were not barred from belonging to prominent clubs and associations, and many were accepted socially by the best gentile society, some assimilating through marriage. This was especially true before the Civil War, when, for instance, the president of the most prominent men's club in Philadelphia was a member of a Jewish family and head of his synagogue. At the same time, Moses Lazarus—father of Emma, whose poem adorns the Statue of Liberty—was one of the founders of New York's patrician Knickerbocker Club, while Joseph Seligman was a founder of the Union League during the Civil War. Even as late as the 1870's, when young Louis D. Brandeis was welcomed into the best Boston society (see Chapter VIII), Jews still belonged to the best clubs in many cities, and a leading society journal could feature the news of a fashionable "Hebrew Wedding" in New York's Orthodox Thirty-fourth Street Synagogue.[8]

Perhaps the most important feature of this second historical period was the development of an affluent and highly aristocratic German-Jewish upper class.[9] Although the more famous family dynasties such as the Lehmans, Warburgs, Schiffs, Strauses, Loebs,

56

Morgenthaus, Ochses, Sulzbergers, Seligmans and Guggenheims eventually settled in New York, they formed a national upper class composed of small local aristocracies in the larger cities, linked together by intercity marriage alliances. Strict class and religious endogamy was characteristic of this class which was based largely on famous founders who came to America during the forties and fifties and made their fortunes in banking, merchandising and mining. The eminent banking house of Kuhn, Loeb & Company, founded in the middle of the century by Abraham Kuhn and Solomon Loeb, typified the dynastic proclivities of this aristocracy. The senior partner during the free-booting Morgan era, Jacob Schiff, came to America from Frankfurt am Main after the Civil War and married one of Solomon Loeb's daughters; Paul M. Warburg, of a Hamburg banking family, married another daughter; and his brother, Felix Warburg, married Jacob Schiff's daughter. These banking families were also intermarried with the Strauses, who along with the Gimbels and Rosenwalds were among the great mercantile families in the nation. But perhaps the Guggenheims were the most interesting family of them all.

The Family Founder was Meyer Guggenheim, who came to Philadelphia from his native Switzerland in 1847.[10] He began by peddling shoe polish on the streets of the city, then branching out into the lace business, and finally laying the cornerstone of his fortune in mining and smelting. As no dynasty is based on money alone, it was fortunate that his wife bore him eleven children, including eight sons. This second generation, well disciplined by their father's weekly family councils on Friday nights to outline family affairs and instill traditions, carried on the dynasty by enlarging the family businesses to include tin mines in Bolivia, gold mines in Alaska, diamond fields in Africa, copper mines and nitrate fields in Chile and rubber plantations in the Congo. They also married into prominent families within their class and faith, and produced twenty-four children. There was only one divorce, which was forced on the youngest son because he had married someone the family considered unsuitable.

The second Guggenheim generation came to maturity just as the second historical period of the Jewish adjustment to the American environment came to a close. This adjustment, to summarize, included a largely Americanized series of German-Jewish communities, dispersed throughout the nation and headed at the elite level by an intercity aristocratic establishment. As anti-Semitism was only sporadic and idiosyncratic, many individuals still participated at the top levels of gentile society, some being assimilated completely through marriage or conversion and others through membership in exclusive clubs and associations. But all this was changed by the flood tide of immigrants from Eastern Europe who came to America after 1880, when a third period of adjustment began.

This new immigration, as we have seen, changed the whole character of American society. It also had a profound influence on the nature of the Jewish community. Just as the Catholic peasant from Italy, Sicily, Poland and Czechoslovakia brought quite different customs, values and traditions to the New World than the earlier, Protestant immigrants from Northern Europe, so the Jews from Russia and Poland were also very different from the Sephardic and German Jews who were already established here as of 1880. It is no wonder that the majority of established citizens, both gentile and Jew, were frankly appalled at this tidal wave of new immigrants, possessed as they were of such alien ways. "One can understand," wrote Nathan Glazer, "the feelings of dismay of the earlier German Jewish immigrants as the Russian Jewish immigration, which had spurted upwards at the beginning of the 1880's, showed no signs of abating, and indeed grew larger. It is as if a man who has built himself a pleasant house and is leading a comfortable existence suddenly finds a horde of impecunious relatives descending upon him."[11]

This horde of impecunious relatives swelled the American-Jewish community to over four millions persons by the end of the 1920's, almost 80 per cent of whom were, by this time, of East European origin. But far more than the increased size of the community was involved. First, there was the concentration of East European Jews in our large cities, especially along the Eastern Seaboard. Thus by 1916, a majority of American Jewry were living in the five cities of New York, Philadelphia, Boston, Chicago and Baltimore (while there were 250,000 Jews in all America in 1880, by 1916, 350,000 were living in New York's Lower East Side alone). Moreover, while the majority of German Jews had been middle class and self-employed, the newer immigrants were largely wage workers concentrated in one industry, garment manufacture. This increase in the size and concentrated location of the newer immigrants, as well as their lower-class occupational pattern, was bound to create unfavorable stereotypes and stimulate anti-Semitism.

And these stereotypes which intensified anti-Semitism now applied to the whole Jewish community. Thus the term "kike," first coined by German Jews as a derogatory stereotype applying to the new Russian immigrants, was now used by gentiles when referring to Jews in general, the cultivated and Americanized German as well as the impoverished and alien garment workers on the Lower East Side. This was, of course, a terrible shock to the established Jews, especially the cultivated elite, some of whom became anti-Semitic themselves. For "the outraged 'German' Jew saw, shuffling down the gangplank, himself or his father, stripped of the accessories of respectability," writes Oscar Handlin, a leading contemporary historian of immigration. "This was what he had escaped from, been Americanized away from; he did not like its catching up with him. ... It was distasteful to incur the ill-feeling of one's fellow citizens on account of these unattractive new Jews; and this unattractiveness, it was frequently pointed out, was 'not so much a matter of religion, but of race and of habits.' "[12]

This new situation might well have precipitated a caste division within the American-Jewish community. For, after all, the differences in "race and habits" as between the newer "Russian" and the older "German" Jews was far greater than the cultural gulf dividing the Americanized German Jews from their gentile neighbors. And indeed there were tendencies toward caste, but the forces of aristocratic assimilation finally won out, and mainly for two reasons. First, increased anti-Semitism among gentiles created new and rigid caste barriers which now excluded all Jews, as well as convinced Christians of Jewish origins, from communal or associational participation in the larger gentile society, especially at the elite level. At the same time, and partly in reaction to new caste barriers raised by the gentiles, a majority of the most influential Jewish leaders within the established upper class, acting on their own ancient traditions of noblesse oblige, took the lead in insisting on the rights of Jews to seek refuge in this country, then assisted them in adjusting to their new life here, and eventually assimilated them into all levels of the American-Jewish community. Oscar Handlin describes the values of the leaders of the German-Jewish community at the turn of the century in the following paragraph:

Of this historic obligation of the rich toward the poor Jews such a man as Jacob Schiff was eminently conscious. Raised in the Frankfurt ghetto and later familiar to the banking circles of Europe, he was a maker of railroad and industrial empires. Riches and power were for him not ends in themselves, but means to assist the Jews in performance of a universal mission. He saw himself, the nogid, or man of wealth, as a shtadlan, or intermediary, between Jews and the rest of the world; and what bound him to Jews everywhere was the conviction "that as Jews we have something precious of high value to mankind in our keeping, that our mission in the world continues, and with it our responsibilities of one for the other." In those words he expressed the sentiments of the successful and powerful men of his generation.[13]

This process of aristocratic assimilation within the Jewish community went through several stages. In the first place, as the nineteenth century came to a close, almost all the charitable resources of the established community went toward aiding the new immigrants from Eastern Europe. And each year the amounts raised and the number of contributors increased. In Philadelphia, for example, the United Hebrew Charities, which raised some $15,000 dollars from about seven hundred contributors in 1870, increased its efforts to raise over $50,000 from more than eight thousand contributors by 1894. These charitable efforts within the established German-Jewish community continued and expanded throughout the early decades of the present century. At the same time, so-called Russian organizations played a larger and larger role in charitable giving, until the two groups, German and Russian, eventually merged. Again taking Philadelphia as an example of a nationwide trend, it was right after the First War that the Federation of Jewish Charities carried on its first combined campaign (over fifty German and Russian agencies cooperated), which set a pattern that has continued down to the present.

The changing patterns of charitable giving, even more so among Jews than among gentiles, are often excellent indexes of change within the elite and the upper-class structures. Thus, while the German-Jewish elite were bearing the main charitable burden at the turn of the century, they were also setting up various caste defenses against the ugliness of the urban melting pot. In much the same way as their gentile peers, they were forming their own exclusive clubs and neighborhoods as well as a series of exclusive summer colonies along the Jersey shore. They also built, in the manner of the Episcopalian gentry, new Reform synagogues, uptown, out in the suburbs and down at the shore. What was happening, in other words, was that both the old-stock gentile and Jewish upper classes, once organized along familistic and communal lines, were now becoming more formal and associational. This was because of the swelling of their ranks as a result of the great expansion of wealth at the turn of the century and the consequent need for formalized institutional ways of assimilating new men and families into the ranks of their respective upper classes. At the same time these exclusive institutions served to protect both upper classes from the rest of the population.

But just as the elite Russian Jews were assimilated into the new and combined charitable organizations after the First War, so the German upper class gradually let down its caste barriers and admitted leading members of the newer immigrant groups into its ranks. In Philadelphia, the leading Jewish country club as well as the most exclusive men's club in the center of the city were both founded and dominated by old-stock German-Jewish families well into the 1930's. By the end of the Second World War, however, these clubs had absorbed leading members of the new Russian-Jewish elite. And today, although there still remains a certain sense of caste superiority among the elder generation of old-stock Jewish families, the members of the younger generation are tending to blend on the basis of common affinity of culture, manners and wealth, rather than on ethnic origins alone.

At this point, I think, it is appropriate to stress the fact that the strength of the American-Jewish community—its low crime, delinquency and divorce rates, for example, as well as its members' extraordinary accomplishments—is at least partly due to its well-articulated class system which, at the same time, has always been combined with both the aristocratic and opportunitarian ideals of assimilation and mobility.

The Elite and the Marginal Man

Winston Churchill once said that in any hierarchical situation there is all the difference in the world between the number one man and number two, three, four and the rest. Thus, while most Americans, like David Levinsky, are living and moving up the class hierarchy within each of our larger religious communities, there exists today an important qualitative difference in the nature of social relationships at the very top levels of society. In other words, while there are

Diagram I

The Triple Melting Pot
and the Class System, 1900 and 1950

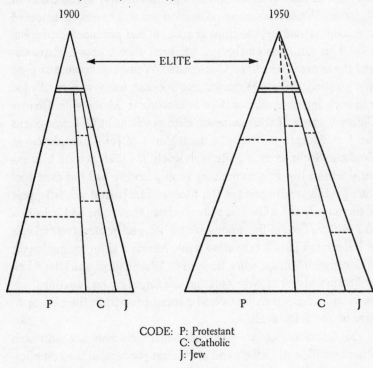

1900   1950

ELITE

P   C   J   P   C   J

CODE: P: Protestant
        C: Catholic
        J: Jew

upper-, middle- and lower-class levels *within the Protestant, Catholic and Jewish communities*, there are Protestants, Catholics and Jews *within the elite*. To put it another way, class tends to replace religion (and even ethnicity and race) as the independent variable in social relationships at the highest levels of our society (see Diagram I).

And this difference as between the elite and the rest of society is more pronounced in the third, as against the first and second generations. Whereas, for instance, Mayor John Francis Fitzgerald was an "FIF" (First Irish Family) within the Boston Catholic community, his son-in-law became a member of the national elite, both as a multimillionaire businessman and Ambassador to the Court of St. James. While the second generation was still emotionally rooted in a *marginal culture*, the third generation had produced a *marginal man*. This same marginality, as has been shown above, characterized the lives of Baruch, La Guardia and Weinberg, because of their elite positions. While Weinberg, for instance, was very naturally led into such intimate relationships as cruising in Maine with Charles Dickey because of their common elite positions at Goldman-Sachs and J. P. Morgan respectively, the majority of Jewish employees at Goldman-Sachs, even at quite high levels, led their private lives entirely within Jewish communities (and probably had not even met their gentile counterparts at the Morgan firm). And similarly, part of the tragedy of La Guardia's life was that, though he had led a rich and convivial social life among his artistic and professional friends of Italian and Jewish extraction while he was a rising young lawyer in Greenwich Village, when he went to Washington, and later when he became Mayor of New York, he was forced by his functional position of leadership either to lead a social life within the elite or to have no social life at all.

The functional necessity that elite members associate with each other regardless of background or religion (or race, as the complications in the lives of such eminent Americans as Ralph Bunche or Marian Anderson attest to), is paralleled in many other areas of life. In residential patterns, for instance, the lower-class Jew will live within an entirely Jewish neighborhood, the middle-class Jew in a predominately, but not wholly, Jewish suburb, while the elite Jew will more likely be found in an almost predominately gentile neighborhood. In New York City, while elite Jews have lived on the gentile East Side of Central Park for some years now, most of the leaders within the Jewish community will be found on the West Side of the Park. And in the fashionable suburbs, especially in the postwar exurbs, gentiles and Jews live as neighbors within elite class enclaves rather than in religious neighborhoods. One would imagine, for instance, that Jacob Schiff's grandson John Mortimer Schiff, who is married to George F. Baker's granddaughter and lives in the fashionable neighborhood of Oyster Bay, on Long Island, would have most of his primary social relationships with his gentile neighbors and in-laws. Recalling Baruch's experiences with his daughters in an earlier era, one wonders how the patronesses of fashionable dancing classes would handle the Schiff children.

The marginal elite member also has to face the problem of club membership. John Mortimer Schiff, as befitting his residence in Oyster Bay, is a member of the best gentile sporting and golfing clubs out on the Island. In town, however, where he is a senior partner, like his father and grandfather before him, in Kuhn, Loeb & Company and a civic leader of some distinction, he does not belong to any of the more patrician men's clubs—even those which his brother-in-law and Oyster Bay neighbor George F. Baker, Jr., lists in his Who's Who biography.

This elite pattern also extends to the socialization of children at school and at college. While public schools are largely neighborhood schools, and thus often ethnically homogeneous, the best private schools cater to a class clientele from all parts of the city and its suburbs, and increasingly tend to include a small nucleus of children from elite Jewish families. The boarding school is, of course, even a more powerful class-assimilating atmosphere for the minority of Jewish youths who go there from wealthy and prominent families. Similarly, the sons of the elite will be living in a far more class-bound atmosphere at Harvard than at the College of the City of New York.

Finally, of course, the class-limited way of life at the top is naturally reflected in the frequency of intermarriages and religious conversions. Thus Baruch, La Guardia and Schiff all married gentiles, as did one of Sidney Weinberg's sons. This pattern was nicely illustrated in the case of the Guggenheims, in the third generation. For while the second generation married into prominent families within their faith and closely knit class, their children not only married gentiles but also established something of a record as far as the frequency of their divorces and remarriages was concerned. This marginal family situation is further complicated by the problem of religious affiliation. Of the members of the Guggenheim family listed in the latest edition of *Who's Who*, none list any religious affiliation, except one, who, in the style of the establishment, lists affiliation in the Episcopal Church (and the Republican Party). Though most elite Jews do not go so far as religious conversion and prefer to live a secular social life outside synagogue or church, one has the definite impression that those who do become Christians prefer the Episcopalian communion, as well as the manners of the communicants, to other Protestant denominations. It is interesting that in Philadelphia, where Quakers tend to be among the city's elite, one often meets Friends of Jewish origins, especially at the more or less one-class suburban meeting houses (while the powerful man of affairs usually converts to the Episcopal ritual, the intellectual convert today—both gentile and Jew—prefers the studied absence of ritual in the Quaker or Unitarian services).

The theory of the triple melting pot, then, must be modified at the elite level in order to take into account the overwhelming factor of class. While in the third generation and at most class levels there is a return to ethnic and religious roots, centered in the suburban synagogue and church, there is a reversal of this trend today at the top levels of national leadership. And the pinch of prejudice will increasingly be felt as more and more non-Anglo-Saxon Protestants rise to this level of society. At the same time, it should be emphasized that this importance of class makes the theory of the persistence of the Anglo-Saxon Ideal—which many sociologists have seen as an important modifying factor in the melting-pot theory—even more important at the elite level than at other social-class levels. This is of course because the nation's leadership is still dominated by members of the WASP upper class, the primary source and carrier of this ideal. The persistence of this ideal and its influence on non-Protestant aspirants to elite status has nowhere been more sensitively expressed than in a recent novel of Jewish life by Myron E. Kaufmann.

While Abraham Cahan's novel, *The Rise of David Levinsky*, painted the classic portrait of an immigrant's rise to affluence within the Jewish community at the turn of the century, Kaufmann's *Remember Me to God*,[14] which Alfred Kazin has called "the most solid and most genuinely created novel of Jewish life in America," is the story of a young Jewish lad, Richard Amsterdam, who goes to Harvard College in the middle of the twentieth century. This pathetic yet touching story of Richard Amsterdam's consuming drive to become a member of the undergraduate establishment of Harvard clubdom includes his inevitable alienation from his highly respectable, suburbanized and Reform-affiliated family; his real and close friendship with Bill Hodge, a Proper Bostonian classmate; his attempted marriage to a rather vacuous debutante; and his moral ambivalence toward his near conversion to Beacon Hill Episcopalianism. His mission in life is outlined in his secret diary, *How to Become a Gentleman—(Handbook)—Anonymous*, in which he catalogues the contrasting Anglo-Saxon ideals of Proper Boston with the middle-class Jewish values he has lived with all of his life, and advocates conversion to the former. He, of course, tries to convert his Jewish friends to his point of view, among them Stuyvesant Gold, a New York intellectual at Harvard who actually has no time for Richard's philo-brahminism. The following excerpt from one of their numerous and lengthy conversations reveals Richard's reverence for the Anglo-American ideal:

"Stuyvesant," *he began leisurely, giving attention to poking his thumb at the glowing tobacco and surrounding ash, which had overflowed a little onto the pipe bowl, "I want you to concentrate on developing a more gentlemanly demeanor, so you won't stick out like a sore thumb. Now, it's not going to be easy, Stuyvesant; let's have that understood. The average Jewish guy isn't 'to the manner born,' so to speak, and he hasn't had it taught in the cradle and the benefit of good schools all his life. Probably his parents never had* a chance to go to college, and probably his grandparents were immigrants from eastern Europe. It's going to take a lot of hard, discouraging work to unlearn all these foreign mannerisms and New York mannerisms of yours and set up some new brain patterns so you'll have some polish. Look at me; I've lived around Boston and vicinity all my life and yet I find I'm still learning. I want you to keep an eye on Bill Hodge. You learn what a gentleman is by watching one. And study the guys from Groton and St. Mark's. Their facial expression. How they modulate their voice. It's always clear and distinct and pleasing to the ear. An American should be proud of his language and handle it with respect, because it's the language of Shakespeare." He took a long draw on his pipe, and then watched the smoke curl before him. "And it might be a good idea for you and your father to try and get some hunting in this summer. Go up to the north woods in New York State—I believe you have north woods up there the same as we do in New England. Get yourself a couple of rifles and lumber jackets and those red hunting caps and go up there with your father for a few weeks and shoot game. . . .[15]

Much like Marquand's ironic treatment of the Protestant establishment, Kaufmann's saga of Richard Amsterdam certainly seems overimpressed with the superficial aspects of upper-class life. Yet, to the outsider, perhaps, these may be the very things that do matter. In this connection, for instance, it is of interest that the autobiographies of Alfred E. Smith, James A. Farley and Edward Flynn all emphasize their efforts to be properly dressed. One observes this same pattern among today's college students: on the Main Line, in Philadelphia, one is impressed that the students at Haverford College, an old and venerable Quaker institution, are almost invariably clothed in a most informal, if not downright sloppy, manner, often sporting straggly, adolescent beards in various stages of growth. A bit further out on the Lancaster Pike, on the other hand, at a newer and rapidly expanding Catholic institution, Villanova University, the students wear coats and neckties, and always appear to be clean-shaven. Similarly, at the University of Pennsylvania in the city, the Jewish fraternities require their brothers to wear coats and neckties, at least in the classroom, while it is often the old-stock Protestants who cultivate the beatnik style. At any rate, young Amsterdam did not take his mission lightly and considered himself a pioneer in the process of assimilation into the American establishment. Thus he tells his real love, a young Jewish girl at Radcliffe, of the seriousness of his mission:

"Don't you see the significance of what I'm trying to do? Our *religion is finally taking its place in this country, and think what it'll mean if I can get up to be a banker and big industrial magnate and run down and advise them in Washington all the time like Mr. Hodge does, and maybe even accept a cabinet post sometime, and at the same time be a Jew that's fully accepted in the inner circles of Boston society. What that will mean for the realization of American democracy, both in terms of my leading those old Yankee families further toward liberalism as a result of my own authority in their different institutions and outfits and everything, and at the same time making them less afraid of minorities by showing them how completely congenial I am. And after I break the ice there'll come Italian guys and colored guys and everything, on any board of directors and in any drawing room. These things are coming, but it's guys like me that push it. I look on it as a mission.*"[16]

In many ways, young Richard Amsterdam's sometimes pathetic confessions of his mission in life goes to the very heart of the problem of American leadership in the second half of the twentieth century. For, while the social organization of the triple melting pot serves quite effectively in assimilating the descendants of the more recent immigrants into most levels of our pluralistic society, there is, at the same time, constant pressure at the top levels of leadership today, which is increasingly composed of hyphenated-Americans of the third generation, to assimilate *all* talented and powerful men, regardless of their origins or religious convictions, into the main stream of traditional authority by ultimately rewarding them with the dignity, security and family honor implied and nourished by membership in an establishment.

The Triple Melting Pot and the Theory of the Establishment

In order to sharpen and elaborate the theory of the establishment, I have attempted to conceptualize, in a series of logical models shown in Diagram II, the past and possible future relationships between the three main ethnic-religious groupings in American society and the two variables of stratification: *social power* (position and power in the functional hierarchy of politics, business, religion, art, etc.) and *social status* (family position and prestige in the social-class hierarchy). Diagram II, in other words, conceptualizes the logically possible relationships between Protestants (WASPs), Catholics and Jews and the social organization of leadership. The *elite* concept, then, refers to those *individuals* at the top of the social power hierarchy (Diagram II, Box a and b); the *upper-class* concept refers to those *families* at the top of the social-status hierarchy (Box a and c); and the *establishment* refers to those leaders within the elite whose families also belong, or are in the process of belonging, to the upper class (Box a).

All social organizations are, of course, hierarchical. For social action depends on the differential distribution of power as between classes and individuals. The essential problem of social order, in turn, depends not on the *elimination* but the *legitimation* of social power. For power which is not legitimized (Box b) tends to be either coercive or manipulative. Freedom, on the other hand, depends not in doing what one wants but on wanting to do what one ought because of one's faith in long-established authority. An establishment (Box a), then, is composed of families who carry traditional authority deriving from the past, and present, power of

Diagram II

The Establishment and
the Triple Melting Pot

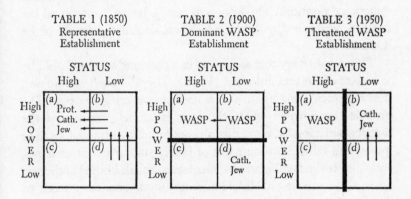

TABLE 1 (1850)
Representative
Establishment

TABLE 2 (1900)
Dominant WASP
Establishment

TABLE 3 (1950)
Threatened WASP
Establishment

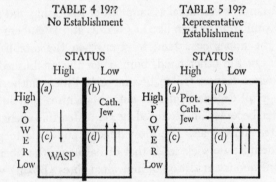

TABLE 4 19??
No Establishment

TABLE 5 19??
Representative
Establishment

KEY CONCEPTS: Elite: Boxes *a* and *b* (High Functional Power)
                 Upper Class: Boxes *a* and *c* (High Social Status)
                 Establishment: Box *a* (Power, Status and Authority)
                 WASP: White-Anglo-Saxon-Protestant
                 Caste: Status without Authority (Box *c*)
                 Aristocracy: Status with Authority (Box *a*)

71

their members. Both Franklin Roosevelt and Fiorello La Guardia, for instance, had power because of their personal qualities and functional positions. The Roosevelt family, however, possessed the kind of established authority which was denied the family of La Guardia.

This is not to say that all leaders in a changing society should be members of the establishment (Box a). They definitely should not. For new men (Box b) are always needed in every generation. The trouble comes when whole classes of new men, because of the accidents of ancestry, are denied the opportunity of translating their power and talent into some sort of family authority. But caste not only denies the families of new men access to established authority; caste also weakens established authority itself because it tends to alienate its supposed beneficiaries by emphasizing their *rights* to privilege (Box c) rather than their *duties* to lead (Box a). Both the Roosevelt family's continual assumption of leadership and the continuous assimilation of men like La Guardia and Weinberg into the ranks of the upper class tend to strengthen the establishment's authority. On the other hand, both when the established fail to lead and when leaders fail to become established, authority is in grave danger of degenerating into authoritarianism, and an organic social order becomes an atomized horde of fearful, alienated and manipulated individuals. The most difficult and delicate problem faced by democratic societies is that of balancing the liberal need for the continuous circulation of individual elites (Box b) with the conservative need for maintaining a continuity of family authority (Box a).

It is the theory of the establishment, then, that the processes of history may be conveniently conceptualized in terms of classes of men and their families circulating counterclockwise on the logical model outlined in Diagram II. When the cycle is complete, and is working without the corruptions of caste, the accomplishments and power of individual leaders are translated into family prestige and the continuity of established authority is maintained. From this point of view American leadership has gone through three more or less distinct periods.

In the first period, from the nation's founding and roughly through the first half of the nineteenth century, positions in the establishment were open to all white men, regardless of ethnic origins (Diagram II, Table 1). Thus, although there was a great deal of anti-Catholicism and fear of "Popery," individual Catholics were assimilated into the upper class on the basis of achievement and manners. The famous anti-Catholic riots in Philadelphia during the 1840's were really anti-Irish, and there was little or no antipathy toward middle-class German Catholics and certainly none toward the few distinguished Catholics who belonged to the upper class. At this time many leading families of Irish and Catholic origins became converts and passed on to their descendants solidly established positions in the Eastern Seaboard upper class. This was the case, for example, for such leading members of the Protestant establishment in Philadelphia as the Drexels of banking eminence (originally Austrian Catholics) or the descendants of George Gordon Meade, Lincoln's choice to lead the Union forces at Gettysburg, who was baptized an Episcopalian at the time of the Civil War, though his ancestors had been staunch Catholics in Ireland and in Philadelphia at the time of the Revolution. And this same pattern of accepting men on their merits and manners and assimilating their families into the establishment was followed, as we have seen, in the case of the Jews. The power of aristocratic assimilation which existed at this time, for example, was implied in a recently published history of the Philadelphia Assemblies—annual balls, attendance at which still marks a family's inclusion within the innermost circles of Philadelphia's upper class and which have been held continuously since George Washington was one's dancing partner. Thus the author of this history was proud to write that "there are on the Subscribers' List of the Assemblies today, families of the following racial strains: English, Welsh, Irish, French, German, Dutch, Swiss, Italian, Spanish, Portuguese, Swedish, and Polish."[17] (What he meant was

73

that the impeccable WASP establishment in the city of Philadelphia was composed of families whose ancestors included Spanish, Portuguese, German and Polish Jews, Irish, French and Italian Catholics, as well as Protestants from all these nations and dominated by those from the British Isles.) In this first historical period, then, the American establishment, though rooted in a mercantile upper class which was exclusive, proud, uniform in manners and certainly less patronizingly democratic in its treatment of the rest of the population than is the case today, was nevertheless still representative of the ethnic and religious composition of the white population.

But all this was to change after the Civil War, when the ethnic composition of American society was radically altered by the new immigration. This second historical period, which reached its peak somewhere between 1900 and the First World War, was marked by an associationally exclusive establishment of White–Anglo-Saxon-Protestants who dominated the leadership of the nation. As this period was such an important turning point in our history and so central to the theory of leadership developed in this book, it has already been discussed in some detail. Here it is only necessary to emphasize that the WASP establishment during this period was still representative of the elite, even though it was increasingly less representative of the population as a whole (Diagram II, Table 2). For this reason the establishment still possessed authority. In other words, it is not necessary, in the short run at least, that an upper class be representative of the whole people. In fact upper-class families are not recruited from the population at all but only from its leadership. The elite, on the other hand, must in the long run reflect and draw on the pool of national talent which inevitably resides in all classes. This is especially true where the people are literate and where a considerable majority have an opportunity for education. As of 1900, there was an authoritative establishment even though there was a more or less closed caste line drawn at the elite level which

74

excluded those hyphenated-Americans of the Catholic and Jewish communities.

The significant difference in the structure of leadership in America in the third, as against the second, historical period is the fact that the caste line is now drawn in a status rather than a power sense, or, as it were, right down the middle of the elite (Diagram II, Table 3). In other words, our open class system has continued to work quite well and has produced a more or less ethnically representative elite. Our status system, on the other hand, has failed to keep pace. The WASP establishment has been forced to share its power while at the same time continuing to hoard its social privileges. In a very important sense, we now have in America, at the elite level of leadership, a *caste-ridden, open-class* society. And the consequent pressure upon the upper class to open its doors to the most talented and polished descendants of the newer immigrants has increased tremendously. For example, whereas the great expansion of the public school system in the first half of the twentieth century was useful in preparing the children of immigrants to rise within the confines of their particular ethnic community, the present boom among the college educated is producing quite different patterns of mobility and attitudes toward the melting pot. For the polished graduate of Harvard in the third generation will surely not be content, as Richard Amsterdam's story tells so well, either to remain within the confines of his ethnico-religious community or to remain forever a marginal man.

At this time it is hard to see how the dynamic tension between the pressures of caste exclusion and of aristocratic assimilation which is now characteristic of the nation's leadership will finally be resolved. Today the situation is an ambivalent one. In the long run, there are two logically possible alternatives: either the WASP establishment will eventually develop into a closed caste, protecting its way of life and privileges while gradually abdicating from its position of leadership (Diagram II, Table 4), or a new aristocracy will emerge with the energy and ability to absorb the most prominent and polished families in the nation, regardless of their ethnic origins or religious convictions (Table 5). These strictly logical alternatives are, of course, only polar tendencies, and reality will fall somewhere in between.

The Tendency to Caste

History is a graveyard of classes which have preferred caste privileges to leadership. The Roman republic, for instance, eventually passed into a democratic despotism largely because the old senatorial aristocracy, in spite of the attempted reforms of the two Gracchi, gradually degenerated into a caste that was unable to successfully absorb the class of Knights, or newly rich urban businessmen. And Tocqueville, as we have seen, pointed out how the British learned from, while the French followed, this Roman precedent. In this country, the eventual decline of the Federalist aristocracy at the beginning of the nineteenth century was, among other things, due to its leaders' failure to learn from the examples of Rome and Paris. While Jefferson and his followers did everything to capture the immigrants' vote, Harrison Gray Otis and the Federalist leaders at the Hartford Convention of 1812, "blind to the realities of pluralist politics to the last gasp, urged a constitutional amendment to bar naturalized citizens from elective and civil office."[18] And as will be brought out in later chapters, the Republican establishment today may also have failed to learn from history.

There are always tendencies toward the caste position (Diagram II, Box c) within any upper class. There are, for example, the well-bred expatriates who live abroad and consider everything American rather common and vulgar; there are the patrician clubmen who so often specialize in genealogy, getting on club admission committees and keeping people out; and there is the growing class of gentlemen-farmers in America, many of them expatriated down on the Eastern shore in Maryland or in the beautiful hunting country around Middleburg, Virginia. One was recently offered an opportunity to reflect on the caste-psychology of this kind of American when, soon after the 1960 Presidential election, a group of Middleburg gentlemen-farmers attempted to block the Kennedy family from membership in the local hunt club. And perhaps it is an ironic sign of our times that Robert Todd Lincoln Beckwith, one of the two last remaining male descendants of Abraham Lincoln, while not listed for any particular accomplishments in Who's Who, is listed in the Social Register, and is a gentleman-farmer in Virginia (Box c).*

But perhaps of greater importance as factors in the decline of the establishment than those persons who have, as it were, resigned from the American experiment is the ever increasing number of business gentlemen who are more interested in success and the protection of their privileged way of life than in leading the community as a whole. They are the successful lawyers who would not consider an appointment to the local bench, or even the Supreme Court (the Philadelphia bar abounds with Proper Protestants while the bench is conspicuous, in recent years, by their absence); they are the favored ones who would not think of dirtying their hands in politics or encouraging their sons to do so. This mood was shown recently in Philadelphia when the exposure of a series of voting frauds rocked the complacency of the city. Thus when the leading local newspaper asked a group of the city's most distinguished citizens to comment on the situation, a leading member of the bar, senior partner in a distinguished law firm and a member of one of the most patrician and talented families in the city, replied: "I know nothing about politics or elections"; another Philadelphia gentleman, also one of the more successful and highly paid executives in the city, could only say: "I haven't followed the situation enough to be intelligent about it"; and a former bank president and head of one of the most affluent and oldest Quaker-turned-

---

* When Robert Todd Lincoln Beckwith, on a visit to Mexico City, was introduced to Benito Juárez, descendant of the great liberator, the Washington *Evening Star* (July 11, 1962) quoted Beckwith as saying: "I never take part in politics. None of the family does."

Episcopal clans in the city had "no comment. I'm not going to get into that situation."[19] Perhaps these comments are understandable reactions to the jungle politics of our larger cities today. But they also reflect the all-too-prevalent attitudes of a class which has been bred, in this twentieth-century America, to succeed rather than to lead.

One of the nation's first plutocrat families, the Astors, provides an excellent example of the forces of caste in America. It is an interesting test case because the same family has followed more in the aristocratic traditions in England. Thus, while the American Astors, once so prominent in the world of Ward McAllister's "Four Hundred," are now known primarily for their wealth and high divorce rate, the British branch of the family sent no less than five of its members to Parliament during the thirties and even today plays a prominent role in both politics and publishing. In this connection, an inspection of the brief biographies of the three Astors listed in a recent edition of *Who's Who in America* (1958–59) was revealing: The late Vincent Astor listed no occupation or profession, noted that he was "now head of the Astor family in the U.S.," and reported that he had three marriages and belonged to fifteen patrician clubs. In contrast, Baron Astor of Hever listed himself as Chairman of the Times Publishing Company and reported one marriage and six club memberships. Viscountess Astor listed her accomplishments as a Member of Parliament and as an authoress. The "blood" was the same, but the environment was different.

The caste-psychology which has led an increasing number of wealthy, talented and educated old-stock Americans to withdraw from power while at the same time protecting their privileged way of life has surely been a factor in the declining authority of the establishment. But the more extreme caste view of the American political process held by those old-stock Americans like Lucius Beebe is potentially far more dangerous. Thus, in a respectable San Francisco newspaper, he commented on the candidates in the last Presidential campaign as follows:

There is a fugitive feeling among Republicans, and responsible people generally, that it would have been a good thing for everybody if Stevenson had been the Democratic nominee instead of a rich mick from the Boston lace curtain district. . . .

The truth of the matter is, whatever clowns, flunkies, and farmers Americans will tolerate in other offices, they have consistently shown that they prefer to have a gentleman, or reasonable facsimile thereof, in the White House. He might be a loud brassy gentleman like Roosevelt I or a class renegade like Roosevelt II or a gentleman ex officio like Harding, but . . . there is a sneaking suspicion abroad in the land that neither Nixon nor Kennedy is quite a gentleman. A good many people are fed up with both parties for not having nominated somebody of gentility, good breeding and manners for the First Citizen of the Republic.

Hostility to Nixon on these grounds has an evasive quality. . . . Prejudice against Kennedy is much easier to pinpoint: it is lace curtain Irish background in a political pigsty so liberally befouled by the late Mayor of Boston and jailbird, James M. Curley, that honest Democrats elsewhere in the land are appalled by it. . . .[20]

Though hardly as blatantly displayed in public, this caste-corrupted view of the late President Kennedy has been, and still is, shared by all too many of the alienated genteel. And, though unfortunate, it is an understandable attitude for one who takes the more generalized view of American society and its government which Mr. Beebe outlines in the next paragraph in this same article:

The electorate has come to realize that, in order to be a candidate, an aspirant for presidential honors must be a congenital liar and that he cannot, and has no intention of delivering a thousandth part, of any of his campaign promises. The voters know damned well that, whomever they vote for and whomever they may elect, they will be taxed more ruinously, rooked more grievously, lose more of their liberties and support more trash in Government offices than before. Wised up by thirty years of continuous short changing and *repudiation of currency, the* American people know pretty well that the enemy is Washington as well as Moscow.[21]

It would be wrong, I think, to dismiss these irresponsible statements as merely the isolated ravings of a resentful mind. For they represent precisely the consequences of the caste point of view when carried to its logical conclusion. And if this conspiritorial view of American society ever comes to be held by the majority of the old-stock upper class, the authority of the traditional establishment will surely be replaced by some form of authoritarianism, whether it be fascism or some form of 100 per cent Americanism.

The Aristocratic Tendency

There is perhaps an all too prevalent tendency toward caste among old-stock families of third- and fourth-generation wealth which, in turn, is so likely to degenerate into the irresponsible view of American society displayed by Lucius Beebe. On the other hand this is by no means the dominant trend. It is hardly conceivable that men who are actively carrying on family traditions of leadership, such for example as Henry Ford II, Thomas J. Watson, Jr., or Nelson Rockefeller, would exhibit the same cynical and irresponsible attitude toward America as those who are obsessed with their own caste superiority. In fact, America is probably now producing more leaders who have had inherited advantages than at any other time in the twentieth century. For we live in an age of radically conflicting social forces, and, along with the alienated genteel and deracinated marginal man, the 1950's also produced such old-stock leaders as Robert Fiske Bradford, a Mayflower descendant, as Governor of Massachusetts; Sinclair Weeks, Secretary of Commerce; Robert Cutler, Assistant to President Eisenhower; Christian Herter and Dean Acheson as Secretaries of State; Henry Cabot Lodge, Ambassador to the United Nations, and his brother, Governor of Connecticut and Ambassador to Spain; John Cabot, Ambassador to Brazil (eleven Cabots are listed in the 1958–59 edition of *Who's Who in America*); one Taft in the Senate and another a leader in civic and church affairs; one Saltonstall in the Senate and another head of Phillips Exeter Academy; a Lowell, a Pulitzer Prize-winner in poetry, and Charles Francis Adams, the head of Raytheon.

And also, at the end of the 1950's, the Democratic Party—the party of the urban ethnic masses, which has its share of aristocratic leaders like Stevenson, Harriman, Acheson and Bowles—finally produced a victory for the second Catholic Presidential candidate in our history. Future historians will certainly look back on the election of John Fitzgerald Kennedy to the Presidency of the United States, in 1960, as a turning point in our history and symbol of a trend toward ethnic aristocracy in America. It was a decisive victory over the forces of caste.

The American people are indeed fortunate that, contrary to the views of men like Lucius Beebe, their political traditions are essentially conservative. Just as Andrew Jackson led a rather crude frontier democracy and yet was himself, both temperamentally and sociologically as master of the "Hermitage," very much in the aristocratic mold of Washington or Jefferson; so, it seems to me at least, President Kennedy was an ideal blend of the old and the new in American leadership. Thus he came to this high national honor, not as the representative of any ethnic machine dominated by political bosses, not as a man who had risen from humble origins, and, above all, not as a man of resentment and alienation who often tends toward extreme positions of either the Left or the Right. Born into a family of unquestioned ability, great wealth, and a two-generation tradition of governmental service (Diagram II, Box b), and educated at patrician Choate School (which produced both Chester Bowles and Adlai Stevenson) and at Harvard University, President Kennedy (Box a) surely followed in the twentieth-century tradition of such Tory reformers as Woodrow Wilson and the two Roosevelts. He was not only essentially conservative politically;

he always talked to the American people from deeply rooted historical convictions, in a dry, factual and typically New England intellectual style, which was probably due, in large part, to his extremely familistic and traditionally religious upbringing. At any rate, just as Nathaniel Hawthorne's sense of American history led him to a deep admiration for Andrew Jackson, so the late Robert Frost, deeply rooted in the individualistic soil of New England Republicanism and hardly sympathetic to the modern welfare state, became an admirer and supporter of John Fitzgerald Kennedy. John P. Marquand, whose creation of *The Late George Apley* was a testament to his understanding of the Anglo-Saxon brahmin mind in America, was also convinced of Kennedy's ability to carry on our best traditions as he (Marquand) understood them. Thus an editor of the *New Yorker* wrote of his last interview with Marquand: "Five days before he died, the week of the Democratic Convention, he surprised us (for we had understood that he was a Republican) by announcing that it was his intention to vote for Senator Kennedy and by contributing, as his share of the talk, a charming and touching personal anecdote about the nominee's grandfather, whom he called Honey Fitz."

The Presidency is the highest office in the Republic, and the Kennedys became the nation's First Family. Just as the Roman republican nobility was composed of descendants of men who had held a consulship, so the Kennedy family's having taken its place at the heart of the American establishment will open up old-stock upper-class ranks to other Catholic families of accomplishment and talent.

As far as Catholics are concerned, there are other indications of changing attitudes within the old-stock establishment. When Henry Cabot Lodge, during the last Presidential compaign, was asked about his views toward having a Catholic in the White House, he was undoubtedly guided in his affirmative answer by the fact that some of his own grandchildren, one of whom may some day seek this office, were being brought up as Catholics; nor would the wealthy heir to fundamentalist Protestant intolerance, Henry Ford II, regard a member of his own Catholic faith as an unworthy candidate for the Presidency solely because of his religion.

The election of President Kennedy, then, marked a definite trend toward a representative establishment (Diagram II, Table 5) as far as the Catholic community is concerned. While anti-Semitism is, of course, something quite different from the antipathy toward Catholics in America, anyone involved in the study of minority relations in this country knows that all hyphenated-Americans (and Negroes as well) tend to share a more or less common marginal situation and feel, in turn, that a breakthrough for one group is a break for all. In other words, even though there is a certain amount of antipathy and rivalry between Catholics and Jews, they both identify with their common exclusion from the WASP monopoly of established prestige and power. If one looked beneath the surface of the Kennedy Administration, which included a Presidential staff and Cabinet (16 Phi Beta Kappas, 4 Rhodes Scholars and one Nobel Prize winner) of Catholic, Jewish and Protestant convictions and diverse ethnic origins, one sensed its awareness of the need to foster an ethnically representative leadership and establishment in this country. More will be said about this awareness on the New Frontier in later chapters. Here it is interesting to note that one of the late President's closest associates, Treasury Secretary Dillon, is a patrician Episcopalian who represents not only the finest type of devoted and talented leadership in America but is also an excellent example of the process of aristocratic assimilation in the third generation.[22]

President Kennedy and Douglas Dillon had much in common: both were of newer immigrant stock; both inherited millions of dollars from fabulously successful fathers who had made their way on their own; both followed their fathers to Harvard University; both were officers in the United States Navy and saw action against the Japanese; both were members of the same club at Harvard, the Spee, where they first met, in 1956, while Kennedy was receiving an honorary degree and Dillon was serving as First Marshal at his class's twenty-fifth reunion.

Douglas Dillon's paternal grandfather was Sam Lapowski, son of a Polish Jew and a French Catholic, who emigrated to Texas after the Civil War, adopted his mother's maiden name of Dillon, prospered as a clothing merchant in San Antonio and Abilene, and finally moved to Milwaukee, where he entered the machinery-manu-facturing business. Sam's son Clarence, born in Texas (1882), was sent East to a private preparatory school in Worcester, Massachusetts, and then to Harvard. Young Clarence Dillon, called the "Baron," was an excellent gambler who took all the gay blades' money and was a respected member of his class. Although he did not make one of the family-tree-conscious clubs, he was taken into the Hasty Pudding in his senior year.

Upon his graduation from Harvard in 1905 (one year behind Franklin Roosevelt) Clarence Dillon returned to Milwaukee and entered business. While spending the weekend with a prominent and wealthy family in the suburbs, he was almost killed in a railroad accident. Rushed to his host's house, he was gradually nursed back to health by their daughter, Anne McEldin Douglas, whom he married the next year and then took off for a two-year honeymoon in Europe.

After a brief business partnership with his brother-in-law in Milwaukee, Dillon moved East to Wall Street, where within five years he had worked his way to the top of William A. Reed & Company. Revolutionizing this conservative firm (now Dillon, Reed), he had much the same success on the Street as at the poker tables at Harvard (he once wrote out a personal check for $146 million to buy the Dodge Brothers Auto Company).

Clarence Douglas Dillon (Clarence has since been dropped) was born in Geneva, Switzerland (1909), and raised in the proper manner of the Eastern Seaboard establishment. He was educated at Groton, where he was an excellent student but not particularly good at games, and then went to Harvard, where he was manager of the football team and graduated magna cum laude, in 1931. Right after graduation he married a handsome and talented Proper Bostonian. His father bought him a $185,000 seat on the stock exchange and took him into his Wall Street firm, where he followed the mores of a competent and conventional banker until the Second War broke out. He joined the Navy, rose to the rank of lieutenant commander, and won the Air Medal and Legion of Merit for his part in the Black Cat operations at Guam, Saipan and the Philippines. Returning from the war, he took a more aggressive part in the affairs of Dillon, Reed and also drifted into politics, working for Dewey in 1948 and leading the draft-Eisenhower movement in New Jersey in 1952. He was made Ambassador to France, in 1953, and Deputy Undersecretary of State for Economic Affairs, in 1957. He then became Secretary of the Treasury under President Kennedy, with whom he had great rapport.

The Dillons live at the very heart of the American establishment. Their six residences—in Washington; at Château Haut-Brion, near Bordeaux, where they produce some of the world's finest claret; at Hobe Sound in Florida; at Dark Harbor in Maine; in New York City; and at the old family place in Far Hills, New Jersey—reveal their sensitive taste in *objets d'art* and Impressionist paintings; Harvard, Groton and Foxcroft have benefited from generous gifts from the family; and Douglas Dillon's club memberships include such patrician and business strongholds as the Racquet, Knickerbocker, Links, River, Recess, Century, and Pilgrims in New York; and the Metropolitan in Washington.

An outstanding member of the WASP establishment in the middle of the twentieth century, the Dillon family provides an excellent witness to the staying power of the American Dream of equal opportunity and aristocratic assimilation. And the talent, wealth and devotion to duty of Douglas Dillon has certainly contributed to the establishment's continuing direction of the nation's leadership. It is indeed a fortunate thing for the nation that the Dillons have been an exception to the general rule of caste-corruption which has excluded countless other prominent and talented families of partly Jewish origins from the establishment. On the other hand, when the Dillons were recently taken into the Chevy Chase Club in Washington, after a number of years on the waiting list, the deeply rooted prejudices of caste were apparently still in full force, as the following circumspect lines written by Arthur Krock at the time reveal: "The most prominent country club in the Washington area, the Chevy Chase Club, has steadfastly maintained a more rigid discrimination than either of the others (Cosmos and Metropolitan), and broader in that it also excludes from membership all Caucasians it assigns to one ethnic group of the population. This barrier was recently lowered for a high Administration official only on the solemn assurance to disturbed traditionalists that his percentage of origin in this group was a maximum of 25."[23]

Unfortunately the values of the traditionalists at the Chevy Chase are in accord with the most prevalent patrician mores in America today. Thus Senator Goldwater, of an old and established Arizona family and presumably acceptable to the majority of old-school traditionalists as far as his political values and style of life are concerned, was about to play a round of golf recently, so the story goes, when he was told that the course was "restricted." When he replied: "I'm only half Jewish, so can't I play nine holes?" his sense of humor was a tragic reminder of Fiorello La Guardia's response to the same set of values.

That two such distinguished gentlemen as Douglas Dillon and Barry Goldwater should be treated dishonorably only serves to dramatize the absurdity of such values. In order to better understand these values, and why they are being challenged today as never before in our history, the chapters which follow will be devoted to an exploration of their historical roots, showing how these values of caste have been in continual conflict with the American Dream as well as that part of the establishment which has always held fast to the ideals of aristocracy.

Thy wish was father, Harry, to that thought.

William Shakespeare

IV

The Ideological Defense of Caste: From Henry Adams to Madison Grant

In the Preface to the second edition of his classic study of the visionary ideals of Puritanism, Brooks Adams devoted more than one hundred pages to an analysis of ancient Judaism through the life of Moses, "the first great optimist and visionary of which any record remains."[1] Any discussion of the attitudes toward Jews in America would then do well to begin with a look at the Puritan mind, which, after all, has been so important in shaping our best traditions.

"The Gentile of American Puritan stock who puts himself in contact with the Hebrew culture finds something at once so alien that he has to make a special effort in order to adjust himself to it, and something that is perfectly familiar."[2] Thus, in attempting to understand the influence of Hebrew on the English language, Edmund Wilson was struck by the strong affinity between Judaism and the Puritanism of early New England. "The Puritanism of New England," Wilson continues, "was a kind of new Judaism, a Judaism transposed into Anglo-Saxon terms. When the Puritans came to America, they identified George III with Pharaoh and themselves with the Israelites in search of the Promised Land. They called their new country Canaan and talked continually of the Covenant they had made with God. Winthrop and Bradford were Moses and Joshua; Anne Hutchinson was pilloried as Jezebel. 'The Christian church so-called,' said a preacher in New Marlborough, Massachusetts, 'is only a continuation and extension of the Jewish church.' 'If we keep the covenant,' said Winthrop, 'we shall finde then the God of Israel is among us.' The Hebrew language, later on in New England, was to be taught as a major subject, not merely in the colleges but even in the schools."[3]

One of the vital aspects of the American Dream has always been our sense of having a moral mission in the world. This sense of mission, though a strong force throughout the major part of the nineteenth century, reached its height in the abolitionist movement. One of the more volcanic abolitionists, Harriet Beecher Stowe, was reared in the typical Puritan, Philo-Hebraic tradition. Her husband, Calvin Stowe, had been a teacher in her father's seminary when they married, and eventually went on from a study of the Bible to the Talmud. Often called "Old Rab" by his wife, Calvin Stowe at one time made a pioneering study of the Talmud, allowed his beard to grow, and habitually wore a rabbinical skullcap. Harriet's own close identification with the Hebraic tradition of the Puritans came out again and again in her stories. "I think no New Englander," she wrote in Old Town Folks, "brought up under the regime established by the Puritans, could really estimate how much of himself had actually been forced by this constant face-to-face intimacy with

Hebrew literature. . . . My grandfather [at family prayers] always prayed standing, and the image of his mild, silvery head, leaning over the top of the high-backed chair, always rises before me as I think of early days. There was no great warmth or fervor in those daily exercises, but rather a serious and decorous propriety. They were Hebraistic in their form; they spoke of Zion and Jerusalem, of the God of Israel, the God of Jacob, as much as if my grandfather had been a veritable Jew; and except for the closing phrase, 'for the sake of Thy Son, our Savior,' might all have been uttered in Palestine by a well-trained Jew in the time of David."[4]

Of all the brahmin intellectuals in Cambridge, none joined the abolitionist cause with such gusto as young James Russell Lowell.[5] The eighth generation of his family in Massachusetts, Lowell was proud of his heredity yet became a reformer in the decades before the Civil War because he believed in the "American Idea," which, in the Unitarian tradition, meant the progress of mankind as a result of the influence of environment. Like most brahmins, Lowell stood aloof from the nativist agitation of the forties and fifties and believed that Negroes, Irishmen, Jews and Poles had the capacity for self-government after sufficient molding in the American environment. Yet Lowell, as with all of his generation of Boston brahmins, inherited two opposing images of the Jew: the noble ancient Hebrew, and the "repugnant" modern Jew. He read Hebrew fluently and still considered the Old Testament the standard of human wisdom as it had been for his Puritan ancestors. On the other hand, while traveling in Europe, he developed an obsession about the new rich Jews emerging from the ghettos into polite society. In fact, he saw Jews everywhere and even claimed that everybody, himself included, was in some way descended from the Jews. Although he had protested against the persecution of Jews in the 1840's, by the end of his life, in the last decade of the century, he was almost pathologically ambivalent toward the peddlers in the streets, and especially the rising class of Jews who were upsetting his ideas of what a homogeneous upper class should be, both here and in Europe. Bewildered, insecure and fearing the Jews, he was yet incapable of the intense anti-Semitism which eventually overtook his younger friend, Henry Adams.

Henry Adams: The Powerless Patrician

Of all Americans, the Adams family had a right to feel an intense possessiveness about the destiny of the United States. Three generations of Adamses had served the nation in the highest offices she had to offer them. But, by their own admission, the sons of the fourth generation somehow failed. And Henry, perhaps the most brilliant of them all, almost reveled in his own failure and in the failure of the American Idea. This failure led him eventually into a worship of the past, especially the eleventh and twelfth centuries, and a hatred of modern urban society, capitalism, the money-power and the goldbugs, and finally above all, and embracing all, the Jews. It would be presumptuous to even attempt to explain the anti-Semitism which eventually took hold of so brilliant a mind as that of Henry Adams. A brief outline of the development of anti-Semitism in his thinking will serve, however, to illustrate a point. For Adams only gradually lost his original faith in environment and the capacities of men for self-improvement and replaced these ideas with the belief in heredity and race. He replaced, as it were, the aristocratic idea (environment makes a gentleman) with the idea of caste (genes make the gentleman).

To begin with, Henry Adams was bred in the Unitarian tradition which held that all mankind was perfectable, or at least capable of improvement. Adams stuck by democracy and this Unitarian optimism as long as he could. In his classic *History of the United States*, he still retained some of this Unitarian optimism when he showed how the American environment was rapidly assimilating the pre-Civil War immigrant. Thus he showed how economic and social mobility reached down to "the lowest and most ignorant class. . . . The penniless and homeless Scotch and Irish immigrant was caught and consumed by it; for every stroke of the axe and the hoe made him a capitalist, and made gentlemen of his children."[6] Adams' wife died by her own hand while he was writing his *History* and he redoubled his efforts to finish it both as a monument to her and in order to drown his sorrows. The *History* was his swan song to the American Dream, but with the death of his beloved wife and the completion of his history in 1890, the dream somehow turned into a nightmare. And the nightmare increasingly was symbolized by the Jew.

"Yet as late as 1880," writes Barbara Miller Solomon, "Jews appeared in Adams' *Democracy* [a novel about Washington society] as upper class Americans with no ethnic stigma. The Schneide-koupons were descended from the kings of Israel and were prouder than Solomon in all his glory. The brother was a rich, versatile amateur, conniving in Washington politics; his activities were typical of other citizens in the nation's capital. His sister Julie was acceptable even to the inner circle of Washington parties. Significantly, Madelaine Lee, the idealistic heroine of the novel, paid tribute to the fluidity of American society created afresh by each generation with no one excluded, not even those who said, 'Abraham is our father.' "[7]

As of 1880, then, Adams was still rather proud of an American establishment which was so capable of replenishing itself in each generation, even to the point of absorbing families of German-Jewish origin. As the century drew to a close, on the other hand, his ideas gradually developed a castelike snobbery, now bolstered with an extreme medievalism which, in turn, served to reinforce his anti-Semitism. In some 750 intimate letters to his personal friends, covering the period from 1858 to his death in 1918, Adams first mentions the word "Jew" in 1896, a year when he was traveling in France collecting material for his great work, *Mont-Saint-Michel and Chartres*.[8]

Adams sought mental refuge in medievalism and the "Virgin"

primarily because of his increasing distrust of modern industrial society as symbolized in the "Dynamo." "I always drift back," he wrote his brother Brooks from Paris, "to the eleventh and twelfth centuries by a kind of instinct which must be terribly strong. . . . The modern world artistically begins with Michael Angelo, and I don't like it."[9] And, as time went on, he increasingly blamed the Jews for all he disliked about his age: The word "Jew" became interchangeable with "new-rich," "businessman," "capitalist" or "goldbug"; and "Jewish" was his private synonym for "greedy," "avaricious" or "materialistic." He knew perfectly well, for example, that August Belmont was an assimilated and highly cultivated Jew, yet he could write to his friend John Hay (addressing him as "Dear Pilgrim") from Paris about the Presidential campaign of 1896 as follows: "Belmont will look in with five other Wall Street Jews to offer you won millione tollars to peat dose tam temocrats mit dier tam Pryan."[10]

Adams was in Paris during the Dreyfus case, which he followed carefully and often referred to in his letters. On the whole, he sided with the anti-Dreyfusards up to the time when Dreyfus was finally shown to be innocent. He never did go along with the conspiracy theory held by many Dreyfusards. He was proud of the French army and glad that it "set its foot on the Jews and smashed the Dreyfus intrigue into a pancake."[11] He was horrified at Emile Zola's defense of Dreyfus in *J'accuse*, and would have liked to see Zola (and "as much more French rot as the island would hold") sent off to Devil's Island along with Dreyfus. He felt that the huge sums of money being spent by the Jews in influencing public opinion in Dreyfus' favor had only resulted in "stimulating the anti-Semitic feeling in France."[12] And he was of course horrified that "all the English and the Americans were with the Jews."[13]

The point is not that Adams was unfair in his attitudes toward Dreyfus ("a howling Jew as you see from his portraits");[14] in the end, he was perfectly willing to "grant the innocence of Dreyfus . . . without question." The importance of the case was that it only

served to reinforce Adams' convictions about the Jews being responsible for all the rottenness of his age. As the Dreyfus case came to a
close, for example, he turned his attention to England and blamed
the Jews for the war against the Boers in South Africa, which was, to
Adams, just another "Jew war."[15]

Inevitably, as Tocqueville clearly saw, privilege without power
breeds resentment and the need for a sense of caste superiority.
Adams' anti-Semitism was curiously tied up with his feeling of
personal failure and alienation from the tone of his times, especially
in America. Thus, as the century closed, he wrote to his brother
Brooks, from Paris: "I don't want to go home. Washington is
repulsive. . . . If I were growing rich, it might be a consideration, but
as far as I know, I am relatively a good deal poorer than I was five
years ago. Nor do I see much outlook. *The Jews have fixed the cards
all round.*"[16]

Surely there is an element of self-hate in all anti-Semitism. The
Adams family had always taken a leading part in the destiny of
America, and Henry's anti-Semitism was indeed a kind of self-hate
born of his abhorrence of the path now taken by "His America." In
fact, the more one contemplates the mind of Henry Adams, the
more one sees it as a symbol *par excellence* of the powerless
brahmin who is finally forced to embrace the idea of caste after
losing faith in aristocracy. And caste has one final defense which
Adams saw clearly when he wrote: "Our sway over what we call
society is undisputed. We keep the Jews far away, and the anti-Jew
feeling is quite rabid."[17]

John Jay Chapman: The Reformer Loses Faith

The critic F. O. Matthiessen considered Henry Adams and John
Jay Chapman "two of our most symptomatic minds." Chapman was
a mixture of Puritan New England and aristocratic New York. The
Puritan strain was very strong. He was a great admirer of William

Lloyd Garrison and wrote a sympathetic and brilliantly perceptive biography of the great abolitionist. While Henry Adams had already turned his back on America and had drifted into his crude anti-Semitism by the late nineties, Chapman still retained his Puritan and philo-Hebraic convictions: "There is a depth of human feeling in the Jew," he wrote in 1897, "that no other race ever possessed. We do no more than imitate it and follow it. David, for instance, and his conduct about Uriah's wife and the child that died—and Absalom—and Jonathan. Compare the Greek—the Chinese, the Roman. These Jews are more human than any other men. It is the cause of the spread of their religion—for we are all adopted in Judah. The heart of the world is Jewish. There is the same spirit in the Old Testament as in the New. That monstrous perversion—that we should worship their God and despise themselves!"[18]

And Chapman had none of Adams' racialism (he once criticized *The Education* for its cynicism and flaunting of family "race-pride"). Though he romanticized the ideal of the gentleman, especially the "family—the club" that was brahmin Boston, Chapman had little sympathy with the fashionable Anglo-Saxonry of his day. In an essay on Kipling in 1899, for instance, he saw through this "Pindar of the Anglo-Saxon forward movement" and found him a "class poet, blazoning an empty race prejudice."[19] In accord with his idealization of the gentleman's role in plutocratic America, Chapman, along with some of his St. Paul's and Harvard classmates, worked devotedly at anti-Tammany reform in New York City. In the course of this work, he became extremely close to Isaac Klein, a hardly literate Jew, whom he came to admire above most men. Yet, in spite of his early admiration for the Hebraic tradition and his friendship with Isaac Klein, Chapman, like Henry Adams before him, eventually lost faith in America and translated his disillusions into a violent conspiracy theory of history which embraced anti-Catholic, anti-Irish, anti-immigrant and anti-Semitic prejudices.

Chapman was horrified at the moral complacency and materialism of postwar America. In an era when a President of the United

States could say that "the business of the United States is business," when moralistic tracts such as E. W. Howe's *The Blessings of Business*, Bruce Barton's *The Man Nobody Knows*, and Roger W. Babson's *Prayers for Business Men* were selling widely, and when most Americans, with Harding, wanted "not surgery but serenity," Chapman, still a Puritan reformer at heart, felt lost at sea and against almost everything. "In the twenties," wrote his son, "my father fought a twilight battle with the present."

But finally Chapman found an emotional anchorage in violent anti-Catholicism and anti-Semitism. His anti-Catholicism had deep family roots, going back to his Huguenot heritage and the St. Bartholomew's Day massacre. His ancestor, John Jay of the Revolutionary period, had proposed that Roman Catholics in New York be deprived of their civil rights unless they swore to the Supreme Court that no pope or priest had the "authority to absolve them from their allegiance to the state." Although he did not join the revived Ku Klux Klan, Chapman was probably its most celebrated supporter as he became a racialist crusader in the twenties. He was also swayed by Henry Ford's Dearborn (Michigan) *Independent* and its crusade against a conspiracy of "World Jewry." In an article in the London *Spectator*, written in 1922, Chapman saw America as a land "wrestling with corruption," "the home of many traitorous cliques," "rocking with Bolshevism in every form," and being led into a dangerous foreign policy by the "Jewish peril."[20] The extent of his tragic flight into this conspiratorial theory of history is illustrated in the following lines from a poem he wrote for the *Ku Klux Kourier*:[21]

> *But see, a sail!—nay more—from every land*
> *They cloud the ocean, conveyed by a crew*
> *Of Master Pirates who have work in hand:*
> *Old Europe's nation-wreckers heave in view!*
> *And lo, to aid them, on our margin stand*
> *Our citizens—the Jesuit and the Jew.*

Yet even in his most fanatic period toward the end of his life, Chapman had the insight to see the dangers and the fallacies of his extreme *anti* positions. In a letter to a French friend he shows, as Henry Adams might have done, how his own anti-Catholicism (and anti-Semitism as well) was in reality a kind of self- or America-hatred: "The decay of life, mind, and character of the American," he wrote, "has got on my brain and has come out in the form of anti-Catholicism . . . and really you know it's easy to become toqué [cracked]—in agitating—anything that is *anti*. It turns into a mystic hostility and this in turn grows very often into 'manie des persecutions.' Men come to believe that they are spied on, followed, and treated with black magic by the organization or sect that they hold in horror."[22]

Madison Grant: Brahmin Racist

John Jay Chapman's friend Madison Grant was probably the last of the brahmin racists and perhaps, therefore, the most blatant. His reaction to one of Chapman's most vitriolic anti-Catholic diatribes, "Strike at the Source," published in *Forum* magazine in 1925 and quickly reprinted in the *Ku Klux Kourier*, shows better than anything else how far the old-stock panic in America had proceeded by the early 1920's. "I have been urging the Forum people," wrote Grant in a letter to Chapman congratulating him on his article, "to get some Protestant to take the position that the *Catholic Church under Jewish leadership*, the Jews and the Communist Labor Party are all international organizations and as such are hopelessly irreconcilable to the principles of *nationalism upon which modern Christendom is founded*."[23] It is indeed hard to believe that an educated man could have written such a fantastically inaccurate diagnosis of the ills of his times. But perhaps he was only carrying to its logical conclusion a proposition held by most proper Anglo-Saxon Protestants in the course of the so-called mongrelization of their previously homogeneous society.

Madison Grant came from an old New York family, all of whom, since Colonial times, had been born within fifty miles of City Hall.[24] His father had been through all the battles of the Potomac and had been awarded the Congressional Medal of Honor. His mother was an heiress who was brought up at the "Gatlands" which is now Belmont Park. Thus Grant came down from Yale in 1887, took a law degree at Columbia, and spent his early manhood as a "typical, New York Society, clubman, belonging to the Knickerbocker, Century, Union, Tuxedo and the Turf and Field clubs." In the patrician tradition of his friend T. R. Roosevelt, Grant was a lover of the land, big animals and the wide-open spaces. He was a founder of both the New York Zoölogical Society and the Save the Redwoods League. He was president of the former society for many years and at the same time was the most active member of the American Bison Society. He was vice president of the Immigration Restriction League and a member of the Society of Colonial Wars (he was an expert genealogist), the National Institute of Social Sciences, American Museum of Natural History, American Defense Society, and the American Geographic Society. Perhaps his most important and valuable work was done as the president of the Bronx River Parkway Commission, from its founding in 1907 to the completion, in 1925, of one of the most beautiful parks in the East. Finally, his active membership in the American Breeders Association and the Eugenics Research Association prepared him for his important role in framing the legislation restricting immigration which was finally passed by the Congress between 1921 and 1924.

Grant was certainly an ideal defender of a vanishing America, and his *magnum opus, The Passing of the Great Race in America,* published in 1916, became the bible of some 16,000 purchasers in the course of several editions. The new science of eugenics, according to Grant, had destroyed the "pathetic and fatuous belief in the efficacy of American institutions and environment to reverse or obliterate immemorial hereditary tendencies."[25] From Grant's point of view, the hordes of Russian-Jewish immigrants were by far the most dangerous and incapable of assimilation. "These immigrants," he wrote, "adopt the language of the native American; they wear his clothes, they steal his name; and they are beginning to take his women, but they seldom adopt his religion or understand his ideals."[26]

Social Science and Social Darwinism

Perhaps one should not be too critical of these brahmin intellectuals. For many of the leading social scientists of their generation also tended to sympathize with the various forms of racialist thinking, were often anti-Semitic, and were strong supporters of immigration restriction. They were evolutionists who were convinced that the Anglo-Saxon millionaires who ruled the nation in their day were the "fittest" men in the world.

After Charles Darwin's publication of his famous book, *The Origin of Species by Means of Natural Selection, or the Preservation of Favored Races in the Struggle for Life*, in 1859, most thinking men in the West became evolutionists. The theory of evolution dealt a fatal blow to the transcendental ideal of the unity of mankind which was founded on the Biblical faith that all men were descendants of Adam and equally brothers under the fatherhood of God. It was, of course, not necessarily the biological theory of evolution itself, but rather its use to bolster by analogy the various forms of Social Darwinism which threatened men's faith in Christianity. As Yale College, for example, was a Christian institution in 1879 (eleven members of the corporation were clergymen), its clergyman president, Noah Porter, was probably right to question the wisdom of William Graham Sumner's using the evolutionist Herbert Spencer's *Study of Sociology* as a textbook in an undergraduate course. For, as he wrote to Sumner at the time, Porter feared that "the freedom and unfairness with which [Spencer] attacks every Theistic Philosophy of society and of history, and the cool yet sarcastic effrontery with which he assumes that material elements and laws are the only forces and laws which any scientific man can recognize" would surely serve to corrupt the faith of his Yale undergraduates.

President Porter may have been right about the consequences of Spencer's evolutionary sociology in breaking down the absolute morality of Christianity. But he was against the trends of his times. And, as more and more men began to accept evolution, moral relativism (whether of a class, racial or cultural variety) soon dominated the most advanced minds in Europe as well as in America. Thus Karl Marx, whose life work might have been called "The Origin of Utopia by Means of Social Selection, or the Preservation of the Favored Proletariat in the Struggle for Life," was a great admirer of Darwin (he wanted to dedicate *Das Capital* in his honor but Darwin refused him permission) and saw morality as largely a product of class interest. But in the year Marx died (1883), the dominant class ideology in America was to be found in the sociology of Herbert Spencer.

"I imagine that nearly all of us who took up sociology between 1870, say, and 1890 did so at the instigation of Spencer," wrote Charles H. Cooley, one of America's leading sociologists, in 1920. "His book," Cooley continued, "*The Study of Sociology*, perhaps the most readable of all his works, had a large sale and probably did more to arouse interest in the subject than any other publication before or since. Whatever we may have occasion to charge against him, let us set down at once a large credit for effective propagation."[28] Spencer's books in the last three decades of the nineteenth century, which was the period of his greatest vogue, sold almost four hundred thousand copies in America.

Following the conflict theories developed in Thomas Malthus' *Essay on the Principle of Population*, Spencer centered his sociology on the idea of "natural selection" in the "struggle for life" and the "survival of the fittest" (a term which he coined). His biological analogies led him to an extreme laissez-faire position which, in turn, produced a conservative bias. Opposed to almost all state interference in the "natural" processes of society, he deplored poor laws, state-supported education, sanitary supervision, regulation of housing, tariffs, state banking regulation and even a governmental postal system. Although he felt that the poor probably deserved to starve, he did allow for a minimum of private charity, especially as it elevated the character of the donors. In other words, both the starving masses and the self-satisfied millionaires were necessary aspects of the laissez-faire struggle for life and the natural law of progress.

Spencer had his greatest vogue in America. Almost every intellectual—from Jack London and Theodore Dreiser to the extreme egalitarian Walt Whitman, the founders of sociology such as Sumner, Ward, Giddings and Cooley, economists like John R. Commons and Thorstein Veblen, and philosophers John Dewey and Josiah Royce—fell under his spell. But most important of all, his theories gave a tremendous boost to the already overwhelming confidence of the capitalist business establishment. Indeed he was a veritable Marx for the millionaires in the Gilded Age. His most prominent disciple was Andrew Carnegie, and the two men were close friends. In his *Autobiography*, Carnegie tells how his fears at the collapse of absolute Christian morality were banished forever after his reading of Darwin and Spencer: "I remember that light came in as a flood and all was clear," he wrote. "Not only had I got rid of theology and the supernatural, but I had found the truth of evolution. 'All is well since all grows better,' became my motto, my true source of comfort. Man was not created with an instinct for his own degradation, but from the lower he had risen to the higher forms. Nor is there any conceivable end to his march to perfection. His face is turned to light; he stands in the sun and looks upward."[29]

Indeed, in the competitive struggle for survival, the American capitalist was certainly the fittest man in the world when Andrew Carnegie wrote those lines. And the most famous capitalist of them all, John D. Rockefeller, was sure of his fitness to lead America in a competitive capitalist system. "The growth of a large business is merely a survival of the fittest," he declared in a Sunday School address. "The American Beauty rose can be produced in the splendor and fragrance which brings cheer to its beholder only by sacrificing the early buds which grow up around it. This is not an evil tendency in business. It is merely the working-out of a law of nature and a law of God."[30]

Just as the fittest millionaires were impressed with the Spencerian sociology, so also were the more orthodox Protestant clergymen of the day. "We need all the Jay Cookes we have and a thousand more," wrote an author in the *Baptist Quarterly* in 1873;[31] "God has need of rich Christians," according to an article in the *Congregationalist* (1869), "and He makes them, and He assigns particular duties to them";[32] and "generally the proposition is true, that where you find the most religion there you find the most worldly prosperity," said Henry Ward Beecher in a sermon to his parishioners, pious and well-to-do merchants in Brooklyn in the 1870's.[33]

At the time, Beecher was the most influential minister in America. In accord with the common sense of his day, and as a "cordial Christian Darwinist," he was sure that "no man in this land suffers from poverty unless it be more than his fault—unless it be his sin."[34] It is no wonder that he denounced strikes as being due to the sinfulness of laborers who were unwilling to "nobly bear" their "self-induced" poverty. "It is said that a dollar a day is not enough for a wife and five or six children," he wrote in the *Christian Union* on the occasion of a railroad strike in 1877.[35] "No, not if the man smokes or drinks beer. It is not enough to enable them to live as perhaps they would have a right to live in prosperous times. But is not a dollar a day enough to buy bread with? Water costs nothing; and a man who cannot live on bread is not fit to live."[36] It is indeed no wonder that, at the Delmonico dinner tendered to Spencer on his visit to America in 1882, Beecher announced in an eloquent oration before this auspicious gathering of millionaires that he had read and admired the famous British sociologist for twenty years.

One of the honored guests at the Delmonico dinner, William Graham Sumner, was America's leading Social Darwinist and disciple of Herbert Spencer. In many ways, Sumner's whole life and family background were a testimony to the values of the Protestant Ethic, middle-class individualism and the survival of the fittest in the struggle for life. His "hero of civilization"—the savings bank depositor and the forgotten man—was surely modeled after his father. For although Thomas Sumner, an English immigrant, never made a large salary as an employee in the shops of the Hartford and New Haven Railroad Company (a pay voucher reveals that he received $34.38 for fifteen days' work in September, 1857), he had saved $1,000 which he gave to his son for his college education at Yale (tuition at Yale College: $45 per annum, additional expenses $230 to $320).[37]

At Yale, William Graham Sumner was both a scholastic and social success. He was elected to Phi Beta Kappa, was a member of the Psi Upsilon fraternity (now the exclusive Fence Club), and was one of fifteen out of the approximately one hundred men in his class to be tapped for Skull and Bones, the senior honor society. He was not popular with the majority of his classmates but was extremely admired by a few friends, among them William C. Whitney, who subsequently married an heiress to the Standard Oil millions and became one of the most successful, and most cultured, members of the generation of business brahmins who ruled America in the Gilded Age.

No doubt owing to his heritage in British Nonconformity and independence, his father's example of thrift and self-reliance, his own rise from poverty to eminence as a professor in a great university, and his friendships with many of the great and successful of his own generation, William Graham Sumner quite naturally became a vigorous proponent of middle-class individualism and laissez-faire economics. He was almost as extreme as Spencer in his advocacy of the weak state and in his opposition to do-gooders and "amateur social doctors" with their socialist plans for "nourishing the unfit." Though he was primarily a champion of the middle class and the "forgotten man" who minds his own business, he was at the same time convinced that the upper classes were the main benefactors of civilization. "The millionaires," he wrote, "are a product of natural selection, acting on the whole body of men to pick out those who can meet the requirements of certain work to be done. . . . It is because they are thus selected that wealth—both their own and that entrusted to them—aggregates under their hands. . . . They may fairly be regarded as the naturally selected agents of society for certain work. They get high wages and live in luxury, but the bargain is a good one for society. There is the intensest competition for their place and occupation. This assures us that all who are competent for this function will be employed in it, so that the cost of it will be reduced to the lowest terms. . . ."[38]

It is no wonder that one Yale benefactor doubled his donation because Sumner's ideas had convinced him that "Yale College is a good and safe place for the keeping and use of property and the sustaining of civilization when endangered by ignorance, rascality, demagogues, repudiationists, rebels, copperheads, communists, butlers, strikers, protectionists, and fanatics of sundry roots and sizes."[39]

But William Graham Sumner was an extremely independent individualist and by no means a consistent ideologist for the status quo or the values of the business establishment. In fact, from the time of his controversy with President Porter over his right to teach Spencer's evolutionary theories to Christian undergraduates at Yale (a controversy which went way beyond the classroom and was argued vehemently in the New York press), Sumner was in constant opposition to various parts of the business community. Perhaps his consistent advocacy of Free Trade created his most bitter enemies. He was also outspokenly opposed to all forms of imperialism. His opposition to the Spanish-American War almost cost him his job at Yale. And, most important from our point of view in this book, Sumner never approved, in contrast to most of his fellow social scientists, of restrictions on immigration. Nor was he a racist: in accord with his fierce faith in the individual, he refused to "judge offhand that some people were not fit for liberty and self-government...."

Racism, Eugenics and Immigration Restriction

While Sumner was no racist, the theories of Social Darwinism were easily perverted into various forms of the Anglo-Saxon complex. Modern racism was founded in the 1850's when a Frenchman, Count Arthur de Gobineau, produced four learned volumes proving that France and Europe were decadent because of the mongrelization of their previously pure, Aryan aristocracies. In a similar vein, Richard Wagner's British son-in-law, Houston Stewart Chamberlain, in his extremely influential *Foundations of the Nineteenth Century* (1900), proved that only Teutons understood the importance of loyalty and leadership, which accounted for German greatness. The works of Wagner and Chamberlain were taken up by Adolph Hitler and his chief racial ideologist, Alfred Rosenberg.

European theorists were usually mistrusted in this country. Yet our scientific community produced its share of racial measurers toward the end of the nineteenth century. With calipers and rulers, hard scientists rather than soft theorists built up elaborate classifications of the "inborn" racial and cultural traits of Nordics, Aryans, Semites, Teutons, Hottentots, Magyars, Negroes, Japanese, Slavs and Anglo-Saxons. With typical scientific thoroughness, one professor even recorded some five thousand measurements on a single skull. By the end of the century most respectable scientists, impressed as always with elaborate statistical tables carried to two or three decimal places, were inclined to agree with this new orthodoxy (at that time even W. E. B. Du Bois acquiesced in the trend). As one might have expected, members of the Anglo-Saxon establishment were bolstered in their faith in themselves by the fact that their measured traits and their "inborn" moral sense were scientifically found to lie at the very top of the evolutionary tree. As an eminent professor at Columbia University put it at the time: "An Anglo-Saxon is a man who *instinctively* knows that liberty cannot survive trade unions and other socialist schemes from Eastern Europe."[40] But perhaps a cynical French pro-Aryan had more insight into the consequences of these new scientific findings when, in the 1880's, he wrote: "I am convinced that in the next century millions will cut each other's throats because of 1 or 2 degrees more or less of cephalic index."[41]

The Eugenics Movement, founded by Darwin's nephew Francis Galton, who first coined the term "eugenics" in 1883, was a natural outgrowth of racialism and Social Darwinism.[42] The eugenicists were interested in the biological consequences of social policy, and they warned the Social Darwinists that the "fittest" were *not* surviving: while millionaires were making money, morons were multiplying; modern medicine was preserving the unfit while modern war was sending the best to the front and keeping the worst at home; and, above all, the old-stock graduates of Harvard and Yale were being rapidly outbred by alien immigrants. The eugenicists had got hold of some useful truths but, unfortunately, by the time of the First War their movement had reached the status of a fad which went too far.

The findings of the eugenicists quite naturally gave support to the opponents of further immigration. One of the most widely read books on this controversial issue was *The Old World in the New*, by Edward A. Ross, which appeared in 1914. Professor Ross, of old-stock Middle Western roots, received his graduate education in Germany and at Johns Hopkins and became one of the pioneers in American sociology. Though he was a strong Progressive who was dismissed from several academic posts for his radical views, he believed in the conventional myth of Nordic supremacy and the need for a program of positive eugenics in order to preserve our Anglo-Saxon Americanism against pollution through immigration.

Professor Ross opened his book, *The Old World in the New*, with a touching quotation, illustrating a friend's idealistic position on the immigration question:

"Immigration," said to me a distinguished social worker and idealist, "is the wind that blows democratic ideas throughout the world. In a Siberian hut from which four sons have gone forth to America to seek their fortune, I saw tacked up a portrait of Lincoln cut from a New York newspaper. Even there they know what Lincoln stood for and loved him. The return flow of letters and people from this country is sending an electric thrill through the dwarfed, despairing sections of humanity. . . . Time-hallowed Old-World oppressions and exploitations that might have lasted for generations will perish in our time, thanks to the diffusion by immigrants of American ideas of freedom and opportunity."[43]

Ross spent the rest of his book showing how wrong his idealistic friend was. After a detailed study of the history and statistics of immigration, he ended with a chapter showing how "Immigrant Blood" was slowly polluting the purer "American Blood," as "beaten members of beaten breeds" swarmed over the beloved land of his own pioneer ancestors. Somewhat obsessed with race, Ross was of course convinced that "the blood being injected into the veins of our people was sub-human"; the newer immigrants were "morally below the races of northern Europe"; and that it all would end in "Race Suicide."

In a chapter devoted to the "East European Hebrews," Professor Ross catalogued all the prevalent stereotypes of his day: thus the Jews "rarely lay hands to basic production"; none can "beat the Jew to a bargain"; at settlement houses "Jewish mothers always want something extra"; in college, "Jewish students always want their grades changed"; Jewish businessmen "are 'slippery' and will 'fail' in order to get rid of their debts . . . so that their readiness to commit perjury has passed into a proverb"; and that, on the whole, "it is certain that the Jews have commercialized the social evil, commercial-

ized the theatre, and done much to commercialize the newspaper."
He was convinced that the "line drawn against the Jews in hotels,
resorts, clubs, and private schools" had nothing to do with "bigotry
or dislike of their religion"; rather, it was justified by "their manners" which were those of "vulgar upstart parvenus." Like Henry
Adams', Professor Ross' antipathy to both Jews and immigrants was
to a large extent part of his generalized mistrust of business values.
Thus he blamed the tragic lack of restrictions on immigration on
"our captains of industry" who give a "crowbar to the immigrant
with a number nine face on a number six head, make a dividend out
of him, and imagine that is the end of the matter."[44]

Yet, after all, as with so much that passes as science in every age
including our own, Professor Ross approached the problem of
immigration with the presuppositions of his own generation of
old-stock middle-class Americans. But in spite of all his racial
theorizing, there are indications that he did feel that the influence
of the American environment might eventually change the so-called
basic, racial traits of the Jews, as the following paragraphs suggest:

*The truth seems to be that the lower class of Jews of eastern
Europe reach here moral cripples, their souls warped and dwarfed
by iron circumstances. The experience of Russian repression has
made them haters of government and corrupters of the police. Life
amid a bigoted and hostile population has left them aloof and thick-
skinned. A tribal spirit intensified by social isolation prompts them
to rush to the rescue of the caught rascal of their own race. Pent
within the Talmud and the Pale of Settlement, their interests have
become few, and many of them have developed a monstrous and
repulsive love of gain. When now, they use their Old-World shove
and wile and lie in a society like ours, as unprotected as a snail out
of its shell, they rapidly push up into a position of prosperous
parasitism, leaving scorn and curses in their wake.*

*Gradually, however, it dawns upon this twisted soul that here
there is no need to be weasel or hedgehog. He finds himself in a new*

game, the rules of which are made by all the players. He himself is a part of the state that is weakened by his law-breaking, a member of the profession that is degraded by his sharp practices. So smirk and cringe and trick presently fall away from him, and he stands erect. This is why, in the same profession at the same time, those most active in breaking down the standards are Jews and those most active in raising standards are Jews—of an earlier coming or a later generation. "On the average," says a Jewish leader, "only the third generation feels perfectly at home in American society." This explains the frequent statement that the Jews are "the limit"—among the worst of the worst and among the best of the best.[45]

Most of the leading social scientists of Ross' generation took a similar position on immigration. "From the 1890's to the 1920's," writes Barbara Miller Solomon, "social scientists—especially Edward Bemis, Thomas N. Carver, John R. Commons, Davis R. Dewey, Richard Ely, Franklin Giddings, Jeremiah Jenks, William Z. Ripley, Edward A. Ross, and Richard Mayo Smith—either directly or indirectly gave aid, counsel, or moral support to the work of the Immigration Restriction League."[46] Founded by three Boston brahmins, the League was but one of many institutions and associations which were erected by the old-stock upper class in order to protect their prestige and position against the rising tide of immigrant power in America at the turn of the nineteenth century.

We are still in power, after a fashion. Our sway over what we call society is undisputed. We keep the Jew far away, and the anti-Jew feeling is quite rabid.

Henry Adams

V

The Social Defense of Caste: The Two Nations in the 1880's

The Civil War was fought, by a nation rapidly becoming centralized economically, in order to preserve the political Union. Although the Union was preserved and slavery abolished, the postwar Republic was faced with the enormously complex and morally cancerous problem of caste, as far as the formally free Negroes were concerned. The solution to this problem has now become the central one of our own age. But the more immediate effect of the Civil War was that, in the North at least, the nation realized the fabulous potential of industrial power. The Pennsylvania Railroad, for instance, began to cut back operations at the beginning of the war, only to realize a tremendous boom during the remainder of the conflict (total revenue in 1860: $5,933 million; in 1865: $19,533 million). But the profits of the war were nothing compared to those of the fabulous postwar years. Between 1870 and 1900, the national wealth quadrupled (rising from $30,400 million to $126,700 million and doubled again by 1914—reaching $254,200 million).[1]

During this same period, wealth became increasingly centralized in the hands of a few. In 1891, Forum magazine published an article, "The Coming Billionaire," which estimated that there were 120 men in the nation worth over $10 million. The next year, the New York Times published a list of 4,047 millionaires, and the Census Bureau estimated that 9 per cent of the nation's families owned 71 per cent of the wealth. By 1910 there were more millionaires in the United States Senate alone than there were in the whole nation before the Civil War. This new inequality was dramatized by the fact that, in 1900, according to Frederick Lewis Allen, the former immigrant lad Andrew Carnegie had an income of between $15 and $30 million (the income tax had been declared unconstitutional in a test case in 1895), while the average unskilled worker in the North received less than $460 a year in wages—in the South the figure was less than $300. It is no wonder that the production of pig iron rather than poetry, and the quest for status rather than salvation, now took hold of the minds of even the most patrician descendants of Puritan divines.

This inequality of wealth was accompanied by an increasing centralization of business power, as the nation changed, in the half century after Appomatox, from a rural-communal to an urban-corporate society. President Eliot of Harvard, in a speech before the fraternity of Phi Beta Kappa in 1888, noted this new corporate dominance when he pointed out that, while the Pennsylvania Railroad had gross receipts of $115 million and employed over 100,000 men in that year, the Commonwealth of Massachusetts had gross receipts of only $7 million and employed no more than 6,000 persons.[2] And this corporate economy was further centralized financially in Wall Street. The capital required to launch the United

States Steel Corporation, for example, would at that time have covered the costs of all the functions of the federal government for almost two years. J. P. Morgan and his associates, who put this great corporate empire together in 1901, held some three hundred directorships in over one hundred corporations with resources estimated at over $22 billion. This industrial age, in which the railroads spanned the continent and Wall Street interests controlled mines in the Rockies, timber in the Northwest, and coal in Pennsylvania and West Virginia, brought about a national economy and the emergence of a national mind.

And the prosperity of this new urban-corporate world was largely built upon the blood and sweat of the men, and the tears of their women, who came to this country in such large numbers from the peasant villages of Southern and Eastern Europe. Whereas most of the older immigrants from Northern and Western Europe had come to a rural America where they were able to assimilate more easily, the majority of these newer arrivals huddled together in the urban slums and ghettos which were characteristic of the lower levels of the commercial economy which America had now become.

Except for the captains of industry, whose money-centered minds continued to welcome and encourage immigration because they believed it kept wages down and retarded unionization, most old-stock Americans were frankly appalled at the growing evils of industrialization, immigration and urbanization. As we have seen, the closing decades of the nineteenth century were marked by labor unrest and violence; many men, like Henry Adams, developed a violent nativism and anti-Semitism; others, following the lead of Jane Addams, discovered the slums and went to work to alleviate the evils of prostitution, disease, crime, political bossism and grinding poverty; both Midwestern Populism and the Eastern, patrician-led Progressive movement were part of the general protest and were, in turn, infused with varying degrees of nativism; and even organized labor, many of whose members were of recent immigrant origin, was by no means devoid of nativist sentiment.

In so many ways, nativism was part of a more generalized anti-urban and anti-capitalist mood. Unfortunately, anti-Semitism is often allied with an antipathy toward the city and the money-power. Thus the first mass manifestations of anti-Semitism in America came out of the Midwest among the Populist leaders and their followers. In the campaign of 1896, for example, William Jennings Bryan was accused of anti-Semitism and had to explain to the Jewish Democrats of Chicago that in denouncing the policies of Wall Street and the Rothschilds, he and his silver friends were "not attacking a race but greed and avarice which know no race or religion."[3] And the danger that the Populist, isolationist and anti-Wall Street sentiment in the Middle West might at any time revert to anti-Semitism continued. As we shall see in a later chapter, Henry Ford, a multimillionaire with the traditional Populist mistrust of the money-power, was notoriously anti-Semitic for a time in the early 1920's.

Nativism was also a part of a status revolution at the elite level of leadership on the Eastern Seaboard. "The newly rich, the grandiosely or corruptly rich, the masters of the great corporations," wrote Richard Hofstadter, "were bypassing the men of the Mugwump type—the old gentry, the merchants of long standing, the small manufacturers, the established professional men, the civic leaders of an earlier era. In scores of cities and hundreds of towns, particularly in the East but also in the nation at large, the old-family, college-educated class that had deep ancestral roots in local communities and often owned family businesses, that had traditions of political leadership, belonged to the patriotic societies and the best clubs, staffed the government boards of philanthropic and cultural institutions, and led the movements for civic betterment, were being overshadowed and edged aside in making basic political and economic decisions. . . . They were less important and they knew it."[4]

Many members of this class, of old-stock prestige and waning power, eventually allied themselves with the Progressive movement. Many also, like Henry Adams, withdrew almost entirely from the world of power. The "decent people," as Edith Wharton once put it, increasingly "fell back on sport and culture." And this sport and culture was now to be reinforced by a series of fashionable and patrician protective associations which, in turn, systematically and subtly institutionalized the exclusion of Jews.

The turning point came in the 1880's, when a number of symbolic events forecast the nature of the American upper class in the twentieth century. Thus, when President Eliot of Harvard built his summer cottage at Northeast Harbor, Maine, in 1881, the exclusive summer resort trend was well under way; the founding of *The Country Club* at Brookline, Massachusetts, in 1882, marked the beginning of the country-club trend; the founding of the Sons of the Revolution, in 1883, symbolized the birth of the genealogical fad and the patrician scramble for old-stock roots; Endicott Peabody's founding of Groton School, in 1884, in order to rear young gentlemen in the tradition of British public schools (and incidentally to protect them from the increasing heterogeneity of the public school system) was an important symbol of both upper-class exclusiveness and patrician Anglophilia; and finally, the Social Register, a convenient index of this new associational aristocracy, was first issued toward the end of this transitional decade in 1887 (the publisher also handled much of the literature of the American Protective Association, which was active in the nativist movement at that time).

The Right Reverend Phillips Brooks—the favorite clergyman among Philadelphia's Victorian gentry, who was called to Boston's Trinity Church in 1869, the year Grant entered the White House and Eliot accepted the presidency at Harvard—was one of the most sensitive barometers of the brahmin mind. Thus, although he himself had graduated from the Boston Latin School along with other patricians and plebeian gentlemen of his generation, he first suggested the idea of Groton to young Peabody in the eighties and joined the Sons of the Revolution in 1891, because, as he said at the time, "it is well to go in for the assertion that our dear land at least used to be American."[5]

113

Ancestral Associations and the
Quest for Old-Stock Roots

The idea of caste dies hard, even in a democratic land such as ours. Our first and most exclusive ancestral association, the Society of the Cincinnati, was formed in 1783, just before the Continental Army disbanded. Its membership was limited to Washington's officers and, in accord with the rural traditions of primogeniture, was to be passed on to oldest sons in succeeding generations. The society's name reflects the ancient tradition of gentlemen-farmers, from Cincinnatus to Cromwell, Washington and Franklin Roosevelt, who have served their country in times of need. Just as the founding of the Society of Cincinnati reflected the rural values of the gentleman and his mistrust of grasping city ways, it was quite natural that the new wave of ancestral associations which came into being at the end of the nineteenth century was a reaction to the rise of the city with its accompanying heterogeneity and conflict. As Wallace Evan Davies, in *Patriotism on Parade*, put it:

"The great Upheaval," the Haymarket Riot, the campaigns of Henry George, and the writings of Edward Bellamy crowded the last half of the eighties. The nineties produced such proofs of unrest as the Populist Revolt, the Homestead Strike with the attempted assassination of Henry Clay Frick, the Panic of 1893, the Pullman Strike, Coxey's Army, and, finally, the Bryan campaign of 1896. Throughout all this the conservative and propertied classes watched apprehensively the black cloud of anarchism, a menace as productive of alarm and hysteria as bolshevism and communism in later generations.[6]

These old-stock patriots, desperately seeking hereditary and historical roots in a rapidly changing world, flocked to the standards of such newly founded societies as the Sons of the Revolution (1883), the Colonial Dames (1890), the Daughters of the American Revolution (1890), Daughters of the Cincinnati (1894), the

114

Society of Mayflower Descendants (1894), the Aryan Order of St. George or the Holy Roman Empire in the Colonies of America (1892), and the Baronial Order of Runnymede (1897). It is no wonder that genealogists, both amateur and professional, rapidly came into vogue. Several urban newspapers established genealogical departments; the Lennox Library in New York purchased one of its largest genealogical collections, in 1896, setting aside a room "for the convenience of the large number of researchers after family history"; the *Library Journal* carried articles on how to help the public in ancestor hunting; and, as of 1900, the *Patriotic Review* listed seventy patriotic, hereditary and historical associations, exactly *half* of which had been founded during the preceding decade alone.

This whole movement was, of course, intimately bound up with anti-immigrant and anti-Semitic sentiments. Thus a leader of the D.A.R. saw a real danger in "our being absorbed by the different nationalities among us," and a president-general of the Sons of the American Revolution reported that: "Not until the state of civilization reached the point where we had a great many foreigners in our land . . . were our patriotic societies successful."[7] The Daughters of the American Revolution was indeed extremely successful. Founded in 1890, it had 397 chapters in 38 states by 1897. That the anti-immigrant reaction was most prevalent in the urban East, however, was attested to by the fact that the Daughters made slow headway in the West and South and had a vast majority of its chapters in New York and Massachusetts.

But, as Franklin Roosevelt once said, "we are all descendants of immigrants." While old-stock Americans were forming rather exclusive associations based on their descent from Colonial immigrants, newer Americans were also attempting to establish their own historical roots. Such organizations as the Scotch-Irish Society (1889), the Pennsylvania-German Society (1891), the American Jewish Historical Society (1894), and the American Irish Historical Society (1898) were concerned to establish ethnic recognition through ancestral achievement. "The Americanism of all Irishmen and

Jews," writes Edward N. Saveth, "was enhanced because of the handful of Irishmen and Jews who may have stood by Washington in a moment of crisis."[8]

The genealogically minded patrician has remained a part of the American scene down through the years. The front page of any contemporary copy of the Social Register, for instance, lists a series of clubs, universities and ancestral associations, with proper abbreviations attached, in order that each family may be identified by its members' affiliations. A recent Philadelphia Social Register listed an even dozen such societies, and a venerable old gentleman of great prestige (if little power) was listed in a later page as follows:

Rittenhouse, Wm. Penn—Ul.Ph.Myf.Cc.Wt.Rv.Ll.Fw.P'83 . . .
   Union League

It was indeed plain to see (after a bit of research on page 1) that this old gentleman was nicely placed as far as his ancestral, college and club affiliations were concerned. He belonged to the Union League (Ul) and Philadelphia clubs (Ph), had graduated in 1883 from Princeton University (P'83), and was apparently devoting himself to some sort of patriotic ancestor worship in his declining years, as suggested by his ancestral association memberships: Mayflower Descendants (Myf); Society of Cincinnati (Cc); Society of the War of 1812 (Wt); Sons of the Revolution (Rv); Military Order of the Loyal Legion (Ll); and the Military Order of Foreign Wars (Fw). And, as the final entry shows, he was living at the Union League.

The Summer Resort and the Quest for Homogeneity

Americans have always longed for grass roots. In a society of cement, the resort movement in America paralleled the genealogical escape to the past. The physiological and physical ugliness of the city streets gradually drove those who could afford it back to nature and the wide-open spaces. Men like Owen Wister, Theodore Roosevelt and Madison Grant went out to the West, and the more timid, or socially minded, souls sought refuge at some exclusive summer resort. In spite of the efforts of men like Frederick Law Olmstead and Madison Grant to bring rural beauty into the heart of the city (Olmstead built some fifteen city parks from coast to coast, Central Park in New York City being the most well known), first the artists and writers, then the gentry, and finally the millionaires were seeking the beauty of nature and the simple life among the "natives" of coastal or mountain communities along the Eastern Seaboard. President Eliot and his sons spent the summers during the seventies camping in tents before building the first summer cottage in Northeast Harbor, Maine, in 1881.[9] Charles Francis Adams, Jr., saw his native Quincy succumb to industrialism and the Irish (the Knights of Labor gained control of the Adams "race-place" in 1887), gave up his job with the Union Pacific in 1890, and finally escaped to the simple life at Lincoln, Massachusetts, in 1893.

The summer resort increased in popularity after the Civil War and went through its period of most rapid growth between 1880 and the First War. Long Branch, New Jersey, summer capital of presidents from Grant to Arthur, was filled with proper Philadelphians and New Yorkers. Further south, Cape May—where Jay Cooke, financier of the Civil War, spent every summer—was the most fashionable Philadelphia summer resort until well into the twentieth century. Boston's best retreated to the simple life at Nahant. Others went to the Berkshires, where large "cottages," large families and large incomes supported the simple life for many years (Lenox boasted thirty-five of these cottages as of 1880, and seventy-five by 1900).[10] Between 1890 and the First War, Bar Harbor became one of America's most stylish resorts. By 1894, the year Joseph Pulitzer built the resort's first hundred-thousand-dollar "cottage," Morgan and Standard Oil partners were the leaders of the community (when a Vanderbilt bought a cottage in 1922, it was the first to change hands in fifteen years; within the next three years, forty-seven such cottages changed hands). Less fashionable, but no less genteel, Northeast Harbor grew at the same time. Anticipating modern sociology, President Eliot made a study of the community in 1890. Among other things, he found that, as of 1881, nonresident summer people owned less than one-fifth of the local real property; only eight years later, in 1889, they owned over half (and total property values had almost doubled).[11]

Just as the white man, symbolized by the British gentleman, was roaming round the world in search of raw materials for his factories at Manchester, Liverpool or Leeds, so America's urban gentry and capitalists, at the turn of the century, were imperialists seeking solace for their souls among the "natives" of Lenox, Bar Harbor or Kennebunkport. Here they were able to forget the ugliness of the urban melting pot as they dwelt among solid Yankees (Ethan Frome), many of whom possessed more homogeneous, Colonial-stock roots than themselves. And these rustic "types" kept up their boats, taught their children the ways of the sea, caught their lobsters, served them in the stores along the village streets, and became temporary servants and gardeners on their rustic estates. But although most old-time resorters were patronizingly proficient with the "Down East" accent, and appreciated the fact that the "natives" were their "own kind" racially, sometimes the idyllic harmony was somewhat superficial, at least as far as the more sensitive "natives" were concerned. Hence the following anecdote circulating among the "natives" at Bar Harbor: "They emptied the pool the other day," reported one typical "type" to another. "Why," asked his friend? "Oh, one of the natives fell in."

But the simple life was, nevertheless, often touching and always relaxing. All one's kind were there together and the older virtues of communal life were abroad; Easter-Christmas-Wedding Christians usually went to church every Sunday; millionaire's wives did their own shopping in the village; and walking, boating and picnicking brought a renewed appreciation of nature. And perhaps most important of all, one knew who one's daughter was seeing, at least during the summer months when convenient alliances for life were often consummated.

When J. P. Morgan observed that "you can do business with anyone, but only sail with a gentleman," he was reflecting the fact that a secure sense of homogeneity is the essence of resort life. It is no wonder that anti-Semitism, of the gentlemanly, exclusionary sort, probably reached its most panicky heights there. Thus one of the first examples of upper-class anti-Semitism in America occurred, in the 1870's, when a prominent New York banker, Joseph Seligman, was rudely excluded from the Grand Union Hotel in Saratoga Springs. This came as a shock to the American people and was given wide publicity because it was something new at that time. Henry Ward Beecher, a personal friend of the Seligmans, reacted with a sermon from his famous pulpit at Plymouth Church: "What have the Jews," he said, "of which they need be ashamed, in a Christian Republic where all men are declared to be free and equal? . . . Is it that they are excessively industrious? Let the Yankee cast the first stone. Is it that they are inordinately keen on bargaining? Have they ever stolen ten millions of dollars at a pinch from a city? Are our courts bailing out Jews, or compromising with Jews? Are there Jews lying in our jails, and waiting for mercy. . . . You cannot find one criminal Jew in the whole catalogue. . . ."[12]

The Seligman incident was followed by a battle at Saratoga Springs. Immediately afterwards, several new hotels were built there by Jews, and by the end of the century half the population was Jewish; as a result, it is said that one non-Jewish establishment boldly advertised its policies with a sign: "No Jews and Dogs Admitted Here." At the same time, other prominent German Jews were running into embarrassing situations elsewhere. In the 1890's, Nathan Straus, brother of a member of Theodore Roosevelt's Cabinet and a leading merchant and civic leader himself, was turned down at a leading hotel in Lakewood, New Jersey, a most fashionable winter resort at that time. He promptly built a hotel next door, twice as big and for Jews only. And the resort rapidly became Jewish, as kosher establishments multiplied on all sides.

Even the well-integrated and cultivated members of Philadelphia's German-Jewish community eventually had to bow to the trend. As late as the eighties and nineties, for instance, leading Jewish families were listed in the Philadelphia Blue Book as summering at fashionable Cape May, along with the city's best gentile families. But this did not continue, and many prominent Philadelphia Jews became founding families at Long Branch, Asbury Park, Spring Lake or Atlantic City, where the first resort synagogues were established during the nineties: Long Branch (1890), Atlantic City (1893), and Asbury Park (1896).[13]

As the East European Jews rapidly rose to middle-class status, resort-hotel exclusiveness produced a running battle along the Jersey coast and up in the Catskills. One resort after another changed from an all-gentile to an all-Jewish community. Atlantic City, for example, first became a fashionable gentile resort in the nineties. By the end of the First War, however, it had become a predominantly Jewish resort, at least in the summer months (the first modern, fireproof hotel was built there in 1902; there were a thousand such hotels by 1930). According to Edmund Wilson, it was while visiting Atlantic City in the winter of 1919 that John Jay Chapman first became anti-Semitic. "They are uncritical," he wrote to a friend after watching the boardwalk crowd of vacationing Jews. "Life is a simple matter for them: a bank account and a larder. . . . They strike me as an inferior race. . . . These people don't know anything. They have no religion, no customs except eating and drinking."[14]

Just before the First World War, resort establishments began to advertise their discriminatory policies in the newspapers. The situation became so embarrassing that New York State passed a law, in 1913, forbidding places of public accommodation to advertise their unwillingness to admit persons because of race, creed or color.

Although the high tide of formal resort society has declined in recent years, the rigid exclusion of Jews has largely continued: As Cleveland Amory has put it:

Certain aspects of the narrowness of the old-line resort society have continued, not the least of which is the question of anti-Semitism. Although certain Jewish families, notably the Pulitzers, the Belmonts and the Goulds have played their part in resort Society—and Otto Kahn, Henry Seligman, Jules Bache and Frederick Lewison have cut sizeable figures—the general record of resort intolerance is an extraordinary one; it reached perhaps its lowest point when Palm Beach's Bath and Tennis Club sent out a letter asking members not to bring into the club guests of Jewish extraction. Among those who received this letter was Bernard Baruch, then a member of the club and a man whose father, Dr. Simon Baruch, pioneered the Saratoga Spa. Several of Baruch's friends advised him to make an issue of the affair; instead, he quietly resigned. "No one," he says today, "has had this thing practiced against him more than I have. But I don't let it bother me. I always remember what Bob Fitzsimmons said to me—he wanted to make me a champion, you know—'You've got to learn to take it before you can give it out.' "[15]

The Suburban Trend, the Country Club and the Country Day School

The resort and the suburb are both a product of the same desire for homogeneity and a nostalgic yearning for the simplicities of small-town life. Just as, today, white families of diverse ethnic origins and newly won middle-class status are busily escaping from the increasingly Negro composition of our cities, so the Protestant upper class first began to flee the ugliness of the urban melting pot at the turn of the century. In Philadelphia, for instance, the majority of the Victorian gentry lived in the city, around fashionable Rittenhouse

Square, as of 1890; by 1914, the majority had moved out to the suburbs along the Main Line or in Chestnut Hill. And this same pattern was followed in other cities.

In many ways Pierre Lorillard was the Victorian aristocrat's William Levitt. Just as Levittown is now the most famous example of a planned community symbolizing the post World War II suburban trend among the middle classes, so Tuxedo Park, New York, established on a site of some 600,000 acres inherited by Pierre Lorillard in 1886, was once the acme of upper-class suburban exclusiveness. According to Cleveland Amory, the Lorillards possessed a foolproof formula for business success which, in turn, was exactly reversed when they came to promoting upper-class exclusiveness. He lists their contrasting formulas as follows:

For Business Success:
1) *Find out what the public wants, then produce the best of its kind.*
2) *Advertise the product so that everybody will know it is available.*
3) *Distribute it everywhere so that everybody can get it.*
4) *Keep making the product better so that more people will like it.*

For Snob Success:
1) *Find out who the leaders of Society are and produce the best place for them to live in.*
2) *Tell nobody else about it so that nobody else will know it's available.*
3) *Keep it a private club so that other people, even if they do hear about it, can't get in.*
4) *Keep the place exactly as it was in the beginning so that other people, even if they do hear about it and somehow do manage to get in, won't ever like it anyway.*[16]

At Tuxedo Park, Lorillard produced almost a caricature of the Victorian millionaire's mania for exclusiveness. In less than a year, he surrounded seven thousand acres with an eight-foot fence, graded some thirty miles of road, built a complete sewage and water system, a gate house which looked like "a frontispiece of an English novel," a clubhouse staffed with imported English servants, and "twenty-two casement dormered English turreted cottages." On Memorial Day, 1886, special trains brought seven hundred highly selected guests from New York to witness the Park's opening.

Tuxedo was a complete triumph. The physical surroundings, the architecture and the social organization were perfectly in tune with the patrician mind of that day. In addition to the English cottages and the clubhouse, there were "two blocks of stores, a score of stables, four lawn-tennis courts, a bowling alley, a swimming tank, a boathouse, an icehouse, a dam, a trout pond and a hatchery. . . . The members sported the club badge which, designed to be worn as a pin, was an oakleaf of solid gold; club governors had acorns attached to their oakleafs and later all Tuxedoites were to wear ties, hatbands, socks, etc., in the club colors of green and gold. . . . No one who was not a member of the club was allowed to buy property."

Tuxedo Park was perhaps a somewhat exaggerated example of an ideal. It certainly would have suggested the conformity of a Chinese commune to many aristocrats seeking real privacy (in the eighties at Nahant, for example, Henry Cabot Lodge built a high fence between his place and his brother-in-law's next door). The upper-class suburban trend as a whole, nevertheless, was motivated by similar, if less rigid, desires for homogeneity. Unlike Tuxedo, however, the country club and the country day school, rather than the neighborhood *per se*, were the main fortresses of exclusiveness. Thus the beginning of a real suburban trend can conveniently be dated from the founding of The Country Club, at Brookline, Massachusetts, in 1882. In the next few decades similar clubs sprang up like mushrooms and became a vital part of the American upper-class way of life. Henry James, an expert on Society both here and abroad, found them "a deeply significant American symbol" at the turn of the century, and an English commentator on our mores wrote:

There are also all over England clubs especially devoted to particular objects, golf clubs, yacht clubs, and so forth. In these the members are drawn together by their interest in a common pursuit, and
are forced into some kind of acquaintanceship. But these are very
different in spirit and intention from the American country club. It
exists as a kind of center of the social life of the neighborhood. Sport
is encouraged by these clubs for the sake of general sociability. In
England sociability is a by-product of an interest in sport.[17]

This English commentator was, of course, implying that the real
function of the American country club was not sport but social exclusion. And throughout the twentieth century the country club has
remained, by and large and with a minority of exceptions, rigidly
exclusive of Jews. In response to this discrimination, elite Jews have
formed clubs of their own.[18] When many wealthy German Jews in
Philadelphia first moved to the suburbs, as we have seen, the famous
merchant Ellis Gimbel and a group of his friends founded one of the
first Jewish country clubs in the nation, in 1906.* After the Second
War, when many Jewish families began to move out on the city's
Main Line, another elite club, largely composed of East European
Jews, was opened.

If the country club is the root of family exclusiveness, the suburban day school provides an isolated environment for the younger
generation. Thus a necessary part of the suburban trend was the
founding of such well-known schools as the Chestnut Hill Academy
(1895) and Haverford School (1884) in two of Philadelphia's
most exclusive suburbs; the Gilman School (1897) in a Baltimore
suburb; the Browne and Nichols School (1883) in Cambridge,
Massachusetts; the Morristown School (1898), the Tuxedo Park
School (1900), and the Hackley School (1899) in Tarrytown, to
take care of New York suburbia.[19] While not as rigidly exclusive as
the country club as far as Jews are concerned, these schools have
been, of course, overwhelmingly proper and Protestant down

* Mr. Gimbel had only recently been "blackballed" by the Union League Club
in the city.

through the years. Few Jews sought admission before the Second War, and since then some form of quota system has often been applied (this is especially true of the suburban schools run by the Quakers in Philadelphia, largely because of their extremely liberal policies of ethnic, racial and religious tolerance).

The greatest monuments are often erected after an era's period of greatest achievement. Versailles was completed after the great age of Louis XIV, the finest Gothic cathedrals after the height of the Catholic synthesis, and the neoclassic plantation mansions after the South had begun to decline. As we shall see below, upper-class suburban homogeneity and exclusiveness are rapidly vanishing characteristics of our postwar era. And when the upper class reigned supreme in its suburban glory (1890–1940), discriminatory practices were genteel and subtle when compared, for example, with the methods of modern automobile magnates in Detroit. The grosser, Grosse Point methods, however, will serve to illustrate (in the manner of our discussion of Tuxedo Park) the anti-Semitic and anti-ethnic values of a suburban upper class, especially at the height of its attempted escape from the motley urban melting pot. As a somewhat tragic, and slightly ludicrous, monument to the mind of a fading era, the following paragraphs from *Time* magazine must be reproduced in full:

Detroit's oldest and richest suburban area is the five-community section east of the city collectively called Grosse Pointe (pop. 50,000). Set back from the winding, tree-shaded streets are fine, solid colonial or brick mansions, occupied by some of Detroit's oldest (pre-automobile age) upper class, and by others who made the grade in business and professional life. Grosse Pointe is representative of dozens of wealthy residential areas in the U. S. where privacy, unhurried tranquility, and unsullied property values are respected. But last week, Grosse Pointe was in the throes of a rude, untranquil expose of its methods of mantaining tranquility.

The trouble burst with the public revelation, during a court squabble between one property owner and his neighbor, that the Grosse Pointe Property Owners Association (973 families) and local real estate brokers had set up a rigid system for screening families who want to buy or build homes in Grosse Pointe. Unlike similar communities, where neighborly solidarity is based on an unwritten gentleman's agreement, Grosse Pointe's screening system is based on a written questionnaire, filled out by a private investigator on behalf of Grosse Pointe's "owner vigilantes."

The three-page questionnaire, scaled on the basis of "points" (highest score: 100), grades would-be home owners on such qualities as descent, way of life (American?), occupation (Typical of his own race?), swarthiness (Very? Medium? Slightly? Not at all?), accent (Pronounced? Medium? Slight? None?), name (Typically American?), repute, education, dress (Neat or Slovenly? Conservative or Flashy?), status of occupation (sufficient eminence may offset poor grades in other respects). Religion is not scored, but weighted in the balance by a three-man Grosse Pointe screening committee. All prospects are handicapped on an ethnic and racial basis: Jews, for example, must score a minimum of 85 points, Italians 75, Greeks 65, Poles 55; Negroes and Orientals do not count.[20]

On reading this questionnaire, one could not fail to see that these Detroit tycoons were, after all, only reflecting their training in the methodology of modern social science. One might prefer the less-amoral world of William James, who once said: "In God's eyes the difference of social position, of intellect, of culture, of cleanliness, of dress, which different men exhibit . . . must be so small as to practically vanish." But in our age, when the social scientist is deified, several generations of young Americans have now been scientifically shown that men no longer seek status "in God's eyes." Instead they are asked to read all sorts of status-ranking studies, often backed by authoritative "tests of significance," which show how one is placed in society by one's cleanliness, dress, and drinking mores. How, one may ask, can one expect these suburbanites, most of whom have been educated in this modern tradition, not to use these methods for their own convenience.

The New England Boarding School

The growth in importance of the New England boarding school as an upper-class institution coincided with the American plutocracy's search for ancestral, suburban and resort-rural roots. At the time of Groton's founding in 1884, for example, these schools were rapidly becoming a vital factor in the creation of a national upper class, with more or less homogeneous values and behavior patterns. In an ever more centralized, complex and mobile age, the sons of the new and old rich, from Boston and New York to Chicago and San Francisco, were educated together in the secluded halls of Groton and St. Paul's, Exeter and Andover, and some seventy other, approximately similar, schools. While Exeter and Andover were ancient institutions, having been founded in the eighteenth century, and while St. Paul's had been in existence since before the Civil War, the boarding school movement went through its period of most rapid growth in the course of the half century after 1880. Exeter's enrollment increased from some 200 boys in 1880, to over 400 by 1905. The enrollment reached 600 for the first time in 1920, rose to 700 in the 1930's, and has remained below 800 ever since. St. Paul's went through its period of most rapid growth in the two decades before 1900 (the school graduated about 45 boys per year in the 1870's and rose to 100 per year by 1900, where it has remained ever since).

It is interesting in connection with the growth of a national upper class, that the founding of many prominent schools coincided with the "trust-founding" and "trust-busting" era. Thus the following schools were founded within a decade of the formation of the United States Steel Corporation, in 1901:

The Taft School in Watertown, Connecticut, was founded by Horace Dutton Taft, a brother of President Taft, in 1890; the Hotchkiss School, Lakeville, Connecticut, was founded and endowed by Maria Hotchkiss, widow of the inventor of the famous machine-gun, in 1892; St. George's School, Newport, Rhode Island, which has a million-dollar Gothic chapel built by John Nicholas Brown, was founded in 1896; in the same year, Choate School, whose benefactors and friends include such prominent businessmen as Andrew Mellon and Owen D. Young, was founded by Judge William G. Choate, at Wallingford, Connecticut; while the elder Morgan was forming his steel company in New York and Pittsburgh in 1901, seven Proper Bostonians, including Francis Lowell, W. Cameron Forbes, and Henry Lee Higginson, were founding Middlesex School, near Concord, Massachusetts; Deerfield, which had been a local academy since 1797, was reorganized as a modern boarding school by its great headmaster, Frank L. Boydon, in 1902; and finally, Father Sill of the Order of the Holy Cross, founded Kent School in 1906.[21]

While the vast majority of the students at these schools were old-stock Protestants throughout the first part of the twentieth century at least, it would be inaccurate to suppose that the schools' admission policies rigidly excluded Catholics or even Jews. Few Catholics and fewer Jews applied (Henry Morgenthau attended Exeter. As he never referred to the fact, even in his Who's Who biography, he probably had a pretty lonely time there). As a matter of historical fact, these schools were largely preoccupied, during the first three decades of this century, with assimilating the sons of America's newly rich Protestant tycoons, many of whom were somewhat spoiled in the style of the late William Randolph Hearst, who had been asked to leave St. Paul's.

On the whole, as will be brought out in a later chapter, these schools have continued to assimilate the sons of the newly rich down through the years. John F. Kennedy, for example, was graduated from Choate School in the thirties, after spending a year at

Canterbury. In this connection, it was a measure of the increasingly affluent status of American Catholics that the nation's two leading Catholic boarding schools, Portsmouth Priory and Canterbury, were founded in 1926 and 1915 respectively.

The College Campus in the Gilded Age: Gold Coast and Slum

The excluding mania of the Gilded Age was of course reflected on the campuses of the nation, especially in the older colleges in the East. In his book, *Academic Procession*, Ernest Earnest begins his chapter entitled "The Golden Age and the Gilded Cage" as follows:

It is ironic that the most fruitful period in American higher education sowed the seeds of three of the greatest evils: commercialized athletics, domination by the business community, and a caste system symbolized by the Gold Coast. . . . A smaller percentage of students came to prepare for the ministry, law, and teaching; they came to prepare for entrance into the business community, especially that part of it concerned with big business and finance. And it was the sons of big business, finance, and corporation law who dominated the life of the campus in the older Eastern colleges. To an amazing degree the pattern set by Harvard, Yale and Princeton after 1880 became that of colleges all over the country. The clubs, the social organization, the athletics—even the clothes and the slang—of "the big three" were copied by college youth throughout the nation. In its totality the system which flowered between 1880 and World War I reflected the ideals of the social class which dominated the period.[22]

It is indeed appropriate that Yale's William Graham Sumner added the term "mores" to the sociological jargon, for the snobbish mass mores of the campuses of the Gilded Age were nowhere more binding than at New Haven. In the nineties, Yale became the first

football factory and led the national trend toward anti-intellectu-
alism and social snobbishness. Between 1883 and 1901, Yale plowed
through nine undefeated seasons, piled up seven hundred points to
its opponents' zero in the famous season of 1888, and produced
Walter Camp, who picked the first All-American eleven and who
produced Amos Alonzo Stagg, who, in turn, taught Knute Rockne
everything he knew about football. By the turn of the century, "We
toil not, neither do we agitate, but we play football" became the
campus slogan. And cheating and the use of purchased papers almost
became the rule among the golden boys of Yale, most of whom lived
in "The Hutch," an expensive privately owned dormitory where the
swells patronized private tailors, ruined expensive suits in pranks,
sprees and rioting, ordered fine cigars by the hundred-lot, and
looked down on those poorer boys who had gone to public high
schools. The Yale Class Book of 1900, appropriately enough, published the answer to the following question: Have you ever used a
trot? Yes: 264, No: 15. At the same time, in a survey covering three
floors of a dormitory, it was found that not a single student wrote his
own themes. They bought them, of course. After all, this sort of
menial labor was only for the "drips," "grinds," "fruits," "meatballs," and "black men" of minority ethnic origins and a public
school education. But at least one gilded son was somewhat horrified at the mores of Old Eli in those good old days before mass democracy had polluted gentlemenly education. A member of the class
of 1879, this young gentleman asked an instructor in history to
recommend some outside reading. The reply was "Young man, if
you think you came to Yale with the idea of reading you will find out
your mistake very soon."[23]

This anti-intellectual crowd of leading Yale men was composed
primarily of boarding school graduates who began to dominate
campus life at this time. Owen Johnson, graduate of Lawrenceville
and Yale (1900), wrote about this generation in his best seller,
Stover at Yale.[24] Stover soon learned that the way to success at Yale
meant following the mores established by the cliques from Andover,

Exeter, Hotchkiss, Groton and St. Paul's: "We've got a corking lot in the house—Best of the Andover crowd." Even in the famous senior societies, caste replaced the traditional aristocracy of merit. Thus a committee headed by Professor Irving Fisher found that, whereas twenty-six of the thirty-four class valedictorians had been tapped by the senior societies between 1861 and 1894, after 1893 not a single one had been considered.[25]

By the turn of the century, the College of New Jersey which had only recently changed its name to Princeton was far more homogeneously upper class than Yale. "The Christian tradition, the exclusiveness of the upper-class clubs, and the prejudices of the students," wrote Edwin E. Slosson in *Great American Universities* in 1910, "kept away many Jews, although not all—there are eleven in the Freshman class. Anti-Semitic feeling seemed to me to be more dominant at Princeton than at any of the other universities I visited. 'If the Jews once get in,' I was told, 'they would ruin Princeton as they have Columbia and Pennsylvania.' "[26]

Football mania and the snobberies fostered by the eating-club system gradually dominated campus life at Princeton. Thus in 1906, Woodrow Wilson, convinced that the side shows were swallowing up the circus, made his famous report to the trustees on the need for abolishing the clubs. Although many misunderstood his purpose at the time, Wilson actually desired to make Princeton an even more homogeneous body of gentlemen-scholars. His preceptorial and quadrangle plans envisioned a series of small and intimate groups of students and faculty members pursuing knowledge without the disruptive class divisions fostered by the existing club system. Wilson was defeated in his drive for reform (partly because of his tactlessness) and was eventually banished to the White House, where he would be less of a threat to the system so dear to the hearts of many powerful trustees.

One should not dismiss Princeton's idea of homogeneity without mentioning one of its real and extremely important advantages. Princeton is one of the few American universities where an honor system is still in force, and presumably works. In this connection, Edwin E. Slosson's observations on the system as it worked in 1910 should be quoted in full:

At Harvard I saw a crowd of students going into a large hall, and following them in, I found I could not get out, that no one was allowed to leave the examination room for twenty minutes. The students were insulated, the carefully protected papers distributed, and guards walked up and down the aisles with their eyes rolling like the search lights of a steamer in a fog. Nothing like this at Princeton; the students are on their honor not to cheat, and they do not, or but rarely. Each entering class is instructed by the Seniors into the Princeton code of honor, which requires any student seeing another receiving or giving assistance on examination to report him for a trial by his peers of the student body. . . . I do not think the plan would be practicable in the long run with a very large and heterogeneous collection of students. It is probable that Princeton will lose this with some other fine features of its student life as the university grows and becomes more cosmopolitan. The semi-monastic seclusion of the country village cannot be long maintained.[27]

In contrast to Princeton, and even Yale, Harvard has always been guided by the ideal of diversity. A large and heterogeneous student body, however, is always in danger of developing class divisions. Like his friend Woodrow Wilson, A. Lawrence Lowell was disturbed by this trend at Harvard at the turn of the century. In a letter to President Eliot, written in 1902, he mentioned the "tendency of wealthy students to live in private dormitories outside the yard" and the "great danger of a snobbish separation of the students on lines of wealth."[28] In a committee report of the same year, he noted how one of the finest dormitories was becoming known as "Little Jerusalem" because of the fact that some Jews lived there.

Samuel Eliot Morison, in his history of Harvard, shows how the college gradually became two worlds—the "Yard" and the "Gold Coast"—as Boston society, the private schools, the club system and the private dormitories took over social life at the turn of the century.[29] "In the eighties," he writes, "when the supply of eligible young men in Boston was decreased by the westward movement, the Boston mammas suddenly became aware that Harvard contained many appetizing young gentlemen from New York, Philadelphia, and elsewhere. One met them in the summer at Newport, Beverly, or Bar Harbor; naturally one invited them to Mr. Papanti's or Mr. Foster's 'Friday Evenings' when they entered College, to the 'Saturday Evening Sociables' sophomore year, and to coming-out balls thereafter."[30] These favored men were, at the same time, living along Mount Auburn Street in privately run and often expensive halls, and eating at the few final clubs which only took in some 10 to 15 per cent of each class. Closely integrated with the clubs and Boston Society were the private preparatory schools. Until about 1870, according to Morison, Boston Latin School graduates still had a privileged position at Harvard, but "during the period 1870–90 the proportion of freshmen entering from public high schools fell from 38 to 23 per cent." About 1890 the Episcopal Church schools and a few others took over. "Since 1890 it has been almost necessary for a Harvard student with social ambition to enter from the 'right' sort of school and be popular there, to room on the 'Gold Coast' and be accepted by Boston society his freshman year, in order to be on the right side of the social chasm . . . conversely, a lad of Mayflower or Porcellian ancestry who entered from a high school was as much 'out of it' as a ghetto Jew."[31]

During most of Harvard's history, according to Morison, a solid core of middle-class New Englanders had been able to absorb most of the students into a cohesive college life which was dominated by a basic curriculum taken by all students. The increasing size of the classes (100 in the 1860's to over 600 by the time Franklin Roosevelt graduated in 1904), the elective system which sent men off to specialize in all directions, and the increasing ethnic heterogeneity of the student body, paved the way for exclusiveness and stratification. By 1893, for example, there were enough Irish Catholics in the Yard to support the St. Paul's Catholic Club, which acquired Newman House in 1912. The situation was similar with the Jews. "The first German Jews who came were easily absorbed into the social pattern; but at the turn of the century the bright Russian and Polish lads from the Boston public schools began to arrive. There were enough of them in 1906 to form the Menorah Society, and in another fifteen years Harvard had her 'Jewish problem.' "[32]

The "Jewish problem" at Harvard will be discussed below. Here it is enough to emphasize the fact that it grew out of the general development of caste in America at the turn of the century. And this new type of caste system was supported by all kinds of associations, from the suburban country club to the fraternities and clubs on the campuses of the nation. Not only were two worlds now firmly established at Harvard and Yale and to a lesser extent at Princeton; at other less influential state universities and small colleges, fraternities dominated campus life.

Although fraternities grew up on the American campus before the Civil War, they expanded tremendously in the postwar period. By the late 1880's, for instance, the five hundred undergraduates at the University of Wisconsin were stratified by a fraternity system which included no less than thirteen houses.[33] As class consciousness increased, campus mores of course became more rigidly anti-Semitic and often anti-Catholic. Bernard Baruch, who entered the College of the City of New York in 1884 (as he was only fourteen at the time, his mother would not let him go away to Yale, which was his preference), felt the full weight of campus anti-Semitism. Although he was extremely popular among the small group of less than four hundred undergraduates, and although he was elected president of the class in his senior year, young Baruch was never taken into a fraternity at C.C.N.Y. "The Greek-letter societies or fraternities," he wrote years later in his autobiography, "played an important part at the college. Although many Jews made their mark at the college, the line was drawn against them by these societies. Each year my name would be proposed and a row would ensue over my nomination, but I never was elected. It may be worth noting, particularly for those who regard the South as less tolerant than the North, that my brother Herman was readily admitted to a fraternity while he attended the University of Virginia."[34] In response to the "Anglo-Saxon-Only" mores which accompanied the fraternity boom in the eighties and nineties, the first Jewish fraternity in America was founded at Columbia, in 1898.

The campus mores were, of course, modeled after the adult world which the students in the Gilded Age were preparing to face. For the large corporations, banks and powerful law firms—in the big-city centers of national power—increasingly began to select their future leaders, not on the basis of ability alone, but largely on the basis of their fashionable university and club or fraternity affiliations. "The graduate of a small college or a Western university," writes Ernest Earnest, "might aspire to a judgeship or bank presidency in the smaller cities and towns; he might get to Congress, become a physician or college professor. Particularly west of the Alleghenies he might become a governor or senator. But he was unlikely to be taken into the inner social and financial circles of Boston, New York or Philadelphia."[35] In the first half of the twentieth century, five of our eight Presidents were graduates of Harvard, Yale, Princeton and Amherst. A sixth came from Stanford, "the Western Harvard," where the social system most resembled that in the East.

The Metropolitan Men's Club:
Stronghold of Patrician Power

When the gilded youths at Harvard, Yale and Princeton finally left the protected world of the "Gold Coast" to seek their fortunes in the Wall streets and executive suites of the nation, they usually joined one or another exclusive men's club. Here they dined with others of their kind, helped each other to secure jobs and promotions, and made friends with influential older members who might some day be of help to them in their paths to the top. Proper club affiliation was, after all, the final and most important stage in an exclusive socializing process. As a character in a novel about Harvard, published in 1901, put it: "Bertie knew who his classmates in college were going to be at the age of five. They're the same chaps he's been going to school with and to kid dancing classes . . . it's part of the routine. After they get out of college they'll all go abroad for a few months in groups of three or four, and when they get back they'll be taken into the same club (their names will have been on the waiting list some twenty-odd years) . . . and see one another every day for the rest of their lives."[36] But, by the century's turn, the metropolitan club was gradually becoming more than a congenial gathering-place for similarly bred gentlemen.

British and American gentlemen, especially after the urban bourgeoisie replaced the provincial aristocracy, soon realized that the club was an ideal instrument for the gentlemanly control of social, political and economic power. For generations in England, top decisions in the City and at Whitehall have often been made along Pall Mall, where conservatives gathered at the Carleton and liberals at the Reform. But perhaps the best illustration of the role of the club in the making of gentlemen, and its use as an instrument of power, was a "gentlemanly agreement" which was made in the late nineteenth century at the frontiers of empire. And it is indeed symbolic and prophetic that it should have been made in racialist South Africa by the great Cecil Rhodes, that most rabid of racialists who dreamed of forming a Nordic secret society, organized like Loyola's, and devoted to world domination. The club served Rhodes well on his way to wealth.[37]

The exploitation of Africa became a full-fledged imperialist enterprise only after Cecil Rhodes dispossessed the Jews. Rhodes' most important competitor in the fight for control of the Kimberley diamond mines was Barney Barnato, son of a Whitechapel shopkeeper, who was possessed by a passionate desire to make his pile and, above all, to become a gentleman. Both Rhodes and Barnato

136

were eighteen years of age when they arrived in Kimberley in the early seventies. By 1885 Rhodes was worth fifty thousand pounds a year, but Barnato was richer. At that time Rhodes began his "subtle" and persistent dealings with Barnato in order to gain control of de Beers. Nearly every day he had him to lunch or dinner at the "unattainable," at least for Barnato, Kimberley Club (he even persuaded the club to alter its rules which limited the entertainment of non-members to once-a-month). At last, Barnato agreed to sell out to Rhodes for a fabulous fortune, membership in the Kimberley Club, and a secure place among the gentlemanly imperialists. While Rhodes had perhaps used his club and his race with an ungentlemanly lack of subtlety, "no American trust, no trust in the world, had such power over any commodity as Rhodes now had over diamonds." But in the end, his dream that "between two and three thousand Nordic gentlemen in the prime of life and mathematically selected" should run the world became the very respectable Rhodes Scholarship Association, which supported selected members of all "Nordic Races," such as Germans, Scandinavians and Americans, during a brief stay in the civilizing atmosphere of Oxford University (the "Nordic" criterion for selection has since been abandoned). In the meantime, his friend Barney Barnato, soon after realizing his dream of becoming both a millionaire and a gentleman, drowned himself in the depths of the sea.

Many such dreams of corporate and financial empire-building have been consummated within the halls of America's more exclusive clubs. The greatest financial imperialist of them all, J. Pierpont Morgan, belonged to no less than nineteen clubs in this country and along Pall Mall. One of his dreams was realized on the night of December 12, 1900, in the course of a private dinner at the University Club in New York. Carnegie's man, Charles M. Schwab, was the guest of honor and the steel trust was planned that night.

In the 1900's the metropolitan club became far more important than the country club, the private school and college, or the exclusive neighborhood as the crucial variable in the recruitment of

America's new corporate aristocracy. Family position and prestige, built up as a result of several generations of leadership and service in some provincial city or town, were gradually replaced by an aristocracy by ballot, in the hierarchy of metropolitan clubdom. In New York, for example, this process can be illustrated by the club affiliations of successive generations of Rockefellers: John D. Rockefeller belonged to the Union League; John D., Jr., to the University Club; and John D. III to the Knickerbocker. Thus is a business aristocracy recruited.

And this associational, rather than familistic, process was certainly democratic, except for one thing. That is the fact that, almost without exception, every club in America now developed a castelike policy toward the Jews. They were excluded, as a people or race, regardless of their personal qualities such as education, taste or manners. It is important, moreover, to stress the fact that this caste line was only drawn at the end of the nineteenth century, when, as we have seen, the members of the upper class were setting themselves apart in other ways. Joseph Seligman's experience at Saratoga Springs was part of a general trend which came to a head again when Jesse Seligman, one of the founders of New York's Union League, resigned from the club in 1893, when his son was blackballed because he was a Jew. Apparently this sort of anti-Semitism was not yet a norm when the club was founded during the Civil War.

Nor was it the norm among the more exclusive clubs in other cities. The Philadelphia Club, the oldest and one of the most patrician in America, was founded in 1834, but did not adhere to any anti-Semitic policy until late in the century. During the Civil War, for instance, Joseph Gratz, of an old German-Jewish family and a leader in his synagogue, was president of the club. The membership also included representatives of several other prominent families of Jewish origin. Yet no other member of the Gratz family has been taken into the Philadelphia Club since the nineties, a period when countless embarrassing incidents all over America paralleled the

Seligman incident at the Union League.* The University Club of
Cincinnati finally broke up, in 1896, over the admission of a prominent member of the Jewish community. Elsewhere, prominent,
cultivated and powerful Jews were asked to resign, or were forced to
do so by their sense of pride, because of incidents involving their
families or friends who were refused membership solely because of
their Jewish origins. Gentlemanly anti-Semitism even invaded the
aristocratic South. As late as the 1870's one of the more fashionable
men's clubs in Richmond, the Westmoreland, had members as well
as an elected president of Jewish origins. But today all the top clubs
in the city follow a policy of rigid exclusiveness as far as Jews are
concerned. This is the case even though the elite Jewish community
in Richmond, as in Philadelphia, has always been a stable one with a
solid core of old families whose members exhibit none of the aggressive, *parvenu* traits given as a reason for the anti-Semitic policies of
clubs in New York, Chicago or Los Angeles.

Yet the inclusion of cultivated Jews within the halls of the Philadelphia or Westmoreland clubs in an earlier day was characteristic
of a provincial and familistic age when the men's club was really social, and membership was based on congeniality rather than, as it has
increasingly become, on an organized effort to retain social power
within a castelike social stratum. George Apley, whose values were
the product of a rapidly departing era, threatened to resign from his
beloved Boston Club when he thought it was being used, somewhat
in the style of Cecil Rhodes, as an agency for the consolidation of
business power. At a time when his clubmates Moore and Field were
apparently violating his gentlemanly code in seeking the admission
of their business associate Ransome, Apley wrote the admissions
committee as follows:

> I wish to make it clear that it is not because of Ransome per-
> sonally that I move to oppose him.

* As a matter of "subtle" fact, there were no "Jewish" members of the Gratz
family left in the city by this time.

Rather, I move to oppose the motive which actuates Messrs. Moore and Field in putting this man up for membership. They are not doing so because of family connections, nor because of disinterested friendship, but rather because of business reasons. It is, perhaps, too well known for me to mention it that Mr. Ransome has been instrumental in bringing a very large amount of New York business to the banking house of Moore and Fields. This I do not think is reason enough to admit Mr. Ransome to the Province Club, a club which exists for social and not for business purposes.[38]

Today many other clubs like Apley's Province, but unlike Pittsburgh's Duquesne, are fighting the intrusion of business affairs into a club life supposedly devoted to the purely social life among gentlemen. "A year or two ago," wrote Osborn Elliott in 1959, "members of San Francisco's sedate Pacific Union Club (known affectionately as the P.U.) received notices advising them that briefcases should not be opened, nor business papers displayed, within the confines of the old club building atop Nob Hill."[39] At about the same time, patrician New Yorkers were shocked at a *Fortune* article which reported that "at the Metropolitan or the Union League or the University . . . you might do a $10,000 deal, but you'd use the Knickerbocker or the Union or the Racquet for $100,000, and then for $1 million you'd have to move on to the Brook or the Links."[40]

In this chapter I have shown how a series of newly created upperclass institutions produced an associationally insulated national upper class in metropolitan America. I have stressed their rise in a particular time in our history and attempted to show how they were part of a more general status, economic and urban revolution which, in turn, was reflected in the Populist and Progressive movements. All this is important as a background for understanding the present situation, primarily because it shows that upper-class nativism in general and anti-Semitism in particular were a product of a particular cultural epoch and, more important, had not always been characteristic of polite society to anywhere near the same extent. This being the case, it may well be true, on the other hand, that new social and cultural situations may teach new duties and produce new upper-class mores and values. As a measure of the success of these caste-creating associations, the following remarks made by the late H. G. Wells after a visit to this country soon after the turn of the century are interesting.

> In the lower levels of the American community there pours perpetually a vast torrent of strangers, speaking alien tongues, inspired by alien traditions, for the most part illiterate peasants and working-people. They come in at the bottom: that must be insisted upon. . . . The older American population is being floated up on the top of this influx, a sterile aristocracy above a racially different and astonishingly fecund proletariat. . . .
>
> Yet there are moments in which I could have imagined there were no immigrants at all. All the time, except for one distinctive evening, I seem to have been talking to English-speaking men, now and then, but less frequently, to an Americanized German. In the clubs there are no immigrants. There are not even Jews, as there are in London clubs. One goes about the wide streets of Boston, one meets all sorts of Boston people, one visits the State-House; it's all the authentic English-speaking America. Fifth Avenue, too, is America without a touch of foreign-born; and Washington. You go a hundred yards south of the pretty Boston Common, and, behold! you are in a polyglot slum! You go a block or so east of Fifth Avenue and you are in a vaster, more Yiddish Whitechapel.[41]

At this point, it should be emphasized that it was (and still is) primarily the patrician without power, the clubmen and resorters and the functionless genteel who, as Edith Wharton wrote, "fall back on sport and culture." It was these gentlemen with time on their hands who took the lead in creating the "anti-everything" world which Henry Adams called "Society." So often, for example, it was the men of inherited means, many of them bachelors like Madison Grant, who served on club admission committees, led the dancing assemblies and had their summers free to run the yacht, tennis and bathing clubs at Newport or Bar Harbor. And these leisurely patricians were, in turn, supported by the new men, and especially their socially ambitious wives, who had just made their fortunes and were seeking social security for their children. In all status revolutions, indeed, resentment festers with the greatest intensity among the new rich, the new poor, and the functionless genteel. And these gentlemen of resentment responded to the status revolution at the turn of the century by successfully creating, as H. G. Wells so clearly saw, two worlds: the patrician and Protestant rich, and the rest.

I hate the narrowness of the Native American Party. It is
the dog in the manger. It is precisely opposite to all the dic-
tates of love and magnanimity; and therefore, of course, opposite to true wisdom. . . . Man is the most composite of all
creatures. . . . Well, as in the old burning of the Temple at
Corinth, by the melting and intermixture of silver and gold
and other metals a new compound more precious than any,
called Corinthian brass, was formed; so in this continent,—
asylum of all nations,—the energy of Irish, Germans,
Swedes, Poles, and Cossacks, and all the European tribes,—
of the Africans, and of the Polynesians,—will construct a
new race, a new religion, a new state, a new literature, which
will be as vigorous as the new Europe which came out of
the smelting-pot of the Dark Ages, or that which earlier
emerged from the Pelasgic and Etruscan barbarism. *La
Nature aime les croisements.*

Ralph Waldo Emerson

VI

The Aristocratic Counterattack on Caste: President Eliot and the Two Roosevelts

In the very decade when the vividness of the American Dream was
beginning to fade, in the year 1886, the Statue of Liberty, a gift of
the French people, was erected on Bedloe's Island in New York harbor. This chapter will be concerned with the values of those aristocrats who saw the dangers in our becoming two nations and who
somehow never lost faith in the American promise to the "huddled
masses yearning to breathe free."

Appearances to the contrary, and in accord with Freud rather than
Marx, no upper-class mind is ever consistent. Nothing human ever
is. At the same time that so many panicky patricians, for example,

were ancestor hunting, forming associations to restrict immigration, building country clubs and neighborhoods to keep out Jews, and doing everything in their power to protect themselves from the ugliness of the urban melting pot, perhaps the finest product of the brahmin mind in America, Harvard College, was adjusting to the new America under the leadership of President Eliot.

Charles W. Eliot: Unitarian Aristocrat

Charles W. Eliot, an impeccable patrician by birth as well as in his brahmin bearing, always played down his ancestry.[1] He was the ideal example of the assimilating aristocrat who never lost faith in the American Dream. He remained a staunch Unitarian in an era when most members of his class were being seduced by the richness of the Anglican ritual. A vigorous and vocal reformer, he eventually attained a nation-wide authority and prestige which, toward the end of his life, elevated him almost to the level of an institution. His strong endorsement of Louis D. Brandeis in the fight over his nomination to the Supreme Court in 1916 was equated, by one of Brandeis' bitter opponents, with an endorsement from God (see below).

But perhaps most important of all, Eliot ran the nation's leading elite-producing institution which, having educated no future Presidents of the United States since the two Adamses graduated in the eighteenth century, produced two Roosevelts under his leadership. It is indeed fortunate for America that these three Harvard patricians, Eliot and the two Roosevelts, interpreted the dominant social forces of the twentieth century quite differently from Henry Adams or Madison Grant and the majority of the members of the class that bred them. But majorities mean nothing at this level of society, for who would deny that the two Roosevelts had more influence on the course of events in their eras than all of the forty or fifty thousand families who considered themselves part of the "Four Hundred."

144

Thus, contrary to the prejudices of so many of their class, these men retained their faith in the American Dream and helped to create an environment which would eventually absorb the immigrant—first, into the main stream of middle-class respectability, then, into leadership positions and, finally, into the ranks of a new, and ethnically mixed, upper class and establishment. In short, these men defended and advanced the ideology of aristocracy as against the steadily retreating, yet always powerful, ideology of caste superiority.

"You and I are about the same age and began life with much the same set of ideas about freedom and democracy," wrote Charles W. Eliot, at the age of eighty in 1914, to his old friend, Charles Francis Adams. "But you have seen reason to abandon the principles and doctrines of your youth, while I have not. So far as I know, my fundamental beliefs are about the same as they were when I was twenty; but I imagine the grounds of my belief to be more solid now than they were then. My fate in this respect seems to me happier than yours; and to my thinking fate is not the right word for it. Your changed beliefs are the outcome of your experience in life, and my unchanged beliefs are the outcome of my experience and observation in life."[2] As a lifelong Unitarian, Eliot never lost faith in environment. He read and reread his favorite philosopher, Emerson, and always kept two complete sets of his works by his side, one at Northeast Harbor and the other at Cambridge. His social and political philosophy was libertarian, utilitarian and strong on uplift and optimism when he became the leader of the "savage and terrible hordes," as John Jay Chapman put it, "who waked up in 1870 to the importance of education." Along with Woodrow Wilson, Eliot had a "truly pious belief in education as a means of self-advancement" and was a "sincere, spontaneous representative of the average American."[3] While Chapman heartily disagreed with Eliot, he thoroughly admired him as one of the great Americans of his age.

President Eliot had no faith in the Populist passion for equality nor the patrician ideal of homogeneity; his idols were liberty and diversity. Like Tocqueville, he understood how equality of conditions was conducive to despotism when he wrote the following prophetic description of the total state: "Under an absolute despotism . . . under which all property is held at the will of the ruler, and every distinction or public station proceeds solely from him, and may at any moment be withdrawn by him, a kind of equality may exist among all the subjects. There is no freedom to rise. . . . Before the one tyrant all subjects are in some sense equal. . . ."[4]

Eliot also realized how a stable, but always open, community of upper-class families served as a protection against the dangers of atomized individualism. "The family, rather than the individual, is the important social unit," he once wrote. "If society as a whole is to gain by mobility and openness of structure, those who rise must stay up in successive generations, that the higher levels of society may be constantly enlarged, and that the proportion of pure, gentle, magnanimous, and refined persons may steadily be increased. New-risen talent should reinforce the upper ranks. . . . The assured permanence of superior families is quite as important as the free starting of such families."[5] While he was troubled by the low Harvard birth rate and urged Yankee procreation, he "believed the American way of life could produce new 'good' families."[6]

In other words, Eliot was a realistic brahmin. Though he realized and often emphasized the evils of great wealth, he thought private property as well as an unequal distribution of income and inherited wealth both right and highly desirable. Provided, that is, that all men should have unlimited opportunities to rise as high as their talents deserved. His famous Five-Foot Shelf, the average man's guide to self-improvement, characteristically began with a volume on Benjamin Franklin, the all-time-champion self-made man. His belief in unity through diversity led to the elective system at Harvard College, and perhaps his major accomplishment, the enlargement of the graduate schools, grew out of his faith in the democratic specialist as against the aristocratic amateur. Thus Eliot transformed a provincial and patrician college into a cosmopolitan and democratic university. And Harvard, incidentally, became our first Ph.D. mill.

It is no wonder that Eliot "became the most impressive foe of the Immigration Restriction League" and once wrote to the Society for Italian Immigration that "the more Italian immigrants that come to the United States the better...."[7] Not only did he favor immigration but, in contrast to most other patrician leaders from Adams to Chapman, he felt that the so-called "American race" was "dying out because of its shortcomings—not because of alien admissions."[8] And he naturally took a dim view of the Eugenics Movement, so dear to the hearts of men like Madison Grant and Lothrop Stoddard. Upon reading *The Crisis in Our Immigration Policy*, written by Robert DeCourcy Ward, one of the three founders of the Immigration Restriction League, Eliot advised one of his professors at Harvard that "one neither should nor could improve human beings by methods which were suitable for horses, dogs and cattle, for the processes of animal breeding are wholly and forever inapplicable to human breeding."[9] Anticipating the Nazi mind, Eliot saw that the *science* of eugenics would reduce men, whether of old or new stock, to the level of animals. "To Eliot," wrote Barbara Miller Solomon, "the descendant of Puritans and the disciple of Channing and Emerson, the upward struggle of man's soul and his responsibility for his brother were realities which superseded the abstract justifications of scientific heredity."[10]

Nor was Eliot insensitive to the problem of anti-Semitism. He wrote several introductions to works on the Jews and counted many among his intimate friends. At Harvard he was always concerned that the "Yard" should be open to the Jews as well as to the members of other minority groups. He even welcomed the possibility of a Jewish president of Harvard, as Norman Hapgood once reported:

He told me frankly why he did not favor the leading possibility, Mr. Lowell, and brought out his own choice, Mr. Jerome Green. I then presented the name of Mr. Louis D. Brandeis. Dr. Eliot was delighted. The question of social prejudice was far from giving him concern. Rather it added to his enthusiasm. On that part of the *subject he said, "I am a Unitarian. It would please me to be followed by a Jew."*[11]

Abraham Lincoln once said that the phrase "the great die young" meant "young in their ideals." Eliot remained true to the ideals of his youth till the end. In fact, though he had hated Catholicism "like poison" when he had visited Rome in his youth, he applauded the appointment, in 1920, of the first Catholic, James Byrne, to the Harvard Corporation (John Jay Chapman was "afire" at this appointment of a man "high up in the Catholic gang").[12] He always kept growing and fighting for what he thought was right and democratic. In some eighty-three articles and addresses, published between his eightieth year and his death at ninety-three, he constantly referred to his hope that he would "never lose faith in democracy." Perhaps, at the same time, he never probed too deeply below the surface of things, for fear of losing faith, as had his Adams friends. "What is there for you and me to do," he wrote a fellow crusader toward the end of his life, "except fight near and tangible evils most of our time, and in the balance try to set forth the moral principles and motives on which alone human progress can be based? For myself," he continued, "I take the most satisfaction in fighting well-recognized evils, like the industrial war, alcoholism, militarism, venereal diseases, and racial discrimination."[13] And when his great friend Woodrow Wilson was defeated, and the League of Nations became a lost cause in America, Eliot, on the eve of his ninetieth birthday, could only say "When do we fight again?"

Charles W. Eliot found the most famous alumnus of his college, Theodore Roosevelt, rather "wholesome, invigorating, and uplifting." In many ways the two men were very much alike. Vigorous individualists and reformers, they enjoyed standing up to each other, especially when they did not agree on an issue. Their correspondence contains a certain amount of informal ribbing ("your colleague the Sultan") on Eliot's part, which was quite unlike his usual aloof and formal way. Eliot's account of Roosevelt's visiting him in the spring of 1905 reveals his sympathetic and amused astonishment at the younger man's informality:

That year was the twenty-fifth anniversary of his class and as he was President I invited him to stay at my house. He appeared very early in the morning, a very warm day in June. He said he was dirty, and he looked dirty, I showed him to his room. The first thing he did was to pull off his coat, roll it up with his hands, and fling it across the bed so violently it sent a pillow to the floor beyond. The next thing he did was to take a great pistol from his trousers pocket and slam it down on the dresser. After awhile he came rushing downstairs, as if his life depended on it, and as I stood at the foot of the stairs I said, 'Now, you are taking breakfast with me?' 'Oh, no,' came the reply, 'I promised Bishop Lawrence I would breakfast with him, —and good gracious! (clapping his right hand to his side) I've forgotten my gun!' Now he knew it was against the law in Massachusetts to carry that pistol, and yet he carried it. Very lawless; a very lawless mind![14]

Theodore Roosevelt: Patrician Cowboy in the Urban Melting Pot

Theodore Roosevelt grew up in the protected world of Protestant patricians and spent his life trying to justify, rather than protect, his inherited advantages. "The men I knew best," he wrote in his *Autobiography*, "were the men in the clubs of social pretension and the men of cultivated taste and easy life." But unlike a majority of his friends and clubmates at Harvard or in New York—gentlemen who looked down on politics as the business of shanty-Irish contractors and immigrant bosses—young Roosevelt entered politics at the bottom, determined to rise into the "Governing Class." Deep down in his heart, he mistrusted and often despised the bourgeois mind, which has, after all, always reveled in luxury, snobbery and the pecuniary values. He preferred the heroic virtues which, in turn, made him the leading progressive aristocrat of his age. Roosevelt, in short, was simply bored with the protected world of privileged patricians which was described in the previous chapter. Thus he wrote:

Personally, the life of the Four Hundred, in its typical form, strikes me as being as flat as stale champagne. Upon my word, I think that for mere enjoyment I would a great deal rather hold my own in any congenial political society—even in Tammany—than in a circle where Harry Lehr is deemed a prominent and rather fascinating person.

I used to hunt at Hempstead. The members of the Four Hundred who were out there rode hard and well, and I enjoyed riding to the hounds with them. But their companionship before and afterwards grew so intolerable that toward the end I would take a polo pony and ride him fourteen miles over before the hunt and fourteen miles back after the hunt, rather than stay overnight at the club. It seems to me that you and I, and those like us, who have in many different ways and with many failures and shortcomings, endeavored in some fashion or other to do our duty and to lead self-respecting lives . . . which, even from the viewpoint of mere enjoyment, is immeasurably above that of the unfortunate creatures who, however well groomed and well cared for, and however luxurious their surroundings may be, yet lead essentially mean, petty and ignoble lives.

I suppose young girls and even young men naturally like a year or two of such a life as the Four Hundred lead; and it has its pretty, attractive, and not unwholesome sides. But I do not think that anyone can permanently lead his or her life amid such surroundings and with such objects, save at the cost of degeneration in character.[15]

Possessed by a nostalgic love of the frontier life* and the great outdoors, and saddened by the sordidness of the rapidly urbanizing world around him, Roosevelt nevertheless plunged into urban re-

* In his *Winning of the West*, Roosevelt took Frederick Jackson Turner's view of the power of the frontier environment to mold character. Thus he believed in a "fused race," bred on the harsh frontier, as the essence of vigorous character. This desire to judge a man on his merits was a frontier- rather than drawing-room-inspired concept.

form as a young man in New York and then spent his later years in the White House trying to elevate and inspire those less fortunate than himself, regardless of their racial, religious or ethnic origins. "I grow extremely indignant," he wrote in a letter to Lyman Abbott, "at the attitude of coarse hostility to the immigrant. . . . I have tried to appeal to their self-respect and make it easy for them to become enthusiastically loyal Americans as well as good citizens. I have one Catholic in my Cabinet and have had another, and now I have a Jew in the Cabinet; and part of my object in such appointments was to implant in the minds of our fellow-Americans of Catholic or Jewish faith, or of foreign ancestry or birth, the knowledge that they have in this country just the same rights and opportunities as everyone else, just the same chance of reward for doing the highest kind of service; and therefore just the same ideals as standards toward which to strive."[16] His attempt to draw members of all races and creeds into the main stream of American life even went as far as the Negro. Thus he entertained Booker T. Washington at the White House, which in that day was open to much criticism. The patrician's typically moral approach to politics (not that Roosevelt could not be extremely opportunistic when he thought it necessary) is illustrated in the following reply to criticism: "There is plenty of room for question as to the wisdom of my having had Booker T. Washington to dinner, and however firmly convinced I may be that I was morally right, I will cheerfully admit that the matter is one for entirely legitimate difference of opinion."[17]

Roosevelt was, of course, very much aware of the position of the Jews in the American social structure. Jews were his co-workers in urban reform in New York, members of his Cabinet, and his friends, and he was very conscious of the need for their being brought into full social and political participation in the life of the community. In a letter* to an exceedingly popular writer of the day, Arthur Train, he

---

* It is of interest that, of the 6,437 Roosevelt letters written between 1868 and 1919 (collected in eight volumes by Elting Morison), Jews are mentioned most frequently after 1900. In fact, of the 1,931 letters written between 1868 and 1900, Jews are mentioned just four times, and then only casually.

reveals a "Boy Scout" and schoolmasterish concern for his country as well as a keen appreciation of the dangers of stereotyping: "That was an admirable story of yours in the current *McClure's*," he wrote. "Will you however permit me one criticism, not in reference to this story, but to the other stories that should go with it. In this story there is a native American scoundrel, which is all right. There is also a meaner Jew scoundrel, which is also all right. But there are native American representatives of manliness and decency; and there also ought to be a Jew among them! It is very important that we shall not give the impression that we are attacking all foreigners qua foreigners. There are exceedingly bad Jews, and exceedingly bad old-stock native Americans. There are exceedingly good men who are Jews, and other exceedingly good men who are native old-stock Americans. It is the same thing with men of Irish and German extraction. I hope you will make the emphasis with all possible insistence as between all men who are good Americans, and all who are bad Americans; and that you will be careful to see that your readers clearly understand that there are Jews and Gentiles . . . on both sides."[18]

Roosevelt, as everyone knows, was forever talking about Americanism; but his idea of Americanism was very different from the defensive and exclusionary brand preached by the members of hereditary societies, the Immigration Restriction League of the membership committees of country clubs. "I do not for a moment believe," he wrote to the German professor Hugo Münsterberg, "that the Americanism of today should be a mere submission to the American ideals of the period of the Declaration of Independence."[19] In fact, Roosevelt's concept of Americanism was not of the static, hereditary sort at all, but closer to the dynamic American Dream which put its faith in the power of environment. For, unlike so many of his class, Roosevelt was on the whole an optimist and a dreamer of dreams about America: "I hold a man worthless who is not a dreamer, who does not see visions."[20] And his visions of the power of the American Dream of all-inclusiveness, in both the life of the nation and in its leadership, will always be remembered by so-called hyphenated-Americans, as best expressed in the following famous statement:

> *I believe that this Republic will endure for many centuries. If so there will doubtless be among its Presidents Protestants and Catholics, and, very probably, at the same time Jews.*[21]

Franklin D. Roosevelt: Democratic Aristocrat

During the fourth decade of Charles W. Eliot's reign at Harvard, Theodore Roosevelt entered the White House and young Franklin D. Roosevelt entered the College. While at Harvard, Franklin Roosevelt, in accord with the mores of his class, led the typical "Gold Coast" life, residing in an expensive dormitory, Westmorely Court, eating at the Groton table during his freshman year, eventually joining the Fly Club, and entering the gay social life of Proper Boston.[22] As he wrote in one letter to his parents: "Last week I dined at the Quincy's, the Amory's & the Thayer's, three as high-life places as are to be found in blue-blooded, blue-stocking and bean-eating Boston!"[23] And in another: "Dined at the 'Fly' with Dr. Hale, Prexy Eliot, Dean Hurlburt, & A. Lawrence Lowell—most interesting—Then had a meeting wrote an editorial & at 11 appeared at the Bigelow's ball at the Somerset—a huge affair— I ushered & had great fun."[24]

But unlike so many young men from his own background, Franklin Roosevelt never let the "Gold Coast" social life become all-absorbing. The Harvard of 1900, in the courses offered and the men who taught them, was brilliant and liberal. And young Roosevelt took full advantage of it. Never satisfied with the usual "gentleman's C," he got through his undergraduate requirements in three years and spent his last year in the graduate school, studying history and economics under such well-known men as Roger Bigelow Merriman, Frederick Jackson Turner and William Z. Ripley. In the College, he had studied under Josiah Royce and A. Lawrence Lowell and done a great deal of writing for George Pierce Baker (mentor of Eugene O'Neill, Philip Barry, Thomas Wolfe and many others) and Charles Townsend Copeland. Among the more interesting of his undergraduate essays was one which appealed to Southern colleges to admit Negroes, as Harvard did at that time, and another which considered the rise and decline of New York's Dutch aristocracy. In this latter prophetic piece, he attempted to show how the lack of "a progressive and democratic spirit" was the main cause of the decline of so many once-powerful families. "One reason, perhaps the chief— for the virility of the Roosevelts is this very democratic spirit," he wrote. "They have never felt that because they were born in a good position they could put their hands in their pockets and succeed. They have felt, rather, that being born in a good position, there was no excuse for them if they did not do their duty by the community, and it is because this idea was instilled into them from their birth that they have in nearly every case proved good citizens."[25] This indeed was a revealing statement of the inner convictions which lay behind the gay and handsome façade of a "Gold Coast" undergraduate.

Possessed of a lifelong genealogical interest, great patrician pride and a prodigious memory for details, Roosevelt loved to discuss his family tree; in this sense and in many others he was a deeply conservative man. But, again, unlike so many others of his class, this interest in ancestry produced an aristocratic sense of duty and need for accomplishment rather than a narrow sense of caste superiority. Thus perhaps his most satisfying accomplishment at Harvard was his work for the *Crimson*. He rose to be editor-in-chief and was writing all its editorials by his senior year. While so many of his friends considered campus activities to be beneath their dignity, Roosevelt made friends with a wide circle in the "Yard" through his position on the *Crimson* and subsequently was elected chairman of his Class Committee upon graduation. This gave him a sense of leadership and accomplishment which he had not achieved at Groton.[26]

Groton School, and especially its headmaster, Endicott Peabody, were, however, vital formative influences in Roosevelt's life. "More than forty years ago," he wrote to the Rector in 1940, "you said, in a sermon in the Old Chapel, something about not losing boyhood ideals in later life. These were Groton ideals—taught by you— I try not to forget—and your words are still with me . . ."[27] Although he had been placed on the school's waiting list at the time of its founding, Roosevelt entered Groton, with one other boy, two years later than the rest of his classmates. As this other boy wrote: "Franklin D. before he went to Groton had never been with other boys very much, had had tutors at home and besides had a father who was quite well on in years when he went to school. He therefore found it difficult at first with these handicaps to adjust himself to boarding school life."[28] This early experience may have given him sympathy for those who were left out.

At the same time, of course, his less than perfect fit and his ambivalence toward the world in which he was reared was shared and doubtless intensified by Anna Eleanor Roosevelt. The product of an unhappy and extremely lonely childhood and "the first girl in my mother's family who was not a belle," Anna Eleanor Roosevelt, at the time when she became engaged to Franklin, was absorbed in good works at the Junior League and the Rivington Street Settlement House in New York. "The feeling that I was useful," she wrote of those youthful days, "was perhaps the greatest joy I experienced."[29] This shy and serious young lady's deeply sympathetic concern for those less fortunate than herself was shared by her handsome and charming fiancé, who had decided to marry her while still in college. And in spite of his doting mother's desire to keep her son by her side, Franklin and Eleanor Roosevelt were married by Endicott Peabody, in New York City, on St. Patrick's Day, 1905.

After finishing law school at Columbia, Franklin joined a conventional New York firm but soon found it unsatisfying. He preferred politics and admired his cousin Teddy who had dramatized for a whole generation the image of the gentleman in public life. Franklin finally decided to follow his famous cousin's example. "It was a fundamental decision," wrote Arthur M. Schlesinger, Jr., in *The Age of Roosevelt*. "For twenty-eight years, he had lived an upper-class life of suitable affability, conventionality, and vacancy. But somehow it had not come off. He had tried to play by the book, but his performance was not convincing. Everybody called him 'Franklin,' an acquaintance said, 'and regarded him as a harmless bust.' It all bored him too much—the chatter, the snobbery, the pomposity, the absorption in money. 'He had the soul and instincts of a journalist, but he was in a social stratum where one must be ordinary, industrious, unread and inarticulate or else be branded as a smarty.' Fortunately he had a way of escape. He was a Democrat, and politics offered and outlet for his ambition, his high spirits, his idealism and his realism."[30]

Although only one Democrat had carried the New York senatorial district which included Hyde Park since the Civil War, Franklin D. Roosevelt, a member of the Republican Club at Harvard and a vigorous supporter of T.R., obtained the Democratic nomination and campaigned against great odds. His victory was the beginning of a long career which carried him to the White House as the leader of a party which was to represent the aspirations and ideals of the millions of hyphenated-Americans (including the Jews, both rich and poor alike) who were seeking acceptance into the main stream of American life and leadership. In this career, Franklin D. Roosevelt, optimist, democrat and reforming genius, was following in the aristocratic traditions of Charles W. Eliot and Theodore Roosevelt. But the story of his relations with the class which bred him, with the urban immigrant masses and with the Jews, will be told in Chapter X. In the meantime, it is important here that he was appointed to his first position in the federal government, as Undersecretary of the Navy, by another reforming patrician, Woodrow Wilson, whom we shall turn to in Chapter VIII.

> It is ideas, not vested interests, which are dangerous for good or evil.
>
> *John Maynard Keynes*

VII

The Intellectual Counterattack on Caste: The Social Gospel, Reform and the New Social Science

When Karl Marx wrote that "the ruling ideas of each age have ever been the ideas of its ruling class," he was oversimplifying the highly complex relationship between ideas and social structure. For, in periods of rapid social change, the most *important* ideas of an age— and the men who produce them—are often in reaction to the *ruling* ideas. This is because contemporary ideologies are usually rooted in the experiences and truths of previous generations. Thus most of the millionaires of Herbert Spencer's generation had grown up in a predominantly rural America where the importance they attributed to heredity in shaping the destinies of men was, after all, quite appropriate. The farmer naturally saw that good seeds brought forth the best fruit and that the quality of his herd depended on his breeding from the best sires and dams. Moreover, in a static small-town world where men were able to observe their neighbors over several generations and where class and ethnic differences in environment were at a minimum, it was obvious that good families prospered and that the bad went "to seed." Even within the same family, black sheep were explained away on the basis of bad blood.

But this hereditarian common sense, born of a rural age and reaching its greatest vogue in the theories of the Social Darwinists and racists, had a hard time surviving in a rapidly industrializing and increasingly urban world, where the social environment of the sordid slums was so obviously debilitating and vastly different from the money-insulated world of the successful. Thus Jane Addams, who was reared in relative luxury in rural Illinois, recalls in her autobiography how, upon first visiting her father's mill at the tender age of seven, she noticed "the curious distinction between the ruddy poverty of the country and that which even a small city presents in its shabbiest streets."[1]

Although this pious and patrician child, who later devoted her life to environmental reform, immediately saw the difference between ruddy rural poverty and the sordid squalor of the city, the orthodoxy which explained poverty as the fault of the poor and wealth a sign of superior moral heredity died hard in America. On the other hand, a New Social Science and a new common sense, grounded in the assumptions of environmental causation, gradually came into their own in the course of the twentieth century: slowly at first, but with increasing momentum in each decade after 1880, a *naturalistic, urban, environmental, egalitarian, collectivist,* and eventually *Democratic* ethic finally undermined the *Protestant, rural, hereditarian, opportunitarian, individualistic,* and *Republican* ethic which rationalized the Natural Right of the old-stock business-gentleman's rule in America between 1860 and 1929. What a rural Republican quite naturally blamed on heredity in the 1870's was confidently blamed on environment by his urban and Democratic grandson in the 1930's.

Environmental Relativism: Ideology of an Urban Age

The seeds of the destruction of many class ideologies have usually been sown by the more socially, if not psychologically, secure members of the establishment. A sense of guilt or injustice at the top has always had a profound influence on social change. Thus it was within the Protestant establishment itself, both here and in England, and at the very height of the Victorian and Spencerian syntheses, that a loss of confidence and quest for change first became manifest: the young Victorian debutante, Beatrice Potter (who, with her husband, Sidney Webb, later became one of the leaders of the Fabian Society and the Labour Party), first went into the London slums in 1883 to work on Charles Booth's famous social survey of living conditions (Booth was president of the Cunard Line), the year her beloved uncle Herbert Spencer was at the height of his popularity among her father's brahmin business friends;[2] and the very same year, Jane Addams, who was traveling abroad on a comfortable inheritance from her recently deceased father, also went into London's East End for the first time. "Nothing among the beggars of southern Italy nor among the salt-miners of Austria," she wrote of the experience, "carried with it the same conviction of human wretchedness which was conveyed by this momentary glimpse of an East End street."[3]

Environmentalism first began to invade the American intellectual community through the Social Gospel and Settlement House movements. Both movements were originally imported from England, where the Christian Socialists, led by Charles Kingsley and Frederick Denison Maurice, were attempting to combat the environmental evils of industrial capitalism (it was Kingsley, not Marx, who first

159

used the term "opium of the people" to describe the traditional use of religion by the governing establishment).

The Settlement House movement began in England when a group of Christian Socialists founded Toynbee Hall in London's East End in 1884. Jane Addams, after two trips to Europe in the 1880's as a leisured observer of social conditions, led the movement in this country with the opening of Hull House in the slums of Chicago in 1889. Soon afterward, her lifelong friend, Lillian Wald, who had lived a spoiled life as the daughter of a prosperous family of German-Jewish origins which had come to America after 1848, decided to dedicate her life to the poor during the depression of 1893 and subsequently founded the famous House on Henry Street in New York. Hull House, Henry Street and a host of other settlement houses in other cities educated a whole generation in social responsibility. And few social workers who went into the slums to work for Jane Addams or Lillian Wald—many of them from secure and fashionable families, like young Frances Perkins or Eleanor Roosevelt*—were able to retain the traditional, hereditarian view of the causes of poverty. As a director of a school of social work put it at the time:

The notion of biological heredity and of innate capacity, as a determining factor, would have a paralyzing effect upon the young social worker, faced as he is with problems of maladjustments of various kinds. Without the hope and courage which the new theories of social causation and social control give, no one would long endure social work.[4]

The new theories of social causation and social control which were so necessary for maintaining the hope and courage of several generations of devoted social workers were originally inspired by the Social Gospel movement. The two principal theologians of this movement were Washington Gladden, whose *Applied Christianity* appeared in 1886, and Walter Rauschenbusch (seventh generation

---

* It was because of Lillian Wald that Eleanor Roosevelt first became interested in social work.

of a line of clergymen), whose *Christianity and the Social Crisis* was published in 1907.[5] The ideas of the Social Gospel were based on the conviction that the saving of individual souls was useless without a parallel effort to Christianize the urban environment. While Washington Gladden, for instance, recognized Herbert Spencer as the greatest living sociologist, he wrote that "we may go far beyond Mr. Spencer's limits and yet stop a great way this side of socialism."

Of all the Protestant denominations, the Episcopal Church ("the Church of wealth, culture and aristocratic lineage") was most receptive to the new Social Gospel.[6] J. P. Morgan's own Rector at fashionable St. George's Church, W. S. Rainsford, had come over in 1880 from England, where he had been a strong follower of Charles Kingsley. The two leading reform organizations within the Protestant Church—the Church Association for the Advancement of the Interests of Labor (CAIL) and the Christian Social Union (CSU) —were founded and led by Episcopalians. Father James Otis Sargent Huntington, founder of the Order of the Holy Cross and a member of the old Knights of Labor, was the first Protestant clergyman in America to devote his life to the labor question. After the Haymarket tragedy, Father Huntington and other church leaders founded the CAIL in 1887. Bishop Henry Codman Potter, Morgan's close friend and at the same time a seasoned and respected arbitrator of strikes and lockouts, was the second president of the CAIL. The Christian Social Union, an American branch of the British organization of the same name, was founded in 1891. A patrician reformer, economist and lay Episcopalian, Richard T. Ely, became the first secretary of the CSU and also took an active part in the rise of the New Social Science.

The rise of the New Social Science paralleled the development of the Social Gospel, Settlement House and political reform movements during the closing decades of the nineteenth century. Many of the early sociologists, like William Graham Sumner, started out to become clergymen. In describing his own intellectual development, the sociologist Charles Horton Cooley recorded his debt to

"Jane Addams and other philanthropic writers." Both Charles A. Beard and John Dewey were at one time associated with Hull House. The alliance between reform and the New Social Science was nicely symbolized when the National Institute of Social Science awarded its Gold Medal to Lillian Wald in 1912. And finally, the close relationship between the Social Gospel and the New Social Science was brought out when the American Economic Association was founded in 1885. Washington Gladden and twenty-two other ministers were among the charter members of the Association, whose original platform, drawn up by Richard T. Ely, declared:

> We hold that the conflict of labor and capital has brought into prominence a vast number of social problems, whose solution requires the united efforts, each in its own sphere, of the church, of the state, and of science.[7]

The need for institutional reform on the part of both church and state, as urged in the platform of the American Economic Association, was a basic assumption of the New Social Science which was outlined in the works of such leaders as William James and John Dewey in philosophy and social psychology, Charles A. Beard and Frederick Jackson Turner in history, Thorstein Veblen in economics, Lester F. Ward and Charles H. Cooley in sociology, Oliver Wendell Holmes, Jr., in the law, and Franz Boas in anthropology. All were opposed to racism, Social Darwinism, imperialism, and all forms of hereditary determinism; and all assumed the malleability of human nature which was capable of responding to improved social conditions; Dewey stated the aims of the New Science in very much the same terms as the Social Gospel movement when he wrote that "there must be a change in objective arrangements and institutions; we must work on the environment, not merely in the hearts of men."

It is important to emphasize the fact that most of the prominent leaders of the New Social Science, like the leaders of the Social Gospel and Settlement House movements, came from within the old-stock and Protestant establishment. Thus Veblen's bitter assaults on the establishment may have been partly grounded in his position as the son of Norwegian immigrants at a time when "Norskie" ranked with "kike" and "dago" as a sneer word; and Boas might have been influenced in his thinking by the fact that he was a German Jew. Yet, on the other hand, Holmes was an impeccable Boston brahmin; Beard's father was the First Citizen of Knightstown, Indiana, where he owned the local bank, the newspaper, the mill, and land which spread out to the horizon; Cooley's father was of old Yankee stock, for twenty years a member of the Michigan Supreme Court, first chairman of the first Interstate Commerce Commission, first dean of the Michigan Law School, and one of the First Family Founders of Ann Arbor; and John Dewey, of solid, middle-class Yankee stock, grew up in Burlington, Vermont. "Where I was raised," he once remarked, "the Hoovers and the Mellons would have had a hard time passing for Americans."[8]

As it illustrates so well the relationship between ideas and social structure, it is significant that this New Social Science took shape at the height of the Spencerian vogue within the establishment, and that its most important ideas—which still lie at the core of social science today—were worked out and published before the First War.[9] Thus Holmes' *Common Law* came out in 1881 and Dewey made his first philosophical contribution the next year; James' famous *Principles of Psychology* was finally completed in 1890; Turner published his essay on the "Significance of the Frontier in American History" in 1893; Veblen's *Theory of the Leisure Class* and Dewey's most widely read book and the earliest statement of his theory of progressive education, *The School and Society*, were both published in 1899; James' *Pragmatism* came out in 1907; Cooley's *Social Organization*, in which he first developed the idea of the "primary group," appeared in 1909; Boas' most influential book, *The Mind of Primitive Man* was published in 1911 and Beard's notorious *Economic Interpretation of the Constitution* in 1913.

The New Social Science
and the Concept of Culture

As law is often the codification of the folkways and mores, it may be no accident that many of the original anthropologists, both here and in Europe, were trained as lawyers. And it is indeed appropriate that Holmes should have been one of the founders of the New Social Science. For his *Common Law* was deeply influenced by the anthropological point of view, especially as set forth in E. B. Tylor's *Primitive Culture* (1871) and H. S. Maine's classic book on comparative jurisprudence, *Ancient Law, Its Connection with the Early History of Society and Its Relation to Modern Ideas* (1861). "The life of the law has not been logic, it has been experience," wrote Holmes, as he brought the widest possible cultural experiences to bear on an understanding of the nature of evolving legal institutions.

The Law, according to Holmes, was not derived from eternal truths about the nature of man or from a set of fixed and formal principles. Rather, it was a product of man's constant adjustments to new and changing sociological situations. Thus the first of his famous dissenting opinions on the Supreme Court was based on the ideas he had developed in his *Common Law*. The case, Lochner v. New York (1905), had been decided in favor of the employer on the grounds that legislation by the State of New York limiting the working day to ten hours was an infringement on the freedom of contract and thus a violation of the Fourteenth Amendment of the Constitution. Holmes took the position that the State of New York had both the right and the duty to experiment with new legislation in response to new conditions in industry (he carefully refrained from making any judgment as to whether the legislation was right or wrong). The following excerpts from Holmes' dissenting opinion nicely illustrate his theory of legal realism or sociological jurisprudence:

This case is decided upon an economic theory which a large part of the country does not entertain. . . .

The liberty of the citizen to do as he likes so long as he does not interfere with the liberty of others to do the same, which has been a shibboleth for some well-known writers, is interfered with by the school laws, by the Post Office, by every State or municipal institution which takes his money for purposes thought desirable, whether he likes it or not. The Fourteenth Amendment does not exact Mr. Herbert Spencer's Social Statics.[10]

Though Holmes held the Constitution and the men who wrote it in high esteem, he thought it should be interpreted anew in each generation. Moreover, it was meant to serve all the people and not just the interests of the business establishment. Thus, in the Lochner dissent, he not only rejected its use as a prop to Herbert Spencer's sociology but also went on to say that it was "not intended to embody a particular economic theory, whether of paternalism and the organic relation of the citizen to the State or *laissez faire.*"[11]

But Charles A. Beard went several steps further than Holmes. He was convinced that the Constitution was an ideological document which always had belonged to the establishment rather than to all the people. He also thought that history should be an experimental and reforming science. Thus his *Economic Interpretation of the Constitution* was an experiment in the writing of history in the interest of reform and from an economic point of view (in the manner of Madison rather than Marx). In a cold and calculatingly objective style, and after a prodigious amount of painstaking research, Beard showed that the Founding Fathers were hardly motivated by Olympian objectivity; rather, they were rich and powerful men who had produced a document designed primarily to protect their own economic interests.

Beard's famous book was a classic example of the methods and values of the New History which were so important a part of the New Social Science.[12] Thus it did not attack the ideas contained in the Constitution directly or from any absolute or logical standards; it debunked, covertly and by implication, these ideas on the basis of their having been founded on the economic interests of the men who produced them. The book was a brilliant example of how the New Social Science which, by assuming the relativity of all knowledge and an extreme environmental determinism, became allied with reform in undermining the status quo. Many conservative members of the establishment immediately saw what Beard was doing. William Howard Taft was enraged and lumped Beard with "all the fools I have run across."[13] The New York Bar Association was horrified. And Warren G. Harding's paper, the Marion (Ohio) *Star*, contained the following headline: SCAVENGERS, HYENA-LIKE, DESECRATE THE GRAVES OF THE DEAD PATRIOTS WE REVERE.[14] Even Holmes did not quite approve of Beard's methods of "belittling" his ancestors through a painstaking investigation of the investment holdings of the Founding Fathers. "It doesn't need evidence that the men who drew the Constitution belonged to the well-to-do classes and had the views of their class," wrote Holmes while reading the book. "Except for a covert sneer I can't see anything in it so far."[15]

Increasingly, in the twentieth century, historians have played the role of intellectual midwives in translating the ideas of a jargon-laden social science into a language that the educated layman can understand. At any rate, after 1913 and partly because of his successful stab at the establishment, Beard became one of the important spokesmen for the New Social Science. At the same time, he freely acknowledged John Dewey as its real leader. "He's the quiet one," Beard used to say, "my friend who looks like your milquetoast uncle and who is undermining the whole world of the nineteenth century with his pragmatism."[16]

Pragmatism—with its emphasis on the relativity of all knowledge, the denial of absolute truth, the experimental nature of all ideas, and the open-endedness of life on this earth—has, of course, been America's major contribution to the history of Western philosophy. Holmes' view of the evolving law as a series of experimental responses to changing social conditions might well have been called legal pragmatism, after the philosophy founded by his friend William James. But James, like Holmes, was no reformer and frankly conceded that it was Dewey who translated his pragmatism into one of the central assumptions of the New Social Science and, at the same time, tied it to the reform movement. "No one has succeeded, it seems to me," James wrote to Dewey, "in jumping into the center of your vision. . . . That is the philosophy of the future, I'll bet my life."[17]

A shy Vermonter who was allergic to publicity and the lecture platform, Dewey produced more than thirty books and eight hundred articles in a stumbling style and became the Herbert Spencer of the New Social Science.[18] In the first half of the twentieth century, his brand of pragmatism—evolutionary environmentalism or instrumentalism—had a profound influence on religion, sociology, economics, morals, criminology, anthropology, law, history and education. "We were all Deweyites before we read him" wrote a Progressive professor and leader of the New Social Science, "and we were all more effective reformers after we had read him." Like Holmes in the law, Dewey pointed out again and again that education was not a matter of educating a fixed human nature in a formal curriculum; instead, an attempt must be made to adjust the whole child to the total cultural environment. Just like the lad from Vermont who learns by doing under his farmer father, Dewey saw that education, like the law, was a matter of experience rather than logic. It is important to point out here that this view of education was infinitely compatible with one of the main tasks of the American school in the first half of this century: the assimilation of the children of immigrants into the main stream of American life. And Dewey's instrumentalism was also, as we shall see, an ideal philosophy for the experimental, rather than dogmatic, political reformers who filtered into the Democratic Party under the leadership of Woodrow Wilson and Franklin Roosevelt.

The New Social Science—whether expressed in the legal theories of Holmes, the philosophy of Dewey, the evolutionary economics of

Veblen or the New History of Beard—must be seen as an inter-disciplinary whole. "We are coming to realize that a science dealing with man has no special field of data all to itself, but rather merely a way of looking at the same thing," wrote Beard. "In the place of a 'natural' man, an 'economic' man, a 'religious' man, or a 'political' man, we now observe the 'whole' man. . . ." And in the twentieth century, the "whole man," as the leaders of the New Social Science conceived of him, was increasingly grounded in sociological and anthropological man. Two of the most important American pio-neers in these two influential disciplines were Charles H. Cooley and Franz Boas.

Although Edward A. Ross was the most popular sociologist of his day (selling some 300,000 copies of his twenty-four books on socio-logical subjects), and although Lester Ward, one of the earliest advocates of social planning and a strong opponent of laissez faire, was the first president of the American Sociological Society, Charles H. Cooley has undoubtedly had a more permanent influence on the sociological tradition.

Cooley, whose intellectual idols were Emerson, Darwin and Goethe, was a strong critic of both Social Darwinism and Eugenics. He had studied under Dewey, whom he greatly admired and whose criticism of Herbert Spencer left a lasting impression.[19] In one of his most fascinating articles, published in 1897, Cooley brilliantly ex-posed the weaknesses in Francis Galton's genetic determinism by showing how genius tended to flower in certain brief historical pe-riods among a people whose racial or genetic qualities had not changed at all (thus Titian, Michelangelo and Raphael were born between 1475 and 1483; and Emerson, Longfellow, Whittier, Holmes, Hawthorne and Poe between 1803 and 1814).[20] Although most of his examples of the relationship between genius and en-vironment were taken from history, Cooley anticipated a great deal of twentieth-century scientific research when he referred to a con-temporary study of the physical characterists of London Jews, which, incidentally, followed the methods of measurement employed by Francis Galton himself. "The West End Jews, who are a well-to-do class, did not differ much from Englishmen of the same class," wrote Cooley.[21] "Those from the East End, employed for the most part in sweat-shops upon the manufacture of cheap clothing, averaged more than three inches less in stature, and were inferior also in size of skull and in every particular covered by the measurements. The intellectual deterioration that goes with this cannot be measured, but that it must exist will hardly be doubted."[22]

Cooley's insights into the influence of environment on the characteristics of different classes of London Jews were soon confirmed by the work of Franz Boas as well as in some of the findings of the psychological testing movement which began with the Alpha tests given to the United States Army recruits during the First War. Although the white recruits from all states made Alpha scores superior to the Negroes', most sociologists have pointed out how these tests show that the Northern Negroes have clearly benefited from environment. Negroes from the states of New York, Ohio, Indiana and Illinois, for example, had higher median scores than the white recruits from Alabama, Mississippi, Arkansas and Louisiana. These tests began a long series of studies of group differences in intelligence, all tending to stress the importance of environment.

The whole tradition of modern sociology has benefited from the insights of Cooley, especially from his emphasis on the importance of the primary group as the molder of a plastic human nature. Thus the Chicago School of Sociology, which had a great influence on the new criminology as well as on social science as a whole during the 1920's and 1930's, showed how certain slum neighborhoods, regardless of the succession of racial or ethnic groups which passed through them over the years, maintained a fairly constant rate of juvenile delinquency and crime. Similarly, the boys' gang, in those neighborhoods where petty crime is socially defined as the norm, leads the healthy and normal, rather than the abnormal, boy into a career of crime. In other words, it is the primary group relationships—in the home, in the play group or gang, and in the neighbor-hood—rather than inborn racial or ethnic traits which lead men into a life of crime and delinquency. And finally, in the tradition of Cooley, the whole modern school of industrial sociology grew up in the 1930's and concentrated on showing how the primary work group was the molder of human behavior and motivation in the plant situation. It is important that this pioneering work in plant sociology which began in the Western Electric works at Haw-thorne, near Chicago, was led by Elton Mayo and his colleagues at the Harvard Business School. For Mayo, though trained as a psychiatrist, was strongly influenced by sociologists like Cooley and especially two Frenchmen, Durkheim and Le Play, and had been on friendly terms with two well-known British anthropologists, Mal-inowski and Radcliffe-Brown. Many of his associates at Harvard, in-cluding W. Lloyd Warner, had also been trained in both sociology and anthropology. In other words, then, it is the concept of *culture* and the importance of *cultural conditioning in the primary group*— whether in the gang in the slum neighborhood, in the plant work-group, in the executive suite, or even in the exclusive private school —which lie at the very core of the social sciences today.

Although modern sociology's emphasis on environmental de-terminism has had a great influence on social reform throughout the twentieth century, especially in breaking down the Anglo-Saxon's convictions of his natural right to rule and in explaining the pathologies of the lower classes (many of whom were immi-grants or their children), it was the new science of cultural anthro-pology which proved to be the reformer's ally par excellence. Ed-ward Burnett Tylor, great Victorian peer of Darwin, Wallace, Galton and Huxley, transformed anthropology from a gentleman's hobby into the modern science of culture.[23] In his famous book, *Primitive Culture* (1871), which had so influenced Holmes, Tylor had written that "active at once in aiding progress and in removing hindrance, the science of culture is essentially a reformer's science."[24] And similarly the brilliant and inconoclastic critic of classical economics, Thorstein Veblen, had seen as early as 1898 that "anthropology was destined to revolutionize the political and social sciences as radically as bacteriology had revolutionized the science of medicine."[25]

In the twentieth century, the science of culture has provided the principal intellectual arguments against the ideas of the racists. Though E. B. Tylor was the founder of the new science, it was Sir James Frazer, an encyclopedic collector of data from all over the world and possessor of a poetic and fascinating style, who did more than anyone else to propagate to the nonspecialist the idea of cultural variation.[26] His classic book, *The Golden Bough*, first published in two volumes in 1890, was widely read in many languages and had an influence on such famous men as Sigmund Freud, in Vienna; Anatole France, Henri Bergson and Emile Durkheim, in France; Wilhelm Wundt, in Germany; Herbert Spencer, Gilbert Murray and Arnold Toynbee, in England; as well as William James, Thorstein Veblen and many others in this country. The significant point about the work of such leading anthropological pioneers as Tylor and Frazer was that, as they roamed the world—in fact, in libraries and in museums—gathering examples of an infinite variety of acquired cultural traits, they had little time even to think of the importance of inborn racial differences. Social heredity and environment, rather than inborn racial differences, seemed a far more plausible basis on which to explain polyandry among the Todas of Tibet, wife-lending among the Eskimos, or the aggressiveness and conspicuous consumption of the Kwakiutl Indians in our Northwest as against the passivity of the Zuñis of New Mexico.

In America, the work of Franz Boas lies at the very core of the New Social Science, its emphasis on environmental reform and its continuing fight against racism.[27] Boas came to this country from Germany to teach at Clark University, and supervised the first Ph.D. in anthropology ever given in America, and went on to teach and inspire such famous anthropologists as Alexander Golden-

171

weiser, Ruth Benedict, A. L. Kroeber, Margaret Mead, Edward Sapir and Robert H. Lowie.

Throughout his life, Boas was a strong critic of racism. His most influential book, *The Mind of Primitive Man*, which grew out of his Lowell Lectures at Harvard in 1910–11, opened with a chapter on "Racial Prejudices" and closed with a discussion of "Race Problems in the United States." The book was called by its admirers "A Magna Charta of self-respect for the 'lower-races.' " Its central thesis, which has guided the research of social scientists down to the present day, was set forth in the following paragraph:

We may now sum up the results of our preliminary inquiry. We have found that the unproved assumption of identity of cultural achievement and of mental ability is founded on an error of judgement; that the variations in cultural development can as well be explained by a consideration of the general course of historical events without recourse to the theory of material differences of mental faculty in different races. We have found, furthermore, that a similar error underlies the common assumption that the white race represents physically the highest type of man, but that anatomical and physiological considerations do not support these views.[28]

Again and again Boas attacked the common-sense norms of his day which considered the Negro to be an inherently inferior race. Thus he wrote at the conclusion of *The Mind of Primitive Man*:

The traits of the American negro are adequately explained on the basis of his history and his social status. The tearing-away from the African soil and the consequent complete loss of the old standards of life, which were replaced by the dependency of slavery and by all it entailed, followed by a period of disorganization and by severe economic struggle against heavy odds, are sufficient to explain the inferiority of the status of the race, without falling back upon the theory of hereditary inferiority.[29]

While he was elaborating his theories in the Lowell Lectures, Boas was also engaged in his most famous empirical investigation, which was the result of the United States Immigration Commission's request for an anthropological study of immigrants. Instead of comparing the characteristics of immigrants and Anglo-Saxons, Boas used a more environmental approach. He carefully measured the changes in certain characteristics of the immigrants themselves (and their children) as their environment changed from Europe to the United States. He concentrated his measurements on East European Jews and Sicilians (considered the least Anglo-Saxon of the immigrant groups), and gave primary attention to the cephalic index (head shape), which was then considered to be an exceedingly stable hereditary characteristic, especially by the racists. Boas' findings were heretical and revolutionary for their day. For he showed that the supposedly unchangeable cephalic indexes of these immigrants and especially their children did alter according to the length of time spent in the American environment. The changes, moreover, were toward a uniform type and more in accord with the measurements of Americans of older stock; the round-headed Russian Jews, for instance, became more long-headed, while the long-headed Sicilians became more round-headed. In other words, utilizing all the trappings of science, including elaborate statistical tables carried to several decimal places, Boas was systematically answering the racial measurers on their own terms. "The adaptability of the immigrant seems to be very much greater than we had a right to suppose before our investigations were instituted," he wrote, "and we are compelled to conclude that when these features of the body change, the whole bodily and mental make-up of the immigrants may change."[30]

Franz Boas' approaches to the problems of race and ethnicity have since become so basic to the orthodoxies of modern social science that it is hard to realize how heretical they were in the first decade of this century. Although he never created a school of followers, two of his students, Margaret Mead and the late Ruth Benedict, both feminists of a sort and therefore receptive to arguments against the inborn inferiority of groups, have probably done more, through teaching and lecturing as well as in pamphlets and in books, than any other American social scientists in modern times to acquaint the general literature public in this country with the importance of the culture concept and its implications for all forms of racialism. Three of their books—Mead's *Coming of Age in Samoa* (1928) and *Growing Up in New Guinea* (1930), and Benedict's *Patterns of Culture* (1934)—have now reached the secure status of popular, as well as scientific, classics (*Patterns of Culture* was one of the first serious books to come out in a paperback edition and was the leading nonfiction paperback for several years during the 1950's). For almost three decades now, few college students have failed to read one or another of these three books which are thoroughly saturated with the ideas of cultural relativity and environmentalism. At the same time, Margaret Mead has for many years been the favorite female philosopher of the League of Women Voters, if perhaps not of the Daughters of the American Revolution.

The Value Implications of the Social Sciences

Darwin's revolutionary theories in biology seemed to deny the validity of our transcendental and Judaeo-Christian traditions. And once this transcendental absolutism was destroyed, there arose two naturalistic alternatives: on the one hand, there were the theories of the Social Darwinists and racists which, implicitly and explicitly, eventually wound up in various degrees of hereditary determinism; on the other hand, and partly in reaction to these hereditarian views, the New Social Science came into its own at the turn of the century. But this new view of man also evolved into a deterministic view of man's fate as a prisoner of his environment. At the same time, of course, all absolute values were destroyed by both the hereditarian and environmental relativists. Although it is too com-

174

plicated a subject to handle here, there is good evidence to support the view that absolute values are logically incompatible with any naturalistic view of man and his social world.

In the meantime, what is of primary interest here is the fact that, in the racially and ethnically mixed urban society of technically free men which America became after the Civil War, the hereditarian view of man increasingly came to deny, and often inadvertently, the traditional ideals of equality of opportunity upon which this country, and especially the Republican Party of Abraham Lincoln, was based. In other words, this view of man was interpreted so as to justify an open and opportunitarian world for the Protestant Anglo-Saxon and a more or less closed world for those of less-favored ancestry. The social implications of Social Darwinism, in fact, were calculated to destroy the very opportunitarian ideals its adherents insisted they were most anxious to defend.

By contrast, the ideas of the New Social Science certainly seemed to imply a far more open world. As Clarence Darrow, who spent his life and legal career in propagating an extreme form of environmental determinism, once said: "Asking how people grew up may make all men equal yet." At any rate and of greatest importance here, it should be readily apparent that the values implied in the New Social Science, in striking contrast to those of the Social Darwinists and Racists, were in accord with the idea of aristocracy, as suggested by Tocqueville, and at the same time wholly opposed to the closed ideas of caste, as advanced by Tocqueville's younger friend, Gobineau. And there is good evidence to support the view that the founders of the New Social Science, in their own personal lives, were convinced that racism, Social Darwinism, and the resultant subtle sanctioning of anti-Semitism, were morally wrong (even in an absolute sense), and hardly in accord with their ideas of aristocracy.

Charles H. Cooley, for example, never looked upon the poor immigrant as unfit to be an American; nor did he feel that the fit capitalist represented the best product of our civilization. Thus he answered the rationalizations of the Social Darwinists as follows:

> Like everything else that has power in human life, the money-strong represent, in some sense, the survival of the fittest—not necessarily the best. That is, their success, certainly no guarantee of righteousness, does prove a certain adaptation to conditions. . . . They are not necessarily the ablest in other regards, since only certain kinds of ability count in making money; other kinds, and those often the highest, such as devotion to intellectual or moral ideals, being even a hindrance. Men of genius will seldom shine in this way, because as a rule, only a somewhat commonplace mind will give itself whole-heartedly to the commercial ideal.[31]

And, summing up modern sociology's objection to the eugenics fad, he wrote:

> Most of the writers on eugenics have been biologists or physicians who have never acquired that point of view which sees in society a psychological organism with a life process of its own. They have thought of human heredity as a tendency to define modes of conduct, and of environment as something that may aid or hinder, not remembering what they might have learned even from Darwin, that heredity takes on a distinctively human character only by renouncing, as it were, the function of predetermined adaptation and becoming plastic to the environment.[32]

The idea of aristocracy, of course, is based on the conviction that it is culture and not genes (caste) which make an aristocrat. Thus James and Holmes, probably the leading aristocratic intellectuals of their own generation, were both opposed to anti-Semitism. "It never occurs to me until after the event that a man I like is a Jew," wrote Holmes to his British friend Pollack, "nor do I care, when I realize it."[33] And on another occasion he wrote to Pollack as follows:

In a few days Brandeis who is next to me in age among the judges will be seventy. That is one lifetime and makes a complete package, with a chance if you are lucky to begin a new one. I think he has done great work and I believe with high motives. To me it is queer to see the wide-spread prejudice against the Jews. I never think of the nationality and might even get thick with a man before noticing that he was a Hebrew. You know the poem: "How odd—of God— To Choose—The Jews."[34]

James was possibly more strongly opposed to anti-Semitism than his friend Holmes. He admired his Jewish friends without reservation and once referred to one of his sons as a "wonderfully beautiful Jewish-looking" child. On another occasion, when a New England hotel which he had formerly visited sent him a circular stating that "applications from Hebrews cannot be considered" he sent the circular back and wrote: "I propose to return the boycott."[35]

Finally, of course, the New Social Science, with its emphasis on environment and faith in reform, was indeed compatible with the aspirations of the urban immigrants of non-Anglo-Saxon ancestry. Thus, in the period between the two world wars, many of the children of immigrants, especially the Jews, were climbing up the traditional American ladder of economic opportunity. And, in striking contrast to the biologically based Social Darwinism which defended the caste superiority of the old-stock establishment, the New Social Science supported and rationalized the minority groups' search for acceptance and respectability. Whether the social sciences were objective or ideological was, in many important respects, beside the point. What was important was the fact that, by the time of Pearl Harbor, thousands of families whose immediate ancestors were recent immigrants had escaped from the slums and attained a reasonably secure middle-class status, in better uptown neighborhoods in most cases, but in the suburbs too. The New Social Science, like the two Roosevelts and President Eliot, was, then, on the side of the future, and the immigrants' response to the American experi-

177

ment was rapidly relegating the caste views of Henry Adams, Madison Grant and the racists to the status of antiquarian myths. But, while the immigrants and their children concentrated on climbing, the sophisticated urban blue bloods as well as, and especially, the Protestant middle classes did not give in without a fight. This was to be the story of the 1920's, the decade of the dying Anglo-Saxon.

Before turning to the 1920's, however, it is important to show how Woodrow Wilson's New Freedom became, in so many ways, the first political expression of the point of view developed by the New Social Science. As Morton White has written of the supporters of the New Social Science:

Its supporters documented and supported their methodological convictions by writing on the concrete questions raised by the social, political, and legal problems of the early twentieth century. Their methodology was not to be wasted and developed for its own sake, and therefore they tried to apply it to specific problems in different fields. They proceeded to formulate a "new psychology," a "new education," a "new economics," a "new history," a "new philosophy," a "new jurisprudence." This was the age of the "news," as Van Wyck Brooks observed, an age which was to see its first political expression in Wilson's New Freedom and its apogee in the New Deal.[36]

Sometimes people call me an idealist. Well, that is why I
know I am an American. America is the only idealistic
nation in the world.

Woodrow Wilson

VIII

The New Freedom:
Wilson, Brandeis
and the Caste Establishment

In America, our greatest political leaders have been more likely to
follow in the British traditions of aristocracy than in the Continental traditions of caste. Reform from the top has, consequently,
usually won out over the forces of revolt from below. Thus, the
patrician reformers who led the Progressive movement eventually
took the steam out of the Populist revolt. And in the twentieth century there has been a continuous thread of aristocratic assimilation
and reform, beginning with Theodore Roosevelt and the Progressives and coming down to the present through his New Nationalism,

179

Woodrow Wilson's New Freedom, Franklin Roosevelt's New Deal and John F. Kennedy's New Frontier.

The age of the "News" began in the second decade of the new century, when the Progressives finally split into the followers of Roosevelt's New Nationalism on the one hand, and Wilson's New Freedom on the other. On the whole, the followers of Roosevelt felt that the trusts were here to stay, that the Sherman Act was an anachronism, and that big government was needed to regulate the power of big business; or, as George W. Perkins—a Morgan partner, organizer of trusts and the largest contributor to Roosevelt's campaign in 1912—would have it, they were for socialism with private property. The followers of Wilson, on the other hand, clung to an older liberalism which stressed a kind of Jeffersonian individualism and the need for regulating business in order to avoid, as Brandeis put it, "the curse of bigness." However, both Roosevelt and the New Liberals (regulated monopoly) and Wilson and the old liberals (regulated competition), agreed on the need for governmental reform and regulation of the economic system.

The decisive year was 1912. Roosevelt bolted the Republicans and ran on a third-party ticket of his own, and Wilson won the Democratic nomination on the forty-sixth ballot, after a long and hotly contested convention at Baltimore. The Presidential contest was actually between two reformers; President Taft hardly bothered to campaign for re-election. Most of the leaders of the Settlement House and Social Gospel movements as well as the leaders of the New Social Science stayed with Theodore Roosevelt; as did such Progressives as Harold Ickes, Donald Richberg, Frank Knox, Henry A. Wallace, George W. Norris, Felix Frankfurter, Francis Biddle, John G. Winant and Dean Acheson, all of whom eventually played important roles in the New Deal; on the other hand, Franklin D. Roosevelt, John N. Garner, Sam Rayburn, Homer Cummings, Dan Roper, Joseph E. Davies, Charles W. Eliot, Bernard Baruch and Louis D. Brandeis all followed Wilson.[1]

Woodrow Wilson's victory set the stamp of aristocratic reform on the Democratic Party; Cleveland had led the financial wing of the party to victory in 1892; Bryan had captured the party for an unsuccessful campaign of revolt in 1896; but Wilson led the Democrats to their first victory in the twentieth century and, in the next four years, took the reforming initiative away from the Republicans, perhaps forever.

Wilson's rise to the White House was symbolic of other changes in the national mood. While both Theodore Roosevelt and Wilson were lay preachers, it was Wilson, a stiff Calvinist like his ancestors (his father and maternal grandfather were clergymen), who symbolized the passing of the intellectual and spiritual leadership in America from the church to the university, from the preacher in the pulpit to the professor in the classroom. Thus, in a very significant sense, Henry Ward Beecher and Phillips Brooks, Washington Gladden and Walter Rauschenbusch, or J. P. Morgan's favorite Episcopal bishops, William Lawrence and Henry Codman Potter, may well have been the last gentlemen of the cloth in American history to exert a real and vital influence on public opinion or on the leaders of economic and political power. And perhaps most important of all, as will be brought out in later chapters, under Wilson's leadership in the White House, both in his domestic policies and in his use of professors and intellectuals during the tragic peace negotiations at Versailles, the academic establishment was brought into the Democratic Party, where it has remained, more or less, to the present day.

At the same time, as the naturalistic view of man increasingly replaced the transcendental, within the secular universities at first and then among the educated public, the New Social Science gradually replaced religion as the dominant interpreter of the nature of human nature and American values. It was during Wilson's first term, moreover, that the ideas of the New Social Science began to be expressed politically in terms of the New Liberalism. The New Liberals, led by John Dewey and Charles A. Beard from the academic community, developed their political ideas in the pages of the *New*

Republic, which was founded in 1914 by three brilliant publicists, Herbert Croly, Walter Weyl and Walter Lippmann.[2] As a measure of the march of intellectual events in America since the turn of the century, it is of interest that William Graham Sumner's Yale classmate and intimate friend, William C. Whitney, became an indirect sponsor of this new journalistic venture which was to do so much to spread the ideas of the New Social Science among educated laymen. For, from its founding, the *New Republic* was subsidized by Whitney's wealthy and socially conscious daughter Dorothy, and her husband, Willard Straight. In the tradition of aristocratic leadership, the Straights felt the need for an independent journal of educated, liberal opinion. As a liberal member of the Morgan firm, in the manner of George W. Perkins, Willard Straight had been impressed by Croly's book, *The Promise of American Life* (1909), whose central theme of "democratic nationalism" called for centralized planning by a responsible elite. At Harvard, Croly had been influenced by Santayana's idea of a "socialist aristocracy" and William James' pragmatism. His book had impressed Roosevelt and foreshadowed Roosevelt's New Nationalism. At any rate, the Straights and Croly decided that the *New Republic* was to be a journal for the education of the elite. Unlike the mass magazines, it was aimed at teachers, professors, civil servants, social workers, enlightened politicians and businessmen who were interested in reform. Like their angels, the Straights, all three editors fulfilled Beard's dictum that reform leaders in America had "better have money, or, next, marry it." Thus Croly, whose parents were militant middle-class reformers who had baptized him in the Comtean Religion of Humanity, had taken a wealthy and socially prominent wife; Weyl, who grew up in the heart of the wealthy German-Jewish establishment in Philadelphia, married into the wealthy Protestant establishment in Chicago (his wife, whom he met at Hull House, was the sister of the socialist novelist Ernest Poole); and finally, young Lippmann came from a wealthy family of second-generation German Jews. The primary purpose, then, of the *New Republic*, supported as it was by members of a *rentier* and leisured class which liberals like Veblen so despised, was an example of journalistic *noblesse oblige.*

Though its founders had supported Roosevelt in 1912, the first Presidential candidate to be officially supported by the *New Republic* was Woodrow Wilson. As an illustration of our thesis that the civil-rights idea of aristocratic assimilation on the basis of culture rather than genes lies at the very core of the liberal point of view in the twentieth century, it is interesting to note that the "first public sign" of the *New Republic*'s support of the New Freedom came after Wilson's announcement of the nomination of Louis D. Brandeis to the Supreme Court, in January 1916. Their support of the nomination was all the more interesting because Brandeis had always been hostile to the *New Republic* and its ideal of democratic centralization as outlined in Croly's *Promise of American Life.*

Woodrow Wilson: Protestant Priest and Aristocratic Anglophile

By the very nature of their position as representatives of all the people, Presidential reformers, contrary to the views of their critics, have usually acted as restraining influences on the zeal of their liberal supporters. In temperament, training and moral conviction, Theodore Roosevelt, Woodrow Wilson and Franklin Roosevelt were conservative forces within the reforming revolutions they were called to lead. (There was every indication that John F. Kennedy followed this tradition.)

Throughout his long academic career Wilson was a liberal in the older nineteenth-century tradition and only moved to the Left and toward the New Liberalism as he was forced to face the problems of power and the need for reform, first as Governor of New Jersey and then as President. He was essentially a Calvinist moralist, rooted in the traditions of the Southern gentleman. His youthful ideal had been Robert E. Lee. Intellectually he was an idealistic, even poetic, Anglophile. "Mr. Wilson," wrote one of his former students, "gave no glimpse of the economic background of the English ruling class. There was always the assumption that these public men were not moved by private gain . . . he was not interested in economics."[3] There was, indeed, no similarity between Wilson's idealization of the disinterestedness of the British aristocracy and Beard's debunking of our Constitutional heroes. Following his idol Edmund Burke and his master Walter Bagehot, Wilson firmly believed that gradual reform was the aristocrat's answer to radicalism and revolution. He "hated the French revolutionary philosophy" and felt that Burke's ideas on freedom and liberty "might serve as a sort of motto of the practical spirit of our race in the affairs of government."[4]

In spite, then, of his well-publicized fight for social reforms at Princeton, Wilson was a conservative by most standards, and certainly by those of the New Social Science and the Progressives. In 1906, as he gradually entered the political arena, he denounced Theodore Roosevelt's "regulative passion" and spoke strongly against the regulation of business and industry by commissions. And his attitude toward the Social Gospel movement was anything but sympathetic. Thus he expressed his position, in 1909, as follows:

> For my part, I do not see any promise of vitality either in the church or in society except upon the true basis of individualism. . . . He, the minister, must preach Christianity to men, not to society. He must preach salvation to the individual, for it is only one by one that we can love, and love is the law of life.[5]

But Wilson gradually changed. Most biographers place the date of his final conversion to a more progressive point of view in the fall of 1910, after his election to the Governorship of New Jersey. It was then that he decided to desert the bosses who had first made his victory possible. After leading a bipartisan Progressive majority in a series of unprecedented reforms in New Jersey and after winning his way to the White House, Wilson showed his changed attitude toward the ideals of the Social Gospel and the more environmentalist point of view in a speech at the YMCA in Pittsburgh, in 1914:

> For one, I am not fond of thinking of Christianity as a means of saving individual souls.... Christ came into the world to save others, not to save himself, and no man is a true Christian who does not think constantly of how he can lift his brother, how he can enlighten mankind, how he can make virtue the rule of conduct in the circle in which he lives.[6]

This Pittsburgh speech was made in the middle of his first term in office, which, according to Richard Hofstadter, resulted in more positive legislation than had been produced at any other time since Alexander Hamilton's day. Thus Wilson moved to the Left as a pragmatic response to the responsibilities of power in a revolutionary age. Yet he retained to the end of his life his original faith in a transcendental and absolute moral law, in which man was "responsible through his own conscience to his lord and maker." In this very important sense, like Franklin D. Roosevelt after him, he acted as a restraining moral force in an age when a majority of the New Liberals were confidently converted to the New Social Science and its naturalistic assumptions about the nature of man.

From his first days in office, Wilson had to face the minorities issue. Because of his Southern background, he at once got into trouble with Negro leaders, especially the NAACP. Several governmental departments dismissed Negroes, and segregation was increased in the shops, lunchrooms and washrooms of the Capital. Wilson publicly affirmed his belief that the total separation of the races was the policy that would bring greatest benefit to the Negroes. In 1915, he made a tactical blunder when he allowed *The Birth of a Nation* to be shown at the White House, thus inadvertently giving his public approval to this violently anti-Negro film. And he almost lost the election of 1916 because of his refusal to play minority politics. In addition to his alienation of the Negroes, he lost the German and Irish hyphenated vote because he stuck by the British as against the Germans in the war and refused to push for the emancipation of Ireland.

The problem of immigration was also a vital issue. For some time, the restrictionists had favored literacy tests for immigrants. Cleveland in 1897 and Taft in February, 1913, had vetoed attempts at such legislation. Organized labor had long led the fight for restriction. This was especially true of the American Federation of Labor, whose leader, Samuel Gompers, was himself an immigrant Jew from London's East End. By 1913, the labor leaders were joined by a number of sociologists and social workers such as Edward A. Ross of the University of Wisconsin, and Robert A. Woods of South End settlement house in Boston. When a new bill requiring literacy tests was introduced in the House in 1913, Wilson was put in an embarrassing position. He was inclined to see the danger that his revered Anglo-Saxon tradition would be upset by immigrants from far different backgrounds (he did not, however, stress the racial but rather the cultural differences between these traditions and those of the vast majority of the newer immigrants). Yet, as he had made certain promises to recent immigrant groups in the campaign of 1912, and as he saw himself as a representative of all the American people, he finally vetoed the bill in 1915, and again in 1917, when, however, it was finally passed over his head by a five-to-one majority.

Although he was undoubtedly ambivalent toward the immigrant and a segregationist in regard to the Negro, Wilson, unlike so many of his class in the North, was not anti-Semitic. In fact, two of his closest associates after 1912 were Bernard M. Baruch and Louis D. Brandeis, both also of Southern origin. As he had himself suffered from the fraternity system at City College, Baruch, who was still young at the time, was first drawn to Wilson during the famous fight over the snobberies of the club system at Princeton. After they met for the first time in 1912, Wilson became Baruch's greatest hero. Not only was Baruch a great admirer of Wilson from the first; he also owed him a great debt for providing a chance for leadership on the national scene as head of the War Industries Board during World War I.

But Brandeis was far closer to Wilson than was Baruch. Drawn to each other from their first meeting in the summer of 1912, it was Brandeis who translated Wilson's ideas of the New Freedom into practical policy. In order to reward his brilliant associate and friend, Wilson finally nominated Brandeis, early in the campaign year of 1916, for a position on the Supreme Court of the United States. This was no casual decision on Wilson's part. Back in 1913, he had finally decided not to have Brandeis in his Cabinet only because of the fierce opposition to the proposed appointment which came from the New England establishment. He also recalled the minor explosion which had occurred the previous year (1915) at the Cosmos Club when Brandeis had been proposed for membership. "Several members of the Club have started an opposition to Mr. Brandeis," Justice Hitz had written to the President, "which bids fair to be successful unless his friends come strongly to his support. The grounds of opposition to Mr. Brandeis are stated to be that he is a reformer for revenue only; that he is a Jew; and that he would be a disturbing element in any club of gentlemen."[7] The President immediately wrote the admissions committee saying that he held Brandeis in "highest esteem" and "his admission to the Club would not only be an act of justice to him, but would add a member of very fine quality to its list." Woodrow Wilson, moralistic aristocrat and practical politician, surely knew that the issue of caste would be a factor in the ratification of his appointment of Brandeis. Yet he was determined, in his stubborn way, to reward his friend with this high appointment as he had failed to do in 1913.

The contrasts between the ideologies of caste and aristocracy, as they developed in America between 1880 and our entry into the First War, are nowhere better portrayed than in the career of Louis D. Brandeis, and especially in the fight over his nomination to the Supreme Court in 1916.

Brandeis and the Brahmin Business Mind

"My friend Brandeis," wrote William E. Cushing to his mother from the Harvard Law School in 1878, "is a character in his way— one of the most brilliant legal minds they have ever had here. . . . Hails from Louisville, is not a college graduate, but has spent some years in Europe, has a rather foreign look and is currently believed to have some Jew blood in him, though you would not suppose it from his appearance—tall, well-made, dark, beardless, and with the brightest eyes I ever saw. Is supposed to know everything and to have it always in mind. The professors listen to his opinion with the greatest deference. And it is generally correct. . . ."[8]

Louis Dembitz Brandeis was born in Louisville, Kentucky, in 1856. His father, a prosperous merchant, had come to America in 1848 from Prague, where his family was of old Bohemian-Jewish stock which traced back to the fifteenth century. After a boyhood in Louisville and two years of study and travel in Europe, Brandeis came to the Harvard Law School, in 1875, where he was soon recognized as the leading student in his class (as late as 1941, Dean James M. Landis stated that Brandeis had made the finest record in the school's history: his over-all average was 97 and he received 100 in three courses and 99 in two others).

As far as young Brandeis was concerned, "the world's center was Cambridge," and after a year of law practice in St. Louis where he was admitted to the bar, he returned to Boston and entered into partnership with his close and devoted law school friend, Samuel Dennis Warren, Jr., brahmin son of a wealthy paper manufacturer. Through Warren and other men he had met at law school, Brandeis at once moved among the best people of "cold-roast" Boston. He had a talent for friendship, loved outdoor life and sports of all kinds and, as he later told one of his junior partners, believed in the need for cultivating "the society of men—particularly men of affairs. . . ." His love of rowing led him to join and become one of the directors of the Union Boat Club. He helped to organize the Dedham Polo Club, was secretary of the Boston Art Club and a steady user of the Turnverein, an athletic club, where he kept "in shape" during the winter months. In town, he lunched at the Exchange or at the patrician Union Club when he was not talking shop with the city's leading brahmin lawyers at their exclusive law club. In spite of his active social life in Cambridge and Boston and his steadily growing law practice, he found time to teach briefly at both Harvard and the Massachusetts Institute of Technology. Though he did not accept President Eliot's offer of a permanent appointment to the faculty of the Law School, he always took a keen interest in the school's development and helped to found the Harvard Law School Association as well as the *Harvard Law Review* (first Treasurer; and a trustee until he went to the Supreme Court in 1916). Harvard also honored him with a Master of Arts and membership in Phi Beta Kappa during those years. And in the meantime, he had become one of the nation's most sought-after corporation lawyers. His clients were men of large affairs who could afford to pay handsomely. By 1905 he was almost a millionaire and had succeeded in his dream of becoming financially independent and free.

But as the nineteenth century waned and his fortune grew, he somehow was not satisfied. A restless germ of reforming idealism lay beneath the external trappings of success. After all, there were all too many other lawyers who were ready to defend the powerful. Who was to defend the poor? He was particularly disturbed by the dangers of monopoly and the growing violence in labor relations. "I think it was the affair at Homestead," he wrote years later, "which first set me to thinking seriously about the labor problem. It took the shock of that battle, where organized capital hired a private army to shoot at organized labor for resisting an arbitrary cut in wages, to turn my mind definitely toward a searching study of the relations of labor to industry."[9]

Beginning sometime in the 1890's, Brandeis gradually began to desert Bourbon Boston and to develop a second career as a celebrated

and beloved, yet deeply hated, "People's Lawyer." He had a passion
for facts and figures and always mistrusted ideology. Never a utopian radical, he fervently believed in gradual reform from the top.
In this connection, it is interesting that some members of the
Cosmos Club, at least according to Justice Hitz's letter to Wilson,
should have been against Brandeis because of his being a "reformer
for revenue only." For his multitudinous efforts at civic and economic reforms included, among other gratuitous services, his acting
as "Unpaid Counsel for the New England Policy-Holders'
Protective Committee (1905); Unpaid Counsel for William B.
Lawrence in the New Haven merger controversies (1907–1913);
Unpaid Counsel for the State in defending hours of labor and
minimum wage statutes of Oregon, Illinois, Ohio and California
(1907–1914); Unpaid Counsel for Commercial Organizations in
I.C.C. Advance Railroad Case (1910–1911); and Unpaid Chairman,
Arbitration Board, New York Garment Workers' Strike, and under
subsequent protocols (1910–1916)."[10] On the whole, he stopped
trying to make money almost entirely after 1912, when his income
from his law firm was $105,758 (which dropped off steadily to
$37,919 by 1916, when he went to the Supreme Court). As he al-
ways preferred the simple life, both at home and in the great outdoors, he and his wife, Alice, never spent more than $10,000 a year
during their more than twenty years in Washington (he gave
$1,496,094.52 to charity between 1905 and his retirement in 1939).
They lived by the following lines of a poem of Matthew Arnold's,
which young Brandeis first discovered on the flyleaf of Alice's diary
a year before their marriage in 1891:

> Life is not a having and a getting;
> But a being and a becoming.

Brandeis came in contact with Jews as a group for the first time
at the age of fifty-four, when he went to New York to help settle
the garment workers' strike in 1910. Like other men of affluence,
he had made token contributions to Jewish causes in Boston and,

because of his own background and experience, he was more or less in favor of assimilation. At the two hundred fiftieth anniversary of the first settlement of Jews in America, in 1905, he praised the contribution to America of people of "Jewish blood" and went on to say that "there is room here for men of any race, of any creed, of any condition of life, but not for Protestant-Americans, or Catholic-Americans, or Jewish-Americans, nor for German-Americans, Irish-Americans, or Russian-Americans. This country demands that its sons and daughters whatever their race—however intense or diverse their religious connections—be politically merely American citizens. Habits of living or of thought which tend to keep alive differences of origin or to classify men according to their religious beliefs are inconsistent with the American ideal of brotherhood, and are disloyal."[11]

But by 1912 Brandeis had lost faith in the forces of assimilation and turned to Zionism. He soon became one of the leaders of the movement in America. The immediate cause of his change at this time was his meeting with an English Jew, Jacob De Haas, who had been closely associated with Theodor Herzl, the father of modern Zionism. His conversion, however, was also due to the increasing anti-Semitism in America at the time. In contrast to his own acceptance into the heart of brahmin Boston Society in the seventies, he was later to observe that the wives of three of his closest business friends in Massachusetts had "never exchanged visiting cards with Mrs. Brandeis." Finally in 1915, in an address called *The Jewish Problem and How to Solve It*, which in the next four years went through five editions comprising fifty thousand copies, Brandeis made his position very clear. The address began by stating that anti-Semitism and Jewish suffering were worse at that time in America than ever before. Brandeis then proceeded to define Jewishness as a matter of "blood," which both sides admit, the non-Jews who persecute those of Jewish faith, and the Jews themselves who take pride "when those of Jewish blood exhibit moral or intellectual superiority, genius, or special talent, even if they have abjured the faith like Spinoza, Marx, Disraeli, or Heine."[12] As might be expected, there were those on all sides, both gentiles and Jews, who strongly disagreed with his position. Yet, as with the almost completely assimilated Herzl, who had been converted to the idea of Zionism by the Dreyfus case, it was perhaps quite natural that a man of Brandeis' temperament and early experience should have responded as he did to the increasing anti-Semitism of his day.

Brandeis was, then, a famous reformer and anti-monopolist, a Zionist and a Progressive Democrat by the time he was nominated for the Supreme Court by Woodrow Wilson on January 28, 1916. The reaction was immediate and intensely partisan. "Impossible!" senators exclaimed. The press of the nation was sharply divided: In New York, the *Sun*, the *Press* and the *Times* were against the nomination and only the *World* supported it; in Boston, the *Transcript* regretted the nomination and the *Post* praised it. To former President Taft, whom Brandeis had supported in 1908, the nomination was a shock: "It is one of the deepest wounds I have had as an American and a lover of the Constitution. . . . He is a muckraker, an emotionalist for his own purpose, a socialist . . . a man who has certain high ideals . . . of great tenacity of purpose, and in my judgement, of much power for evil. . . ."[13]

Within twenty-four hours of the nomination, a Senate subcommittee was appointed to sift the mounting charges. The first protest heard by the committee came from the agrarian Middle West, and the last from a simon-pure reformer who asserted that, in 1906, Brandeis, the so-called People's Attorney, had conspired with the Boston Consolidated Gas Company to defeat the people's interests. The day before the hearings closed on March 15, the American Bar Association launched an all-out attack with a statement signed by William Howard Taft, Elihu Root, Joseph H. Choate, Moorfield Storey, Simeon E. Baldwin, Francis Rawle and Peter W. Meldrim, all distinguished lawyers and former presidents of the Bar Association. "The undersigned," the brief statement read, "feel under the painful duty to say to you that in their opinion, taking into view the reputation, character, and professional career of Mr. Louis D. Brandeis, he is not a fit person to be a member of the Supreme Court of the United States."[14] One gentleman who testified at the Senate hearings in favor of Brandeis made a pretty fair estimate of the legal establishment's feeling when he said: "By way of explanation, may I say that we have what I may call an aristocracy of the Boston Bar. I do not use the word at all offensively; on the contrary, they are high-minded, able, distinguished men. But they can not, I think, consider with equanimity the selection of anybody for a position on the great court of the country from that community who is not a typical, hereditary Bostonian."[15]

Hereditary Boston was represented in a petition against Brandeis' appointment, which was published on February 11, and signed by fifty-five citizens, including President A. Lawrence Lowell of Harvard, Charles Francis Adams and other leaders of the Protestant establishment. A younger lawyer in the Brandeis office drew up a chart showing the social and economic relationships between the members of this prestige group; it outlined in minute detail (anticipating the modern science of "sociometry" by some decades) each petitioner's connections with "State Street Officers, Trustees and Bankers, the Somerset Club, and Large Corporation Connections and Advisors." In response to the publication of this chart, Walter Lippmann, in the *New Republic*, probably caught the "sense of the establishment" at that time when he wrote that Brandeis was "a rebellious and troublesome member of the most homogeneous, self-centered, and self-complacent community in the United States. It was a special community that found Mr. Brandeis untrustworthy, the powerful but limited community which dominated the business and social life of Boston. He was untrustworthy because he was troublesome. He was disloyal, if at all, to a group. All the smoke of ill-repute which had been gathered around Mr. Brandeis originated in the group psychology of these gentlemen and because they are men of influence it seemed ominous. But it is smoke without any fire except that of professional group antagonism. . . . They come of a proud line and are jealous of a noble tradition."[16]

Not all of Boston, by any means, was against the appointment. Ten of the eleven members of the Harvard Law School faculty were for Brandeis, and former President Eliot wrote "that the rejection by the Senate would be a grave misfortune for the whole legal profession, the Court, all American business, and the country." And another reformer who had worked with Brandeis (and Eliot) in the Massachusetts Savings Bank Insurance League, the Reverend A. A. Berle, wrote to Senator Chilton that the establishment in Boston, "simply cannot realize, and do not, that a long New England ancestry is not prima facie a trusteeship for everything in New England. That is in my judgement the real spring of most of the opposition."[17]

The fight over Wilson's nomination of Brandeis dragged on for almost five months. "Communiques from Europe's war fronts competed unsuccessfully for headlines," as editors, lawyers, columnists, politicians and social reformers joined in the nation-wide debate. The final vote of the subcommittee was an anticlimax; party regularity ruled, as the ten Democrats on the committee outvoted the eight Republicans on May 24 in a meeting which lasted eight minutes. On June 1, regularity ruled again in the Senate when the nomination was confirmed by a vote of forty-seven to twenty-two; all save one of the Democratic Senators voted to confirm; all Republicans, except La Follette and Norris and one other, were against confirmation. Thus Brandeis became the first Jew to become a member of the Supreme Court of the United States. And it was not long before the phrase "Holmes and Brandeis dissenting" became part of the progressive fight to liberalize Constitutional interpretation.

The Brandeis affair was important for several reasons. It marked, in the first place, a victory for reform and a defeat for the Republican establishment. The final confirmation in the Senate, as well as the party regularity of the vote, was another indication that the reforming initiative in America had definitely passed to the Democratic

Party. And finally, the affair highlighted the nature of the business-brahmin mind. For although the fact that Brandeis was a Jew had not been publicly referred to by his distinguished opponents, in the style of the gentleman, there was little doubt that ancestry and anti-Semitism were factors in the case.

Brandeis, who had translated Woodrow Wilson's ideals into policy during the crucial years between 1912 and 1916, was a major figure on the Supreme Court during the New Deal years. His belief in the living law and the usefulness of dissenting opinions as educational devices formed a vital part of this second age of transition under Franklin Roosevelt. But Brandeis was by no means a continuous dissenter. In the 528 cases which came before the Court during his term in office, he followed the majority 454 times. He strongly supported the decision to abolish the NIRA, which showed his respect for private property and his opposition to overall planning. Though he admired Roosevelt and generally sympathized with the New Deal, he strongly opposed the court-packing plan of 1937. In other words, Brandeis was no radical, but a reformer who emphasized the duties as well as the rights of property. In a rapidly changing age, he felt that continual reform was the only answer to violent revolution. He had, above all, a passion for the freedom of the individual in a world of increasingly complex institutions. Surely Woodrow Wilson would have found it highly appropriate that Alpheus Thomas Mason should conclude his exhaustive biography of this angular, aristocratic and Lincolnesque Jew with the following evaluation: "If we hold with Burke," Mason wrote, "that the standard of a statesman is the 'disposition to preserve and the ability to improve, taken together,' then Brandeis met that test."[18]

Gradually, toward the end of Wilson's first term in the White House, and especially after the fight over Brandeis' nomination to the Supreme Court, intellectuals and liberals of both the old and new variety turned to Wilson and, as Walter Lippmann wrote in the *New Republic* at the time, to "the only party which at this moment is national in scope, liberal in purpose, and effective in action." Walter Lippmann, always a weather vane of intellectual trends, was the first of the New Liberals to strongly declare for Wilson. During the summer, most of them followed his example, including such prominent leaders as Jane Addams (who had seconded T.R.'s nomination in 1912), Lillian Wald, Washington Gladden, Lincoln Steffens, John Dewey, Charles A. Beard and many others who were eventually to play prominent roles in the New Deal years. Thus, in spite of some personal and private reservations, Woodrow Wilson, who had made the transition from the conservative nineteenth-century liberalism of his academic years to the New Freedom of his early years in public office, finally became the leader of the New Liberalism. And apparently the nation had been going through the same transitional process.

But the war and the postwar reaction were to reverse the trend, at least on the surface of political and social life, for more than a decade. Perhaps Francis Biddle, Attorney General of the United States under Franklin D. Roosevelt, one of the founders of the Americans for Democratic Action, and now on the Board of the American Civil Liberties Union, revealed the tone of the twenties, at least within the Protestant establishment, in the following incident which he recalls in his autobiography:

When Franklin Roosevelt, a member of the Fly, resigned as Assistant Secretary of the Navy in 1920, Guy Murchie, who was running the graduate dinners, asked me to be toastmaster at a banquet given in Franklin's honor. Murchie had secured two or three speakers, and wanted me to get one more. I was fortunate enough to persuade Felix Frankfurter, then a professor of the Harvard Law School, to fill the bill. As chairman of the War Labor Policies Board during the First World War, he had come to know Roosevelt well. When several of the members of the club would not go to the dinner, and one refused to speak to me because I had asked Frankfurter to speak, I realized how strongly anti-Semitic feeling permeated Harvard clubs. I felt deeply humiliated that this could have happened.[19]

Such had been the fate of the French nobility. The political element had disappeared; the pecuniary element alone remained, and in some instances had been largely increased.

Alexis de Tocqueville

IX

The Anglo-Saxon Decade: Success without Leadership

After the First World War, the aristocratic idealism of Woodrow Wilson was soon replaced by the bourgeois realism of Harding, Coolidge and Hoover. Thoroughly defeated in his tragic efforts to persuade the American people of their duty to assume the leadership of a new world community symbolized in the League of Nations, Wilson spent his last days in the White House in virtual seclusion, a broken and beaten man. He had indeed been prophetic when he had once remarked to young Franklin Roosevelt that "it is only once in a generation that a people can be lifted above material things."

Rejecting Wilson's call to world leadership, Americans now turned to isolationism and the avid pursuit of success. And it is no wonder that, during the 1920's, the business establishment, especially the statesmen of big business, attained a position of authority and public adulation unique in the nation's history. The Anglo-Saxon business brahmin, often referred to as a "robber baron" or "malefactor of great wealth" in an earlier day, now reigned supreme. While even the elder Morgan had on occasion deferred to the priestly authority of Bishop Potter or the Reverend Rainsford, business itself now became a religion, and the finest tribute one could pay a clergyman was to say he would have made a good businessman. With an unerring sense of the mood of his times, Bruce Barton, one of the senior partners in a famous advertising firm and himself the son of a clergyman, produced the leading nonfiction best seller of the Coolidge era. In *The Man Nobody Knows: A Discovery of the Real Jesus*, he showed how Jesus Christ was "the most popular dinner guest in Jerusalem," an "outdoor man" and a great "executive" who "picked up twelve men from the bottom ranks of business and forged them into an organization that conquered the world." An era that worshipped salesmanship and success was naturally receptive to Barton's ingenious theme that "the parables were the most powerful advertisements of all time," and that Jesus Christ, as "the founder of modern business," would surely have been a "national advertiser today."

But the decade of business and ballyhoo, which reached its apex in the complacent reign of Calvin Coolidge, was born in violence and buried in the Crash of 1929. While all Americans, regardless of racial or religious affiliations, had been unified against a common enemy in an idealistic war to save democracy, the disillusioned isolationism which took over at the war's conclusion fostered the reassertion of the divisive forces of caste. The unifying slogan "Hang the Kaiser" was now replaced by an hysterical hunt for anarchists and Bolsheviks, and an antipathy to the supposed un-Americanism of Catholics, Jews and organized labor.

Nineteen-nineteen was a year of violence. More than a million men went out on strikes which shook the nation. Proper Bostonians patrolled the streets in place of a striking police force. In the bitter steel strike, the managers set a pattern of divisiveness by contriving to stir up bitterness between the Serbian, Polish and Italian members of its labor force. In this year of fear, the *Nation*, the *New Republic* and the *Freeman* were classified as "revolutionary" by officials of the American Defense Society, and solid citizens pointed with alarm to the League of Women Voters, the Federal Council of Churches and the Foreign Policy Association. Both the American Communist Party and the American Legion came into being, while the Ku Klux Klan was revived, no longer as a White conspiracy to keep the Negro in his place, but as a Protestant crusade against the un-Americanism of Catholics and Jews. And then the anarchists took it upon themselves to bomb the enemies of the people: first, the Mayor of Seattle found a bomb in his mail "big enough to blow out the entire side of the County-City building"; the next day, a bomb blew off the hands of a colored maid in the home of a senator from Georgia who was Chairman of the Immigration Committee which was considering restricting immigration to keep out Bolshevism; a clerk in the New York Post Office uncovered some thirty-six bomb packages addressed to leading government officials and capitalists, including Justice Holmes, J. P. Morgan and John D. Rockefeller; and finally, as the year came to a close, a bomb blew up in front of the Washington residence of the "Fighting Quaker" reformer and Attorney General, A. Mitchell Palmer, who now became the leader of the "Big Red Scare."

The year 1920 opened with Palmer Raids in thirty-three major cities which placed some six thousand citizens behind bars and set a new record for executive transgression of individual Constitutional rights; the Prohibition amendment went into effect in January and soon made gangsters of the more ambitious sons of recent immigrants; anti-Japanese hysteria raged in California; Henry Ford launched his famous anti-Semitic campaign; a holdup-murder, which was not important enough to be reported in the New York Times, was committed at South Braintree, Massachusetts; and the American electorate, led by the Protestant establishment, chose "normalcy" with Harding in an election year in which the Democratic Party suffered its worst defeat since the Civil War.

The nationalist panic was also affecting the intellectual community. In 1921, while most young sophisticates were applauding H. L. Mencken's rollicking diatribes against democracy, the ideology of racism increased in tempo. A new edition of Madison Grant's Passing of the Great Race was issued and widely sold (it went relatively unnoticed by the general public when first published in 1916). At the same time, Henry Fairfield Osborn, friend of Grant and a leading member of a prolific Groton-Princeton clan whose family seat still sits, like a prince's castle on the Rhine, atop a rugged crag overlooking the Hudson River, brought the Second International Congress of Eugenics to New York for a series of well-publicized meetings.* William McDougall, transplanted Englishman, ardent eugenicist and the most eminent psychologist of his generation, published a book, Is America Safe for Democracy?, which argued for a racial interpretation of the army intelligence tests given during the war (see the environmental interpretation, Chapter VII) and questioned whether democracy would survive the mongrelization of a Nordic civilization. At the same time, George Horace Lorimer's Saturday Evening Post was popularizing both Grant's ideas and the similar scientific findings of Lothrop Stoddard, Proper Bostonian and Harvard contemporary of Franklin Roosevelt, whose book The Rising Tide of Color Against White World-Supremacy became an "international sensation" when it came out in 1920. It is of interest that, in the first issue of Time magazine (Vol. 1, No. 1, March 3, 1923), Charles Scribner's Sons took a whole page on the inside of the back cover to advertise

* For interesting notes on other members of the clan, Fairfield Osborn (Our Plundered Planet, 1948) and Frederick Osborn (Preface to Eugenics, 1940) see Who's Who in America, Vol. 30, 1958–59, p. 2102. Also see Frederick Osborn's comments on eugenics in the next chapter.

Stoddard's sensational book. By that time, *The Rising Tide of Color* had already reached its fourteenth edition.

The End of Immigration

In this hysterical climate of postwar opinion, it was no wonder that the American people were ready for legislation against further immigration. As we have seen, presidents Cleveland (1897), Taft (1913) and Wilson (1915), as representatives of all the people, had felt it their duty to veto earlier attempts at restriction through literacy tests. But the panicky Protestant establishment now had more sympathetic ears in Washington. The Republicans took control of Congress in 1919, and an energetic nativist from the State of Washington, Albert Johnson, was made Chairman of the House Committee on Immigration. The first quota bill, highly prejudiced in favor of immigrants from Northern Europe, passed both houses during the last days of Wilson's term in office. The President let it die by withholding his signature. "The ailing, rejected chief of state never explained his silent scorn, and his available papers provide no clue to it," wrote John Higham. "Did he still remember his iron-clad promises to the immigrants in 1912? Did his mind turn back to the cosmopolitan ideals that echoed through his earlier vetoes of the literacy test? Whatever the case, Wilson's disapproval was an anachronism in the world of 1921."[1]

Soon after Harding's inauguration, the restriction bill was reintroduced at a special session of Congress. It passed the House in a matter of hours without a record vote, passed the Senate by seventy-eight to one, was immediately signed by the President, and became law in May, 1921. Although the bill was a temporary measure, from that date onward large-scale immigration would cease to be a major factor in our history. In the course of the next few years, Representative Johnson worked continuously for the passage of more permanent legislation. In his work he was guided by two patrician volunteers from New York, Madison Grant and Captain John B. Trevor, as well as a newly appointed Senator from Pennsylvania, David A. Reed.

Representative Johnson was much impressed with the racialist theories of Madison Grant. The two men carried on a constant correspondence and met frequently both in New York and in Washington. At least as far as their racial ideals were concerned, the rough and ready politician from the Far West and the fastidious Eastern socialite got on famously. And so it was with John B. Trevor, Harvard man, member of New York's best clubs, including the Knickerbocker and Union, and fellow trustee of the Museum of Natural History with Madison Grant and Henry Fairfield Osborn. Captain Trevor, who always used his military title (in a gentlemanly style more prevalent after the First War than today), had been a commanding officer of Military Intelligence in New York immediately after the war, through which he became extremely interested in the various radical movements on the Lower East Side. He was troubled by the fact that Jews often led these movements. His experience interested Johnson, who had Trevor sit continuously in the Washington committee meetings after 1921.

Senator David A. Reed, of a patrician background similar to Grant and Trevor, was appointed Senator from Pennsylvania in 1922 and served continuously until defeated in the New Deal landslide of 1934. The Reeds were one of the original steel dynasties of Pittsburgh. James Hay Reed, the Senator's father, had been Carnegie's lawyer and an original organizer of the United States Steel Corporation, on whose board he sat for two decades. Senator Reed, graduate of fashionable Shady Side Academy and Princeton and a long-respected member of the Duquesne Club, carried on a Pittsburgh First Family tradition of extreme conservatism. He was usually an ally of Philadelphia's Boies Penrose and an enemy of the more liberal wing of Pennsylvania Republicanism, represented by Gifford Pinchot. As a trustee of Princeton, one of the original group of Ivy League gentlemen who went through officers training at

Plattsburgh before the First War, and possessed of a distinguished war record, it was only natural that he should want to keep America free from excessive mongrelization.

Under the leadership of Senator Reed and Representative Johnson, permanent legislation was finally passed in 1924. In that year, President Coolidge, who had previously written an article on the dangers of race-pollution for *Good Housekeeping* magazine, called for some final and permanent restrictive legislation in his annual message to Congress. Big business, which had always been against restriction because of its need for a cheap and expanding labor supply, finally conceded that immigration was essentially a racial and not an economic problem and discontinued its active opposition (mechanization and the migration of Negro labor from the South had freed the businessman from dependence on the immigrant). The American Federation of Labor and its leader Samuel Gompers, although not quite happy about weighting immigrant quotas against Southern and Eastern Europeans, agreed that "our dominant racial characteristics should be preserved." The Ku Klux Klan, of course, vigorously supported the legislation. At any rate, the Johnson-Reed Act, which set up rigid national origins quotas based on 2 per cent of each foreign-born group residing in the United States as of 1890 (before the flood tide of immigration from Southern and Eastern Europe had reached its peak), was finally passed by the Congress. In spite of the fact that it abrogated our gentleman's agreement with Japan and rather offensively cut immigration from the so-called undesirable areas to the bone, the bill was signed by Coolidge. Thus ended the dream of America as a land of hope and opportunity for the toiling and oppressed masses of the Old World. It was indeed the end of an optimistic and humanitarian epoch in American history. Yet this so-called Nordic victory was certainly a popular triumph, supported by the vast majority of the American people of all classes and various economic interests. But most important was the fact that this was the *last surge of active nativism in this country to be led and strongly supported by the old-stock Eastern upper class*. (McCarthyism, which was to come later, was to be directed against this class.)

Immigration Restriction and Anti-Semitism

The nativism which finally lead to the restriction of immigration was strongly permeated with anti-Semitism. Indeed many have felt that anti-Semitism was one of the major causes of the change in immigration policy. For example, Burton J. Hendrick, in his book *Jews in America* which was published in 1923, wrote that the immigration law of 1921 was "chiefly intended—it is just as well to be frank about the matter—to restrict the entrance of Jews from eastern Europe." And John Higham, in his brilliant book on American nativism, has more recently written:

A postwar wave of persecution in central and eastern Europe was bringing the United States 119,000 Jews during the fiscal year 1920–21, and the sponsors of the suspension bill made as much of this condition as they dared. From an official in the State Department known as a pronounced anti-Semite, Johnson secured a report paraphrasing comments by American consuls overseas on the pernicious character and gigantic proportions of Jewish emigration. According to this document America faced an inundation of "abnormally twisted" and "unassimilable" Jews— "filthy, un-American, and often dangerous in their habits." The House Committee on Immigration appended these comments to its own report in favor of the suspension bill and used them to suggest that the present immigration was largely Jewish. This strategy made a strong impression. It left a conviction in various quarters that the chief purpose of the immigration law of 1921 was to keep out the Jews.[2]

Anti-Semitism was also part of the Big Red Scare which marred the immediate postwar years. Unfortunately there was a real, if exaggerated, sympathy with the Russian Revolution among many

East Side Jews. At the same time, the most infamous anti-Semitic document of the twentieth century—*The Protocols of the Elders of Zion*—was brought to New York by Czarist army officers. The Protocols, forged by the Russian secret police at the beginning of the century, first circulated in this country among nativist groups in an English translation and only came before the general public when Henry Ford's Dearborn *Independent* began its famous anti-Semitic campaign in the twenties. Ford, an American folk hero, disillusioned by the war and the failure of Wilsonian idealism, and possessed of a long-standing mistrust of bankers and cosmopolitan sophisticates, quite naturally fell for the idea of a Jewish conspiracy to rule the world. "I know who makes wars," he once said. "The international Jewish bankers arrange them so that they can make money out of them. I know it because a Jew on the peace ship told me so."[3]

Bernard Baruch, who reached the height of his formal career of public service as chief of the War Industries Board under Wilson, became the prime focus of Ford's attack on the Jews, which began with a series on "The Scope of Jewish Dictatorship in the United States." An exposé of "The Jewish Copper Kings" termed Baruch the "most powerful man in the world." Baruch, incidentally, had no copper holdings at all. "Banner headlines screamed Baruch's name," writes Baruch's biographer. "Baruch read the charges in his office one morning, then went home. He found his wife broken, shaken, his daughters crying. Bitterness came over him and an overpowering sense of helplessness—because of what Ford was, and what those dear to him had to endure. It was not for himself that he suffered."[4] Although Baruch has often denied the fact, his biographer was probably right when she wrote that "the net result of the Ford campaign was to lose the Democratic Party and, incidentally, the country, the open services of Bernard Baruch, and, indirectly at least, to drive him into the back-stage role he was thereafter to play."[5]

That the hysterical brand of Anti-Semitism carried to its "Paper

Pogrom" extreme by Henry Ford should have deprived the nation of such a talented man as Baruch was indeed a loss to the nation's leadership. Far more important, however, was the persistent, though less spectacular, exclusion of talented Jews from the highest levels of status achievement, which was intensified and formalized during the twenties.

Caste and the Corporate Economy

The increasingly rigid exclusion of Jews from the establishment during the twenties was due to the changing nature of both the Jewish and gentile communities. On the one hand, Jews steadily moved up the ladder of economic and political power in the course of this prosperous decade and quite naturally strove for social acceptance, primarily in education but in other ways too. But at the same time the American social structure became increasingly urban and corporate, which meant, in turn, that social status became less a matter of family standing in a local community and more a matter of one's affiliations in associations which carried prestige on a national scale. Social standing became, as it were, centralized and collectivized. A member of the hypothetical Jones family, for example, with a mansion on the hill and a family firm on the other side of the tracks, whether in Muncie, Indiana, or Newburyport, Massachusetts, needed no Ivy League degree or exclusive club affiliations to legitimize his secure social position in the local community. On the other hand, in a metropolitan-managerial society, J. Arnold Jones II, Yale 1922, vice president of a national corporation with exclusive metropolitan and country club memberships at his home office base, in Chicago or Detroit, as well as out-of-town memberships in the Yale and Links clubs in New York, has all the qualifications for a secure *national* and *associational*, rather than *local* and *familistic*, social position. Thus Charles Gray, the hero of J. P. Marquand's novel *Point of No Return*, was placed in his home town of Newburyport by his family's position and reputation, but, down in New York, he was ranked by the fact that he had graduated from Dartmouth rather than from Harvard or Yale. In this mobile world of New York, moreover, Charles Gray was also faced by the executive migration from suburb to "better" suburb, from country club to "better" country club, as he chased the grail of rootless success. In this same vein, the Lynds found in their second study of Muncie, Indiana, *Middletown in Transition*, that it was during the twenties that the country-club crowd, "now more self-consciously upper-class," had taken form. At the same time, local managers of nationally-owned firms were moving into this country club crowd for the first time.

It was during the twenties that the managerial society first began to dominate the establishment. One of the most important and seminal books to be published during the interwar years, for example, was *The Modern Corporation and Private Property* by A. A. Berle, Jr., and G. C. Means. The core of the argument in this book was that, on or about January 1, 1930, the two hundred largest non-financial corporations in the United States controlled between 45 and 53 per cent of the total corporate wealth (other than banking), between 35 and 45 per cent of the total business wealth (other than banking), and between 15 and 25 per cent of the total national wealth. These two hundred corporations, moreover, had grown in size and importance during the twenties. Twenty-eight of them, for example, had been acquired in mergers by another company on the list between 1920 and 1927, while no less than twenty-two mergers within the list had taken place in the years 1928–29.[6]

On the whole, although criticized in detail and revised by further research, the Berle and Means thesis has stood the test of time. They have been most legitimately criticized for placing too much emphasis on heavy manufacturing, railroad transportation and public utilities, which do not represent the majority of opportunities for employment today. On the other hand, it is just these areas of the economy which the Protestant establishment tended to dominate (along with commercial banking and insurance), while the less-favored ethnics, especially the Jews, were forced into the consumer and soft-goods parts of the economy, into retail and wholesale trade, into entertainment and communications. A Groton and Harvard man might become a manager of General Motors or the Pennsylvania Railroad but not the local Chevrolet dealer, the owner of a nation-wide fleet of trucks, or a radio entertainer. The Jews especially became concentrated in the peripheral areas of the economy where a large risk-factor was involved. Included here were new fields, old ones once considered unimportant, and such fields as amusement and entertainment, or the liquor industry, all usually considered beneath the dignity of proper members of the establishment. And even in the fields where both gentiles and Jews were to be found, it was often the local rather than the national firm which was Jewish. The local store, for example, was usually run by ethnic or Jewish entrepreneurs while the national chain was gentile-controlled; the large insurance companies, operating on a national and international scale, were dominated by the establishment, even though countless insurance brokers, operating in a highly competitive local market, were often Jews.

The Berle and Means thesis of increasing bureaucratization was, in short, infinitely appropriate as far as the members of the old-stock establishment were concerned. And the growth of the large corporation had inadvertently produced somewhat of a caste situation in which the national corporations were run by managers chosen on a merit system, which actually meant that they possessed the proper college, ethnic and club affiliations, while, at the same time, the objective criteria of survival in a free market tended to test primarily the marginal, ethnic entrepreneurs, among the most successful of whom were Jews. It was at least ironic that the very members of the Protestant and Republican establishment who vocally defended the virtues of free-market competition as the best test of excellence were, at the same time, creating a caste-protected merit system which exclusive colleges, suburbs and clubs were now being called on to protect.

Caste and the Campus

In a rapidly developing, managerial society, the proper college degree became the main criterion for potential elite status. It is no wonder that college enrollment increased from 156,756 in 1890 to 1,100,737 by 1930 (proportion of 18–21 year olds in college: 3 per cent in 1890; 12 per cent in 1930). More important here was the fact that it was during the twenties that certain institutions of high prestige, such as Harvard, Yale and Princeton (and Stanford on the West Coast), became all important as upper-class-ascribing institutions. I have documented this trend in more detail elsewhere, but perhaps the following figures will illustrate this important point: in a sample of gentlemen listed in the 1940 social registers of San Francisco and Philadelphia, for example, it was found that, of those who had graduated from college before 1900, 35 per cent of the San Franciscans had gone to Harvard, Yale and Princeton or Stanford while 24 per cent of the Philadelphians had gone to the "Big Three"; on the other hand, of those graduating after 1920, 58 per cent of the San Franciscans and 57 per cent of the Philadelphians had gone to these prestige institutions. As another instance of the trend, a majority of the San Franciscans had gone to the University of California before 1920, while Stanford only became a prestige institution in educating a majority after that date (though Proper San Franciscans like to think of Stanford as the "West Coast Harvard" it is probably more accurate to equate Cambridge with Berkeley and Palo Alto with Princeton).[7] Princeton, of course, became a class institution primarily in the twenties, when the proportion of undergraduates who were Episcopalians (the College of New Jersey had always been Calvinist), sons of alumni and products of private schools all reached their heights (of the forty-four members of the

Princeton football squad in 1927, all had graduated from private schools). It is certainly appropriate that F. Scott Fitzgerald, whose art was concentrated on the mores of the Anglo-Saxon establishment during its greatest days, should have been a perennial Princetonian and football fan.

And of course there were no Jews to speak of at Princeton in those days, except for a few from extremely wealthy families, one of whom (modeled on a grandson of old Meyer Guggenheim) Hemingway dissected in The Sun Also Rises. There were also a few rich and socially ambitious Jews at Yale, where the majority of the others were "townies" from New Haven who were accepted in order to accommodate the local community and were no problem socially simply because, as it were, they did not count. At Harvard the situation was different. Thus, in 1922 right in the midst of the argument over immigration and Henry Ford's propagation of the Protocols plot, President Lowell urged the Corporation to adopt a quota system in order to solve the "Jewish Problem."

It is unfortunate that an educator of A. Lawrence Lowell's stature and essential liberalism in many areas should be remembered for his attempt at introducing exclusionary practices at Harvard. In so many ways he possessed none of the tribal qualities of his class.[8] He was not a member of any undergraduate club at Harvard, although his bearing and background would presumably have assumed it. He was a great defender of academic freedom as against control by the business community, as seen, for instance, in his staunch defense of Harold Laski's defense of the Boston police strike. He had also worked tirelessly during his entire administration to bridge the gap between the Yard and the "Gold Coast," by first introducing Freshman Commons and finally creating the House Plan. On the other hand, Lowell certainly was on the side of those who took a narrow view of the establishment's righteousness in the Brandeis affair and the Sacco and Vanzetti case. His role in the effort to keep Brandeis off the Supreme Court has already been referred to. The case of Sacco and Vanzetti is too complicated to deal with here, except to say that it was Lowell who first convinced Governor Fuller, in a letter, that sincere men who had no sympathy for anarchists were troubled by the fact that perhaps Sacco and Vanzetti had not had a fair trial. Lowell himself was not in sympathy with Judge Thayer's paranoid attitudes and indiscreet behavior, and yet his committee reported to the Governor that they were of the opinion that justice had honestly been done. In other words, though the prejudices of his class may have influenced him in his conclusions (as whose do not?), Lowell was certainly no rabid anti-Semite or hysterical opponent of immigrants and anarchists; he felt, rather, that justice had been done in the Sacco-Vanzetti case and that a quota system was in the best interests of Harvard College. In this latter connection, Lowell had seen a private school run by one of his friends destroyed because of the lack of a quota system: the school, which had begun as a gentile school, soon became an all-Jewish school because of the policies of its head; and then, because of this, the Jewish parents withdrew their children. He did not want this to happen to Harvard, and, though quotas were perhaps not morally justified, Lowell may have been sociologically right at the time.

At any rate, Lowell was openly and honestly advocating a policy which was prevalent in almost all the Eastern colleges at the time. Nicholas Murray Butler (who loved the rich with a passion), for example, cut down the proportion of Jews at Columbia from 40 to around 20 per cent within two years, at the opening of the twenties.[9] Almost all the other private Eastern colleges, as well as other types of institutions all over the nation, had some kind of covert or overt restrictions on the number of Jewish students admitted. Within the Ivy League, the University of Pennsylvania (perhaps because of the Quaker influence) had no rigid restrictionary policies. On the other hand, the Jews who were admitted were definitely relegated to a second-class position within the student body. There were "A" (gentile) and "B" (Jewish) fraternities; two interfraternity councils; two interfraternity balls; in short, there were two rigidly separated caste worlds. All this is changed today, but at least one administrator was recently rather horrified to find that, upon visiting and talking to an alumni group in a Midwestern city, there were no Jews present at the meeting although many prominent Jewish alumni lived there.

Quota restrictions, though, were entirely in accord with the whole mood and social structure of the tribal twenties. There is no need here to go into the extreme practices of our medical schools. Down to the present, the practice of medicine in America has always been associated with high social prestige (much higher for example than in England), and the medical schools have been highly successful in restricting the admission of Jews. The law schools, on the other hand, have on the whole been open. As in the corporate world of business, however, the brilliant Jewish graduate of Harvard Law or Columbia was unable to obtain a position with the small group of large law firms with a corporate clientele of national importance. The Jew was by and large relegated to the highly competitive local scene, and invariably worked for himself, if not for the very few leading Jewish firms. Finally, and one tends to forget it because of the extreme changes in this area which have come about since World War II, the product of a graduate education, if a Jew, was hardly able to secure a tenure appointment at any good university in most disciplines: English, history, chemistry, sociology and engineering departments were, for various reasons, the most rigidly exclusive (no Jew ever held a tenure appointment in any English department at the "big three" until the Second War). It is of course appropriate that anthropology, with its discipline in transcultural values, was rather an exception to this prevalent rule.

Caste in the Suburb and Club

While the suburban trend in America, especially within the upper class, began to take shape back at the turn of the century, the pace was considerably stepped up during the 1920's. In a systematic analysis of Proper Philadelphians, for example, it was found that, while a majority of them still lived within the city before the First War, by 1930 most families had migrated to the suburbs (the more fashionable private schools, for instance, moved to the suburbs during this period). The suburban trend, as has been pointed out earlier, was an excellent answer to the ugliness of the heterogeneous urban melting pot. And, at least during the twenties, upper-class suburbs remained secure in their WASP homogeneity.

In the meantime, the more successful members of the Jewish community who still preferred an urban way of life were seeking better addresses uptown. And, while a majority of the old-stock families were moving out to the suburbs, those who remained engaged in a battle to keep Jews out of the more fashionable neighborhoods in the city. In New York the twenties witnessed a running battle along Park and Fifth avenues. "Within the single month of May, 1925," wrote Heywood Broun, "the Jewish real estate speculator, Benjamin Winter, bought the famous château of Mrs. William K. Vanderbilt at Fifth Avenue and Fifty-second Street and the mansion of Vincent Astor at Fifth Avenue and Sixty-fifth Street. As if to make the change more emphatic, he turned the site of the latter over to his co-religionists for the erection of Temple Emanu-El."[10]

The suburban movement was, of course, accompanied by a great boom in country clubs. By 1929 there were 4,500 clubs in the nation, the highest level ever attained before or since. It is no wonder that Sinclair Lewis' George F. Babbitt, a business go-getter whose god was Modern Appliances and who lived in a Dutch Colonial house in Floral Heights (only recently leveled by a developer's bulldozer), was inwardly resentful that his own membership in the Outing Golf and Country Club marked him as a notch below those who played at the Tonowanda Country Club: "You couldn't hire me to join the Tonowanda, even if I did have the hundred and eighty bucks to throw away on the initiation fee." As Lewis knew and John O'Hara outlined with his usual eye for detail in his best novel, *Appointment in Samarra*, middle-class mores of the twenties centered on the golf course and the clubhouse where newly emancipated women and their husbands engaged in an interminable round of Saturday night dances, sexual experiments, and compulsive drinking out of hip flasks. And the country club became the final index of one's arrival and a bastion of neighborhood exclusiveness. Heywood Broun, for example, once asked a realtor about his policy toward accepting Jewish residents in a suburb on Long Island: "Would you sell to a Jew," asked Broun? "I should say not," was the answer. "None of them gets in here. I simply tell them the section is restricted and we can't sell. But even if they managed to get a lot and build there, it would do no good. They would be ostracized and excluded from any enjoyment of the place. There is a community club which controls the beach and all social affairs, and they would never get into the club."[11]

Both Adam Smith's economics and the game of golf came out of Scotland toward the close of the eighteenth century; and more than a century later, America's business brahmins reigned supreme in their avid pursuit of success, trusted the leadership of the nation to the Invisible Hand and consummated many of their best deals in the privacy of the nineteenth hole.

Caste and the Criminal Culture

But the era of success-striving under the leadership of the Invisible Hand, based as it was on the theory that public virtue was a product of private vice, sometimes had some seamy consequences. And after a solid core of respectable old-stock Protestants had pushed through the Prohibition amendment, largely to curb the drinking mores of the "inferior" ethnic masses who filled the saloons in the city slums, the free market now included an overwhelming demand, even among the "best people," for alcoholic beverages. By late January, 1920, according to one account of the Prohibition era, "women began to invade the speakeasies. . . . Young people began to carry flasks and to break out in whoopee parties at which a popular game was to see who could first get plastered. They helped their elders handle the distilling and brewing apparatus in their homes, saw them guzzle liquor, making drunken passes at one another's wives and husbands, and nursing hangovers. They heard little conversation that didn't deal with the high cost of booze, the difficulty of controlling fermentation, the proper quantity of yeast, and the sterling qualities of 'my bootlegger.' "[12] And, as might have been anticipated, many ethnics of ability and enterprise, who were naturally denied access to success in the respectable world of the managerial merit system, became sterling bootleggers for the country-club crowd. "All I ever did," Al Capone once said, "was to sell beer and whiskey to our best people. All I ever did was to supply a demand that was pretty popular."[13]

Anti-Semitism was by no means the only manifestation of the caste corruption which was intensified in this country during the twenties. For below the respectable, and increasingly managerial, corporate and country-club world, and below the legitimate world of the ethnic entrepreneur, there lay a highly institutionalized criminal culture. One professor in Chicago has accurately described the origins of this culture as follows. "A typical criminal of the Capone era," he told a British author, "was a boy who had taken on the pattern of the successful mobster, the pattern that surrounded him. He wasn't out of step. He was a regular guy. He'd seen what was rated as success in the society he had been thrust into—the Cadillac, the big bank-roll, the elegant apartment. How could he acquire that kind of recognizable status? He was almost always a boy of outstanding initiative, imagination and ability; he was the kind of boy who, under different conditions, would have been a captain of industry or a key political figure of his time. But he hadn't the opportunity of going to Yale and becoming a banker or a broker; there was no passage for him to a law degree at Harvard. There was, however, a relatively easy way of acquiring those goods that he was incessantly told were available to him as an American citizen, and without which he had begun to feel he could not properly count himself as an American citizen. He could become a gangster."[14]

Al Capone, undoubtedly one of the organizing geniuses of his generation in America, was born in Naples, Italy, and brought to this country by his parents, who settled in an Italian tenement section of Brooklyn. Al grew up fast, learned about life in the famous Five Points Gang, married a handsome and devout Irish-Catholic girl at the age of fifteen, and soon afterward was on his way to wealth and power. Although Al never dreamed of going away to Yale University it was perhaps symbolic that he got his first job from a Mr. Frankie Yale, racket and liquor boss of Brooklyn, gunman mercenary and national head of the Mafia, who ran an infamous joint at Coney Island, the Harvard Inn.

After a brief education under Professor Yale of the Harvard Inn, Al went to Chicago, where he made millions of dollars, became a hero to millions of Americans and, during much of the 1920's, ran the city, which the best people had left to the Invisible Hand and the machine politicians. And, at the height of his power in 1930, when the soup kitchen had replaced the speakeasy, he showed his gallant sense of *noblesse oblige* by feeding large masses of his city's most destitute citizens at his own expense.

Capone, of course, had the normal American's desire for respectable status as well as success. Thus in spite of his great wealth and power, he was unusually sensitive to his foreign origins (which he denied) and his low-caste position in society. Hating his nickname "Scarface" and embarrassed by his foreign-sounding real name, Capone, for many years, insisted on being called Anthony Brown by his associates. Perhaps it was this underlying sense of inferiority which led him to cultivate an exaggerated air of swashbuckling dignity. He surrounded himself with a court of gentlemen-in-waiting who were always kept in peak physical form for their rigorous duties. "The Big Fellow hires nothing but gentlemen," said one of his crack troops. "They have to be well dressed at all times and have to have cultivated accents. They always have to say 'Yes, Sir' and 'No, Sir' to him."[15] Capone was also a solid family man who brought up his son in the style of the establishment to which he himself was forever denied access. Thus young Anthony Capone, after a private school education, was sent to Yale. And one of the few times Capone came out of his virtual seclusion in the 1940's was to attend Anthony's marriage to a "Society Girl" in Nashville, Tennessee.

In many ways, then, Al Capone was following in the tradition of the American Dream of the self-made man. Indeed, except for its being forever relegated to an inferior caste position, perhaps the Capone family was not really so different from those of the old-stock "robber barons" of an earlier era. And in our day of collectivized overconformity (fostered by the country club as well as the state), it is no wonder that the American gangster, like the lone cowboy, has become a folk hero in the manner of the Arthurian legends of old. For, after all, they were "the last of the rugged individualists," as the weak and vacillating intellectual called the Neanderthal Killer in Robert Sherwood's brilliant play, *The Petrified Forest*.

The 1920's marked the last decade in American history in which the members of the WASP establishment, protected by countless caste barriers from the rest of the people, had everything more or less their own way. But the saddest thing about the existence of caste in a professed democracy is its corrupting effect on those who supposedly benefit most from it. For indeed, while the members of the proper business establishment reigned supreme, they surely failed to rule (Coolidge spent more time napping while in the White House than any other President before or since). The best people abdicated, as it were, from leadership in their efforts to display their rights to success. And historians will look back upon this decade as one of adolescent irresponsibility which deeply corrupted the American soul. Samuel Insull, incidentally a teetotaler and the son of two rabid temperance crusaders, was, after all, only an extreme example of the predominant tone of his times. Thus a Chicago lawyer and son of a one-time attorney general looked back on the twenties and said: "Capone was relatively innocent compared with some of the men who dominated business and public life then—and I'm thinking particularly of Samuel Insull, who conducted his financial operations like a ruthless brigand. There were businessmen who supported honorable political and civic standards, yet who were seduced and bought by Insull. It was the great abandonment of honesty and integrity in public life brought about by Insull that had as a by-product the moral climate in which Capone ascended."[16] Or as another Chicagoan, a respected middle-aged banker today, put it: "During the twenties my daughter said to me, 'You've always taught me to respect law and the Constitution, and here you are making your own gin,' and I had no answer."[17]

The Intellectual as Artist: Fratricidal Revolt

But the last Anglo-Saxon decade, when hordes of middle-class Babbitts were joining clubs, deriding differences and denouncing dissent, was also an age of passionate individual revolt among intellectuals. The Social Gospel was replaced by the gospel according to Freud. The self-sacrifices demanded by the illusions of love and leadership surrendered to the apparently more realistic and self-satisfying pursuits of sex and success. The educated minority were bored by the earnest "kept liberalism" of the New Republic and preferred being entertained by the sneering cynicism of H. L. Mencken. And, above all, this decade of the dying Anglo-Saxon, as Mencken called it, produced the second great renaissance in American literature.

It was sociologically appropriate that the "lost generation" should have produced such a powerful literature. For indeed they belonged to the last generation in which the establishment still possessed a sense of intimacy and homogeneity and confidence on the surface at least, which may well be a vital prerequisite of artistic creation. Just as a homogeneous, provincial and transcendental New England produced our first great literary generation just before industrialism and materialism caused its decline, so the members of the lost generation came to maturity in a period of national transition from Anglo-Saxon and provincial homogeneity to ethnic and cosmopolitan heterogeneity. Thus, for example, Edmund Wilson, Philip Barry, John Dos Passos, F. Scott Fitzgerald, Robert E. Sherwood, Thornton Wilder, Stephen Vincent Benét, William Faulkner, Ernest Hemingway and Thomas Wolfe were all born within five years of one another at the turn of the century; all came from solidly middle-class and primarily old-stock, Protestant families; and all save Hemingway and Faulkner, who never went to college, were educated at Harvard, Yale or Princeton at a time when these campuses were small and relatively homogeneous communities, permitting an intimacy among students and between students and members of the faculty who prided themselves on teaching the young.

Yet they were rooted in an Anglo-Saxon and business establishment which was in the process of disintegration at the very hour of its greatest prestige. In striking contrast to the smug feelings of the best people, with their fervent faith in the smiling side of life, the blessings of the eternal business boom and the reign of Harding, Coolidge and Hoover, the artists of this generation, identifying themselves with Kipling's "legion of the lost" and "cohort of the damned," were obsessed with violence and a sense of doom, disaster and despair. Theirs was no genteel tradition. Possessed of deep middle-class roots, they were outsiders by choice and conviction. And, as such, they led a passionate revolt from the prevailing values of their age in a manner which makes the present generation of intellectuals, so often outsiders by inheritance, seem mild and conforming. But it may well be true that, while the outsider by inheritance makes an excellent, analytic critic, it is the disenchanted member of the establishment who tends most often to be the creative artist; perhaps the lost generation saw the tragedy in a world they still believed in, while the present generation sees only the pathos in a world they are alienated from.

Of all the members of this last creative generation, F. Scott Fitzgerald has left us the best portrait of the establishment. Though Fitzgerald was partly an outsider by the fact of his Catholic inheritance on his mother's side (his father came from shabby-genteel Protestant stock), he nevertheless identified with, and wrote most intimately about, the American rich who, as one of his characters put it, were "after all, all there is." No one has left us a more vivid picture of the essential violence and decadently self-destructive values which pervaded the country-club and Ivy league establishment of the twenties. Thus all Fitzgerald's gilded Yalemen were doomed to destruction. On May Day, 1919, his Gordon Sterrett, once voted the best-dressed man in his class at Yale, blew his brains out after a party at the Ritz; the "hard malice" of Tom Buchanan, "the best end ever produced at New Haven," destroyed his own marriage and Gatsby as well; and Dick Diver, whose career at Yale closely resembled Fitzgerald's at Princeton, was finally defeated, spiritually and emotionally, by the compulsively destructive, millionaire expatriates—the sick Nicole and her vicious sister.

Fitzgerald was fascinated by the charming and established world based on "animal magnetism and money" which ran from Princeton and New Haven to Paris and the Côte d'Azur, to the Plaza and the Ritz and to the Green Light, at East Egg down on Long Island. In his best novel, *The Great Gatsby*, he created the classic portrait of this establishment's encounter with the rising New Man. Thus Jay Gatsby—who once went to Oxford, old sport, and had apparently made a fortune in bootlegging under the expert tutelage of Wolfsheim, the famous fixer of the 1919 World Series—bought himself a great mansion at West Egg, where he settled down to watch the Green Light across the bay on the estate of Tom Buchanan and his wife, Daisy. It was upon Daisy that Gatsby had centered all his idealistic dreams ever since they had first met and fallen in love during the war, at a dance at an officer's club in Daisy's home town in the South. And while waiting and watching, Gatsby gave his famous parties. Fitzgerald's brilliant description of his rootless and destructive guests, who had nothing in common but their vulgarity and money, will forever remain the classic portrait of what has since come to be known as Café Society. But if Gatsby's world symbolized the New Man's corruption of the American Dream of Success, the Buchanans stood for the corruption of this dream by the establishment: "They were a careless people, Tom and Daisy—they smashed up things and creatures and then retreated back into their money or their vast carelessness, or whatever it was that kept them together, and let other people clean up the mess they had made. . . ."[18]

And Tom Buchanan was impressed with his caste superiority as well as his inherited money. "Have you read 'The Rise of the Colored Empires' by this man Goddard," he asked Nick Carraway, the narrator of *Gatsby* and Fitzgerald's alter ego, in the course of a casual dinner table conversation. "This fellow has worked out the whole thing," Tom continued. "It's up to us, who are the dominant race, to watch out or these other races will have control of things. . . . This idea is that we're Nordics. I am, and you are, and you are . . . and we've produced all the things that go to make civilization—oh, science and art, and all that. Do you see?"[19]

Nick Carraway, who is living on the Gatsby estate, finally brings Daisy and Gatsby together again at one of the famous parties. In the meantime, Tom is steadily becoming more dissolute and insecure, eventually realizing that both his mistress and wife "are slipping precipitately from his control." Then he meets Gatsby for the first time at East Egg. He and Gatsby, Daisy, Nick and Jordan Baker (Daisy's best friend and "incurably dishonest" lady golfing champion) are sitting around having drinks. When Tom becomes increasingly ugly and aggressive toward Gatsby, Daisy asks him to "please have a little self-control." Tom explodes—and the party breaks up after he has made the following panicky plea for the preservation of caste solidarity:

"Self-control!" repeated Tom incredulously. "I suppose the latest thing is to sit back and let Mr. Nobody from Nowhere make love to your wife. Well if that's the idea you can count me out. . . . Nowadays people begin by sneering at family life and family institutions, and next they'll throw everything overboard and have intermarriage between black and white."

Flushed with his impassioned gibberish, he saw himself standing alone on the last barrier of civilization.

"We're all white here," murmured Jordan.

"I know I'm not very popular. I don't give big parties. I suppose you've got to make your house into a pigsty in order to have any friends—in the modern world."

Angry as I was, as we all were, I was tempted to laugh whenever he opened his mouth. The transition from libertine to prig was so complete.[20]

Though he identified with them as individuals in his personal and charming way, as all great artists must, Fitzgerald nevertheless hated what both sides of the caste divide, both the Gatsbys and the Buchanans, stood for, with all the passion and power his talent could command. Thus, in their last talk together, with Gatsby in his flaming pink suit standing beside the swimming pool where he would soon be shot to death, Nick Carraway, referring to Daisy's world, sums up the tragedy of the twenties as he leaves to go into New York:

"They're a rotten crowd," I shouted across the lawn. "You're worth the whole damn bunch put together."

I've always been glad I said that. It was the only compliment I ever gave him, because I disapproved of him from beginning to end. . . .[21]

It is significant that Fitzgerald, after suffering through more than a hundred rejection slips, finally sold his first story to the Smart Set, in 1919. While the Saturday Evening Post and the American magazine were glorifying the businessman and the money-mad values of

the day, the *Smart Set* (and then the *American Mercury*, after its
founding in 1924) was the bible of the better-educated classes, who
roared and cheered the antidemocratic and antibusiness diatribes of
the sage of Baltimore, H. L. Mencken. As one looks back on the
twenties, it is indeed indicative that Mencken—who hated women
and motherhood, boobs and babbitts, Jews and immigrants, and
especially democrats like "Whining Woodrow" and "Roosevelt the
Younger"—should have held a position in American criticism and
letters like that of George Bernard Shaw in England. The following
paragraph from his *Treatise on the Gods*, for example, was typical
of his style.

> The Jews could be put down very plausibly as the most unpleasant
> race ever heard of. As commonly encountered they lack many of the
> qualities that mark the civilized man: courage, dignity, incorrupt-
> ibility, ease, confidence. They have vanity without pride, volup-
> tuousness without taste, and learning without wisdom. Their forti-
> tude, such as it is, is wasted upon puerile objects, and their charity
> is mainly a form of display.[22]

Mencken saw the caste lines which were developing on every
side in America all too clearly. But unlike Madison Grant, and more
like the later Henry Adams, he hated both sides of the caste divide
with equal passion. He liked nothing better, for instance, than to
shock the concerned Christian community by referring to President
Wilson as the "perfect model of the Christian cad" or to shock
smug Angles and Saxons by reminding them that they were of
course most purely represented in the Bible and hookworm belts.
The following lines from *Prejudices: Fourth Series* (published in
that fateful year of 1924) nicely indicate his views of the Anglo-
Saxon Decade:

> The descendants of the later immigrants tend generally to move
> upward; the descendants of the first settlers, I believe, tend plainly
> to move downward, mentally, spiritually and even physically. Civili-

zation is at its lowest mark in the United States precisely in those areas where the Anglo-Saxon still presumes to rule. He runs the whole South—and in the whole South there are not as many first-rate men as in many a single city of the mongrel North. Wherever he is still firmly in the saddle, there Ku Kluxery flourishes, and Fundamentalism, and lynching, and Prohibition, and all the other stupid and anti-social crazes of inferior men. It is not in the big cities, with their mixed population, that the death rate is highest, and politics most corrupt, and religion nearest to voodooism, and every decent aspiration suspect; it is in the areas that the recent immigrants have not penetrated, where "the purest Anglo-Saxon blood in the world" still flows. . . . The normal American of the "pure-blooded" majority goes to rest every night with an uneasy feeling that there is a burglar under the bed, and he gets up every morning with a sickening fear that his underwear has been stolen.[23]

Other critics had much the same views about the twenties as Mencken. The literary critic Van Wyck Brooks, himself of much more secure old-stock ancestry than Mencken, was horrified at the values of his age, as the following notes from his fictional journals of Oliver Allston indicate:

Fascism and suicide,—equally negations of life,—appear most frequently in those who have had "all the advantages."

The "revolt of the masses,"—yes,—but who are the masses? The Iroquois of Princeton, the Mohawks of Yale, the red-painted Mic-macs of Harvard, who are so pleasant until they are threatened and then behave like other barbarians.

I say that the gilded savages who swarm in the country clubs,—those cardboard imitations of English aristocracy in its surface-aspects,—do more to debase standards, intellectual and moral, than the so-called masses have ever had a chance to do.

The mass-mind in high places, that is the thing to attack and the point at which to attack it.[24]

It is no wonder that a majority of American intellectuals felt that perhaps some kind of eternal justice had been done when the unquestioned rule of the country club–business establishment came to an end as of the stock market crash in 1929. "The Slump began, and . . . a darkness seemed to descend," wrote Edmund Wilson. "Yet, to the writers and artists of my generation who had grown up in the Big Business era and had always resented its crowding-out of everything they cared about, these years were not depressing but stimulating. One couldn't help being exhilarated at the sudden unexpected collapse of that stupid gigantic fraud. It gave us a new sense of freedom; and it gave us a new sense of power to find ourselves carrying on while the bankers for a change were taking a beating."[25]

Remember, remember always that all of us, and you and I especially, are descended from immigrants and revolutionists.

Franklin Delano Roosevelt

X

The Caste Establishment Reacts to F.D.R.

The American people's faith in the business establishment collapsed almost completely after 1929. "In the late twenties the words of a Morgan partner were given more publicity than those of the President or Secretary of State," wrote Professor Cochran in his recent analysis, *The American Business System.* "In the early months of 1933," he continued, "the term 'bankster' classed these erstwhile paragons of respectability with the underworld and President Roosevelt in his inaugural address promised to drive the money-changers from the temple."[1] The individualistic undercurrents of the intellectual, sexual and religious revolt which paralleled the country-club

226

conformity and business Babbittry of the twenties erupted in a collective wave of political and economic reforms in the course of the next decade.

And these reforms produced a major change in the structure of the American political establishment. Between the presidencies of Abraham Lincoln and Herbert Hoover, the Republicans remained the majority party in a nation whose citizens were still predominantly rural, small-town and old-stock Protestant in origins and whose aspirations were focused on the individualistic pursuit of business success. Between the Crash in 1929 and the landslide election of 1936, the Democrats, under the leadership of Franklin Roosevelt, became the majority party in a nation increasingly composed of an urban and ethnically mixed electorate whose aspirations were more likely to be expressed in collective and political terms, largely because so many of them were denied access to success at the core of the business and corporate power structure.

It was appropriate that the last man to be sent to the White House by the Republicans while they were still the majority party should have been a man of the stature and character of Herbert Clark Hoover.[2] For Hoover represented, in the highest and best sense, all the virtues of the last Anglo-Saxon–Protestant generation to dominate the American political establishment. Born in a small town in Iowa where the only Democrat was the town drunkard, and deeply rooted in the Protestant-Rural-Republican ethic of self-help and individualism, Hoover was a professional expert on government yet an essentially reluctant amateur in politics. Above all, he was an outstanding example of the American self-made man who could proudly say, in 1914, that his "aggregate income from professional activities in various countries probably exceeded that of any other American engineer." Possessing the traditional Calvinist's faith in monetary success as a reward for virtue and a sign of one's election by the Deity, Hoover at the same time instinctively equated failure with sin and feared the common people. "Thank God," he said during his last Presidential campaign, "we still have a government in

Washington that knows how to deal with the mob." Hoover's mind and sentiments were understandably rooted in a past era when Anglo-Saxon Protestants and gentlemen-businessmen ruled the Nation and the World. "The happiest period of all humanity in the Western World in ten centuries," he once wrote, "was the twenty-five years before the First World War." And it was no wonder that he felt that the "new deals" of the Democrats "would destroy the very foundations of our American system," as he put it at Madison Square Garden in 1932, in one of his last, bitter speeches of the campaign.

The virtues of Franklin Delano Roosevelt were quite different from those of Herbert Clark Hoover. Possessed of substantial inherited wealth, reared in the protected world of Groton and Gold Coast Harvard, and a relative failure in the few business ventures he attempted, Roosevelt had the typical patrician's lack of respect for the money-power. "Government by organized money," he once said, "is just as dangerous as Government by organized mob." While Hoover came to the White House after a brilliant career as an engineer and appointed public servant, Roosevelt spent virtually his whole adult life in the political arena. The fact that Roosevelt proved to be a gifted, charismatic leader rather than a systematic administrator like Hoover, only served to endear him to the urban ethnic masses who had long been bred in the tradition of personal leadership ("Boss Rule"), as against the rural-Protestant preference for a weak executive and adherence to abstract principle. Indeed Roosevelt was ideally suited, in temperament, experience and background, to bridge the gap between the values of a rising urban frontier and those of a receding rural Protestantism. Loving the land as his Knickerbocker ancestors had done for generations, he was an essentially conservative man (like most Progressives, he was deeply concerned with Conservation all his life). Yet he also came to know and sympathize with the aspirations of the voters of the urban melting pot who lay at the very heart of New York politics. While Hoover, a congenital pessimist, looked to the past, the essentially

optimistic patrician from Hyde Park could understand big Tim
Sullivan of Tammany Hall when he said that "the America of the
future would be made out of the people who had come over in steer-
age and who knew in their hearts and lives the difference between
being despised and being accepted and liked."

The Urban-Ethnic Revolution

The transition from the twenties to the thirties, from Hoover to
Roosevelt, from Wall Street to Washington, and, above all, from a
business-dominated to a government-dominated society was indeed
a social revolution of major proportions. The immediate cause, of
course, was the collapse of the economy and the Great Depression.
But the revolutionary mood of the thirties was also the product of
other social forces which had been gaining momentum throughout
the first three decades of the century. Of importance here were the
following: (1) between 1900 and 1930 the majority of American
people came to live in cities; (2) while old-stock Protestants still
dominated rural America, ethnic heterogeneity marked the city;
(3) the newer immigrants who came to America after 1880 were
predominantly urban dwellers; (4) because of the shortage of labor
during the First War as well as the closing of the gates to cheap
labor from overseas immediately afterward, Negroes and poor-
whites from the South migrated to our large urban industrial areas
in the North; (5) and finally, the children of these migrants to the
urban frontier, educated in the public schools, slowly improved their
economic position and sought to take their place in the political life
of the nation as they came of age in the thirties. In other words, the
political reforms instituted by the New Deal in order to bring the
nation as a whole out of the Great Depression were, at the same
time, strongly supported by the members of racial and ethnic
minority groups, the vast majority of whom were still to be found
at the lowest levels of the economic pyramid. The economic battle

to liquidate the Depression was fused with the minority battle to liquidate both the heritage of slavery and the second-class status of the hyphenated-American. And the Northern wing of the Democratic Party, which had been kept alive ever since the Civil War by the political machines run by the sons of Irish immigrants, now became the party of the whole urban melting pot, made up of Poles, Italians, Jews and Czechs as well as the swelling tide of deracinated Negroes and hillbillies from the South. Just as Andrew Jackson had once transformed the Democrats into majority status as the hero of the Scotch-Irish immigrants to the Middle Western frontier (often referred to as "foreign savages" and "liars" by members of the resentful Federalist establishment), so Franklin Roosevelt became the hero, as Samuel Lubell has put it, of the heterogeneous mass of new arrivals on the Urban Frontier.[3]

It was the twentieth-century urban revolution which made the Democrats the majority party. The revolution, which began before the age of Franklin Roosevelt, found its first national leader in Alfred E. Smith (whom Roosevelt nominated in 1924 and supported in 1928). It was under Smith that the Democrats first broke the Republican hold on the urban North. In the twelve largest cities in the nation, for example, the Republican pluralities of 1,638 million in 1920 and 1,252 million in 1924, were translated into a small Democratic plurality of 38,000 votes in 1928. The Smith nomination, when "The Sidewalks of New York" was added to "Dixie" as a symbol of the new Democratic Party, was the first stage in a revolution which Roosevelt consummated in the four years between 1932 and 1936, when the Democratic plurality in these twelve major cities was increased by over 80 per cent (1932: 1,910 million; 1936: 3,608 million).[4]

If the members of the urban minority groups could identify with Al Smith, both with his record and his East Side brogue, they also had faith in the sincerity of the aristocrat from Hyde Park when he once said: "If I could do anything I wanted for twenty-four hours, the thing I would want most to do would be to complete the melting pot." And, on the whole, since Smith and Roosevelt, ambitious members of minority groups have sought careers within the Democratic Party. In 1928, for instance, a Providence tailor named Salvatore Pastore rented a store and started an "Al Smith for President" club. His stepson John, studying law at night school at the time, was uncertain whether he was a Republican or a Democrat. By 1933, however, there was little doubt that a struggling Italian-American lawyer belonged in the Democratic Party; thirteen years later John Pastore became the first Governor of Italian descent in the nation, and in 1950, the first Italian-American to sit in the United States Senate.[5]

Although the New Deal concentrated on economic reforms in the whole community, there was also a concern for minorities. Catholics and Jews were brought into the higher levels of government as never before: of the 214 federal judges appointed by Harding, Coolidge and Hoover combined, only 8 were Catholics and 8 Jews; of the 196 Roosevelt appointments, 51 were Catholics and 8 Jews. Roosevelt named the first Negro and the first Italian American to positions on the federal bench. In 1936, the National Association for the Advancement of Colored People, which had not publicly endorsed a Presidential candidate since endorsing Theodore Roosevelt in 1912, came out for Franklin Roosevelt. And although the majority of American Negroes had voted for Hoover in 1932, they had turned Lincoln's picture to the wall and replaced it with one of Franklin Roosevelt by 1936.[6]

The members of the Jewish community were the most urban of all the minority groups and were also the most successful in rising up the ladder of opportunity. Discriminatory practices—in education, in employment, in white-collar jobs, and in the professions—continued, and in many areas became more intensified, throughout the Depression. Yet, by the end of the thirties, most sociological studies of religious groups showed that proportionately the Jews tended to be better educated and more prosperous than Protestants or Catholics. In fact, the Jews were most similar to the Episcopalians and Presbyterians, the elite Protestant denominations, as far as education and occupation were concerned. But in spite of their success, they did not necessarily vote according to their economic interests and remained extremely loyal to the aspirations of the Democratic Party. In the election of 1940, for instance, even the wealthiest Jewish neighborhoods, according to Lubell, supported Roosevelt to an overwhelming extent. And an extensive survey of its college-educated readers made by Time magazine in 1947 was even more revealing. Thus while only 34 per cent of the Protestant readers and 39 per cent of the Catholics were pro-New Deal in their opinions, the Jewish college-graduates were 66 per cent in favor of the New Deal. At the same time, while a large proportion of these Time readers considered themselves to be political independents, 45 per cent of the Protestants, 22 per cent of the Catholics, as against only 6 per cent of the Jews, considered themselves to be Republicans.[7]

Schizophrenia in the Establishment

In a conservative and stable democracy such as ours, the establishment must, over the long run, reflect the composition and aspirations of the whole people. Thus the significance of the so-called Roosevelt revolution, like the Jacksonian revolution before it, was that it produced a kind of schizophrenia within the ranks of the establishment. Those who believed in the aristocratic ideal of assimilation and service to the whole people responded to the threat of violent revolution by supporting the reforms of the New Deal (even when they did not become formal Democrats). Those who clung to the idea of caste protection and the pursuit of individual success were more likely to have become a part of a rich and resentful opposition. It is interesting, in this respect, how history so often repeats itself. Thus, for example, in the early nineteenth century, Charles Jared Ingersoll, whose father had been a highly successful lawyer, staunch defender of the Federalist establishment

The Caste Establishment Reacts to F.D.R.

and Vice Presidential candidate on the Federalist ticket in 1812, became one of Philadelphia's leading Democrats and great admirer of Andrew Jackson in his fight with the banking establishment, led by Nicholas Biddle. And a century later, his great grandson, R. Sturgis Ingersoll, a First Family leader in the city's cultural and civic life, was Pennsylvania Chairman of the Democratic Victory Fund Campaign in 1932, and never quite took the fervently anti-Roosevelt and antireform position so prevalent among his Proper Philadelphia peers.

It is important to emphasize the fact that this schizophrenia in the establishment took place in an era of violent world revolution, fortunately only a potential here at home but a tragic actuality abroad. It took place at a time when Stalin, Mussolini and Hitler ruled a large part of the "civilized" world, and when revolution finally brought Franco to power in Spain. In America, the rootless and resentful were turning to communism on the Left, to the Minute Men and Silver Shirts, Khaki Shirts and White Shirts, and the American Nationalists on the Right, as well as to the increasingly popular demogoguery of such would-be dictators as Father Charles E. Coughlin, Dr. Francis E. Townsend and Huey Long. In the early thirties, moreover, many intellectuals had lost faith in democracy itself. "The rejection of democracy," wrote Ralph Barton Perry, "is nowadays regarded as evidence of superior wisdom." "To attempt a defense of democracy these days," wrote an eminent professor, "is a little like defending paganism in 313 or the divine right of kings in 1793." At the same time, some of the "best people" admired Hitler's disciplined dictatorship and handling of communism. (They also soon found out that a first-class passage aboard one of the luxury liners of the North German Lloyd steamship line possessed all the advantages of their favorite country club. "Thank God," some were heard to say at the time, "since Hitler there are no more Jews on the *Bremen* and the *Europa*.") David A. Reed, Senator for the Pennsylvania establishment, who had worked so effectively for the restriction of immigration in the early twenties

233

and was soon to become a prominent member of the Liberty League, could say on the floor of the Senate: "I do not often envy other countries their governments, but I say that if this country ever needed a Mussolini it needs one now"; and even the magazine *Vanity Fair*, hardly an organ of revolution, suggested: "Appoint a Dictator."[8]

But perhaps the ultimate example of the old-stock establishment's descent into despair and alienation from the democratic process was to be seen in the attitudes of Demarest Lloyd, son of the reforming crusader, Henry Demarest Lloyd, whose *Wealth Against Commonwealth* had been one of the most influential books of the Progressive era.* Thus Demarest Lloyd—one-time chairman of the National Immigration Legislative Committee of Patriotic Societies, vice chairman of the American Coalition of Patriotic Societies, member of such economic defense organizations as the Taxpayers Union and the National Republic Builders, and soon to become one of the leaders in the Liberty League's frantic fight to save Constitutional government from the un-American ways of Franklin Roosevelt— had apparently lost all faith in democracy by 1932, when he called for some sort of modern Directory, reminiscent of the French Revolution: "Popular government is a perilous extravagance in time of emergency," he wrote in his magazine *Affairs*. "The present situation is more destructive than war and much more difficult to handle. ... It is quite apparent that unless confusion is to become chaos, Congress, like a long line of unfit rulers in the past, should abdicate. ... It should delegate its powers and functions to a small group, not over a hundred of the most well-informed, intelligent and patriotic men in the country...."[9]

Yet Franklin Roosevelt somehow never seemed to lose faith in

---

* There were many other alienated old-stock gentlemen of Demarest Lloyd's generation. Nicholas Roosevelt was a Liberty League leader in the thirties, and today T.R.'s son Archibald B. Roosevelt is a leader among those seeking to root out subversion at Harvard as a trustee of the Veritas Foundation (see their popular publication, *Keynes At Harvard, Economic Deception as a Political Credo* [seventh printing, July, 1962]).

the democratic process. And those members of the establishment who stood by the New Deal believed him when he made the following statement during the campaign of 1936: "The most serious threat to our institutions comes from those who refuse to face the need for change. Liberalism becomes the protection for the far-sighted conservative. . . . 'Reform if you will preserve.' I am that kind of conservative because I am that kind of liberal."[10]

Roosevelt and the Aristocratic Ideal

A great American aristocrat, Oliver Wendell Holmes, Jr., once remarked that "if a man says: 'It is all very well to talk about being a gentleman, what I want to do is succeed,' it is hard to give any other answer except that our preferences differ. . . ."[11] The preferences of those members of the establishment who went down to Washington during the thirties were indeed quite different from those who remained at home to protect their privileges, along the Wall and Walnut streets of the nation. Francis Biddle knew both worlds, for he was born and bred within the very heart of the Philadelphia Republican establishment before he finally went to Washington and became a New Dealer. During the twenties, Biddle had a highly successful, conventional and lucrative law practice. Partner in one of the leading Proper Philadelphia firms, he personally handled "The Railroad" account (the Pennsylvania Railroad was to Proper Philadelphia what Harvard was to Proper Boston). And he was a member of the best clubs and served on the most fashionable boards of directors.

Yet, intellectually and temperamentally, Biddle never exactly fitted into the mold. He and his wife had always stood somewhat apart from the fashionable world which, as he put it, "spread out along the Main Line, played golf at the country clubs, knew what they wanted in life and got it."[12] They were understandably bored by the "formal dinner parties where the same faces appeared and reappeared each year, each season a little older, the cautious well-bred talk, the amiable and routine minds, not so much disillusioned as devoid of curiosity and passion. . . ."[13] Biddle's final revolt from the values of the Philadelphia establishment had long been a latent possibility. After graduation from the Harvard Law School, he had served as a clerk under Justice Holmes, and in 1912, much to the horror of his Philadelphia friends, he had been an ardent worker for Theodore Roosevelt. Though he first registered as a Democrat in 1932, he had supported and worked for Al Smith in 1928. And as a new boy at Groton he had strongly admired Franklin Roosevelt, then a sixth-former. At any rate, when he accepted the chairmanship of the Labor Relations Board and finally went to Washington in 1934, he and his wife soon felt perfectly at home among their new associates who preferred issues and ideas to the conventional gossiping about golf and grouse shooting. Though Biddle, like so many men during the early New Deal years, often worked to the point of collapse, and at a far smaller salary than his law practice had provided, he once described this new experience as providing:

. . . a deep sense of giving and sharing, far below any surface pleasure of work well done, but rooted in the relief of escaping the loneliness and boredom of oneself, and the unreality of personal ambition. The satisfaction derived from sinking individual effort into the community itself, the common goal and the common end. This is no escape from self; it is the realization of self.[14]

In the course of transforming the Democrats from a minority into a majority party, Franklin Roosevelt went outside the traditional party organization (incidentally losing Jim Farley in the process) to form a broad coalition of independent leaders, all of whom were agreed on the need to raise the moral tone of the nation's leadership by rescuing it from the narrow consequences of business domination. While Theodore Roosevelt had tried, unsuccessfully, to rescue the Republican Party from the "merchant mentality" which was only too likely to regard everything merely from the standpoint of

The Caste Establishment Reacts to F.D.R.

"Does it pay?" the New Deal was finally successful in its appeal to all those Americans who felt isolated and alienated from the business culture—farmers, laborers, intellectuals, minority-group members, Southerners, Negroes, and idealistic educated women.

And it was those leaders who, like Francis Biddle, still believed in Theodore Roosevelt's Progressive tradition, rather than formal Democrats, who eventually formed the inner circle of New Deal command. Thus Franklin Roosevelt's Cabinet as well as the heads of the regulatory agencies included men like Harold Ickes, Henry Wallace, Bronson Cutting, John G. Winant and the first woman ever to be appointed to a Cabinet post, Frances Perkins, none of whom had been formal Democrats before 1932. Henry Wallace, for instance, was a third-generation Iowa Republican, whose father had been Secretary of Agriculture under Hoover. Harold Ickes, the typical moralist in politics (sometimes, like many ardent New Dealers, humorlessly and self-righteously so), had been Chicago's leading Progressive Republican ever since Theodore Roosevelt's day. Though Franklin Roosevelt was himself rather cautious and conventional as far as race relations were concerned, he let Harold Ickes, who had been President of the Chicago NAACP, act as a kind of informal Secretary of Negro Relations: among his other accomplishments in fostering civil rights, Ickes ended segregation at the Interior Department and brought Negro architects and engineers into the PWA (many leading Negroes today, such as William H. Hastie and Robert C. Weaver, were first brought into government at that time).

From the beginning, Eleanor Roosevelt was openly and vigorously identified with the cause of minorities, especially Jews and Negroes. Her resignation from the Daughters of the American Revolution after their refusal to allow Marian Anderson to sing in their hall, her resignation from the Colony Club in New York because of their treatment of her friend, Mrs. Morgenthau, and her later refusal to fulfill an engagement in Lancaster, Pennsylvania, because the country club where she was to speak explicitly excluded Jews from membership, were all witnesses to her convictions. But, then, one must remember that, from Harriet Beecher Stowe to Eleanor Roosevelt, educated women have always identified with minorities who, like women themselves, have been discriminated against because of inherited physical characteristics.

It was, of course, in accord with the spirit of the New Deal that a woman like Frances Perkins should be given a Cabinet position. A typical brahmin reformer and Progressive Republican all her life, she had early fled the debutante routines of polite society to devote herself to reform and social work, first under Jane Addams in Chicago and then under Robert Wagner and Al Smith in New York.[15] And others like her were also brought in. During the early New Deal days, for instance, Frances Perkins shared a house in Washington with the widow of the sculptor Charles Cary Rumsey, also an ardent New Dealer and social reformer. Mary Rumsey, Averell Harriman's older sister, had once horrified her social set by enrolling at Barnard College, where she majored in sociology. Both her polo-playing and banker brother and she had been Republicans up to 1928, when they voted for their friend Al Smith. They both voted for another Democratic friend in 1932. Although Averell Harriman had been one of the original organizers of the Business Advisory Council (still the government's liaison with the top echelons of the business community) as well as an administrator of NRA, his friends say that his later development of an ardent identification with the Democratic Party, as well as his liberal convictions, was rooted in the memory of his older sister whom he greatly admired. (Mrs. Rumsey was killed in a riding accident during the thirties.)[16]

Franklin Roosevelt was not an intellectual. He was always more interested in human beings than in abstract humanity (in this respect, quite different from Woodrow Wilson and more like his uncle Ted). And his ability to inspire individuals, as Francis Biddle has written, surely "brought into the service of the country the ablest group of men the government had ever known." He was unusually fond of appointing sympathetic Republicans to high office.

The Caste Establishment Reacts to F.D.R.

John Gilbert Winant of New Hampshire, one of the more interesting of his Republican appointees, was an excellent example of the New Deal's appeal to the aristocratic temperament in America.

Born into a wealthy and aristocratic New York family, Winant married an heiress of an old Princeton clan whose father had been Eleanor Roosevelt's father's law partner.[17] Upon graduating from St. Paul's, Winant went to Princeton, where he eventually withdrew before graduating in order to campaign actively for Theodore Roosevelt in 1912. He then returned as a master to St. Paul's, where he founded the student self-government system and became a hero to the boys of T. S. Matthews' generation (some would say that Winant has been the only authentic great man the school has as yet produced). In World War I, Winant joined the Air Force, where he rose from private to squadron commander, was shot down seven times, and decorated for gallantry in action. After the war, he returned to New Hampshire, where he served in both houses of the legislature before leading a Progressive revolt within the Republican Party against the conservative forces led by the publisher Frank Knox and the New Hampshire Manufacturers Association. In a campaign for the Governorship in which it seemed as if he had talked casually and informally (he was a dismal public speaker) with almost every voter in the state, Winant won and became the youngest governor in the United States at that time. He went on to serve for three terms (like Roosevelt, he broke an ancient precedent against a third term) and brought the state out of a severe economic crisis with a series of reforms, many of which anticipated similar New Deal measures by almost a decade. By 1933, there was a brief "Winant for President" boom among Republican leaders who felt he might rejuvenate the national party. Many looked upon him as another Lincoln, whom he resembled in style, convictions and angular appearance to an uncanny degree.

But Winant gave up all personal political ambitions to go to Washington in the service of Roosevelt, whom he admired to an overwhelming extent. He took a major part in organizing the Social

Security Program. An ardent democrat with a sincere love of, and faith in, the average man, Winant was convinced that Social Security was the very heart of the New Deal. When he thought that the Landon campaign was threatening the program, he resigned from his appointed position and actively campaigned for Roosevelt's re-election. But he never became a formal member of the Democratic Party. He wanted to stress his disinterested position of service to the nation as a whole and, when Roosevelt offered him a Cabinet post as a reward for his support, he refused. "I did not think, since I had fought for what I believed to be a non-partisan measure," he wrote at a later time, "that I should accept a party appointment."[18]

Winant, however, did accept Roosevelt's appointment as American representative to the International Labor Organization, at Geneva. He was shortly elected director and, in this capacity, traveled all over Europe, talking to all sorts of people of high and low estate. As a consequence, he became one of the first Americans to see the dangers of war and Nazism. At a time when so many of his class were amused at the little man with the Charlie Chaplin mustache and pleased with the new policies of the North German Lloyd, Winant was publicly announcing his refusal to use any German ship in his trips abroad. As a result of this wide experience in Europe, Winant was appointed Ambassador to England. From the first, he had the complete confidence of both Roosevelt and Churchill and provided a vital leadership during those tragic and trying days of the destroyer deals, Lend Lease and the Battle of Britain. And the English people loved him. When he was replaced by Averell Harriman, their sentiments were best expressed by the London *Daily Express*: "Second only to President Roosevelt, Mr. Winant has seemed to us the personification of the finest part in America's character. We shall miss that tall, thoughtful, awkward-seeming man."

The thread of friendships and commonly held convictions which increasingly brought more and more aristocratic democrats and reformers into government service under the two Roosevelts and Woodrow Wilson makes a fascinating story which will some day be told in more detail. What is important here is not their statistical significance but the stature and moral convictions of this handful of old-stock members of the inner circles of the New Deal. For they inspired countless others of lesser stature than themselves which, in turn, slowly sowed the seeds for a real break in the traditional, if often indirect, control of the American political establishment by Anglo-Saxon–Protestant businessmen. And what brought these men and women into the service of the nation during the New Deal years was a profound belief, in accord with the values of Justice Holmes, that our best American traditions would never be preserved by a class of gentlemen who were primarily motivated by the narrow pursuit of success and the perpetuation of their privileges. They were convinced that the nation had other and more important business than business. (An interesting example of these aristocratic "threads of friendship" was Herbert Claiborne Pell, one of Roosevelt's Hudson River neighbors. Brought up among the rich at Tuxedo Park and Newport, Pell lost all faith in the business mind during the twenties. "The destinies of the world," he once wrote, "were handed them on a plate in 1920. Their piglike rush for immediate profits knocked over the whole feast in nine years. These are the people, with an ignorance equally only by their impudence, who set themselves up as the proper leaders of the country." Pell thought both aristocrat and bourgeois totally selfish—in accord with his background—but the aristocrat at least thought of his grandsons, while the bourgeois thought only of himself. Today, Pell's son is continuing an aristocratic tradition as a leader of the younger generation of New Frontiersmen down in Washington as Democratic Senator from Rhode Island. See Chapter XIII.)[19]

Roosevelt and the Ideology of Caste

When Roosevelt took office on March 4, 1933, the nation was prostrate. Some thirteen million Americans were unemployed, many of them huddling in Hoovervilles across the land, and even former members of the solid middle class were selling apples on street corners, a symbol of the last gasp of the free-enterprise system. In the morning, Roosevelt and the members of his Cabinet attended a service at St. John's Episcopal Church, led by Endicott Peabody of Groton. His inaugural speech opened with a plea for action and ended with an appeal to God for guidance in the days to come. Then, beginning with the Bank Holiday and the famous Hundred Days, in which he "sent fifteen messages to Congress, guided fifteen major laws to enactment, delivered ten speeches, held press conferences and cabinet meetings twice a week, conducted talks with foreign heads of state, sponsored an international conference, made all the major decisions in domestic and foreign policy, and never displayed fright or panic and rarely even bad temper,"[20] Roosevelt gradually brought the nation back to some sense of common purpose and faith in the future. The gregarious and optimistic atmosphere in the White House was now very different from what it had been in those seemingly distant days of lonely Herbert Hoover or napping Calvin Coolidge.

At first, many members of the business community, despairing of their own failures and unable to imagine any other course of action themselves, went along with the New Deal experiments, though sometimes reluctantly. Many unpuritanical leaders of big business were relieved when Roosevelt did away with Prohibition, among them the extremely affluent supporters of the AAPA (Association Against the Prohibition Amendment) who voted for both Smith in 1928 and Roosevelt in 1932. The business community, of course, was immediately aware that its accustomed power and authority were being threatened by increasing federal regulations. The Security and Exchange Act, for example, horrified Richard Whitney, Groton-Harvard-Clubman-Sportsman and president of the New York Stock Exchange, who firmly believed that this country had been "built on speculation." And he led a well-financed fight against any federal regulation (as a symbol of the tragic irony of the period, Endicott Peabody was eventually to visit his 'old boy' with some regularity at Sing Sing). But all was not yet lost. For, in spite of increasing governmental control, the early New Deal reforms centered on the National Industrial Recovery Act which was, after all, an experiment in centralized planning under the co-operative leadership of big business and government.

The honeymoon, however, was an all too brief one. After the Supreme Court declared the NRA to be unconstitutional, the New Deal turned away from centralized planning toward a compensating economy. The liberal "brain trusters" from the economics department of Columbia University who had been close to Roosevelt since he had been Governor of New York were gradually replaced by more conservative men from the Harvard Law School, who were inspired by the decentralizing philosophy of Louis D. Brandeis and who were brought down to Washington by Felix Frankfurter. This change toward a more conservative emphasis should have pleased the business community. But the new theories called for "pump priming" and a government-regulated redistribution of wealth in order to encourage the masses to consume rather than the few to save. Partly as a consequence of this new theory, and partly to ward off the effectiveness of the rising demagoguery of Huey Long and the Communists, Roosevelt finally called for new income- and inheritance-tax legislation. "I am fighting Communism, Huey Longism, Coughlinism, Townsendism," he told a Hearst reporter in 1935. "I want to save our system, the capitalist system; to save it is to give some heed to world thought of today. I want to equalize the distribution of wealth."[21]

The new income and inheritance taxes proposed by Roosevelt were taken as stabs at the very heart of the moneyed establishment. As a matter of ironic fact, it was partly the tax issue which led a large segment of the American rich first to support Roosevelt, in 1932, and then to hate him, by 1936. Prohibition, for instance, became a vital issue among the rich during the twenties and early thirties for two main reasons: first, and perhaps of lesser importance, it hurt their patrician pride to be forced into breaking the law of the land (set by an amendment to the Constitution, which they professed to hold sacred); secondly, so they soon saw, it cost them money: Pierre du Pont, for example, who poured his money and influence into both the Association Against the Prohibition Amendment which supported Roosevelt and the American Liberty League which later tried to defeat him, once sent out a letter under his signature, to a selected list of large taxpayers, which read in part as follows:

As our average tax collections for the years 1923–26 from individuals and corporations were $1,817,000,000, resulting in a considerable surplus, it is fair to say that the British liquor policy applied in the United States would permit of the total abolition of the income tax both personal and corporate.[22]

Soon after repeal, the AAPA died a natural death, and the American Liberty League took its place in the hearts of establishment leaders like Pierre du Pont. The Liberty League, founded in the summer of 1934, was a nonpartisan (open to both Democrats and Republicans) organization devoted to defending the Constitution (after the deletion of the "General Welfare" clause) and saving the American Way of Life from New Dealers, Communists and the inevitable dictatorship of Franklin D. Roosevelt. For the two years of 1935 and 1936, its activities produced headlines almost daily. From its headquarters in the National Press Building (thirty-one rooms and fifty staff members, the finest money could hire, as compared with the Republican national headquarters with its twelve rooms and seventeen staff members) its staff flooded the nation with pamphlets (Government by Busybodies; Will It Be Ave Caesar; The Way Dictatorships Start; Abolishing the States). Never had such a concise summary of conservative political thought been written in the United States since the Federalist era. Though from the first the League got more publicity than it did followers among the people, it never lacked money. In 1935, for instance, it raised nearly as much money as both national committees combined, and it spent over half a million dollars trying to defeat Roosevelt in 1936. Fewer than half a dozen bankers, industrialists and businessmen contributed over half the League's funds for 1935 (almost 30 per cent from the du Ponts alone); thirty wealthy men contributed two thirds of the money collected in 1936 (one dollar in five came out of du Pont pockets).

At the opening of the campaign year of 1936, the high-water mark of the Liberty League crusade to preserve Americanism from the alien philosophies of the New Deal was a well-publicized dinner at the Mayflower Hotel in Washington on January 25. That evening some two thousand guests, "the greatest collection of millionaires ever assembled under one roof" (including an even dozen du Ponts), gathered to hear Alfred E. Smith discuss the administration of his one-time ally and friend. Introduced as plain "Al Smith of America," the guest of honor proceeded to pin the Communist label on the New Deal: "The young brain-trusters caught the Socialists in swimming and they ran away with their clothes. . . . There can be only one capital, Washington or Moscow. There can be only the clear, pure, fresh air of free America, or the foul breath of Communist Russia. There can be only one flag, the Stars and Stripes or the flag of the godless Union of the Soviets. There can be only one national anthem, the Star-Spangled Banner or the Internationale. . . ."[23] The polite applause was deafening. "It was perfect," said Pierre du Pont.

The millionaires' dinner at the Mayflower was indeed an ironic reminder of another dinner, held just about a half-century earlier, when the millionaires of Andrew Carnegie's generation gathered at Delmonico's in New York City to honor the visiting British Social Darwinist, Herbert Spencer. For, in the meantime, the world had changed beyond recognition. And while Henry Ward Beecher had expounded at Delmonico's the faith of a confident establishment which still possessed both affluence and authority, Al Smith appealed to the Mayflower millionaires in the shrill voice of alienation and resentment, desperation and despair, born of a futile attempt to justify the affluence and an establishment which had lost its author-

245

ity. The irony was doubly compounded by the fact that Smith had once stood as a symbol of the ideals and aspirations of millions of patriotic Americans who had come to this country in the years between the dinners at Delmonico's and the Mayflower. And when he rose to defend the millionaires who professed to possess a monopoly on patriotism, he had apparently forgotten the recent immigrants as well as his previous reply to Herbert Hoover's questioning of his own Americanism. "The cry of socialism," Smith said in a speech in Boston in 1928, "has always been raised by powerful interests that desire to put a damper upon progressive legislation."[24]

"To a philosophy that was at once a combination of Social Darwinism, laissez-faire economics, Old Testament apocalypse, and Constitution and ancestor worship," writes George Wolfskill in his recent history of the League, "the Liberty League now often added a savage hatred of the man who came to symbolize their torment and frustration."[25] The Liberty League was an organized manifestation of the more generalized hatred of Roosevelt which took hold of the American rich during the New Deal years. "Regardless of party and regardless of region, today, with few exceptions," reported *Time* magazine in April, 1936, "members of the so-called Upper Class frankly hate Roosevelt." It was said that the protective family of the aging J. P. Morgan kept newspapers with pictures of Roosevelt prominently displayed away from him because of their upsetting nature. And there was the unforgettable Peter Arno cartoon in the *New Yorker* at the time, picturing the inevitable clubmen sitting in the picture window and saying, "Let's go down to the Translux and hiss Roosevelt." Hating "That Man" had, by this time, replaced gout as the *rentier* establishment's special disease.

The authority and prestige of the Protestant establishment had always been anchored in the business community. While Roosevelt concentrated his attacks on the so-called economic royalists and money changers, the hatred of Roosevelt had far deeper origins than mere economics, as anyone who dined out in polite society at the time knows—anyone, that is, who remembers being called a Jew- or nigger-lover for making even a mildly favorable comment on "That Man, Rosenfelt." In his book, George Wolfskill sums up the attitudes of the Roosevelt Haters as follows:

> In their thesaurus of hate, Roosevelt was a "renegade Democrat," an "extravagant," "destructive," "vacillating," "unprincipled charlatan." A "cripple," an "invalid" lacking physical stamina, a captive, psychologically, who was morally "weak," intellectually "shallow," unbelievably "gullible," a "dupe" (surrounded by "radicals," "crackpots," "quarterbacks," and "foreign-thinking brain-trusters, some of whom were better known in Russia than in the United States"). Nor was this the worst of it. From Newport to Miami, from Wall Street to Park Avenue, in country club locker rooms, the cathedral-like hush of bank offices, in board rooms and carpeted law offices, in hotel suites and cabin cruisers the broad stories passed: Roosevelt was an inveterate liar, immoral (hadn't you heard about his affair with Frances Perkins?), a syphilitic, a tool of Negroes and Jews, a madman given to unbroken gales of immoderate laughter, an alcoholic, a megalomaniac dreaming his dreams of dictatorship.[26]

Caste resentment was a definite part of the hate campaign. Some very respectable establishment money, for example, went to support the work of William Dudley Pelley, who had established the Foundation for Christian Ethics, Galahad College, and who also published a violently anti-Semitic paper, *Liberation*. Roosevelt, Pelley insisted, was really a Jew of Dutch ancestry who had been foisted on an unsuspecting electorate by the Elders of Zion.[27] A great deal of the anti-Roosevelt resentment, of course, was centered on his wife. For example, on the occasion of Eleanor's visit to Washington's Howard University to address the Women's Faculty Club, she was photographed along with two young R.O.T.C. officers. The resulting "nigger pictures" had a wide circulation.[28] But perhaps most revealing of the caste resentment which characterized so much of the antipathy toward the whole New Deal was the following bit of doggerel about Franklin and Eleanor:

> You kiss the negroes
> I'll kiss the Jews,
> We'll stay in the White House
> As long as we choose.[29]

The anti-Semitic and racial undertones which marked so many of the anti-Roosevelt stories and which soon became an obsession among the members of the country-club establishment were not accidental. Wit and humor, as Freud has told us, are usually manifestations of unconscious, deeply rooted and often repressed psychological drives. Thus, this period of irrational and acute hatred of Roosevelt and the tone of the tales through which it was expressed, provide an excellent clue to the causes of the schizophrenia in the American establishment which began in the thirties and has continued to the present day. On the one hand, for example, the universalistic conviction that all men should be judged on their merits—and not their antecedents, their race or their religion—lay at the very core of the constellation of ideas and ideals which united former Progressives and independents of old-stock origins behind the New Deal reforms. On the other hand, the hatred of Roosevelt, shared by the majority of the members of the WASP establishment was surely due to deep-seated caste values and an irrational fear, if not horror, of social and racial equality. These differing attitudes toward race and religion have been emphasized here primarily because the important divisions over economic and political philosophies have so often been, and rightly, emphasized by others. That the upper-class antipathy to the Roosevelt regime was not entirely economic is apparent in the following statement:

For quite a while I have lived in a commuter community that is rabidly anti-Roosevelt and I am convinced that the heart of their hatred is not economic. The real source of the venom is that Rooseveltism challenged their feeling that they were superior people, occupying by right a privileged position in the world. I am convinced that a lot of them would even have backed many of his economic measures

if they had been permitted to believe the laws represented the fulfillment of their responsibility as "superior people." They were not
permitted that belief. Instead, as the New Deal went on, it chipped
away more and more of their sense of superiority. By the second
term, it was pressing hard on a vital spot and the conservatives were
screaming.[30]

The hatred of Roosevelt was even strong enough to overcome the
bonds of the old school tie. And Groton alumni were not above circulating countless stories about the traitor to their caste. In this connection, it was interesting that Groton School celebrated its fiftieth
anniversary just as the anti-Roosevelt mania was beginning to develop. The school's founder and headmaster, Endicott Peabody, had
voted for Hoover in 1932. But he eventually came to defend his
most famous former student to countless alumni who wrote him of
their antagonism toward the President. In fact, things went so far
that Peabody finally felt it necessary to warn all alumni who were
planning to return to the school for the fiftieth-anniversary celebrations that they should not do so if they were not prepared to be
polite to the President and Mrs. Roosevelt. And on another occasion, at the exclusive Union Club in New York City, the Rector
injected a sober note into a jolly gathering of the Groton Family
when he said at the end of a brief, after-dinner speech to his old
boys: "In national crises like the present one, we get pretty excited
and perhaps we give vent to expressions that later we are sorry for. I
believe Franklin Roosevelt to be a gallant gentleman. I am happy to
count him as my friend."[31] Silence reigned.

The aging Rector also participated in another ceremonial occasion
which was the very personification of the schizophrenia which split
the establishment during the thirties. For, as "Grottie" custom demanded, he assisted at the marriage ceremony which united the
President's third son and a beautiful member of the du Pont clan.
Franklin D. Roosevelt, Jr., who of all the sons most closely resembled his father in looks and charm of manner, had been a Senior

Prefect and leading athlete at Groton, where he first met Ethel du Pont at a school dance.[32] The courtship of this famous and golden couple, which took place during the height of the Liberty League crusade, of course produced constant headlines. Finally, in the early summer of 1937, after the President's victory over the du Pont–led Liberty League, and in the midst of his controversial attack on the nine old men of the Supreme Court, three hundred carefully chosen guests—including famous Democrats and members of the Roosevelt family, on one side of the aisle, and the more anonymous members of the du Pont clan and their socialite friends, on the other side—gathered at Christ Church, Christiana Hundred, Delaware, to witness the "Wedding-of-the-Year," as *Time* magazine described it in a cover story at the time. If there was ever any personal hostility to the match on the part of either family, it was politely and thoroughly submerged. This patrician restraint practiced on both sides of the aisle, however, could not hide the fact that the families and guests at the Roosevelt–du Pont wedding symbolized the nature of the opposing leadership in perhaps the greatest battle between the ideas of caste and aristocracy since the defeat of the Federalist establishment by Andrew Jackson. For, in the twentieth century, if the Roosevelts had been an outstanding example of the humanistic leadership of the forces of aristocratic assimilation, the du Ponts surely stood for the idea of the single-minded, and scientific, pursuit of success, ever since the first Pierre Samuel Dupont, a Parisian watchmaker's son, rose to power and influence during the Ancient Regime and founded the house of du Pont de Nemours after his ennoblement by the King.[33]

Well connected (both Jefferson and Franklin were family friends) when they came to America and settled on the banks of the Brandywine in 1802, the clan du Pont (in the French tradition and unlike so many other rootless millionaires' families who left their source of wealth and settled for the social whirl of New York and Newport) has sunk deep roots in one of the nation's smallest states, which it has controlled down through the years as perhaps no other family has ever done in America. The clan has always produced at least one *paterfamilias* in each generation, who usually ran the business and ruled the family with an autocratic hand.

From its very beginning the clan has been both prolific and caste-conscious. In 1934, for instance, the Social Register listed some 73 du Pont adults, compared to 31 Mellons, 28 Harrimans, 27 Rockefellers. Down through the years the number of consanguine marriages has been unusually high. One *paterfamilias* was forced to issue an edict against the practice. Yet Pierre Samuel, the last of the patriarchal rulers of the family, married his own mother's niece. In this connection, it is of interest that when Pierre's mother married into the family there was a slight stir; for, while she was the beautiful daughter of the trusted company bookkeeper and also of French stock, she was at the same time partly Jewish. She was immediately accepted, however, when the *paterfamilias* paid her a social call soon after the marriage.

In so many ways, Pierre Samuel Dupont was an ideal *paterfamilias* for the age of Roosevelt when the family so needed protection from the grasping hands of the federal government. He first took over the leadership of the family and company during the First War. Almost overnight, he transformed "the staid and ancient tribe of du Pont into a dynasty of overwhelming wealth and power." Pierre and his close associates, despite dividends paid to themselves and other stockholders (458 per cent on the par value of the stock), emerged from the war with a surplus nest egg of some $90,000,000.

At any rate, Pierre and his intimate associate, John Jacob Rascob (who had begun his career as a $45-a-week stenographer for Pierre), went scouting for ways to invest their surplus cash. Rascob finally found General Motors. Within a few years, the du Ponts had control of this great automobile empire which had been built up by another gentleman of French descent, William Crapo Durant. Thus by 1934, the year the Liberty League was founded, the Barons on the Brandywine had become the leading financial and manufacturing dynasty in the nation: In that year, the net income of General Motors and du Pont combined (GM: $94,679,131; du Pont: $46,-701,465) easily surpassed that of the nation's first money-maker,

251

American Telephone and Telegraph ($125,351,768). "The Du Pont group," wrote John Jacob Rascob in 1934, "controls a larger share of industry, through common stock holdings, than any other group in the United States . . . including the Rockefellers, the Morgans, or the Mellons."[34]

It gives one a sense of history, as well as a realization of the continuing applicability of sound social theory, to speculate on how Alexis de Tocqueville (whose own father was in jail at the same time as the first du Pont de Nemours; both were saved from the guillotine by a hairbreadth because of the death of Robespierre) would have viewed the values of those who shared his beloved French blood as they fought to preserve their privileges against the onslaughts of the Roosevelt revolution. Though he would undoubtedly have been proud of the accomplishment of these descendants of the Old Regime, it is at the same time safe to say that his theory of the causes of the French Revolution would have led him to condemn the caste spirit of the du Ponts and to condone the aristocratic spirit of the Roosevelts. But today, on the other hand, Tocqueville would also see the possible usefulness of dynasties like the du Ponts, as "secondary powers" and guardians of freedom, in an age that has gone far beyond the Roosevelt revolution on the road toward the omnipotent state. Like Aristotle before him, Tocqueville was always aware of the need for balance and the moderate mean: in the depths of a depression, the balance of power surely needed tipping in the direction of Washington, as against Wilmington or Wall Street; this may not be the case today.

Schizophrenia within the Business Community

The principal significance of the New Deal was that it produced a kind of schizophrenia within the ranks of the old-stock Protestant establishment. On the whole, but not entirely, this division of loyalties was between those members of the establishment who stood in the Progressive and antibusiness tradition which began with T. R. Roosevelt and came to a head in the New Deal coalition, and those who followed the leaders of the business community, who by and large continued to dominate the Republican Party as well as such organized opposition groups as the American Liberty League.

It would be inaccurate, however, to leave the impression that the American business community as a whole was united in its antipathy toward the New Deal. One of the Morgan senior partners, Thomas W. Lamont, for example, saw the short-sightedness of the Liberty League crusade and remained a supporter of his old friend Franklin Roosevelt. But Lamont was an extraordinarily complex and resourceful man. According to Ferdinand Lundberg, whose *America's 60 Families* has become a classic study of the American rich, Lamont had been "the brains of J. P. Morgan and Company throughout the postwar period and was a mentor of Woodrow Wilson in Wilson's second administration as well as of Herbert Hoover throughout his fateful single term in the White House, has exercised more power for twenty years in the western hemisphere, has put into effect more final decisions from which there has been no appeal, than any other person."[35] As one might expect, Lamont, even though he was often openly critical of Roosevelt's economic policies, was quick to see the essentially conserving nature of the New Deal. Thus, in 1934, he told Harry Hopkins that he considered Roosevelt a "bulwark of sane politics" and that he expected him to remain in office until 1940, or perhaps 1944. "When people complain to me of the amount of money that the government has been borrowing," Lamont continued, "I always answer it by saying: 'Well, if the country was willing to spend thirty billion dollars in a year's time to lick the Germans, I don't see why people should complain about its spending five or six billion dollars to keep people from starving.' "[36] But perhaps Lamont was only a far-sighted conservative who had taken the elder J. P. Morgan seriously when he had once said that he made it a policy "never to sell America short."

Lamont was certainly an exception within the heart of the Protestant establishment which centered on Wall Street, and in insurance and banking, in heavy industry, and in large manufacturing establishments such as du Pont and General Motors. For the real schizophrenia within the ranks of the business community came, by and large but of course not entirely, from the conflict between this old-stock concentration in the older, more production-oriented seats of economic power and the newer consumer and communications branches of the business community. Thus, not only were those leaders in communications (radio and motion pictures), in retail sales, and especially in the new electronic appliances, more likely to support the New Deal economically because of its efforts to redistribute wealth and place purchasing power in the hands of the masses of consumers; it was the members of the newer ethnic minorities, especially the Jews, who supported the New Deal because they had taken the lead in developing these newer, consumer fields, partly because of the caste monopoly of the older centers of production and commercial banking maintained by established members of the old-stock upper class.

The nature of the schizophrenia which divided the business establishment during the thirties was nicely illustrated in the career of Gerard Swope.[37] He and such men as Owen D. Young and Alfred P. Sloan, Jr., were leaders of the managerial revolution which took place in American business leadership between the two wars. These new industrial statesmen were highly sensitive to the rising consumer democracy and also interpreted their leadership of the large corporation world as implying a quasi-public trust which required a sense of corporate *noblesse oblige* (Sloan, incidentally, led GM in a style- and consumer-conscious drive which eventually took the leadership of the automotive industry away from Henry Ford, who continued to insist on an engineering and production approach to his customers).

Gerard Swope graduated from the Massachusetts Institute of Technology with a degree in electrical engineering, in 1895 (along with his classmate, Alfred P. Sloan, Jr.). But he soon switched

254

from engineering to sales as he worked his way up to the presidency of General Electric, a position which he held between 1922 and his first retirement in 1939 (for a brief period during the war, he returned to GE after Charles Wilson was called to Washington).

From the beginning, Swope was a new kind of businessman and, as such, was often called a "radical" by his peers. He was, for instance, the only major industrial leader to attend the funeral of Samuel Gompers. And he instituted all kinds of reforms at GE, including a voluntary unemployment insurance plan and the encouragement of unionization among his employees. Yet in spite of his reforms, which were understandably called socialistic by some, Swope was also a genius at turning out a profit.

By and large, Swope was a political independent and Progressive who supported Wilson and the two Roosevelts, while turning to Willkie in 1940. And he was, unlike Sloan of GM who could be counted on to support most of the du Pont causes like the Liberty League, an active and sympathetic representative of business down in Washington during the New Deal years. As a member of the Industrial Advisory Board of the NRA, first chairman of the Business Advisory Council, chairman of the Coal Arbitration Board, and a member of the first National Labor Board and the Advisory Council on Social Security, Swope was called, by one of the inner circle of New Deal intellectuals, George Creel, ". . . the only industrialist who counted among the brain-trusters."

After his first retirement from GE, Swope continued to play a major role in various positions of public service. As Chairman of the New York Housing Authority, for example, he increased the number of rooms built under the project from 8,000 to 37,000 and at the same time reduced the average price per room from nine dollars to seven. Then, after the war, he accepted Mayor La Guardia's nomination to a directorship in the Health Insurance Plan of Greater New York, in spite of its being branded as "socialized medicine."

Swope's sense of social responsibility was developed early in his career. While at M.I.T. he eagerly attended the lectures of Louis D. Brandeis, who continually stressed the fact that business was a public service. Then, during his early business career, he lived at Hull House where, after a hard day's work, he taught algebra and electricity to immigrants. Here he also met his future wife, Mary Dayton Hill, one of the new women in the style of Frances Perkins and Mary Harriman, who had graduated from Bryn Mawr, where she had become a disciple of John Dewey. After their marriage, the Swopes continued their interest in reform by purchasing a house in the slums of St. Louis and living there while Swope was working his way up the ladder in the shops of Western Electric.

It was also important that Swope was not a member of the old-stock establishment and thus was more able to sympathize with the Roosevelt revolution. For, though few members of the public knew it, Swope was born of immigrant parents, and his grandfather had been the chief rabbi of Thuringia and the first Jew ever to receive a Ph.D. from the University of Breslau. The few who did know, however, were presumably members of the watchful and caste-conscious admission committees of the "best" businessmen's clubs in Chicago and New York. For the only first-rate club membership held by this admittedly top leader in American business between the two wars was the more aristocratic Metropolitan Club, in the nation's capital.

In San Francisco, the inner circle of the commercial and banking establishment—led by W. H. Crocker, graduate of Yale, and head of the city's First Family and President of the Crocker First National Bank—went to the top of Nob Hill for lunch at the Pacific Union Club. But Amadeo Peter Gianinni was never one of them. Born the son of an immigrant hotel keeper in San Jose on San Francisco Bay, Gianinni eventually became the Morgan of the new age of mass democracy. Way back in 1904, when he started his banking career, in an era in which the Morgan firm dealt only with the giant trusts and large investors, Gianinni resolved to become the banker of "the little fellow." And for many years his Bank of Italy was patronized largely by immigrants who had never seen the inside of a bank before and had traditionally hidden their spare cash in a sock under the mattress. Gianinni's success was, in many ways, a measure of the immigrants' progress in America. When he resigned from the chairmanship of the board at the Bank of America in 1945, the day of his seventy-fifth birthday, his firm had just passed the Chase Bank of New York to become the largest commercial bank in the world.

Although he had voted for Cleveland in his youth, "A.P.," as he was affectionately known throughout the Bay area, usually stood aloof from politics, as befitted his position as a rising banker. In the crisis year of 1931, however, the leaders of the commercial community, headed by W. H. Crocker, expected him to actively endorse his old friend Herbert Hoover. But they were somewhat upset when Gianinni, after a long chat with Roosevelt, Joseph P. Kennedy and James A. Farley, who were then touring the West, announced to the local press that he hadn't "decided to support anybody yet." Finally, at the suggestion of the local establishment, Hoover called Gianinni on the telephone from the White House and asked for his public support. "Well, I'm sorry, Mr. President," Gianinni politely replied, "but I'm not in politics at all."[38]

The banking panic in California grew steadily worse. Finally the Governor closed all the banks in the state, on Friday, March 3, the day Roosevelt left New York for Washington. The next day, A. P. Gianinni, along with thousands of his fellow citizens in San Francisco, listened to the inauguration ceremonies over the radio. In *Biography of a Bank*, Marquis James described his feeling as follows:

A. P. Gianinni was an absorbed and approving observer of the inauguration of Franklin D. Roosevelt, the most momentous occasion of its kind since 1861. He liked Roosevelt's words. "The only thing we have to fear is fear itself." Gianinni himself had used somewhat the same words time and again in California. Gianinni warmed to Roosevelt's excoriation of "the unscrupulous money changers . . . [who stand] indicted in the court of public opinion. . . . They only know the rules of a generation of self-seekers. They have no vision, and where there is no vision the people perish." The speaker promised "action, and action now," to remedy the state of affairs. "Happiness lies not in the possession of money; it lies in the joy of achievement, in the thrill of creative effort. The joy and the moral stimulation of work no longer must be forgotten in the mad chase of evanescent profits." The Californian had damned Wall Street in much the same fashion, and his life was an exemplification of the new leader's philosophy concerning the possession of wealth.[39]

Consummation of the Urban-Ethnic Revolution

At the height of the Liberty League crusade, A. P. Gianinni and another San Franciscan, Rudolph Spreckles, progressive civic reformer and head of the sugar clan, suggested to Roosevelt that a counterorganization be formed. Apparently the President thought the plan unwise. Or perhaps he was confident of victory and knew that actually the League was one of his greatest assets. At any rate, he campaigned against the League rather than the Republican Party and Alfred M. Landon, who personally went along with much of the New Deal anyway (and had once remarked that "we have too many stuffed shirts in the Republican organization").

The President opened his campaign in late September with a highly successful speech at Syracuse in which he repudiated the support of the Communists, emphasized his position as a far-sighted conservative ("Reform if you will preserve") and then told a charming story to illustrate the attitudes of his short-sighted conservative friends in the business community. "In the summer of 1933," he said, "a nice old gentleman wearing a silk hat fell off the end of a pier. He was unable to swim. A friend ran down the pier, dived overboard and pulled him out; but the silk hat floated off with the tide. After the old gentleman had been revived he was effusive in his thanks. He praised his friend for saving his life. Today, three years later, the old gentleman is berating his friend because the silk hat was lost."[40] He closed the campaign with a swing through Pennsylvania and Maryland, with a brief look at Wilmington, Delaware, "just to assure myself that the du Ponts are not broke," and ended up with a mocking, teasing, gloves-off speech at Madison Square Garden: "For twelve years this nation was afflicted with a hear-nothing, see-nothing, do-nothing Government. . . . Powerful influences strive today to restore that kind of government with its doctrine that the Government is best which is most indifferent. . . . Never before in history have these forces been so united against one candidate as they stand today. They are unanimous in their hatred for me—and I welcome their hatred."[41] Most Americans knew that Roosevelt was referring to the well-publicized leaders of the Liberty League.

Republican hopes were high in September, after a victory in Maine, where du Ponts and other members of the League spent thousands of dollars. And, after all, the *Literary Digest* poll, as well as the scientific findings of a leading Harvard statistician, had predicted a Landon victory. But on Election Day an old political myth was exploded ("As Maine goes, so goes the nation"), science was confounded and the "economic royalists" defeated, when the American people gave Roosevelt the largest Presidential plurality in history. Thus the urban-ethnic revolution was peacefully and democratically consummated in the four historic years between 1932 and 1936. In spite of the Liberty League, perhaps because of the narrow short-sightedness of its leadership, the forces of aristocratic assimilation had been given a boost, at the polls if not yet in the country clubs, in the never ending conflict with the forces of caste exclusion.

> An aristocracy in the days of its strength does not merely conduct affairs; it still directs opinions, gives their tone to the writers and authority to ideas. In the eighteenth century the French nobility had entirely lost this part of its supremacy.
>
> *Alexis de Tocqueville*

XI

The Intellectuals Abandon the Caste Establishment

In our materialistic age it is unfashionable to attribute too much autonomy to ideas as independent, rather than dependent, variables in the social and political process. On the other hand, it is impossible, I think, to have any real understanding of the New Deal years, and the schizophrenia within the ranks of the old-stock establishment during that period, without taking into account the climate of intellectual opinion at the time.

As far as the American intellectual community was concerned, the twenties were years of psychological and moral revolt from Puritan values, Main Street mores and the complacency of a cold business culture. It was an individualistic decade dominated by artists. The more collectivist and political thirties, on the other hand, were years of radicalism and reform, dominated by social scientists and socially conscious artists. The decade witnessed the decline of Freud and the rise of Marxism, as sex gave way to sociology, and internal conflicts were projected on various crusades to correct the evils of the external environment. H. L. Mencken went out of vogue (the *American Mercury* closed shop in 1934) and concerned intellectuals turned to the more politically oriented magazines of the Left. But above all, the common man, who had been just another "booboisie" and an object of scorn among the smart set, now came into his own among intellectuals of the Left who saw him as one of a chosen class, as they pinned their faith on secular religions preaching sociological salvation. And Vassar girls, having discovered the religion of art in the Village, along with sex and gin in darkened speakeasies, now came out into the open air of political and economic controversy, marching on picket lines in the cause of labor and class justice.

Perhaps the truest symptom of the differing moods of the two decades was that Edmund Wilson should have published *Axel's Castle*, a literary study of such high priests of the religion of art as Proust, Joyce and Gertrude Stein, in 1930, and *To The Finland Station*, an historical analysis of the creators of the religion of revolution, from Michelet and Marx to Lenin, in 1940. "From the fall of 1930 to the spring of 1934," Wilson has written of his career, "I spent a good deal of time reporting political and industrial events, and thereafter, till 1940, writing a study of Marxism and the Russian Revolution, so that I did not give the literary events of these years as much attention as I had given to those of the twenties or as I was afterwards to give to those of the forties."[1]

Concern for economic and political issues and sympathy for the Left, then, formed an important part of the intellectual's value system, both here and in England, during the thirties. By the end of the decade, most of the members of the American intellectual community, many of whom had first turned to the Democratic Party under Woodrow Wilson (some turned to Foster and the Communists in 1932, and to Norman Thomas and the Socialist Party in

1936), eventually allied themselves with the party of Franklin Roosevelt. "More than any other man who has been President within the memory of any of us now living," wrote Sherwood Anderson of Roosevelt, "he has made us feel close to him."

But the intellectual climate of opinion which had moved from revolt in the twenties to a more or less extreme radicalism in the early thirties, had turned toward reform by the end of the decade. Thus Sherwood Anderson, as well as Edmund Wilson, John Dos Passos and other leading intellectuals, voted for the Communist Party in 1932. Like the supporters of the Liberty League, they had lost faith in the democratic process and the possibilities of reform. Both the extreme Left and the extreme Right were hypnotized by either-or abstractions: for the League the only alternatives were pure capitalism or Communism (i.e., the New Deal and Roosevelt); for the radical Left the alternatives were pure socialism or the preservation of capitalism (i.e., the New Deal and Roosevelt). As in most revolutionary situations, unfortunately, concrete issues were polarized into abstractions, both by those who wanted nothing changed and those who wanted everything changed. Thus Al Smith, in his Mayflower speech to the Liberty Leaguers, saw the only alternatives as between "Washington or Moscow, the Star-Spangled Banner or the Internationale." While, just six months earlier, the editors of the *New Republic* had urged that "either the nation must put up with the confusion and miseries of an unregulated capitalism, or it must prepare to supersede capitalism with socialism. There is no longer a feasible middle course."[2] Both the radicals and the reactionaries, of course, were following the politics of despair.

Schizophrenia and the Sacco-Vanzetti Case

The radicalism of the early thirties and the intellectual's break with the values of the old-stock establishment came in the final days before the execution, in the summer of 1927, of two immigrant anarchists for murder in connection with an armed robbery at South Braintree, Massachusetts, back in 1921. Personal revolt was now given an external anchor in the class struggle, as it were, and the Sacco-Vanzetti Case became a legendary part of the radical myth of the thirties.

Unfortunately, like the Dreyfus case in France, the central issue of legal justice was lost sight of in the course of the world-wide and partisan ideological argument which the case aroused. As far as this book is concerned, it is not a question of whether justice was done. What is relevant here is the fact that the case became a matter of social justice centering around the issue of ethnicity and caste. It dramatized the plight of the dispossessed immigrant. And in the summer of 1927 the American establishment was split wide open over whether Sacco and Vanzetti were finally convicted on the basis of valid legal evidence or because they happened to be immigrant anarchists and a threat to the old-stock establishment's authority. On the whole, according to Francis Russell's recent book on the case, those who were solidly middle-class Republicans and read the Boston *Herald* in the morning and the *Transcript* in the afternoon thought the two "anarchist bastards," as they were unfortunately referred to by Judge Thayer, were probably guilty. University professors and other liberals, on the other hand, thought the trial at least unfair, and readers of the *New Republic* or the *Nation* were convinced that the two men were innocent. Granville Hicks, who was teaching at Smith College at the time, has written how town and gown were at swords' points over the case. And Francis Russell, who was then growing up in a Boston suburb, recalls how his father, a solid Republican lawyer, was convinced that Sacco and Vanzetti were guilty. At the same time, Russell's Aunt Amy, a social worker at the Elizabeth Peabody House, was equally convinced of the two men's innocence, as were all her co-workers. One of the proudest moments in Aunt Amy's life was when she was arrested and taken off to jail for picketing in front of the State House (she was only sorry that the policeman handled her with such politeness and deference).[3]

The case provided a social cause upon which the intellectuals could project their smoldering resentment against the whole business establishment. Edna St. Vincent Millay, for example, had come down from Vassar to the Village in the twenties to worship at the shrine of art and revolt. And just like Aunt Amy, she, along with John Dos Passos, Dorothy Parker and other intellectuals, was hauled off to the Joy Street Jail for picketing in front of the State House. Besides organizing the picketing, the Sacco-Vanzetti Defense Committee secured over half a million petitions from all over the world. The protesting petitioners in this country came largely from college campuses and law schools (both faculty and students) and included many college presidents as well as such distinguished persons as Senator Robert La Follette, Norman Thomas, Robert Hutchins, Harry Emerson Fosdick, Jane Addams, H. L. Mencken, Alfred Landon (he was a reader of the New Republic), and John Dewey.

The final conviction and execution of Sacco and Vanzetti was seen by their defenders as an indictment of the whole "system" and especially the arrogance of the defenders of the old-stock establishment. Intellectuals all over the nation identified with the eloquence of the half-educated immigrants. "I know the sentence will be between two classes," said Sacco just before Judge Thayer read the death sentence to the court, "the oppressed class and the rich class, and there will be always collision between one and the other...."[4] And the more intellectual Vanzetti, who unlike Sacco protested his innocence to the end, painted a vivid portrait of the suburban, country-club establishment which has lingered in the liberal mind to the present day: "We know that you have spoke yourself and have spoke your hostility against us, and your despisement against us with friends of yours on the train, at the University Club of Boston, on the Golf Club of Worcester, Massachusetts...."[5] And it forced men like Gardner Jackson, Secretary of the Defense Committee, and William G. Thompson, solid member of the Boston Bar and defense attorney for the accused, to despair and finally to desert their class. "It forced me," wrote Robert Morss Lovett, "to accept a doctrine which I had always repudiated as partisan tactics—the class war." "All right," said John Dos Passos, "all right, we are two nations."

As far as the significance of the Sacco-Vanzetti case is concerned, it is important, I think, to emphasize several things. In the first place, it is important to see that, by and large, that part of the American elite which had previously supported Woodrow Wilson's appointment of Brandeis to the Supreme Court also supported the cause of Sacco and Vanzetti (Senator Robert La Follette, for example). At the same time, those who identified with the New England establishment's opposition to Brandeis also supported the conviction of the two immigrant anarchists (President Lowell, for instance). This more or less consistent alignment of attitudes and values, over the years, serves to emphasize the fact that the schizophrenia within the establishment, which erupted during the thirties and continues to the present day, was deeply rooted in the ethnic conflicts of the whole twentieth century. It was not an invention of Roosevelt and the New Deal.

It is also important to emphasize the fact that the Sacco-Vanzetti myth—and myth is always a far more powerful impetus to action than reality, especially among "rational" intellectuals—was dramatized, by both radicals and conservatives, as a class war when actually, as in most revolutionary situations, it was primarily a conflict in values within the leadership community itself. For it is those leaders who interpret the will of the people, rather than the people themselves, who dramatize and create revolutions. It was Dos Passos and other intellectuals—not the residents of the "side streets" of South Braintree—who saw the Sacco-Vanzetti case as a class war between the "two nations" (and they were not immune to the Communist leaders' ability to manufacture martyrs). When Francis Russell was working on his recent book on the case, for instance, he was rather surprised to find that "all South Braintree still firmly believed that

Sacco and Vanzetti were guilty." As one South Braintree resident in his sixties who remembered the case shouted at Russell: "Why do you people still come around writing sweet stuff about those two gangsters? Why are you wasting your sympathy on them when you got none at all for that poor Mrs. Parmenter [the murdered man's wife] that lost her husband? They raised thousands of dollars for those two Eyetalians, and she got nothing. Afterwards she had no money, she lost her house. No one ever gave her a thought. . . ."[6] There was, then, no more sympathy for the "wiser-than-thou professors of Harvard and Yale" along the streets of Charlestown, Brockton and South Braintree than among the defenders of the establishment on Beacon Hill. As one representative of the side-street mind, speaking to the local Kiwanis Club at the time, put it: "It is an impressive fact that the nearer we get to the scene of this murder the more convinced are the people that these men are guilty. . . . The citizens of Norfolk County know these men are guilty. On the other hand, in those domains where foreign and un-American principles are in vogue, such as Russia, Harvard, Argentina, Wellesley, China and Smith, they are sure these men are innocent. . . ."[7] And though Bishop Lawrence had his dignified doubts about the justice of the case, and while Professor Hocking, preaching at Boston's liberal Community Church, was sure that the two defendants "were as innocent as you or I," perhaps Billy Sunday had a realistic understanding of the side-street mind. "Give 'em the juice," roared Sunday as he pounded on the pulpit. "Burn them if they're guilty. That's the way to handle it. I'm tired of hearing these foreigners, these radicals, coming over here and telling us what we should do."[8]

In attempting to place the Sacco-Vanzetti Case in more objective perspective, I do not intend to minimize its importance as a mythic event which prepared the liberal mind in America for the revolutionary decade of the thirties. My purpose, rather, is to emphasize the fact that the case was more an example of schizophrenia within the ranks of the establishment itself than a matter of class conflict, which so many radical intellectuals, and especially the Communist propagandists, were so intent on having one believe at the time. For civil liberties are almost always defended and valued by members of an elite and not by the masses of men; by reformers and not by radicals. And this is of great importance, I think, because it partly explains why the revolutionary changes which were brought about in this country during the thirties never degenerated into a totalitarian dictatorship. The New Deal was led from the top by reformers who were alienated from the caste values of the old-stock Republican establishment but who were at the same time firmly rooted in a tradition of civil liberties. The nature and source of leadership may make all the difference between reform and the retention of freedom, and revolution which so often descends into despotism.

The New Social Science and Liberal Orthodoxy

At any rate, the liberal intellectual community's alienation from the values of the old-stock Republican establishment, dramatized in the Sacco-Vanzetti myth, was reinforced by the collapse of the business system soon afterward. Many "lost their bearings," as Edmund Wilson put it, and, "impressed by the achievements of the Soviet Union," entered the Communist Party for brief periods. Few, however, were able to stand the stultifying rigidity of party discipline for any length of time (seven thousand members or one-third of the party, resigned after the election of 1934). And in the meantime, a strictly native brand of radicalism was coming to the fore, led by the editors of such liberal magazines as the *New Republic* and *Common Sense*, and such patriarchs of the Progressive-Liberal tradition as John Dewey and Charles A. Beard.

Alfred Bingham was an excellent example of an American aristocrat who turned to the Left during the thirties. Son of a highly conservative United States Senator from Connecticut and a graduate of Groton and Yale, Bingham visited Russia in 1931 and was much impressed with what he saw there. After his return from Russia, he founded *Common Sense* (1932) and then wrote *Insurgent America* (1935), one of the most influential books of the decade. Although convinced that his father's world was doomed, Bingham was nevertheless unwilling to accept the Communist solution as applicable to the American situation. He felt that there was still life in the middle class and looked forward to some kind of technological utopia, in accord with the predictions in Edward Bellamy's *Looking Backward*.

It was symptomatic of the spirit of the thirties that, early in 1935, when Beard, Dewey and Edward Weeks of the *Atlantic Monthly* made independent selections of the most important books of the last half-century, *Das Kapital* (first English edition, 1886), *The Golden Bough* (1890), and *Looking Backward* (1888) headed each list.

Edward Bellamy was an incorrigible idealist, a child of the Enlightenment who believed in the natural goodness of man, and also a materialist who was repelled by the vulgar individualism of the Gilded Age. In *Looking Backward*, Edward Bellamy created a utopian world dominated by One Big National Trust, run by experts (social engineers) in the interests of all rather than for the profit of the few. In this materialistic paradise, he visualized the efficient production of an ever increasing supply of consumer goods, more and more skyscrapers, bigger and better restaurants, streets covered with waterproof material in wet weather, the abolition of the servant problem, compulsory retirement for all at age forty-five, and "music by telephone." While this utopia "out-socialized the socialists," it had great middle-class appeal because Bellamy carefully dissociated himself from Red Flag Socialism ("the word socialist is one I could never quite stomach") and visualized the gradual advent of a material paradise, without revolution or class war, and free of all intolerance. The replacement of the profit motive and organized greed by the scientific method would, of course, eventually "eliminate all crime, waste and fraud." But above all, the new society was to allow men to express their true nature. "Human nature," as one of the characters in *Looking Backward* put it, "in its essential qualities is good, not bad . . . men by their natural intention and structure are generous, not selfish, pitiful, not cruel, sympathetic, not arrogant, godlike in aspirations, instinct with divinest impulses of tenderness and self-sacrifice, images of God indeed, not the travesties upon Him they seem. . . ."

Looking Backward soon became the most popular American book since *Uncle Tom's Cabin*. By 1890, it was still selling at the rate of ten thousand copies a week and was being translated into many languages. Bellamy's Boston friends founded a magazine, the *Nationalist*, to propagate his ideas, and Nationalist clubs spread throughout the nation and abroad. *Looking Backward* became the bible of Progressives: Thorstein Veblen read it aloud to his wife, and Henry Demarest Lloyd was convinced that "we must now achieve the Social Utopias of Christ, Thomas More, Mazzini, Bellamy and Howells. . . ."

In many ways, of course, Bellamy popularized in fictional form the basic assumptions and ideals of the New Social Science which Beard, Dewey, Veblen and other serious scholars were developing at the same time. As an indication that these ideas had reached the status of secure orthodoxies, *Looking Backward* had a great revival in the early thirties and new Bellamy societies sprang up all over the land. Heywood Broun wrote a "Back to Bellamy" column. And, as another index of the Bellamy influence, it is interesting that an admirer and biographer of Bellamy was Arthur E. Morgan, idealistic engineer, leader in the Unitarian Church and the progressive-education movement, president of Antioch College, and chairman of the Tennessee Valley Authority in its New Nationalism phase.

But the importance attributed to *Das Kapital* and *The Golden Bough* was even more indicative of the dominant place now held by the social sciences in the intellectual climate of opinion of the thirties. Both books laid great stress on environment, rather than race or heredity, as the independent variable in the formation of personality, the creation of religions and value systems, and in determining the direction of social change. Indeed, the environmental concepts of *culture* (anthropology), *class* (sociology) and *ideology* (sociology) were central to the liberal *Weltanschauung* of the 1930's. Just as the Freudian theory of ideas had shown that *truths* were largely *rationalizations*, rooted in the emotional life of the individual thinker, so the findings of social science now convinced men that *truths* were merely *ideologies* projecting or reflecting the cultural conditioning of classes of intellectuals.

These views of truth, of course, were thoroughly grounded in the scientific findings of experimental psychology. Thus the concept of the conditioned reflex was discovered before the First War when a brilliant and aristocratic Russian of the old regime, I. P. Pavlov, showed that dogs do not associate by rational thought or according to any inborn instincts, but largely as a result of their conditioning. At the same time, in this country, a rural South Carolinian, John B. Watson, who mistrusted philosophic introspection and the existence of any such thing as an inner conscience, founded Behaviorism which, by the end of the twenties, was not only the most fashionable school of psychology in this country but also became the central theory of human nature upon which the great industry of advertising was being built. It was no wonder that Pavlov was treated with great deference and respect by the Bolshevik revolutionists, and that Watson eventually left Johns Hopkins to become a vice president of one of the nation's most successful advertising agencies. Faith in conditioning became the basis of social control in the new manipulative society, composed of citizen comrades in the U.S.S.R. and citizen consumers in the U.S.A.

The central ideas of the New Social Science, largely developed before the First War (see Chapter VII), finally came into their own as the dominant view of man and society, in the course of the thirties. The decade witnessed the complete triumph of naturalistic relativism over transcendental absolutism; theology was replaced by anthropology; and the universalism of the inner consciences of men gave way before the particularistic conditioning of the external environment. The popularity of Marxian socialism on the Left was quite understandable because it was, after all, only an extreme example of a naturalistic environmentalism which most educated men in the West adhered to anyway. For they now shared John Dewey's faith in the plasticity of human nature and the possibility of progress if only the environment could be reformed or transformed through social engineering in order to allow the natural goodness of human nature to express itself fully, unfettered by the harmful conditioning of a competitive, bourgeois culture.

As the founder of modern anthropology, E. B. Tylor, and Thorstein Veblen had predicted back in the nineteenth century, the idea of culture, now reinforced by scientific psychologies, was indeed a revolutionary concept. And it is important to see that the New Deal's efforts to change the economic and cultural environment, largely through legislating greater equality of conditions between classes of men, were a reflection of the whole intellectual climate of opinion at the time. In almost every area of intellectual endeavor—in the theories of crime, in law, in religion, and in the arts—there was general agreement as to the sickness of the bourgeois society and the need for environmental reform.

The leaders of organized religion, for example, were alienated from the business establishment and calling for change. In 1934, when 21,000 clergymen were asked whether capitalism or a "cooperative commonwealth" was more in accord with the ideals of Jesus Christ, only 5 per cent chose capitalism; of the other 95 per cent, 10,000 came out for a "drastically reformed capitalism," and 6,000 declared outright for socialism. At about the same time, the Protestant Episcopal House of Bishops resolved that Christ demanded a new order "which shall substitute the motive of service for the motive of gain." The hierarchies of the Church had indeed come a long way from the ideas of Henry Ward Beecher or Bruce Barton's theories of Jesus Christ as the "first businessman" which were so wildly popular during the Coolidge era.

In literature also there was a radical criticism of the social environment from the point of view of environmental naturalism. Among the important books of the decade, none were more symptomatic of the mood of the times than John Dos Passos' *U.S.A.* trilogy, published between 1930 and 1936, and the works of James T. Farrell, whose trilogy *Studs Lonigan* (published between 1932 and 1935) won a Book-of-the-Month-Club prize in 1937. Dos Passos finally embraced a theoretical Marxism because of his aesthetic disillusionment, first with the brutalities and futilities of industrial civilization and then with the injustices of the Sacco-Vanzetti case. His was an aristocratic revolt from the whole success ethic which he had learned from his family (his father was a first-generation millionaire and highly successful lawyer) and his education at Choate School and Harvard ("get A's in some courses but don't be a grind be interested in literature but remain a gentleman don't be seen with Jews or socialists and all pleasant contacts will be useful in Later Life say hello pleasantly to everybody crossing the yard . . .").[9] In the *U.S.A.* trilogy, Dos Passos painted in vivid strokes the environment he so resented, but even the main characters tended to be rather weakly drawn stereotypes (white-collar girls, public-relations counselors, or radical laboring men). And all of them, whether of high or low estate, were eventually defeated by the evils of "the system."

While John Dos Passos represented the revolt of the aristocratic aesthete, James Farrell was probably the best example of a group of proletarian writers (John Steinbeck, Clifford Odets, Richard Wright and Nelson Algren, for example) who came to the fore during the thirties. It was, of course, far more natural for men who had themselves grown up among the lower classes to see the evils of environment in corrupting the characters of men (by and large, the successful rationalize their position in biological terms, and the failures their position in terms of environment). Farrell was one of the best-educated novelists of his generation, especially in philosophy and the social sciences. And he consequently broke away from his Catholic heritage with its transcendental faith in free will and embraced the naturalistic determinism of the social sciences. Most of his characters were passive, and often pathetic, products of a world they never made.

Though, as Farrell himself has pointed out, this naturalistic view of man had been explicitly outlined by Emile Zola and had had one of its leading exponents in Theodore Dreiser (whose best work was done, and often suppressed, before the First War), it is nevertheless important to see that, by the decade of the thirties, this view of man had pervaded virtually the entire intellectual community. Most educated men were reading with approval the work of Dewey, Beard, Veblen and Boas, and their followers in the social sciences like Robert and Helen Lynd, Ruth Benedict, Margaret Mead, and Thurman Arnold (professor at the progressive Yale Law School and Assistant Attorney General in 1938), whose books *The Symbols of Government* (1935) and *The Folklore of Capitalism* (1937) brilliantly combined the cultural determinism of the social sciences with the legal realism and sociological jurisprudence of Holmes, Brandeis and Roscoe Pound.

Environmental naturalism, of course, served the interests of the downtrodden and especially the cause of recent immigrants who were struggling to assimilate into the main stream of our national life and culture. Indeed, in attributing the differences between men as being due to their cultural conditioning rather than to any innate racial or ethnic characteristics, the assumptions of social science were apparently in accord with the idea of aristocracy rather than caste. After all, George Bernard Shaw, who dramatized the advanced ideas of his time for the educated members of the middle class just as Voltaire had once done for the educated aristocrats of his day, had read and been impressed by Pavlov before writing his most successful play, *Pygmalion* (1912), in order to show that fair ladies could be produced even from cockney genes if only the science of cultural conditioning were properly applied.

But, as was shown in earlier pages, scientific naturalism cut two ways. While our own social scientists were working with the assumptions of the plasticity of human nature and the importance of environmental conditioning, social scientists across the Atlantic in Germany (one of the most literate and scientific cultures on earth) were coming to just the opposite conclusions. Thus, if the Marxian inspired revolution in Russia and the reforms supported by social science in this country were based on the assumptions of more or less extreme forms of environmentalism, the Nazi ideologists were, at the same time, elevating the concept of race as the major assumption in support of their attempts at a world counterrevolution. The naturalistic views of the nature of man finally came of age in the 1930's, in the radical dreams of environmental utopias on the one hand, and the reactionary dreams of a racial utopia on the other.

If *Mein Kampf* was the old testament of Nazi scientism, Alfred Rosenberg's *Myth of the Twentieth Century* was the new testament. Outlined in 1917, finished in 1925, and first published in 1930, this new testament of Nazism went through 142 editions and sold over 700,000 copies by 1938. "The Myth of the Twentieth Century," according to Rosenberg, "is the myth of blood, which under the sign of the Swastika unchains the racial world-revolution. It is the awakening of the race soul, which after long sleep victoriously ends the race chaos."[10]

Perhaps it was inevitable that the racial scientism of Nazi Germany should have reached its most fantastic and antihuman peak in its policies of anti-Semitism. For Rosenberg's theories were in direct revolt against environmentalism: German morals and culture could never be acquired by Jews or Slavs, whose stock was so innately inferior to that of their Nordic neighbors. And it was this extreme view, and the attempts at the "final solution" of the world's problems through racial segregation and extermination, that drove so many intellectuals here and in England into the Popular Front movement against fascism as the thirties came to a close and the Second World War began. Many leading social scientists came out of their ivory towers and lectured and wrote pamphlets against the whole concept of racialism. In the course of this highly emotional counteroffensive, some even went so far as to say that there "was no such thing as human nature" or "race."

Professor E. A. Ross' autobiography, *Seventy Years of It*, published in 1936, provided an interesting index of the changed climate of intellectual opinion in this country since the turn of the century (see Chapter IV for Ross' earlier views). Thus Professor Ross, who had the courage to admit his loss of "faith in Race as the key to social interpretation," wrote the following interesting paragraphs in an age which was passing through both the pragmatic Roosevelt reforms as well as the fanatic Nazi revolution:

> In an article I published in The Independent for November, 1904, "The Value Rank of the American People," I characterized some of our immigrants from Eastern Europe as "the beaten members of beaten breeds." I rue this sneer.
>
> Difference of race means far less to me now than it once did. Starting ... with the naïve feeling that only my own race is right, all other races are more or less "queer," I gained insight and sympathy until my heart overleapt barriers of race.
>
> Far behind me in the ditch lies the Nordic Myth, which had some fascination for me forty years ago....[11]

Even ardent eugenicists were forced to modify extreme positions they might have once held because of the use and misuse of eugenics by the Nazis. Thus, in a definitive analysis of the eugenics movement, one of its aristocratic leaders, Frederick Osborn, was probably influenced by the majority of his colleagues in the social sciences when he judiciously wrote as follows:

> But belief in the influence of heredity over-reached itself when it was used—as it still is all too often—to justify the continued domination of some particular caste.... So resentment on the subject of hereditary classes is very near the surface. It is well to have it so in a country that is both liberal and democratic. Democracy needs all the leadership which can be found, and leadership is to be found in every class....

Americans, more than any other people, have hoped to improve man by improving his environment. Few of us have failed to take some part in this noble effort. . . . Recently it has come to be recognized that eugenics is not in opposition to efforts to improve the environment, but in many cases a necessary supplement to their success. . . .[12]

The leftward trend and emphasis on environment, both in this country and in England, then, was partly a reaction (and over-reaction) to the tragic, hereditarian ideologies of National Socialism. If the left-wing intellectual could rightly be blamed for his all too easy sympathy for Marxian socialism, the so-called "best people" within the establishment were equally guilty of a too easy sympathy for the Nazis. While the intellectual Left tended to see fascism behind every move of the business establishment, the members of the Liberty League saw every New Deal reform as an example of communism. If the average American intellectual tended to be pro-Semitic (and at the same time rigidly anti-Catholic), so the average member of the country-club set was naturally anti-Semitic.

Fortunately, however, the American people entered the Second War as a more or less unified nation. And the thirties passed without any violent revolution, as Franklin D. Roosevelt succeeded in guiding the nation along a conservative and reforming course which avoided the ideological rigidities of either Berlin or Moscow, of either the Liberty League or the Communist Party U.S.A. And most intellectuals would finally have agreed with the aristocratic theory implied in the following statement made by Roosevelt in the course of his campaign for the Presidency in 1932:

Say that civilization is a tree which, as it grows, continually produces rot and dead wood. The radical says: "Cut it down." The conservative says: "Don't touch it." The liberal compromises: "Let's prune it, so that we lose neither the old trunk nor the new branches."[13]

276

The blood-dimmed tide is loosed, and everywhere
The ceremony of innocence is drowned;
The best lack all conviction, while the worst
Are full of passionate intensity.

William Butler Yeats

XII

The Postwar Status Revolution: The Caste Establishment on the Defensive

Walter Bagehot, in the introduction to his brilliant analysis of the British Constitution observed that the political battles culminating in the Reform Bill of 1832 were not really "won" or made a permanent part of the British social structure until the 1860's. His point was that economic and social reforms are usually accomplished, in the long run, more through generational change than simply through political enactments. Similarly, I think, it is also true that the economic reforms of one generation tend to produce status conflicts in the next. Thus, the class revolutions of the Depression years have been translated into the status revolutions of our age of affluence. The class conflicts of the thirties produced a radical Left, while the caste conflicts of the forties and fifties have now produced a radical Right.

The Postwar Status Revolution

There are many indications of this change in generational interest. The important Supreme Court decisions before the war were primarily concerned with economic issues and class conflict, focusing on the proper interpretation of the Fourteenth Amendment. Since the war, the most controversial decisions have had to do with civil rights, the status conflicts of a multigroup society, and the interpretation of the Bill of Rights. While the liberals in the thirties saw the Constitution, following Charles A. Beard, as the defender of a cynical conspiracy to protect the economic privileges of the business community, in the forties and fifties these same men have come to revere the Constitution as the eternal guardian of civil liberties. While the radical Left once saw their dreams of reforms frustrated by the "nine old men," the radical Right now wants to "impeach Earl Warren." In both cases, of course, the Constitution and the Court were only serving the function they were designed to serve, protecting minorities and preserving the long-range view.

There were many other examples of this new emphasis on civil rights. Whereas the subject of "civil rights" does not appear in the indexes of any of the three volumes of Arthur M. Schlesinger, Jr.'s brilliant *Age of Roosevelt*, it would be hard to imagine this to be the case in a comparable history of our postwar period. As another indication of the growth of interest in civil rights, it is interesting that the membership rolls of the NAACP dropped during the business boom from 90,000 in 1921 to 21,000 in 1929, rose slowly during the New Deal Years to some 50,000 by 1940, and then jumped to almost 500,000 by 1960. In sports, a man named John Roosevelt Robinson led a major revolution in our national pastime, and another talented Negro, Levi Jackson, was elected captain of the Yale football team and tapped for Skull and Bones ("If my name had been reversed, I never would have made it," said Jackson, with a smile, which illustrated both his sense of humor and how members of minority groups are all too aware of their common opposition to the forces of caste). And finally, it should be remembered that, while President Roosevelt set up a Fair Employment Practice Committee during the war, it was President Truman who really put teeth in it (the first State FEPC law was put through in New York in 1945). And it was Truman who first integrated our armed services, during the Korean war, and—for the first time in American history—ordered that prominent Negroes be officially invited to the top social events of his inauguration in 1948.

If the civil-rights issue was playing an increasingly important role in our domestic politics, it was also becoming a more and more vital international issue. For the racial revolution is very closely allied to the world economic revolution. Racial humiliation is as degrading as poverty, and aspirations for racial dignity as important as those for a higher standard of living. And, as everybody knows by this time, the Americans around the world who segregate themselves from the "natives" in isolated islands of country-club narcissism have done more to neutralize the efforts of our expensive foreign-aid programs than all the Communist propaganda put together. For it is not only a question of meeting the rising levels of economic expectation among the lower classes in the underdeveloped nations of Latin America, Asia and Africa; it is of equal, and perhaps even greater, importance that American leaders learn to accept a world *elite* revolution, in which the upper classes in underdeveloped nations, whose members are often polished and cultivated graduates of Oxford, the Sorbonne and Harvard, will surely no longer stand for the traditional Anglo-Saxon assertions of caste superiority. But, unfortunately, the country-club narcissism of Americans abroad is but a reflection of our racial and caste values here at home.

The nature of this problem was revealed when Angier Biddle

Duke of the Department of State was forced to resign from the distinguished Metropolitan Club, in Washington, because its admission policies interfered with his interpretation of his duties as Chief of Protocol.

A product of both the plutocratic (Duke) and aristocratic (Biddle) traditions in this country, Duke's own career nicely illustrates the contrast between the caste and aristocratic values as defined in this book. After graduating from St. Paul's and coming down from Yale without a degree, he spent the prewar years as a more or less typical clubman and socialite in New York's Republican, Social Register caste which extends from Southampton and Tuxedo Park to Palm Beach. After a distinguished career in the army during the war, he returned to use his great talents and energy in a wide variety of positions of public responsibility, both governmental and private, especially in the field of international relations. Perhaps it was natural that he should eventually take an active interest in politics as a Democrat. He had long admired his uncle Anthony Drexel Biddle, who had been one of Franklin Roosevelt's trusted public servants. At any rate, after serving as U.S. Ambassador to El Salvador under presidents Truman and Eisenhower (1952–53), Duke returned to New York, where he took an increasingly active part in Democratic Party politics (Chairman, New York State Democratic Convention Committee, 1954). He contributed money and campaigned vigorously in 1960 for his good friend Senator Kennedy, and hoped to be rewarded with an important post in the government. With his new dedication to serious public service, he was hardly pleased when he was offered the cookie-pushing, protocol position, which would have been more appropriate in his socialite days (he turned the job down twice). He finally accepted the position when Secretary Rusk convinced him that his responsibilities would extend far beyond the purely ceremonial.

Rusk was right. The present office of the Chief of Protocol is no longer a cookie-pushing section of State but a veritable department of international human relations.[1] Under Duke's leadership, the section doubled in size, and is now doing more social research and engaging in more delicate social action than many departments of sociology in our larger urban universities. In the past, the protocol section limited itself largely to formal apologies for embarrassing incidents which non-Anglo-Saxon diplomats have always encountered in this country. But with so many newly established African embassies in Washington, Duke had to introduce positive programs of social change. He not only had to change diplomatically the housing and restaurant prejudices of semisegregated Washington; his reforms reached out all over the nation, especially along Route 40, which had come to be known as "Incident Highway" because so many diplomats had been refused service in restaurants while traveling between the U.N. and the Capital.

But the new Chief of Protocol, debonair as Fred Astaire and wise to the ways of the world, is no radical. "I hated all that publicity over my resignation from the Metropolitan, especially as I think it is the finest club I've ever belonged to," Duke said in an interview. "I just do not feel I can go along with their policy of automatically extending an honorary membership to the British Ambassador while at the same time categorically refusing the Ambassador from Sierra Leone, for instance. As much as I hated to do it, I had to take a stand on this issue as long as I intended to do the best job I knew how for the country." Duke, in other words, is convinced that caste has no place in a world where aristocratic assimilation is now demanded, both at home and abroad, in a world revolution of major proportions.

Duke is only one example of a whole new generation of old-stock aristocrats who went to Washington to serve in the Kennedy Administration, just as an older generation had once done in Roosevelt's day. The nature of this second Democratic generation, and its contribution to building a new and ethnically heterogeneous establishment in this country, will be discussed in some detail in the next chapter. In the meantime, I should like to show how the schizophrenia in the American establishment, which began with the New Deal, degenerated still further in the tragic era of McCarthyism.

Caste, Conspiracy and McCarthyism

The American democracy, ethnically heterogeneous, egalitarian, highly mobile, and insecure in so many ways, has always been all too prone to accept the conspiracy theory of history. The very use of the term "Hundred Per Cent Americanism" implies a suspicion of conspiracy among those less American than thee and me. The American people were, of course, unified during the Second World War in their common opposition to an evil conspiracy led by the Nazis and the Japanese. But our wars have usually been followed by periods of nativist hysteria and panic directed against internal conspirators. After the First War, as we have seen, the nation repudiated all the ideals Woodrow Wilson stood for and then proceeded to go on an hysterical hunt for anarchists, bombthrowers, Communists, and various other lower-class conspirators, which ended in the final closing of the gates to immigration in 1921–24. After the Second War, however, the expected hysteria and nativism were focused, not on lower-class conspirators or the un-Americanism of Catholics and Jews, but rather, and perhaps with far more destructive consequences, on the conspirators within the ranks of the old-stock and respectable upper class. This was indeed something new.

It all began in the summer of 1948 when Whittaker Chambers, an admitted ex-Communist agent, bravely risked a hard-won respectable career as a senior editor at *Time* magazine when he accused Alger Hiss of treasonable activities in passing on information to Communist agents during the New Deal years (1934–38). Alger Hiss' fastidiously respectable bearing and Social Register background, his friendship with the "best people"—including Dean Acheson and John Foster Dulles, who had recommended him as president of the Carnegie Endowment for International Peace—his probably overplayed part in both the New Deal leadership and the subsequent formation of the United Nations, all attested to his secure position within the old-stock establishment. And he was fervently defended, and his case financed, by some of the "best people." "A striking number of socialites and corporation executives," writes Eric Goldman, "who hated the New Deal, not to speak of Communism, doggedly defended the image of Alger Hiss, the respectable success, against the image of Whittaker Chambers, the grubby upstart."[2] After all, if a man like Hiss was a traitor, whom could one trust? Most important of all, the tragic tale of Alger Hiss soon became a symbol of "twenty years of treason" to the ideals of Americanism led by New Deal "eggheads." At the same time, the eggheads also fell for the theory of conspiracy: many refused to face the evidence, and most never forgave Richard Nixon for his part in the case. At all events, the Hiss case made fascinating and frightening headlines for over a year before his final conviction for perjury on two counts, in January, 1950.

And it was in that same month of January, 1950, that an obscure Senator from the State of Wisconsin (he was mostly known for his work in behalf of the Pepsi-Cola and Lustron corporations), while dining at the Colony Restaurant in Washington, hit upon the idea that there was political mileage and publicity to be made out of the issue of Communism in High Places.

Senator Joseph R. McCarthy was the most ruthless and skillful demagogue ever to rise to power on the national scene in America.[3] Born of humble Irish-Catholic parents, and driven by resentment, he was, from the beginning, willing to go to any lengths in order to attain his ends. He was a New Deal Democrat before turning to the Republican Party ("It was an advantage to be a Republican with a Democratic name"). He deceived his first law partner when he ran for office after they had both agreed it was his partner's turn; he smeared his opponent with lies about his unfitness for office because of old age; he first went to the Senate by defeating the distinguished son of the great La Follette, after a pseudo-patriotic campaign built on his false war record and, incidentally, with the support of the Communist Party in Milwaukee; and then, years after the war, he was awarded the Purple Heart for a leg injury he had suffered in a crossing-the-Equator party, and the Distinguished Flying Cross for twenty-five missions against the enemy, which he never made. But the Senator was liberated from ordinary morality and delighted in the grand falsehood.

After his discovery of the threat of communism while dining at the Colony restaurant in Washington, McCarthy went to the Republican campaign headquarters, where he asked to be placed on their Lincoln's Birthday speaking list. His first assignment was to speak to a small, women's Republican club in Wheeling, West Virginia. Pointing to some papers in his hand, his characteristic way of suggesting that he had concrete evidence gathered by careful research, he announced that he had the names of 205 (or 81 or 57) Communists in the State Department. The exact details of what he said that night will never be known; the speech was conveniently misplaced. But the State Department was an ideal target, for, as every red-blooded American knows, it has always been heavily staffed with blue-blooded Ivy Leaguers from privileged families along the Eastern Seaboard. That McCarthy was off on a crusade to uncover an old-stock conspiracy was made clear by the following paragraph he later had inserted in the Congressional Record:

The reason why we find ourselves in a position of impotency . . . is the traitorous actions of those who have been treated so well by this nation. It is not the less fortunate or members of minority groups who have been selling this nation out but rather those who have had all the benefits the wealthiest nation on earth has had to offer—the finest homes, the finest college educations, and the finest jobs in the government that we can give. This is glaringly true of the State Department. There the bright young men who are born with silver spoon [sic] in their mouth are the ones who have been worse [sic].[4]

The crusade against conspiracy was on. Within a month of the Wheeling speech, "McCarthyism" was added to the language, and by the end of the summer no man was closer than McCarthy "to the center of American consciousness or more central to the world's consciousness of America." All who opposed him, and tragically few dared, were soon driven from power. He began with Millard Tydings, Maryland patrician of enormous wealth, possessed of an authentic record of great heroism in the First War, and a member of the Senate's inner circle. Though Franklin Roosevelt had failed to defeat Tydings, whom he considered a reactionary, in 1938, the forces of McCarthyism, by smearing him as pro-Communist, drove him out of office in 1950. And for four years, presidents Truman and Eisenhower had to take into account McCarthy's possible reactions to any of their plans for action, both at home and abroad.

At the very core of the conspiracy, of course, were two important leaders in foreign policy, George C. Marshall and Dean Acheson. Thus Senator McCarthy found Marshall, the South's greatest aristocrat since Robert E. Lee, to be a man "steeped in falsehood . . . who has recourse to the lie whenever it suits his convenience . . . and [part of] a conspiracy so immense and an infamy so black as to dwarf any previous venture in the history of man. . . ."[5] And Acheson, whom the red-blooded McCarthy found to be a "pompous diplomat in striped pants, with a phony British accent," was especially vulnerable after his hardly public-relations-minded refusal, because of Christian principles derived from a reading of Matthew, 25: 34–36, to turn his back on Alger Hiss. And for four years, anyone who disagreed with McCarthy automatically was branded a member of the treasonous "Acheson Gang."

The final round in this tragic era of treason and conspiracy came when some 20 million Americans were mesmerized by McCarthy's television investigation of the integrity of the United States Army, in the course of which General Ralph Zwicker, hero of the Battle of the Bulge, was called by McCarthy a "disgrace to the uniform" and a "shielder of Communist conspirators," and Secretary of the Army Stevens, impeccable, old-stock Yankee-Yaleman, was subject to a humiliating and disgraceful public cross-examination.

McCarthyism surely represented a brand of traditional populism which has, of course, always been prone to seize on some conspiratorial theory of history. For the Senator was popular among the people, if not among the better-educated classes. In a Gallup Poll, taken in January, 1954, 50 per cent of the respondents were found to have a "favorable opinion" of his work, only 29 per cent were opposed, and the rest had "no opinion."[6] In another study, he was found to be most popular among manual laborers and small businessmen and least popular among professionals and executives.[7] That McCarthyism was partly grounded in an appeal to ethnic resentment against the arrogance of the old-stock establishment was nicely indicated when the old-stock Republican Senator from Massachusetts, Henry Cabot Lodge, asked the Democratic Governor Paul A. Dever how people felt about McCarthyism. "Your people don't think much of him," Dever replied, "but I'm afraid mine do."[8] Indeed, Governor Dever's followers in the Boston Irish-Catholic community, who had bitterly battled the old-stock brahmins symbolized by the Lodges for several generations, were avid supporters of Senator McCarthy's campaign against the Hiss-Acheson, egghead conspiracy. Joseph P. Kennedy, for example, was not only a personal friend of McCarthy but had also contributed financially to his campaign for re-election in Wisconsin.[9] At the same time, his son Robert Kennedy admired McCarthy personally and served on his committee, at least until Cohn and Schine, whom he distrusted from the beginning, finally went too far in their book-burning tour of Europe. In fact, if McCarthy had come into Massachusetts to campaign for Lodge (which he told Joseph P. Kennedy he would have to do if asked) he might have swung enough Irish-

Catholic voters away from the Democratic Party to defeat John F. Kennedy.[10] It is a tribute to Lodge that he stood by his principles rather than win at any cost and did not make the request (Lodge and McCarthy, as might be expected, had no love for one another).

What was new about McCarthyism, then, was that it was a calculated attack on the loyalty of members of the Anglo-Saxon establishment rather than members of minority communities. There were, for instance, no traces of the usual populist theories of a Jewish Conspiracy. Two of McCarthy's closest associates, in fact, were Jews of the new, postwar generation who apparently turned to a cynical conservatism in reaction to the "bleeding-heart liberalism" of so many of their fathers' generation in the thirties. Thus Roy Cohn,* educated at private schools and Columbia, was the son of a successful Democratic Judge in New York, and David Schine, a graduate of Andover and Harvard, was the spoiled heir to a hotel-chain fortune. At a massive rally at Madison Square Garden, these two Jews were enthusiastically cheered and suggested as possible Presidential candidates by the assembled crowd of McCarthyites. All this is not to say, of course, that the Jewish community supported McCarthyism. On the contrary, the vast majority of Jews were violently opposed. For, in the first place, they had always strongly identified with the liberalism of the New Deal, and secondly they feared McCarthy as a possible leader of outright fascism. Even though the late Senator Lehman openly challenged McCarthy, few other prominent Jews—for much the same reasons as Lodge's successor as Senator from Massachusetts—were in a secure enough position to speak out against the Senator from Wisconsin.

* Cohn, who participated in the Rosenberg case, had been involved in the Communist conspiracy long before McCarthy entered the picture. In this connection, it is indicative of the climate of opinion at the time that the Rosenberg case, which apparently involved far more dangerous examples of espionage than the passing of classified documents between Hiss and Chambers back in the thirties, did not attract McCarthy nor make anywhere near the same stir in the headlines as the Hiss case.

The Function of an Establishment

In so many ways the rise of McCarthyism was a test case for the theory of the establishment which has been developed throughout this book. In the first place, McCarthy's demagoguery was allowed to go so far partly because it came at a time when established authority was declining in America and being replaced with what I have called, in an earlier chapter, the manipulative society. Cleveland Amory, whose own roots are deep in the New England old-stock establishment, has documented the rise of this new society which he has, in accord with the tone of our times, not been averse to exploiting for his own profit. Thus he and his associates have recently compiled what they call a *Celebrity Register*. Here some two thousand members of the postwar international elite are listed in alphabetical order which finds the philosopher Mortimer Adler followed by Polly Adler, Dwight Eisenhower preceding Anita Ekberg, ex-President Herbert Hoover following torch singer Libby Holman, Pope John XXIII coming after Mr. John the hat designer, and Bertrand Russell followed by Jane Russell. The criteria for inclusion in this atomistic elite were highly objective and in accord with the latest quantitative values of social science. "We think we have a better yardstick than the *Social Register*, or *Who's Who*, or any such book," Amory and his associates cynically explain. "Our point is that it is impossible to be accurate in listing a man's social standing—even if anyone cared; and it's impossible to list accurately the success or value of men; but you *can* judge a man as a celebrity —all you have to do is weigh his press clippings."[11]

Senator McCarthy was able to produce the heaviest pile of "press clippings" of them all. He was able to dominate and intimidate the atomized leadership of the supposedly most powerful nation on earth for almost half a decade precisely because he was an amoral master of publicity in a manipulative society. Apparently, moreover, the "indiscriminate objectivity" of a free press, one of the major means of public relations in a manipulative society, proved to be no more of a protection against McCarthyism than the power of the popular will. In fact, though most of the owners and reporters were opposed to McCarthy, the faith of the American press in fact rather than truth actually contributed to his rise to power. Richard Rovere reveals the absurdity of the manipulative society in the following description of the press' reaction to McCarthy's methods:

He [McCarthy] knew how to get into the news even on those rare occasions when invention failed him and he had no un-facts to give out. For example, he invented the morning press conference called for the purpose of announcing an afternoon press conference. The reporters would come in—they were beginning, in this period, to respond to his summonses like Pavlov's dogs at the clang of a bell —and McCarthy would say that he just wanted to give them the word that he expected to be ready with a shattering announcement later in the day, for use in the papers the following morning. This would gain him a headline in the afternoon papers: "NEW MCCARTHY REVELATIONS AWAITED IN CAPITAL." Afternoon would come, and if McCarthy had something, he would give it out, but often enough he had nothing, and this was a matter of slight concern. He would simply say that he wasn't quite ready, that he was having difficulty in getting some of the "documents" he needed or that a "witness" was proving elusive. Morning headlines: "DELAY SEEN IN MCCARTHY CASE—MYSTERY WITNESS BEING SOUGHT."[12]

No wonder that even the staid and conservative New York Times looked back upon its own coverage of the McCarthy era and admitted that it had done its readers a great, if unavoidable, disservice through its objective reporting of fact.

Unfortunately, the manipulative society which made McCarthyism possible, if not inevitable, was a tragic symptom of the schizophrenia which first split the establishment during the New Deal years and which widened during the age of conspiracy after the war. For McCarthy was after all only carrying to its logical conclusion a theory of conspiracy which many respectable members of the old-

stock establishment had held ever since Al Smith had been cheered
by his millionaire audience at the Mayflower Dinner in Washington in 1936, when he told them that the followers of "Moscow"
were in control of the federal government. After the war, moreover,
that part of the old-stock establishment which centered in the wing
of the Republican Party led by Senator Taft was still consumed by
a violent hatred of all the New Deal and Roosevelt had stood for.
And the cries of "twenty years of treason" began to circulate among
the respectable members of the best clubs and executive suites of
the nation. In the meantime, Senator Taft had been rightfully hurt
by his party's rejection of his leadership in favor of Thomas E.
Dewey in 1948, and horrified at Truman's subsequent victory. Thus,
while Taft had always been a good loser as well as a good winner,
and had rarely been given to holding personal grudges, this was
indeed, as a sympathetic biographer has put it, "The Sad, Worst
Period" in his life.[13] And so he lent his great prestige to a tacit endorsement of McCarthy (Taft was probably the only man in the
Senate both respected and feared by McCarthy). Taft once said
that McCarthy should "keep on talking and if one case doesn't
work out he should proceed with another."[14]

Neither Taft nor the followers of his point of view, of course,
approved of McCarthy's methods. But, so they argued, his ends
were sound. Yet it is just the means which make all the difference
between democracy and totalitarianism. Many of his admirers were
saddened that a great conservative like Taft did not come out against
the methods of McCarthyism. And it was hard for many to believe
that he really thought that his fellow Yaleman (both Taft and
Acheson were members of the Yale Corporation at the time) was
capable of knowingly tolerating Communists in the State Department. At all events, McCarthyism fed on the mistrust and suspicion
which were inadvertently fostered by the followers of Taft's point
of view.

In the last analysis, a unified establishment is probably the major
bulwark against the demagogue. And accordingly, the hysterical era

of McCarthy finally came to an end only after the return to power of the Republican Party under Eisenhower. For the Republican Party, in spite of our having been a Democratic nation since 1936, still represented the core of the old-stock Protestant establishment in this country. As Ralph W. Burgess, Deputy Secretary of the Treasury under Eisenhower and formerly of the National City Bank, said: ". . . our kind of people are now in power."[15] For eight years this old-stock confidence was constantly reinforced each time the press reported the President's golf scores as he played on the best and most exclusive courses in the nation.

Though it could be argued that Eisenhower reigned rather than ruled, there is good reason to believe that his two terms in office were needed at the time, both in order to restore a sense of tranquillity among the "best people" and to appease the hysterical groups within the party which had been without the responsibility of power for far too long a period. When Eisenhower settled the Korean war, for example, Harry Truman remarked: "I would have been crucified for that armistice." In a similar vein, Walter Lippmann, who supported Dewey in 1948 and Eisenhower in 1952, has recently gone so far as to suggest that the whole McCarthy issue might have been avoided entirely if Dewey had won in 1948 instead of Truman. Lippmann's views were, of course, entirely in accord with our theory of the establishment's function as a protector of freedom against the onslaught of demagoguery.

Yet some of the worst examples of McCarthyism, including the antics of his assistants, Cohn and Schine, in disgracing us abroad, took place during the early years of Eisenhower's reign, before the authority of a responsible establishment and its ability to silence the cries of conspiracy and treason were demonstrated in the case of Charles Bohlen's nomination as our Ambassador to Moscow. Bohlen was one of our leading Russian experts. His whole career had been in the Foreign Service. He was an impeccable member of the old-stock establishment by both birth and breeding. He was a nominal Republican, but he had unfortunately taken part in the

Yalta Conference, which had now come to symbolize the ultimate in the treasonable betrayal of the nation by the Roosevelt-liberal conspiracy. Bohlen, moreover, refused to join in the condemnation of Yalta, which he defended as having been in the best interests of the nation at the time. Here was an ideal target for McCarthy who immediately organized a movement to oppose Bohlen's nomination. Bohlen was appropriately branded a "security risk" and a member of the "old Acheson Gang" by McCarthy, who now pressed for Bohlen's submission to a "lie detector" test.[16]

It was Eisenhower's theory that the Congress should rule while the President reigns, and by and large throughout our history Congress has ruled when the establishment has been in power in Washington, while strong presidents, from Jackson to Franklin D. Roosevelt, have come to the fore when the establishment's authority has been challenged. At any rate, after his historic meeting with Eisenhower at Morningside Heights during the 1952 campaign, Senator Taft assumed the leadership of the Republican establishment in the last and, perhaps, greatest years of his life. Taft had always believed in the betrayal theory of the Yalta Conference. And he strongly disapproved of the Bohlen appointment. Yet he had a passion for Republican order and immediately took it upon himself to push through the Bohlen appointment. He carefully read through the FBI files (which, in our horrifying age of mistrust and rapidly declining privacy, contained detailed records of the "questionable" guests the Bohlens had privately entertained at dinner from time to time) and then announced that the case was closed, and Bohlen's loyalty established, as far as he was concerned. The confirmation of Bohlen's appointment went through the Senate with as little delay as possible. This was the beginning of the end of McCarthy.

Classical liberal theory to the contrary, then, there is little empirical evidence in history to support the theory that either a free people of a free press is, in the long run, sufficient, though both are indeed necessary, guarantors of freedom against the rise of dictatorial demagoguery. Though economic security may be valued and understood by the many, there is good reason to believe that civil liberties and freedom of expression are more highly valued by the few. McCarthy was feared far more in the university than on the assembly line. A demagogue, moreover, appeals to the *demos* by definition. And as long as a free press is guided by a theory which supports the reporting of fact, whether it be true or false, it is hardly in a position to do anything but provide the demagogue with publicity, which Franklin Roosevelt himself once said was beneficial whether it was for or against him. The final protector of freedom, on the other hand, may very well be a unified establishment from within which the leaders of at least two parties are chosen, who, in turn, compete for the people's votes of confidence, from differing points of view and differing standards of judgment, yet both assuming the absolute necessity of using fair means in accusing their legitimate opponents of fallibility rather than treason. An establishment, in other words, may be the best protection against a conspiracy theory of history. It is well to remember, for instance, that both Henry Wallace (in 1948) and the Birch Society candidates (in 1962) did well in the rootless communities of Southern California, where there is no established authority and where conspiracy theories (from both the Left and the Right) have consequently always had a wide appeal.

It is indeed significant that Sir Winston Churchill, unlike our less-worldly conservative, Senator Taft, thought the rise of McCarthyism dangerous enough to write an eloquent anti-McCarthy passage into Elizabeth II's Coronation speech. But perhaps he was only reflecting his own Tory traditions of freedom which, as Tocqueville saw, have always been protected by a cohesive establishment, slow to cry treason and always able to absorb new men of power within its ranks.

All nobility in its beginnings was somebody's natural superiority.

Ralph Waldo Emerson

XIII

The 1960's:
The Quest for a New
Aristocratic Establishment

There was every reason to believe that the Eisenhower victory in 1952 was needed to restore a sense of responsibility and power within the Republican Party and a measure of tranquillity among the people as a whole. At the same time, however, the members of the intellectual community, who had been more enthusiastic about Adlai Stevenson than about any other Presidential candidate in the twentieth century with the possible exception of Woodrow Wilson, were deeply depressed. There were exceptions, among them Walter Lippmann who, as has been pointed out above, thought the country needed a Republican victory, especially in order to rid itself of

McCarthyism. "If Eisenhower had lost in 1952," he said when interviewed in 1961, "the Republicans would have followed McCarthy. After being out of power for 20 years, they would have gone mad."[1]

The two Republican terms in the White House have usually been attributed less to the party than to the charismatic leadership of President Eisenhower and his ability to appeal to all the people. They were also due, I think, to a deep yearning in this country, as well as in many other Western democracies, for a return to conservatism. Witness, for instance, the postwar leadership of such tory conservatives as Macmillan, de Gaulle and Adenauer in Europe. The Republican Party, however, while it represents a combined establishment of business as well as a majority of the members of the old-stock upper class, still has not been able, like the Tories in England for instance, to establish itself as the majority party, in spite of the conservative mood of the people.

In the meantime, the Democrats are still the established party politically. By 1960, when they returned to power under the leadership of John F. Kennedy, the Democrats had come to represent a political tradition which had been in the process of developing in this country in the course of almost three decades, and especially since the re-election of Franklin Roosevelt in 1936 (and this tradition stretched even farther back as a minority movement under the leadership of Theodore Roosevelt and Woodrow Wilson). Adlai Stevenson, one of the more philosophically mature conservatives to come upon the American political scene in this century, described this development as follows, in 1952:

The strange alchemy of this has somehow converted the Democrats into the truly conservative party of this country—the party dedicated to conserving all that is best, and building solidly and safely on these foundations. The Republicans, by contrast, are behaving like the radical party—the party of the reckless and the embittered, bent on dismantling institutions which have been built solidly into our social fabric. . . . Our social-security system and our

Democratic party's sponsorship of the social reforms and advances of the past two decades [are] conservatism at its best. Certainly there could be nothing more conservative than to change when change is due, to reduce tensions and wants by wise changes, rather than to stand pat stubbornly, until like King Canute we are engulfed by relentless forces that will always go too far.[2]

John F. Kennedy's victory in 1960 represented a return to power of an essentially conserving political tradition. The fighting faiths of one generation have a way of becoming conservative assumptions in the next. A decade after Adlai Stevenson made the statement quoted above, Walter Lippmann wrote, in the New York *Herald Tribune*, as follows: "Though Mr. Kennedy is a progressive and a liberal, he is also a profound conservative, and only the befuddled theorists find that strange and hard to understand."[3] In other words, President Kennedy stood for both continuity and change, the essence of any dynamic conservatism. The symbolic significance of his being sent to the White House by the American people in the 1960's has already been discussed in an earlier chapter. Several things, however, should be emphasized here.

In the first place, the fact that President Kennedy was the first non-Protestant to enter the White House in our history was of great importance. It was of even more importance that the Kennedy administration represented both the second generation of Democratic majority-party rule as well as the first generation of American political leadership to have grown up entirely in the twentieth century. Thus President Eisenhower calmly reigned as representative of a generation still dominated by the Protestant establishment, which was slowly passing from the stage, while President Kennedy represented a younger and more heterogeneous generation of American political leaders who were just coming to power (within both political parties, of course). McCarthyism, for example, was surely oriented toward exposing the past rather than planning for the future. In many ways McCarthy was the product of America's last innocent generation's fratricidal fight over its adherence to already-lost illusions. It was no wonder, in an era which witnessed the Rosenberg, Oppenheimer and Hiss cases, the Yalta re-evaluations and the Korean and Cold wars, that cries of conspiracy and treason filled the air and opened wide the door to one form or another of McCarthyism. Perhaps Eisenhower was needed to calm the hysteria of an old, tired and disillusioned generation of leaders who would not, and perhaps could not, face the future and were consequently engaged in a schizophrenic conflict over their pasts. Indeed it was no accident that the affluent fifties began with the purposeless publicity-seeking of McCarthy and ended with a nation-wide debate, in the pages of the Luce publications as well as in formal hearings in the Congress, over our lack of a sense of National Purpose. It will be no easy task, but perhaps the generational change in leadership which marked the election of 1960 will eventually produce a renewed sense of purpose in America.

The Two Democratic Generations

The new generation of Democrats differed in almost every way from the generation of Franklin Roosevelt. For the two generations came to maturity in very different worlds. Roosevelt's generation was born in an age of innocence and security at the turn of the century, when an Anglo-Saxon establishment ruled the nation and the world; they went away to college, where they naturally assumed the leadership due their social position (the "Gold Coast" ruled Harvard); they went away to training camps like Plattsburgh, where Ivy League gentlemen prepared to be officers in the last idealistic war to end all wars; they turned to the Democratic Party under Wilson, especially after the party of their fathers deserted the ideals for which they had fought; having discovered sex and Freud, they went on an irresponsible spree in the twenties; and finally, armed with the easy optimism of John Dewey if not Marxism, they led a brilliant and idealistic reform movement against poverty and economic in-security at home and then produced the unconditional surrender of "all the evil forces in the outside world" in the Second War, only to be faced with an era of reaction in the late forties and fifties, often articulately led by conservative ex-New Dealers, as well as ex-Marx-ists and ex-Communists of the more extreme Right.

The Democrats of the second generation were very different men, bred in a very different world. Coming to maturity in an urban, Augustan age, marked by fierce, and often cynically manipu-lative, struggles for power, they were far removed from rural and republican America where amateur aristocrats, from Washington and Jefferson to the two Roosevelts, were called, like Cincinnatus of republican Rome, to serve the nation in time of need. Forced to struggle for power like the Caesars of old, they tended to be realists rather than idealists, professionals rather than gentlemen-amateurs. They were born during the war which spelled the begin-ning of the end of the Pax Britannica and they came to maturity during the Depression years, when established authority was rapidly retreating before the fanatic ideologists of fascism and communism abroad and the New Deal and Liberty League at home; they went to college, where leadership was awarded to the swift rather than the polite, and where the "Gold Coast" was rapidly vanishing or being relegated to an inconspicuous and minor role; and, above all, they went to war with no illusions, and were trained as officers in a highly competitive atmosphere of talented men from diverse ethnic back-grounds (the aviators of this generation were the product of the most aristocratic, rather than castelike, selective process this nation, or the world, had ever witnessed). They came back from all parts of a war-torn world to rise to the top in a postwar era in which all illusions, if not ideals, were surely dying. Thus their spiritual and in-tellectual mood, whether they were gentiles or Jews, was far closer to the neo-orthodox Christianity of Reinhold Niebuhr (or his spirit-ual kin, Martin Buber, the existentialist Jew) than to the optimistic and naturalistic scientism of John Dewey. Perhaps Arthur M.

Schlesinger, Jr., the Court Philosopher of the Kennedy Administration, has best expressed the conservative mood of his generation in the following paragraph:

> But the Christian millennium calls for a catastrophic change in human nature. Let us not sentimentalize the millennium by believing we can attain it through scientific discovery or through the revision of our economic system. We must grow up now and forsake the millennial dream. . . . Given human imperfection, society will continue imperfect. Problems will always torment us, because all important problems are insoluble: that is why they are important. The good comes from the continuing struggle to try and solve them, not from the vain hope of their solution.[4]

And, ironically enough, this second generation of philosophically conservative realists, struggling to defend our traditional freedoms in a cold war which will surely last for more than a generation, were opposed by a radicalism on the Right which was crying out for unconditional surrender, in the utopian style of Rooseveltian idealism.

But perhaps the most important difference between the two generations was the fact that, while the Protestant patricians of Roosevelt's generation sincerely believed in assimilating the members of minority groups into the main stream of American economic life and leadership, they were at the same time incapable of accepting the members of minority groups as their social equals. Although both Franklin and Eleanor Roosevelt sincerely wanted to complete the melting pot, they were never really at ease socially with the Farleys, the Flynns or the Al Smiths. It was not so much a matter of ethnic snobbery, as it was that their backgrounds and education were so divergent. The Roosevelts were, of course, very close to their Dutchess County neighbors, the Morgenthaus, who were after all of the old-stock and German generation within the Jewish community. Yet on the whole, there was just a touch of the condescending Lady Bountiful in Eleanor Roosevelt, which was entirely in accord with her Victorian background. Thus Ambassador Kennedy, who always deeply resented being referred to as an "Irish American," once expressed his feelings toward Mrs. Roosevelt in the following blunt statement to the press: "She bothered us more on our jobs in Washington to take care of the poor little nobodies than all the rest of the people down there put together. She's always sending me a note to have some little Susie Glotz to tea at the Embassy."[5] And although Franklin Roosevelt was continually amused by the wit and brilliance of Kennedy's mind, in the last analysis he preferred to relax with what Jim Farley, with a touch of resentment, once called the "Hasty Pudding Cabinet" as he watched them sail away for a brief vacation with the President on Vincent Astor's yacht.

What one generation begins is often left to the next generation to complete. The New Deal revolution marked the beginning of both an ethnic democracy and an ethnic elite in this country. The Kennedy Administration brought to Washington a talented and extremely ambitious group of leaders and their families who represented the beginning of an ethnically heterogeneous establishment. The men who surrounded Kennedy on the New Frontier, as has been pointed out in an earlier chapter, were surely social peers of great ethnic diversity. There was, moreover, no old-stock dominance or ethnic condescension. The minority-group members among them, a generation or more removed from Roosevelt's ethnic associates, shared a common educational background at the best universities (most often Harvard) with their friends of the old-stock establishment.

Perhaps of even greater importance, I think, was the fact of their having shared a common war experience. Most of them were officers in hierarchical organizations which were, at the same time, led by the most ethnically heterogeneous elite in the nation's history. Indeed, it is hard to believe that shallow ethnic prejudices could have survived in the minds of men, whether from Back Bay, Park Avenue, Brooklyn or the Bronx, who had once shared the risks and dangers of war together in the intimate atmospheres of the ward room on a carrier in the South Pacific, or in the officers' mess of a

bomber squadron in Britain. In fact, I visualized the possibility of
an ethnically mixed establishment, which underlies the theory of
American leadership developed in this book, during my own experiences in the ward rooms and officers' clubs of the South Pacific. At
any rate, the American ideal of equality of opportunity in a hier-
archically organized social structure had never been so nearly realized as in the selection of reserve officers who led our armed forces
during the Second World War. It is hard to believe that down in
Washington on the New Frontier the accidents of birth meant
much to leaders of men who had shared a common war experience,
a common educational background and common ideals about our
democracy. As an artist friend—son of a clergyman who was Dean of
the Princeton Chapel for many years, classmate of John F. Kennedy
at an Officers' Candidate School in the Navy, and a veteran of over
twenty months of the Pacific war—said to me some six months
before the President's assassination: "I love everything about the
New Frontier, and whatever Kennedy does, whether I agree or not,
seems part of me and of my generation."

The Kennedy Family
and the Democratic Establishment

While elites are composed of talented individuals, an establishment is always rooted in the family. The Kennedys may very well
take their place in the tradition of the great political families of older
stock like the Adamses and Roosevelts, Lodges and Tafts. The
family founder was, of course, the late President's father, Joseph P.
Kennedy. It was his buccaneering ways in business and finance
which produced the family fortune. And he was probably no more
ethically fastidious than the adventurous sea captains and merchant
princes of the early nineteenth century who founded the older
Massachusetts families of Cabot, Peabody, Lodge and Lowell.
"From the beginning, Joe knew what he wanted—money and status

for his family," said one who knew him intimately in Washington during the New Deal. "He had the progenitor's sense: to him, his children were an extension of himself. Therefore, what he did, he did with them always in mind." Joseph Kennedy made all his sons independently wealthy, one of the greatest assets for freedom of action in a democracy. Moreover, and equally important considering how many second-generation playboys our society has been capable of producing in this century, he gave them a strong sense of duty toward their country and a consuming desire for political leadership. "None of my children," he once said with pride, "has the slightest interest in making money: not the slightest."[6]

The Kennedys are not only a talented, prolific and independently wealthy political clan; they are also important, and of timely significance, because of the fact that their extended family includes representatives of a wide variety of contemporary elites in this country: thus members of the Hollywood celebrity elite, so often rootless outcasts from the centers of stolid communal authority in America, are brought into the Kennedy establishment through the Peter Lawfords and their position at the heart of the Frank Sinatra "clan"; the old-stock upper class is represented in Sargent Shriver, Yaleman member of an old Maryland family; and, of course, the late President's gifted wife, though born of Wall Street and Catholic wealth much like the Kennedys', is also the stepdaughter of a member of old-stock and brownstone New York which has been dissected so well in recent years by the author Louis Auchincloss.

In democratic ages, as Tocqueville once wrote, one tends to underestimate the ability of men and families to influence the course of history. Yet the Kennedys are, I think, in an excellent position to assimilate the members of a wide variety of contemporary elites into some sort of new and stable establishment. In fact, they are very much in the Whig tradition of aristocracy which Tocqueville so admired. For it was the old Whig families, in eighteenth- and early nineteenth-century England, who had so much to do with the blending of the old-landed with the new-commercial wealth which eventually formed the backbone of the establishment in the Victorian era. One is immediately reminded of the Kennedys upon reading the following description of the sporting and democratic Whig aristocracy, in Lord David Cecil's *Melbourne*:

The Whig lord was so often as not a minister, his eldest son an M.P., his second attached to a foreign embassy, so that their houses were alive with the effort and hurry of politics. . . . Whig society itself was a sort of club, exclusive, but in which those who managed to achieve membership lived on equal terms; a rowdy, rough-and-tumble club, full of conflict and plain speaking, where people were expected to stand up for themselves and give and take hard knocks. . . . Born and bred citizens of the world, they knew their way about it by a sort of infallible instinct. And they had an instinctive mastery of its social arts. Their negligence was never boorish; it arose from the fact that they felt so much at home in life that they were careless of its conventions. . . . For they possessed—it was their chief charm—in the highest degree, the high spirits of their home.[7]

There is probably a very close correlation between the structure of an establishment at any given time and the tempo of leisure-time social activities. Thus, on the one hand, a caste society will usually produce a relatively formal and low-pressure Society. For men and women who have known one another since childhood, and whose ancestors have intermarried for generations, there is often very little to talk about except sports and the market, child rearing and the mild extramarital affairs of the overly-bred-bored, or how so-and-so, who was president of his class at St. Grottlesex, is now quietly drinking himself to death.

In an assimilating aristocracy, on the other hand, when talented and ambitious men and women from very different backgrounds are brought together by a passionate commitment to the present, the temperature of social life is bound to rise, and sometimes even to get out of hand. Washington Society on The New Frontier was not unlike that of the Gilded Age when the new-rich Yankee plutocrats were knocking at the gates of the old Four Hundred. Both reminded one of Versailles, when the Sun King was creating a national bureaucracy which blended the old *noblesse* of the sword with the striving new *noblesse* of the robe. Similarly, the exuberance of the New Frontier was a product of the blending of the old- and new-stock members of the nation's first twentieth-century-bred generation of political leaders to come down to Washington.

There was, of course, a great deal of the manipulative society down on the New Frontier; too great a preoccupation with the image rather than the man; and perhaps too great a preference for political power at the expense of moral authority (especially where the rights of Negroes were concerned). But, on the other hand, it is not my purpose here to judge the moral righteousness or the political policies of the New Frontier coalition. Rather, it is the sociological composition of its leadership which is my main concern. And the Kennedy clan set the tone for a great deal of the private, informal and family-centered life on the New Frontier. It will be the children (and grandchildren) of this young generation of leaders —having been schooled together in and around the nation's capital, having gone away together to Exeter or Andover, Harvard or Radcliffe, and finally having intermarried—who will, in the long run, lay the foundations for a truly representative establishment in this country. This may well be the most important, if unplanned, consequence of the composition of the generation of New Frontiersmen. For an establishment is never created by revolution or deliberate design, but only through a slow evolutionary process over several generations.

The New Frontier was more receptive to the arts and the artist than previous administrations. This may have been partly due to the temperament and background of the President's wife. It is also true that patronage of the arts has usually been characteristic of newly rising classes. In this country, moreover, it has been increasingly true in this century that members of minority groups, rather than the older stocks, have gone into the arts. This unfortunate castelike character of the arts has been intensified since the war as the members of the old-stock upper class have tended to withdraw from the cultural life of the city into the suburban sporting life.

The receptiveness to the arts down in Washington under President Kennedy, then, was partly due to the ethnic composition of a rising generation of leaders. It was due also to what Walt Whitman Rostow, himself a leading member of the New Frontier, has called the "Buddenbrooks Dynamic" which had been operating among the members of the old-stock upper class since the war (the first generation seeks money; the second, social and civic position; while the third goes into music and the arts in general). In this country, following this pattern, many members of the third and fourth generation, born to the mores of the Republican old-stock upper class, deserted the business civilization for careers in the arts or in teaching. As a result of their new friendships with members of minority groups as well as to their new convictions, they almost always sympathized with the ideals of the Democratic Party (as it has taken shape since Wilson and Roosevelt). Only recently, for instance, I was discussing this generational problem with the wife of an artist and teacher in Philadelphia. She and her husband, both admirers of President Kennedy, live in a community dominated by artists and intellectuals. Each summer, however, she takes her family to a resort which her old New England family has dominated for several generations. "It is so good for the children," she said to me, "and I myself feed on the sense of family continuity which I find there. But both my husband and I are only too glad to leave at the end of the summer. . . . Their values are so different . . . and though I hate to say it, their persistent, and often unconscious, anti-Semitism seems to bother me most of all. . . ."

Like their friends in the arts or in teaching, men of inherited wealth in America are increasingly seeking a sense of personal fulfillment in government service. Their family firms have been sold, and the life of the organization man surely has little appeal. Nor do the large and conventional law firms which their fathers or grandfathers founded—engaged as they are in defending large and impersonal organizations or figuring out the subtle technicalities of tax avoidance—hold much hope for personal fulfillment. And the Kennedy style acted like a magnate in drawing this kind of gentleman to Washington. Thus there were probably more men of second- and third-generation inherited wealth—and of the Eastern Seaboard upper class like Angier Biddle Duke—down in Washington at all levels of the New Frontier bureaucracy than at any other time in our history (even including the generation of Franklin Roosevelt). The style also appealed to Republicans of this generation and class, among the more well known of whom were McGeorge Bundy and Douglas Dillon, old Grotonians and former supporters of Eisenhower, who became two of the late President's closest associates.

Aristocracy and the Democratic Establishment

Groton School has, in many ways, been a great conserver of the best aristocratic traditions in this country.* One has the impression that its founder, the late Endicott Peabody, would have been proud of the fact that one of his old boys, Dean Acheson, not only stood up for his Christian convictions as to the duties of friendship in regard to Alger Hiss, but also became a leading elder-statesman-without-portfolio in the Kennedy Administration. The Rector would also be pleased that two of his grandchildren took part in the continuing American experiment in democracy as active members of the new Democratic generation.

Endicott Peabody, a Boston lawyer and political reformer rather than professional Democrat, is now Governor of Massachusetts, having squeaked through by less than a five-thousand-vote margin in

---

* Groton was the first of the St. Grottlesex schools to accept Negro students. Its faculty now includes a Jew, which may go a long way to explode some of its students' home-grown stereotypes.

306

the course of Edward Kennedy's landslide victory in the race for the United State Senate. Some may have had their doubts as to Peabody's qualifications for the Governorship. At any rate, he is typical of the new generation of old-stock Democrats. At Harvard he was a leader on the campus and an All-American guard (1941) in his senior year (he was probably the last member of the old-stock upper class to achieve this honor). During the Second War, he served as a lieutenant on a submarine, where he won the Silver Star for leading raiding parties aboard Japanese craft, often engaging in hand-to-hand combat. He returned from the war determined to enter politics. In contrast to many of his resentful friends in the Republican establishment—who seemed to go out of their way during the campaign to stop him on the street in order to tell him that they were, of course, not going to vote for him or his running mate—Peabody is now getting a chance to practice what he long has preached: "I want to play my part in shaping the world, and I don't believe in hiring mercenaries to do it."[8]

Endicott Peabody's older sister, Marietta Endicott Peabody Tree, also played her part in the second-generation Democratic establishment.[9] A convinced liberal, Marietta has been one of the Democratic Party's most inspired organizers and fund raisers for some time now. She has also served the party officially as Committeewoman from the Ninth Assembly District in New York, and the nation as a representative to the Human Rights Commission of the United Nations, where she is now an official member of the United States Delegation (appointed by President Kennedy, in 1961). Since her conversion to the Democratic Party during the war, she has been active in many liberal, civic causes, especially in the fields of civil rights and race relations. According to her *Who's Who* biography, for example, she was one of the founders of Sydenham Hospital, the first interracial hospital in New York City. At one time or another, she has been an active member of the Fair Housing Practice Panel of New York City, the Puerto Rican Board of Guardians, the

National Urban League and the New York Chapter of the National Conference of Christians and Jews.

Marietta Peabody grew up in the heart of the Proper Philadelphia Republican establishment, in the suburb of Chestnut Hill, where her father was the rector of one of the most prosperous Episcopalian congregations in the nation at that time.* She was always admired by the boys in the neighborhood, especially after she knocked down one of the bigger bullies among them. While at St. Timothy's School, outside Baltimore, she took an ardent interest in politics and dreamed of someday becoming a senator (she was a vocal supporter of Herbert Hoover, in 1932). After a year at a finishing school abroad, she came back to the University of Pennsylvania, where she majored in political science and international relations. She left college in 1939, after her junior year, to marry a wealthy and conservative New York lawyer.

After her husband joined the army, Marietta saw him only infrequently. In the meantime, she took a job as a researcher for an editor of *Life* magazine. "It turned into a marvelous education," she said later of the experience. "I had to know by heart the voting records of almost every United States Senator and the heads of all the important committees in the House. It was then, after memorizing those senatorial and House voting records, that I became a passionate Democrat."[10]

After the war, Marietta's extremely liberal values proved to be incompatible with her husband's conservative Republicanism, and she eventually obtained a Reno divorce, over the fierce opposition of her parents (her father was a Bishop of the Episcopal Church and a Harvard Overseer).** She then married Arthur Ronald Lambert

---

* A solid and conservative class background is often an excellent stimulus to revolt. Thus it is interesting that the liberal Democratic Senator from Pennsylvania, Joseph Sill Clark, grew up in the inbred atmosphere of Proper Philadelphia and is now a resident of Chestnut Hill.

** Republicans of the old-stock establishment like to point out how so many prominent Democrats of their own class (especially Franklin Roosevelt's children) are divorced, and hence, of course, quite unstable. There is indeed a high

The 1960's

Field Tree, an Anglo-American multimillionaire and descendant of two of Chicago's pioneering and most distinguished family founders. The Trees sailed almost immediately for England, where they took up residence at Dytchley Hall, Tree's stately country house near Oxford. A Conservative Member of Parliament for thirteen years before his defeat in the Labour landslide after the war, Tree was a good friend of Winston Churchill and knew everybody. And as mistress of Dytchley Hall, Marietta Tree kept open house and entertained all the important figures in British politics as well as many from the Continent.

The Trees eventually returned to New York, where Marietta was in an ideal position to bring the Whig tradition of aristocracy, and its love of people of talent and wit regardless of background, to the Park Avenue wing of the Democratic Party, and eventually to the party as a whole. In many ways she was bred for the role. In addition to her experience in England, she had been trained in her grandmother Parkman's distinguished Boston salon, which equaled that of her more famous contemporary, Mrs. John Lowell Gardner of Fenway Court.

Marietta first got into Democratic Party politics through her friend Earl Brown, Negro member of the Council of the City of New York and an assistant editor of *Life* magazine. Taking Brown's advice, she worked within the regular party organization from the beginning instead of following her natural impulses to work for reform from without. She became an active member of the Lexington Democratic Club, where she wrote speeches, raised money, and even served as campaign manager for a local candidate (she once broke a strict rule of protocol when she left a dinner in honor of

---

divorce rate among old-stock Democratic leaders. But, on the other hand, one must remember that these old-stock Democrats are still sociologically marginal; and sociological marginality often has to be paid for in various amounts of personal pathology. Conversion to the Democratic Party in adulthood in the manner of Marietta Tree's experience, moreover, often means adherence to values which conflict with the parental and class values of one's youth, upon which one's first spouse was chosen.

309

England's Queen Mary at an early hour in order to be with her candidate and co-workers on election night).

In recent years, the Lexington Democratic Club has played an important role in New York City politics, where the Reform Democrats, made up primarily of college-educated liberals, have been struggling to take control of the party from the traditional machine politicians. Whether they will succeed in the long run remains to be seen. What matters here is the fact that reform politics within the Democratic Party, much like the world of the arts and culture, has become an important area of New York life where affluent and educated, old-stock Protestants and Jews have come together in the interest of a common cause. Glazer and Moynihan, in their excellent recent book on the New York melting pot, found that "the reform movement in politics has already become one of those areas of city life in which people of different backgrounds, from different groups, come together not as representatives of groups, not to bargain for group rights and positions, but to work in a common task as individuals. This happens often enough in New York business, but there the common end is gain. The fact that it happens in politics, where the common end is a general good, is a cause for satisfaction. This is after all the only real basis of 'integration'—common work in which one's group characteristics are not primary and therefore of no great account."[11]

The Tree house on Seventy-ninth Street soon became an important meeting place for Reform Democrats. "It beat the back rooms by a block," said Earl Brown in recalling those gatherings. "We were trying to raise money for something. I remember the tickets to this party at Marietta's house cost twenty dollars, but people crowded in from the Lower East Side, Harlem and all over. The catering and the champagne were from '21.' When Governor Harriman and I wanted to talk privately, the only place we could find was in the house's sub-subbasement. I shall never forget the sight of the Trees' English butler, Collins, dying by stately inches at the thought of what that mass of Democrats could do to the house, or of Ronnie

Tree, stiff, perspiring and apprehensive. And all the time Marietta was sashaying around as if it were a picnic in Central Park."[12] Tree himself apparently was pleased to have his wife take an interest in Democratic politics: "Although I am, of course, completely divorced from politics now, I find that English Conservatives and American Democrats are indistinguishable in their aims."[13]

It was during the second Stevenson and the Kennedy campaign that the Tree salon became a central meeting place for Democrats of all kinds and degrees of political opinion and social background. The Harvard wing of the party, led by John Kenneth Galbraith and Arthur M. Schlesinger, Jr. (a close friend of the Trees), were, of course, important in setting the intellectual tone of the party meetings. A stimulating atmosphere of conversation and ideas was also provided by such leading newspaper people as James Reston of the *Times*, James Wechsler of the New York *Post* and Alicia Patterson Guggenheim of *Newsday*. At the same time, writers, columnists, commentators, TV executives, intellectuals and the many lively arts were represented by such salon regulars as Edward R. Murrow, Doris Fleeson, Eric Sevareid, Alistair Cooke, Edward Morgan, Theodore White, Moss Hart, Kitty Carlisle, David Lilienthal, Earl Brown and even some Republicans like Henry and Clare Boothe Luce (one suspects from having read *Time* magazine during the last three years that perhaps Henry Luce was not quite so antagonistic toward President Kennedy as, according to T. S. Matthews, he apparently once was toward Roosevelt and Acheson). "Marietta," said Adlai Stevenson, "gives the party status and prestige. When you find someone closely identified with the intellectual and aristocratic communities who is also a positive, active, working Democrat, it tends to encourage everyone in the party."[14]

It is easy (especially in an age which is convinced that the "power drive" is the basis of human nature) to interpret the interest in Democratic politics of a beautiful and worldly woman like Marietta Tree as nothing more than her desire to set the fashion at the center of the stage. But this, I think, is only a small part of the truth. For her whole character and training are rooted in the ideals of an ancestral line which goes back to Cotton Mather's "Zion in the Wilderness" on Massachusetts Bay and to the fierce Puritanism of early Salem which Nathaniel Hawthorne (who married Sophia Peabody) described in *The Scarlet Letter*. And perhaps Marietta Tree's values are not really so very far removed from those of Harriet Beecher Stowe, who did so much to start a racial revolution which Marietta is trying to play some part in completing. Both were products of the stern authority of the Hebraic-Puritan God of their ancestors. Thus Marietta once explained the origins of her reforming and liberal values as follows: "I am impelled by a feeling that I have so many blessings I must try to pay for them in hard work for the community and in gratitude for being an American. I have to try and pay my debt to God."[15] And it is members of the old-stock establishment like Marietta Tree, with their moral convictions as to the need for racial and ethnic equality of opportunity (including a strong antipathy to anti-Semitism), who best represent the ancient Anglo-Saxon tradition of aristocratic assimilation.

Although rarely articulated explicitly or publicly, for obvious reasons of tact, one of the most deep-seated convictions which unite the second generation of old-stock Democrats is that anti-Semitism is morally wrong. We have seen how this was also characteristic of Franklin Roosevelt's generation and how anti-Semitism was always close to the surface in the Right's reaction to the New Deal, and especially their pet hate, Eleanor Roosevelt. In other words, one of the most important things which divide the members of the old-stock upper class who are also Democrats from those who have remained in the Republican tradition of their ancestors is their differential responses to the gentlemanly agreements as far as Jews are concerned. By and large the Republicans are more inclined to remain bystanders when it comes to the subtle and informal, yet rigid, policies of exclusion at their club or place of work, while the Democrats are not. It was, for example, no accident (and perhaps not entirely candid) that President Kennedy made every effort to discourage the press from photographing him on the golf course both during the 1960 campaign and afterward. It is often the little and seemingly harmless things in life which point to larger and more important values, and every one of the hundreds of times that President Eisenhower was photographed on the golf course served as a symbolic reminder of the subtle policies of exclusion practiced by the overwhelming majority of golf clubs in the nation.

The Liberal Political Establishment and Established Communal Authority

It may be a law of policial evolution in a stable democracy that innovating examples set by the Left must always await acceptance by the Right before becoming a part of established community values and practices. Although the second generation of Democrats were established politically as the majority party (by a slim margin to be sure), and although, as Adlai Stevenson has pointed out, they had come to represent the conserving political forces in the nation, they did not, and perhaps could not, represent the authority of an establishment. It may thus be inevitable that the Kennedy Administration, a brilliant but unstable coalition of sociological minorities, should have been preoccupied with the manipulation of its public image. For, in the long run, a really authoritative establishment must be firmly anchored in the solid, and stolid, property interests of the community. These interests, by and large, except in the South, are still represented by the Republican Party. At the same time, unfortunately, the Republicans will continue to run the danger of degenerating into a radical Right so long as their leaders are unable to appeal to the majority of the electorate over a considerable period of time—and not only with the intermittent charisma of a leader like Eisenhower.

This is indeed, as Walter Lippmann has implied time and again, an unhealthy situation. Just as an automobile needs both a brake and an accelerator, so a healthy democracy needs both conservative and liberal political forces which are in working order. We had, in the young New Frontier coalition, a vigorous and responsible party. It was, moreover, their function as liberals to be innovators and accelerators of change. Yet, perhaps one of the reasons why the New Frontier was unable "to get us moving again" was the very fact that President Kennedy was too conservative and responsible in temperament. On the other hand, owing to the vacuum on the conservative Right, he may have had to be. For it must be remembered that the two great reforming periods in this century—the first two years under Woodrow Wilson and the first hundred days under Franklin Roosevelt—were both liberal reactions to an established authority which needed reform. Both the intellectual Left and liberal political reformers may need *an enemy in established authority*, which they surely do not have today. The brake in the contemporary American political machine is defective. The Republicans represent the established property interests of the community but they have not been able to translate this into established political authority. There are, of course, complicated reasons for this, which need not be gone into here. But many of these reasons stem, I think, from the central thesis of this book, which is that the solid property interests of this country, or rather the Anglo-Saxon–Protestant representatives of such interests, have lost political authority because there are now a large number of affluent, talented and ambitious men of property who have been alienated from the Republican Party as a result of the caste values of the conservative establishment's community, if not party, leadership. In the next chapter, this matter will be considered in more detail.

If wealth is the obedient and laborious slave of virtue and of publick honours, then wealth is in its place and has its use. But if this order is changed, and honour is to be sacrificed to the conservation of riches, riches, which have neither eyes nor hands, nor anything truly vital in them, cannot long survive the being of their vivifying powers, their legitimate masters, and their potent protectors. If we command our wealth we shall be rich and free. If our wealth commands us, we are poor indeed.

Edmund Burke

XIV

Caste and the Corporation

Both the tragic era of McCarthyism and the election of the first non-Protestant to the Presidency in 1960 were of a piece. They were symptoms of the ethnic revolution at the elite level of leadership. President Kennedy's breaking of the caste barrier surrounding the Presidential establishment should make it much less likely that in the future there will be a revival of the type of ethnic resentment upon which McCarthy thrived. It is even more important to see that Kennedy's victory in 1960 will, in the long run, serve to bring many affluent and capable Catholic leaders in this country into the conservative ranks of the Republican establishment. Thus Catholics,

315

regardless of their class interests, voted overwhelmingly for Kennedy. A wealthy Palm Beach Catholic who had voted the straight Republican ticket since 1928, for example, voted for Kennedy in 1960, as he put it, because "the Catholics ought to be given a chance." But he did not necessarily intend to support the Democrats in the future. Once the caste line has been broken, ironically enough, affluent and conservative Catholics will be more likely in the future to support their class (Republican), rather than their caste (Democratic), interests. In the long run, caste interests are best dissolved by the forces of aristocratic assimilation.

The caste line, on the other hand, continues to be drawn as far as elite Jews are concerned. This is the case, as we have seen, in spite of the fact that elite Jews are increasingly, in the third generation, behaviorally assimilated through education at the best private schools and colleges, and are unusually talented and successful in many important and strategic occupations and professions. As a result, there has been a great postwar boom in gilded ghettos, centered around opulent synagogues and country clubs in the upper-middle-class suburbs of all our major cities. At the same time there is an ever increasing number of talented and sensitive Jews, often married to gentiles and with only nominal ties to the Jewish religious community, who find that life in the gilded ghettos comes more and more in conflict with the type of social life demanded by their elite positions. Caste exclusion not only hampers their contribution of community leadership as a whole, it also becomes increasingly dysfunctional as far as established communal authority is concerned.

An often overlooked phenomenon, moreover, has further emphasized the dysfunctional aspects of elite anti-Semitism. Ever since 1933 the American leadership community has been the beneficiary of one of the greatest talent migrations in modern times. Perhaps no accurate measure of the refugees' contribution to our society, most of whom have been Jews, will ever be obtained. The sociologist Maurice Davie and his associates have found that these new citizens made unusual contributions in the fields of law, medical science, language and literature, chemistry, economics and social science, mathematics, history and philosophy. By 1946, according to Davie, over three hundred of these distinguished refugees, in spite of the barriers of language, culture and discrimination, were already listed in *American Men of Science* and/or *Who's Who in America*.[1] Among them were 38 physicists (6 Nobel Prize winners), 42 mathematicians, 38 chemists (2 Nobel Prize winners), 58 persons in the medical sciences (1 Nobel Prize winner), 9 astronomers, 8 psychologists, 7 meteorologists, 12 social scientists, and 4 engineers. But numbers are never important at the elite levels of society. Who would deny that our whole postwar world might not have been different (if not obliterated) had Albert Einstein (to say nothing of men like Enrico Fermi or Edward Teller) not crossed the Atlantic in the thirties as refugees from the caste policies of the European dictatorships. And this talent migration has continued throughout the postwar period. The National Science Foundation has recently reported that between 1949 and 1961 a total of 43,523 scientists and engineers entered this country as immigrants. Few people are aware that to a remarkable degree the nation's pool of top scientists has been fed by this type of immigration.[2]

Jews—both native-born members of the second and third generation and the large group of talented and cultivated refugees from Europe—then, make up an important, influential and perhaps indispensable part of the contemporary American leadership community. This and the following two chapters will attempt to show how two vital American institutions, the corporation and the club, systematically exclude Jews from top leadership positions in the former and from membership in the latter; how these policies of caste work against the translation of conservative communal authority into Republican political power; and how, on the other hand, the aristocratic assimilation of Jews into the contemporary educational community inadvertently contributes to the continuing political power of the Democratic Party, and is slowly changing tradi-

tional anti-Semitic attitudes among members of the younger generation, regardless of whether they be Democrats or Republicans.

The Corporation as Community

Established communal authority in America has increasingly come
to be centered in the large national corporation. In an earlier chapter it was shown how the members of the local and established
upper class, educated at private secondary schools and Ivy League
universities, began moving into managerial positions in national
corporations during the 1920's. In the course of the past two decades,
according to Professor Thomas Cochran, this managerial group was
not only "the most rapidly growing segment of our population," but
by mid-century it "had the education, nation-wide contacts, and
company resources at its command that allowed it to set manners,
attitudes and habits of living" which influenced the whole society.[3]

Rather than a single purpose association organized for producing
a profit, the modern corporation, especially since the Second War,
has become a *community* with a whole system of folkways, mores
and values which now absorb more and more of the life and loyalties
of its employees and especially its managers. It is highly significant,
for example, that since the war an increasing number of novelists,
from Cameron Hawley (*Executive Suite*) to the late J. P. Marquand, have turned to the corporate community as a social setting
for the traditional novel of manners. While Marquand could still
use the life of George Apley to satirize the stable community norms
of brahmin Boston as of the First World War, some of his best
characters (for instance, the sincere Willis Wade) have been drawn
against the social norms of the post World War II corporation
community. And many other novelists have followed his example.
The social sciences have also come to see the large corporation as a
social rather than solely an economic system. Thus it is appropriate
that *The Organization Man*, by William H. Whyte, Jr., became one

of the most important books in the postwar period. In contrast to
The Modern Corporation and Private Property, written by Berle
and Means in the early thirties, which concentrated on the economics of the large corporation, Whyte's book was the first systematic study of the mores and folkways of the large corporation
management community.

Normative authority has thus been gradually moving from the
territorial to the corporate community. This transformation of communal authority was recently highlighted in the City of Philadelphia
when the United Fund drive changed its methods of solicitation.
Several years ago a new policy was introduced whereby citizens were
urged to make their annual contributions, not at home in their local
neighborhoods, but at their place of work. This experiment was a
great success. It was immediately obvious that the social pressures
to conform at the office were far stronger than the pressures to conform in the local neighborhood. The corporate collection of dona-
tions to the United Fund has now become established practice.

There is every reason to see why the corporate community has
come to dominate the social as well as the business life of its employees. For, along with the growth of the modern welfare state, the
corporation has also been increasingly engaged in all sorts of social
activities, including baseball, basketball and bowling facilities,
beauty parlors and charm schools, salary savings and retirement
plans, and even psychic salvation in the increasing number of
cases in which clergymen and psychiatrists have been added to the
staff. Indeed the top officials in the executive suites of the large
corporation are rapidly assuming the roles of stewards and trustees
for the social and economic welfare and security of their employees.
In this new climate of corporate feudalism, executive *noblesse
oblige* has gradually replaced the rugged individualism of an earlier
day. In a recent and brilliant analysis of the twentieth-century capitalist revolution, A. A. Berle, Jr., has summed up his impressions of
the function of the corporation in the modern world as follows:

To anyone who studies and even remotely begins to apprehend the American corporate system . . . the corporation, almost against its will, has been compelled to assume an appreciable part of the role of the conscience-carrier of twentieth-century American society. Unlike other great groups which have attempted a major part of this task, the modern corporation has done so without intent to dominate and without clearly defined doctrine. The revolutionists who made the Communist Party in the Soviet Union knew more or less what sort of structure they proposed to build, and had at least a glimmer of theory why they wished that result, ghastly as it seems to American thought. The Catholic Church, in the splendid medieval days when it attempted to construct a suprarational society, was tolerably clear in its objectives. . . . No one, however, has made a blueprint of the community desired by Standard Oil of New Jersey or Sears, Roebuck & Company, by the Southern Pacific Railroad, or by Ohio Edison, least of all the corporations themselves.

Yet it seems the aggregate of their day-to-day decisions do form life and community. They do play a notable part in the physical basis on which life is lived. They build or shift or direct frameworks of human experience within which great masses of men live. Indirectly they affect an even greater peripheral group. They do enter into those community institutions, now including colleges and schools and philanthropies, which are the proudest product of American life. To the extent, therefore, that corporation managements, knowingly or unknowingly, reflect a philosophy, they have become a powerful force.[4]

As men like Berle and Whyte have clearly seen the corporate community has increasingly become a new source of conformity in a nationally organized society where loyalties and normative sanctions are breaking down at the level of the local community. The corporation is also providing a new moral conscience on a national, and perhaps even on an international, scale. Indeed the modern corporation, perhaps unwittingly, is playing a vital and revolutionary role in gradually creating a world community.

320

Ethnic Homogeneity and Overconformity

At the same time, there is the ever present danger of a kind of compulsive overconformity developing in the executive suite. While Whyte and others have stressed this danger in their various works on the postwar corporation mores, they have not emphasized the fact that conformity may well be due to the castelike homogeneity of the modern executive suite. At a time when the total elite structure in America is increasingly heterogeneous as far as ethnic origins are concerned, the large corporation executive suite is still mainly composed of managers of an Anglo-Saxon–Protestant background. The most recent and systematic studies of large corporation leadership tend to show that top management is predominantly Protestant, with Catholics poorly represented, and Jews virtually excluded.[5] This pattern of homogeneity and Protestant exclusiveness is so strong that even such corporations as Sears, Roebuck and the Radio Corporation of America, which went through much of their growth under Jewish leadership, are now following the pattern set by industry as a whole.

Management recruiting policies, moreover, seem to be perpetuating this religio-ethnic homogeneity in the executive suite. Rather than taking young men out of college or business schools on the basis of their drives or talents alone, management too often tends to be guided by other criteria, such as physiognomy, manner of dress, pleasing (conforming) personality, accents and antecedents. There is, of course, good evidence to show, as Chester I. Bernard has emphasized, that "communion" and "social compatibility" or "comfort in social relations" are conducive to producing a successful management team. But a good thing may be carried too far. One has the impression, and it is an impression backed by some recent scientific surveys, that even where educational background, acquired manners and other desirable and compatible personal traits are possessed by Jews or men of Jewish origins, these men are not selected because of caste criteria. One of my seniors at the Wharton School of Finance and Commerce, educated at private schools, tall and handsome, a good student though not a grind, and possessed of a quiet charm of manner, went to New York for an interview with a prospective employer. He had previously been selected by the on-campus management recruiter. After his interview in the New York office, he was taken out to lunch by some junior executives. All went well. Then, on the way back from lunch, as he recalled it, one of his hosts casually asked him what fraternity he belonged to. He named his fraternity, which happened to be the leading all-Jewish fraternity on the campus (the fraternity discriminates against the "New York type" as they put it, but my friend was from the South). He still wonders why he did not get the job, for the evasive letter which soon followed his visit to New York gave no clear reason for the company's decision. This is, of course, no isolated case, and, over the years, I find it is often boys from the best homes and with the finest manners and morals who face such problems.*

Such problems are, apparently, also faced by the highly screened graduates of the Harvard Business School. Today, about one graduate in seven is of Jewish origins. Yet, of the middle-aged "retreads" who come back to Harvard each year for the Advanced Management Program (selected by the companies who send them and not by Harvard), only one in about two hundred are Jews (usually from Jewish firms). Sometimes, as one might imagine, these Jews spend a lonely year at Harvard.

While on a recent teaching visit to the West Coast I ran into such a case. I was visiting an old friend and refugee from the solid Philadelphia Republican business community. He was president of his own company, was incidentally a Democratic convert, and was proud

* The campus recruiting policies of many of our large corporations have changed considerably in recent years. Many of my best Jewish students have taken jobs with large, and previously all Anglo-Saxon, firms. Few of the really ambitious will remain in these firms, however, if they find that country and metropolitan club membership (see Chapter XVI) are prerequisites for acceptance into top management positions outside of research.

to have just hired his first Negro salesman. He lived in a suburb which was dominated by young Ivy League immigrants from the East who have, since the war, become an important part of the younger generation of business and professional leadership in San Francisco. One of his neighbors, who was partly Jewish, had been sent back to the Harvard "retread" program in preparation for top management responsibility. I was told by my friend that the neighbor's wife had suffered a minor nervous breakdown which was partly precipitated by their year at Harvard. Unlike her husband, she was a protected Protestant before marriage and, therefore, had not experienced the subtle anti-Semitism which was so deeply, if often unconsciously, a part of the value systems of her husband's adult classmates at Harvard and their wives.

The psychological damage to the personality of Jews which results from even such apparently harmless and unconscious anti-Semitism as marked the Harvard "retreads" is of course of moral significance. And it is just as morally damaging to those on one side of the caste divide as those on the other. Most important, however, is the fact that the excessive homogeneity of ethnic background, religious convictions and political attitudes which is created by the policies of top management today may result in their taking an unrealistic view of modern American society. Before he wrote *The Organization Man*, William H. Whyte, Jr., began his dissection of the nature of modern executive leadership with a series of articles in *Fortune* magazine which were eventually published in his book, *Is Anybody Listening?* One of his central theses in this book was that management was still seeing American society from the point of view of its rural Protestant values even though we had long since become an ethnically heterogeneous and urban nation. This type of management myopia has since been formally and rationally corrected. Yet one wonders if it is actually possible for leaders to possess an emotionally realistic view of our society when, day after day, at home, in the office and at the club, their most intimate social relations are limited to contact with a homogeneous caste of men exactly like themselves. On the contrary, caste exclusiveness in an otherwise open and changing society will only lead to resentment and unconscious fears of change, and even of new ideas.

Caste and Xenophobia

Acceptance of change and new ideas demand imagination and a reasonable capacity for abstract thinking. Today, as the management process becomes more and more a matter of planning and mathematical programming utilizing computer technology to an ever greater extent, the need for leaders who are skilled in the handling of abstract problems will necessarily increase. At the same time, all studies of the relationship between personality and social structure show that where men of varying backgrounds and points of view come together and associate in more or less intimate social relationship, abstract thinking and imaginations tend to be stimulated. Throughout history, urban and heterogeneous cultures have always been more productive of ideas than rural and homogeneous ones. Similarly, a sacred and caste-protected executive suite may be less conducive to creative thinking than one with more cosmopolitan and secular make-up. One does not have to be a sociological determinist to see that continual ethnic inbreeding leads to mental stagnation. In this connection, a professor at the Harvard Business School who has been studying the career lines of twenty-five Jewish and twenty-five gentile graduates has tentatively reached some interesting conclusions: the companies with no Jewish managers, he notes, are more likely to be led by organization men and to "put considerably more store in adjustment and modesty and lack of troublesomeness. The companies hiring Jewish boys, on the other hand, are much more tolerant of positive qualities that might be troublesome, such as intelligence, aggressiveness, and so on. I get the feeling that what they are telling us is that 'we are willing to try and get along with someone that will not fit into the job easily in

order to get a gain in creativity, motivation and intelligence!' "⁶
Homogeneity is, after all, more comfortable but, in the long run, it
may be stultifying. It is thus significant that American Motors,
under the leadership of George Romney, a Mormon, was the first of
the Detroit companies to counter the small-car threat from abroad
and at the same time—in an industry which is unusually addicted to
ethnic homogeneity of management personnel—also took the lead
in employing Jewish managers.

One of the most dangerous consequences of caste in the executive
suite is that it fosters a xenophobic fear and stereotyping of the outsider. The vast majority of corporation executives are of course not
active anti-Semites. The sociological fact of caste, however, fosters
anti-Semitic attitudes, which stereotype the Jew as an outsider and,
in its extreme form, as less than human. As long as the Jew remains
an outsider, the stereotype will be reinforced. For anti-Semitism is,
contrary to conventional common sense, not overcome through
friendship or pleasant relations with Jews. Rather, it is only overcome, in the long run, when Jews are seen in the role of *insiders*—
when one's close associates are Jews, some of whom will then
become friends while others will be heartily disliked. In other words,
until the caste line as a sociological fact is de-institutionalized, as it
were, no amount of individual contact or developing friendships
between Jews and gentiles will counteract the dehumanizing stereotype.

Xenophobia and the Radical Right

Anti-Semitism, however mild and gentlemanly, which fosters the
dehumanization of Jewish-gentile relationships, paves the way, in
turn, for the active anti-Semite. All available evidence points to the
fact that the Nazi anti-Semite had his way in Germany largely because of the prevalence of gentlemanly anti-Semitism. At the
moment, it seems safe to say that active anti-Semites are still a small

and ineffective minority who are distasteful to the vast majority of
Americans. Yet I am convinced the radical Right is a real and
potential threat in this country today—in many ways more dangerous than McCarthyism. For unlike McCarthyism, which appealed
to the caste resentment of rising ethnic minorities, the present radical Right is grounded, on the whole if not entirely, on the resentment of old-stock Protestants who feel threatened by a conspiracy
of rising racial and ethnic minorities (among them Jews). This new
radical right, I am afraid, has a large number of latent, if not yet
overt, anti-Semites within its ranks and leadership. There has been,
for example, no open anti-Semitism within such movements as the
John Birch Society or Dr. Frederick C. Schwarz's Christian Anti-
Communist Crusade. But there is a danger that, in a crisis, both
might go the way of Gerald L. K. Smith's Christian Nationalist
Crusade which summed up the nature of the conspiracy against the
American Republic as follows:

1. The preservation of our Christian faith against the threat of
Jew Communism, a conspiracy to abolish Christian civilization and
the Church of Jesus Christ.
2. The preservation of our national sovereignty against the Jew-
financed plot of World Government.
3. The preservation of our racial self-respect against a campaign
to mongrelize our race and mix the blacks with the whites.
4. The preservation of our national independence against the
threat of Jew Zionism which attempts to dictate both our domestic
and foreign policies.
5. The preservation of our national tradition threatened by the
immigration flood.[7]

The personal psychology which sees a conspiratorial threat behind every issue, then, is one of the most dangerous consequences of
the sociological forces of caste. Though the vast majority of leaders
in the corporate establishment today have little sympathy with the
radical Right, there is a danger that their continuing caste isolation

326

may ultimately lead them to embrace some conspiratorial theory of society. Unfortunately, there are already more than a few highly respected members of the community and leaders in the postwar military-industrial complex who have been active supporters, in one way or another, of various movements on the extreme Right. What else but a conspiracy theory of American society, for example, would prompt one of the nation's leading industrial statesmen, himself a graduate of the Massachusetts Institute of Technology, to give large sums of money to an obscure college in Arkansas whose main claim to educational excellence is its organization and support of a crusade against Communists in our midst. It is indeed tragic that so many have failed to learn from the experiences of one of prewar Germany's leading industrialists, Fritz Thyssen, who was eventually forced to flee, in horror and disgust, from a conspiratorial movement he had helped to bring to power. In his autobiographical confession, *I Paid Hitler*, Thyssen wrote:

> For ten years before he came to power I supported Hitler and his party.... I did in fact bring about the connection between Hitler and the entire body of the Rhenish-Westphalian industrialists. It is common knowledge that on January 27, 1932—almost a year before he seized power—Adolf Hitler made a speech lasting about two and a half hours before the Industry Club of Dusseldorf. The speech made a deep impression on the assembled industrialists, and in consequence of this a number of large contributions flowed from the resources of heavy industry into the treasuries of the National Socialist party.[8]

It would be wrong, as the conspiracy theories of the orthodox Left would have it, to say that Hitler was brought to power against the will of the German people by the big-business community. On the contrary, Hitler was a popular demagogue who appealed to all classes, especially lower-middle-class shopkeepers. He obtained financial support only from those big businessmen, like Thyssen, who had lost all faith in democracy and saw Hitler as their protector against the Communist conspiracy.* Like Mr. Welch of the Birch Society, who has openly damned democracy as inevitably leading to communism, Hitler ended his speech to the industrialists of Dusseldorf with a familiar sophism: "The economic parallel of political democracy is Communism."

Finally it should be a significant warning to those who take mild anti-Semitism mildly that, though he admitted that he had "not attached much importance to the anti-Semitic brawls of the National Socialists" before 1933, Thyssen finally withdrew his support from the party and eventually fled Germany because, as he piously put it, his "Catholic conscience" finally could not stand the immorality and beastliness of Nazi anti-Semitism.

Any complex and changing society is bound to produce its share of men and women whose paranoiac fears of conspiracy draw them to the demagogue. Their numbers are bound to increase in an era of protracted conflict and fear such as ours. But as Thyssen eventually found out, and as anyone dedicated to the democratic process (cumbersome and infinitely frustrating as it always is) should know, the simplifying demagogue preaching hate and crying conspiracy will always go too far, especially if allowed to come to power. Thus Hermann Goering, whom many honorable British and American gentlemen found to be quite a charming host when they visited his deerstalking parties in the Schorheide during the thirties, once told Thyssen that he thought Alfred Rosenberg's *Myth of the Twentieth Century* (the Nazi racial bible) was "completely idiotic."[9] Yet he eventually played his part in making the myth a realistic nightmare. Caste, in other words, is a dangerous and insidious thing. Though gentlemanly anti-Semitism seems harmless enough on the surface, it is deeply dehumanizing, perhaps more so for those who guiltily go along with the gentlemanly mores than for those who are convinced anti-Semites.

* According to Thyssen himself, few big businessmen had any connection with Hitler's rise to power. Herr Krupp von Bohlen, head of the munitions family, violently opposed Hitler from the start and only did business with him after the fact of his power had been firmly established.

328

Caste and the Corporation

It is important to emphasize the potential dangers of caste and gentlemanly anti-Semitism in a nervous age which is all too susceptible to the conspiracy theories of the radical Right. It is not that the leaders in the contemporary, corporate community hold these theories to any appreciable extent; it is, rather, that if they are not convinced of the kind of world they want and are willing to work for, they are all the more vulnerable and susceptible to the arguments of demagogic leaders with radical theories who, in the end and perhaps too late, they will come, like Thyssen in Germany, to repudiate with repugnance. In other words, "without intent to dominate and without clearly defined doctrine" themselves, as Berle put it in the passage previously quoted, the best of men may become unwitting partners in producing a world they surely will not want.

Established Communal Authority and Political Power

But of even more importance for the stability of our society are the dysfunctional consequences of caste in inhibiting the restoration of the authority of a conservative establishment. A radical Right thrives on the insecurities of a manipulative society which, in turn, are largely due to the continuing discontinuity between *established communal authority* and *established political power*. As was emphasized in the previous chapter, the Democratic Party in the North, no matter how conservative and responsible, simply does not represent established authority in most communities. Back in the thirties, established political power passed to the Democrats partly because the business establishment failed the nation economically. Today, however, our large corporation economy has certainly been successful in supplying the endless stream of goods and services which the American people so admire. Yet the corporation managers have failed to translate their undoubted communal prestige and authority, both economic and social, into majority political power. The reasons are many but they all flow, I think, from the fact that the corporate establishment has failed in its aristocratic function of assimilating into their ranks new men of power and ambition from the Jewish and other minority communities. Equality of opportunity in an open and freely competitive society, as opposed to equality of conditions in a planned society, has surely been the professed ideology of the business community and the Republican Party since the days of Abraham Lincoln. But this ideology has been denied in fact by the closed caste policies of the executive suites of the nation. As a result of caste conventions in the community, leaders of the Republican Party have quite naturally failed to retain their position as the "conscience-carriers" of our heterogeneous twentieth-century society.

The sweeping Kennedy victory in the city of Philadelphia in 1960 proved an excellent example of this failure. After the election, a group of concerned Republican leaders both from politics and business made a careful study of the reasons for their defeat. According to their own findings, the primary reason was not the difference in economic philosophy between the two parties but rather the Republican Party's failure to assimilate minority group members into its ranks. As one businessman–political leader put it at the time: "The local GOP has failed to broaden the base of our party to bring in other than Anglo-Saxons." "The Republican Party," he continued, "cannot win unless it opens its doors—its heart and mind—and lets these people in."[10]

It is now a fact of political life that minority-group members tend to dominate the electorate in large cities like Philadelphia. Political power is a reflection of the composition of the community. But it may be even more sensitive to the composition of communal leadership. Minority-group members, in other words, tend to follow the example set by their leaders. Even though they often do not comprehend the complexities of many political issues, they can and do understand and identify with the concrete social and occupational insults their most talented leaders have had to suffer so often at the hands of the Anglo-Saxon establishment which still dominates the Republican Party. This is especially true of members of the Jewish community. As long as the leaders of minority groups are denied the equality of opportunity which is supposedly the central core of the Republican Party's philosophy, and as long as the Republican Party is led and supported by those who actually mean equality of opportunity only for those like themselves, it is only natural, and an expression of their sense of dignity, that minority-group leaders and their followers should continue to support the Democratic Party.

In this connection, it is instructive to look at the contrasting backgrounds of the larger contributors in Philadelphia to the Republican and Democratic campaign committees in 1960. On the one hand, most of the larger contributors to the Democratic Party were minority-group members (largely Jews) who were also individual entrepreneurs. It is worth noting that one consequence of caste exclusion in the large corporation executive suite is that, while old-stock Protestants will take the path of least resistance and most security by going to work for the large corporation, minority-group members must of necessity strike out for themselves as individual entrepreneurs. This of course means that they will usually make more money if successful and, moreover, that they will be able to be more independent in politics and to spend more time working for the party they have chosen. It is also ironic that the party of free enterprise tends, in any community, to have more members who are working as salaried bureaucrats in large corporations (the executive suites of large utilities such as Bell Telephone, for example, are usually staffed with Christians only) while the party which is supposedly against free enterprise and unregulated competition (Democrats) is in fact supported by free-enterprising entrepreneurs rather than bureaucratic managers. In other words, the Republicans are shutting out talented potential leaders from their ranks, men who believe in and are actually practicing free enterprise, but who are alienated from the party because of its caste values.

It is surely hard to justify the corporation as the "conscience-carrier of twentieth-century American society," so long as its policies at the management level are dominated by caste considerations. In recent years, for example, there has been considerable talk among top management people that there should be more attention paid to politics; the management point of view, so their thinking goes (and correctly, I think), is not getting over to the electorate; it has even been suggested that executives be encouraged to take a more active part in politics. On the other hand, perhaps it would be better for these management experts to *stick to their last*. For it has been the central contention in these pages that, should the large corporation leaders make a concerted effort to make their management personnel truly representative of today's rising talent, regardless of ethnicity or race (eventually), they would do more toward influencing the American electorate in the direction of management's point of view than all the millions of dollars they now spend on publicizing the "Corporate Image" or selling the Republican Party on Madison Avenue.

What is good for the Republican Party is also good for General Motors. More respect for the sincerity of the Republican Party's claim to represent all the people—a claim any party which expects to become the established majority party must make—would result, for example, from the resignation of several leading executives from their clubs because their admission committees refuse to admit one of their friends to membership because of his ethnic or Jewish background. Indeed, for one man of real stature in the American business community and the Republican Party to stand up and be counted on this issue, thereby surely alienating some members of the business community, would be worth more than all the campaign oratory and money spent in advertising combined. Unfortunately all too many of America's business leaders still feel somewhat like the Coca-Cola Company executive who was once quoted as making the following comment on his company's stand, or lack of a stand, on the racial issue: "Our problem is to walk a very fine line and be friends with everybody. I've heard the phrase 'Stand Up and

Be Counted' for so long from both sides that I'm sick of it. Sure we want to stand up and be counted, but on both sides of the fence. For God's sake, why don't they let us go on selling a delicious and refreshing beverage to anybody who's got a gullet he can pour it down."[11]

But if what is good for General Motors is also good for the country, and indeed there is every reason to agree that this is not only true but of vital importance to the health of our society, modern management must, whether it wants to or not, take more philosophical stands on such issues as racial integration and anti-Semitism. Top managers must be "uncommon men" and take the lead rather than wait to be pushed by FEPC legislation, the NAACP, the Anti-Defamation League, or the American Civil Liberties Union. Moreover, if management waits until the state takes the initiative it will have the statism it deserves. The national corporation must now be seen as a moral community whose duty it is to set standards on a national scale. It is in the best American traditions, which many think it is now the conservative's duty to defend, that morals should emerge spontaneously from communal life and not be legislated by the state. The downfall of every civilization comes, not from the moral corruption of the common man, but rather from the moral complacency of common men in high places.

It is indeed a sociological anachronism that caste exclusion, rather than aristocratic assimilation, should still dominate the moral values of this important sector of American society, whose leaders, especially since the war, have at the same time revived so many aspects of the old aristocratic ideal of *noblesse oblige*. This aristocratic ideal of responsibility is perhaps nowhere better illustrated than in the initiative now taken by corporate management in the support—through gifts, scholarships and research funds—of privately endowed educational institutions. Yet the close co-operation which now exists between these two vital American institutions only serves to emphasize certain fundamental ideological differences between the university and corporate communities. These differences are many

333

and various, and some are unfortunately the result of mutual misunderstanding. The differences in their attitudes toward caste exclusion, as against aristocratic assimilation, however, are real and fundamental. For it can safely be said that, primarily in the years since the war, the intellectual community in America, which increasingly centers in the university, has gone a long way toward assimilating the Jew.

> The primary concern of American education today is not
> the development of the appreciation of the "good life" in
> young gentlemen born to the purple. . . . Our purpose is to
> cultivate in the largest possible number of our future citi-
> zens an appreciation of both the responsibilities and the
> benefits which come to them because they are Americans
> and are free.
>
> *James Bryant Conant*

XV

Aristocracy on the Campus

Stereotypes always contain an element of truth. As the stereotype
would have it, while General Motors went to Washington in 1953,
Harvard University was sent there in 1961. In the election of 1960,
the American intellectual community not only supported John F.
Kennedy, they were also almost universally opposed to the Republican candidate. As Walter Lippmann, who this time supported the
Democrats, put it in an interview after the campaign: "Nixon would
not have attracted new brains to Washington. The intellectuals
were overwhelmingly for Kennedy—brains, you know, are suspect
in the Republican party."[1]

335

Aristocracy and the Faculty Club

It would of course be absurd to say that the universities possess a monopoly of brains in this country. On the other hand, the brains in the universities and the brains in business are, on the whole, used for very different purposes and operate from very different value premises. These differences are partly due to the ethnic composition of the membership in the two communities as well as their differing convictions regarding racial and ethnic equality. Whereas the business leaders who lunch at Philadelphia's Union League are uniformly nominal Christians and predominantly old-stock Protestants, it would be hard to find a more ethnically, racially and religiously heterogeneous elite in America than the one found lunching at the faculty club at the University of Pennsylvania (or at any other major university today). And, while virtually every member of the Union League probably supported Nixon in 1960, a safe majority of the faculty members at the University probably voted for Kennedy. This difference in political values has sociological roots in the fact that, in contrast to the business community, the leaders in the universities are now being drawn from all segments of our heterogeneous society.

But this has not always been so. Throughout the thirties and well into the forties, our major universities were still staffed almost entirely by old-stock Protestants. Except for a few fields like anthropology, it was almost impossible for a Jew to obtain a tenure position on the faculty. At Harvard, Yale, Princeton and the University of Pennsylvania, for instance, there had never been a tenure professor in English until the Second World War. According to Heywood Broun's study of anti-Semitism referred to in an earlier chapter, departments of sociology were among the worst offenders as far as anti-Semitic hiring policies were concerned.[2] In every field and department, however, the changes since the war have been tremendous.

It would be safe to say that today no faculty at any leading university can afford to be anti-Semitic in its hiring policies. Even English departments have now been forced by the postwar competition for talent, as well as by changes in convictions, to hire talented scholars regardless of their Jewish antecedents. At the University of Pennsylvania, for instance, I was talking about these changes recently with a full professor in the English Department, who also happened to be of old-stock Protestant origins if not convictions. The following remark was typical of the changed climate of opinion in the University today as compared to before the war: "It is not that some of my best friends are Jews," the professor said, "as a matter of fact, most of my best friends are."

Or take the discipline of sociology, which is my own field of interest. As noted earlier, it was largely a Protestant monopoly up until the Second World War. Today, a significantly large proportion of the most talented and productive sociologists in America also happen to be of Jewish descent (they are not usually active members of any Jewish religious community). In this connection, it is significant that, up to and including the period of the Second War, all the presidents of the American Sociological Society, the highest professional honor in the field, were gentiles and largely of old-stock Protestant ancestry. Since the war, the society has elected its first Negro president, and the presidency has by now had several Jewish incumbents. A rapidly growing discipline, sociology simply cannot afford to exclude Jews (even if its leaders should so desire, which, with minor exceptions they do not). Perhaps the following is of interest here: As the 1960 Presidential campaign got under way, I received, as presumably did many of my colleagues, a little brochure announcing the formation of a "Scholars for Nixon" organization. A casual glance at the professors who were sponsoring this new organization was revealing. It was not entirely accidental, I think, that the Nixon sponsors listed on the letterhead included an eminent sociologist who, in the considered but unspoken opinion of many members of the profession, has had a rather difficult time maintaining the traditional prestige of the department of sociology which he heads in a distinguished university, partly because of his rather exceptional, at least nowadays, propensity for hiring only gentiles, preferably those who fulfill his conception of the "clean-cut" Anglo-Saxon stereotype. One tends to forget that it is little incidents such as this, multiplied many times in many areas of life, which, in the long run, sway the votes of even educated people who cannot afford the time for a detailed study of political issues. Nixon had, of course, no way of knowing that these were the values of his eminent sponsor from sociology. It is indicative of the differing values of our two parties, nevertheless, that this man should have turned out to be a Republican in a profession where Republicans are all too rare (one leading sociologist of my acquaintance who has always been a supporter of the Republican Party, once facetiously attributed his continued support to the fact that he always seems to take the side of the underdog—which Republicans are in most faculty clubs).

The faculty communities today in America, then, are much less likely to represent ethnic ivory towers than is the case in most executive suites. In contrast to the homogeneity of the top leadership at General Motors, Bell Telephone or du Pont, the Harvard faculty community is today an infinitely cosmopolitan one, with representatives from various races and religious groups. Even the Board of Overseers at Harvard, certainly representative of the ultimate in communal authority and prestige, has changed with the times. As of 1900, for example, the board was composed of twenty-five gentlemen, all save six of whom were Bostonians, and all of whom were of old-stock Protestant antecedents. The first member of the Harvard Corporation from the Catholic community was elected in 1920. By 1925, the geographical dominance of Proper Boston was broken, as seventeen of the thirty board members lived outside Boston, in many cities from New York to San Francisco. And in 1960 the board was still representative of the nation's elite as a whole: thus the thirty members included the late John F. Kennedy and other men of authority from varied backgrounds: a Cabot and a Peabody from Proper Boston, a Rockefeller from New York, and men of Jewish origins like Meyer Kestenbaum and Stanley Marcus (even though ethnically representative, the Overseers are still predominantly Republican, according to such authorities as John K. Galbraith and Arthur M. Schlesinger, Jr., which I think, in contrast to these eminent scholars, is probably a good thing as it may tend to nicely balance the predominantly Democratic leanings of the faculty).

The aristocratic assimilation, especially since the war, of talented individuals from all segments of society into the faculty elites of the nation is one of the most important contemporary witnesses to the staying power of our traditional ideal of equality of opportunity. In striking contrast to the caste-limited corporate elites, the major universities are now drawing on a truly national pool of talent. Though all large organizations face the usual dangers of institutionalized conformity, a group of talented men from widely varying backgrounds should, in the long run,* prove to be more creative than a comparable, but caste-limited, leadership group. Above all, the university elite today may well be in a better position to take a more realistic view of our heterogeneous and rapidly changing society. It is hardly realistic, for instance, for the members of our corporate elite, through the Republican Party, to claim to be the best and most vocal representative of our traditional opportunitarian, as against equalitarian, values when, at the same time, they are in practice not upholding them, at least as far as the assimilation of non-Anglo-Saxons into their leadership ranks is concerned.

Aristocratic Elite Selection on the Campus

Perhaps of even more importance than the changing composition of the faculty elite since the war, is the fact that the American student community is changing in the same direction. The large university community in America has since the Second War become one of

---

* I say *in the long run* because, at the moment, the highly competitive and heterogeneous atmosphere in the academic world may well produce too much success-striving and promotion-publishing with too little emphasis on lasting accomplishment.

339

the most important elite-selecting and elite-producing institutions in the whole free world. Truly the sun never sets on the alumni of Harvard University. As a result, the student community in Cambridge today has changed sociologically beyond recognition from the days when Franklin Roosevelt was an undergraduate, and, as was described in an earlier chapter, a small class of "Gold Coast" patricians ruled the roost. As former President Conant indicated in the lines quoted at the opening of this chapter, while Harvard was engaged at the turn of the century in educating the sons of the Anglo-Saxon establishment along with a small minority of talented youths from less privileged backgrounds, it is today educating and training a highly ambitious and carefully selected student body from all classes, from all over the world, from a wide variety of racial, religious and ethnic groups—and only partially leavened by a minority of the more talented members of the traditional Eastern Seaboard establishment. Rather than educating a privileged elite to better perform their duties, it is now training an ambitious elite to accept the responsibilities which will go with the privileges and power they will eventually acquire.

As never before in our history, the large corporations are now depending on the universities for the selection and training of their future managers. In a recent exhaustive study, *Big Business Leaders in America*, by W. Lloyd Warner and James Abegglen, this trend has been documented in some detail. Not only has there been a steady increase in the proportion of college graduates among the ranks of top management; Warner and Abegglen also found that these managers were also most likely to have been graduates of high-prestige institutions. Thus, of their sample of 476 top executives who went to college, 86 had received their undergraduate training at Yale, Harvard and Princeton alone (statistically this number should have been 2 rather than 86).[3] And a large proportion of the rest were graduates of a few other high-prestige universities and colleges, such, for example, as the Massachusetts Institute of Technology and the Wharton School at the University of Pennsylvania.

Aristocracy on the Campus

Since the close of the Second World War, these prestige institutions have constantly tried to make their undergraduate student bodies, like their faculties, as representative of the population as a whole as possible. At the Wharton School, for instance, almost four-fifths of the undergraduates, according to informal polls taken in my own classes for over a decade or more, have had at least one grandparent born outside the boundaries of the United States. This indeed represents a systematic policy of aristocratic assimilation, as caste on the campus has steadily retreated before the modern admissions policies which stress individual accomplishment rather than family background.

Before the Second War, for instance, the typical prestige college took an entering class with an average aptitude score of 500, or about the middle of the whole college population.[4] As a former member of the admissions committee at Princeton put it, they rarely turned down an applicant with "good character and adequate scholastic preparation." Adequate scholastic preparation often meant private schooling and the "character" requirement often meant the proper ethnic and non-Jewish affiliations. It is no wonder that a new professor at Princeton in 1940 should have made the following comment upon meeting his first class: "It was like looking at a room full of siblings."

Today, on the other hand, sibling similarity no longer marks the entering classes at our prestige institutions. Their average aptitude scores have risen to about 625, which is at the top 10 per cent of all those examined or the top 4 per cent of the age group as a whole (at Princeton, Columbia and Amherst, the average scores are in the neighborhood of 650 or the top 2 per cent of the age group). And the Jewish quotas have also been relaxed (only M.I.T. has made a clear statement regarding the nonexistence of quotas of any kind). At Princeton the token Jewish population body which existed before the war has now risen to about 15 per cent of the total student body. Within the Ivy League as a whole, the Jewish population has risen by almost 50 per cent.

341

The trend toward more and more aristocratic assimilation has of course meant a decrease in the proportion of private school candidates who are accepted each year. At a place like Princeton, for instance, the more than two-to-one prewar preponderance of private school freshmen has now been reduced to almost half and half. The change since the 1920's has been even more dramatic. Whereas all the members of the Princeton football squad were private school products in 1927, only ten members of a squad of sixty-four players in 1962 were privately educated. Moreover, while the provincial squad of 1927 was drawn mainly from the Eastern Seaboard, the 1962 players came from twenty states, ranging from Texas, California and Washington, to the Middle West, and down to Mississippi and Florida. Watching the Princeton team last fall, I was reminded of the author James Farrell, who made a point of measuring the progress of the melting pot by noting how the "Fighting Irish" of Notre Dame gradually absorbed more and more players of Polish and Italian backgrounds, and eventually Negroes. The Princeton team of 1962, dominated as it was by heroes of Irish, Italian, Greek and Polish origins, was a veritable elite melting pot and not unlike the Notre Dame team of 1932 as far as ethnic origins were concerned.

Aristocracy and the Private School

The private schools themselves have been changing rapidly. Thus Exeter and Andover, the two leading secular schools, have far more heterogeneous student bodies than was the case before the war. While Jews have always been accepted, there is now a sizable Jewish minority at each school. Both schools have recently introduced a series of Saturday religious services with rabbis brought in from the outside. In a fairly recent issue of the *Exonian*, "The Oldest Preparatory School Paper in America," there was a stimulating example of ethnic aristocracy at work in modern America. In the first place, the president of the *Exonian* was Michael Lerner, and the managing editor, Michael de K. Riesman, both sons of two of the nation's leading Jewish intellectuals. A photograph on page 3 showed an Exeter student, who happened to be a Negro, in the process of pinning the captain of the wrestling team of Milton Academy. On the front page, the intellectual and political stimulation of student life was reflected in the headlines: *Urban League Expert to Give Cum Laude Talk; Negative Wins Debate about Congo; Socialist Candidate to Talk . . . On Purpose of His Party; Government Has Right to Censor Mails; Dramat Winter Production "Darkness at Noon."*[5]

No doubt the close personal relations which are now taking place among boys of widely different backgrounds and religious traditions is an important part of the stimulating and creative atmosphere at Exeter. The school is continually reaching out into the whole of American society in order to continue its traditions of aristocratic assimilation. Of the 170 scholarship boys at the school in 1962, for example, fifty were initially recommended to Exeter by a selective group of circulation managers of newspapers all over the country.[6] And following the ideals of Emerson, Exeter is training these boys in the Puritan ideal of its founders who "respected work as such, scorned softness and believed in discipline." It is hardly surprising that one of the former newspaper boys now at the school, Charles Ascheim of the Pittsburgh *Press* (who had never heard of Exeter before being recommended for a scholarship), should say of his experience there: "My ambitions were heightened a little."[7] Today the ethnic Horatio Algers growing up in Pittsburgh would probably find it easier to develop their talents at such schools as Exeter or Andover than attempt to climb through the hierarchy at U.S. Steel, where Duquesne Club affiliation (see the next chapter) seems to be the ultimate requirement for top management positions.

And many other top preparatory schools are following these policies of aristocratic assimilation. Even Groton and St. Paul's schools have changed rather radically since before the war, when

343

they were bastions of old-stock exclusiveness. "We reach out to the world of which we are a microcosm," wrote the Rector of St. Paul's in a report to the alumni in the autumn of 1960. "Twenty countries are represented here in one way or another. *Every segment of American society* is here. Nearly a fourth of the student body is on formal scholarship in varying amounts."[8] Yet perhaps the administration and faculties of these schools are still somewhat more liberal than the parents who send their children there. In this connection, it is of interest that, while a majority of the students at St. Paul's (following the values of their parents) voted for the Republican candidate in 1960, as the student body has done in every election since the Civil War (Lincoln was defeated at the mock election at the school in 1860), the faculty turned in a majority for John F. Kennedy. Such are the dynamics and discontinuities of generational change.

This ethnic aristocracy of talented and ambitious young people now attending the best universities and colleges as well as such schools as Exeter and Andover (and, to an increasing extent, such schools as Groton and St. Paul's) provides a dramatic witness to the staying power of the American Dream of equality of opportunity. Indeed it is no accident that these ideals of aristocracy have not gone unnoticed by American Marxists, who rightly see the opportunitarian ideal as the worst enemy of their ideals of equality of conditions. Thus one of our leading Marxist thinkers, Paul M. Sweezy (himself a graduate of Exeter and Harvard), has recently pointed out the dangerous role now played by the preparatory schools and colleges "as recruiters for the ruling class, sucking upwards the ablest elements of the lower classes and thus performing the double function of infusing new brains into the ruling class and weakening the political leadership of the working class. . . . It is this aspect of the American educational system," he continued, "involving as it does fairly generous scholarships and other forms of assistance for the bright poor, which is often and *least deservedly* praised as democratic."[9] What a Marxian finds so dangerous, Tocqueville found desirable.

344

The Fraternities: Caste or Aristocracy

In recent years, there has been a considerable amount of comment upon the conservative trend on the campuses of the nation. There is indeed such a trend. One of its manifestations is the fact that the extreme Right has a hard core of followers on most campuses. Though these extreme groups represent an important movement among the younger generation, and although some of the more interesting students fall into this category, I shall not discuss them here. The more moderate majority of the student body, however, seems to be more conservative too. On the whole, this conservatism represents a revolt of the younger generation against the dogmatic liberalism of their fathers in the economic and political spheres. At the same time, this conservative generation is vitally concerned with the status revolution and increasingly tends to embrace the values of racial and ethnic equality. Its mood is best reflected, not in terms of the "sit-in" liberals of more extreme convictions, but rather in terms of its slow but steadily growing disenchantment with traditional fraternity values and other excluding campus mores. For example, one of my more reflective students, of a conservative economic and political outlook, is working to transform the rigid caste line within the fraternity system at the University of Pennsylvania. His case is of particular interest for its contrast to his old-stock heritage—his great-grandfather once excluded Treasury Secretary Henry Morgenthau from his private Tuxedo-like preserve in the Catskills.

Since the war, fraternities and exclusive campus clubs as well as other aspects of the "Gold Coast" and fraternity row mentality—which, as we have shown in an earlier chapter, grew up primarily between 1880 and the Crash in 1929—have come under constant attack both from college administrations and the student body as a whole. It is indeed typical of this generation that countless campus battles have been waged, not over such ideological abstractions as the virtues of socialism or the labor movement, or even over fascism or

345

communism, but simply over concrete incidents which have threatened an older generation's ideal of Aryan or Anglo-Saxon brotherhood. The pattern is simple: a group of young men in a fraternity—right after the war they were often veterans who had fought for their country before returning to the campus with its prewar mores—happen to like or admire a young Negro or Jew and quite naturally see no reason why they should not ask him to join their group; an invitation is issued and a solemn pledge is made; but the alumni are horrified at this callow disregard for their hallowed ideals of Aryan brotherhood; the local chapter is reprimanded and eventually, if it does not repent and break its pledge with its new friend, it is often suspended from affiliation with the national brotherhood. This pattern has been repeated on countless campuses all over the land and, since the war, has been gaining momentum. Newsweek magazine, for example, has recently summed up the campus mood as follows:

At California's Stanford University, the Alpha Tau Omega chapter is feuding with its national organization. The issue: It pledged four Jewish students in violation of the national charter and now is threatened with disbarment.

At Williams College in Massachusetts, Beta Theta Pi tapped a Negro for membership and was ordered by the national hierarchy to halt all initiations pending an investigation.

These two recent incidents on campuses at either end of the nation were more than regrettable outbreaks of discrimination. They were part of a complex evolution in today's U.S. college life, summed up in this question: Is the old fraternity handshake losing its grip? The fact is that the traditional image of the fraternity of the '20s, rooted in snobbism and hell-raising, is crumbling in the face of spreading sophistication and intellectual seriousness on most U.S. campuses. Youngsters are beginning to snipe at reactionary leadership in the national organizations; colleges and universities are demanding that local chapters sign non-discriminatory pledges and are trying to force campus houses into mature, productive channels.

More significant, at many schools the actual prestige of fraternities seems to be gradually withering.[10]

In spite of the growing dissatisfaction of both administrations and students, the fraternity system, especially in large and impersonal university campuses without adequate dormitory space, will probably remain in force for some time to come. It is significant nevertheless that at Yale University—where snobbism and rah-rah barbarism, in the days when Walter Camp's football teams ruled the roost and Dick Stover's crowd of Andover men ran the campus, once set the tone for the nation—the "Gold Coast" life of fraternity and club is now being threatened as never before. Thus two houses, Chi Psi and York Hall, have only recently closed their doors, and a third, St. Elmo's, is now up for sale.

These changes at Yale are significant because, in their study of the composition of the modern executive suite referred to above, Warner and Abegglen found that Yale had been the leading producer of top executive talent. Yet one wonders if the Yalemen now entering business will be as willing as their fathers to endure the stultifying atmosphere which the excluding social life of modern businessmen's clubs now provide. As we have shown in an earlier chapter, their patrician and wealthy fathers found it to be entirely proper to work on intimate terms with someone like Sidney Weinberg—to sail and cruise with him in the summer and to entertain him in their homes—and, at the same time, not even dream of asking him to join one of their favorite clubs. But it would be hardly proper, so their fathers would argue, to ask their friends at the Links Club, for instance, to accept a man whose parents were immigrant Jews and whose formal education stopped after graduation from a Brooklyn public school. On the other hand, Sidney Weinberg's two sons, educated at one of the best preparatory schools in the nation, Deerfield Academy, and at Princeton University, hardly had such background handicaps. Today, in other words, it would surely seem less than human for old friends at Deerfield,

347

Exeter or Andover to suddenly break off their friendships upon facing the club or fraternity systems at Yale, Princeton or Stanford, just because one or another of them happened to have Jewish parents. And this is just exactly where the new conflicts on the campuses of the best and most exclusive universities are now taking place. The brothers in the better gentile fraternities are *not* insisting on taking Jews into their ranks; rather, they are insisting on their rights, indeed their sense of human dignity, to take in their old friends from school or new friends on the campus who happen to be Jewish in *origins* (we stress *origins* only because so many of these conflicts arise over boys who have no Jewish convictions or ethnic characteristics and who, moreover, are often converts to Christianity). At the author's own university, for instance, a fraternity only recently pledged a boy who had been a friend of many of the brothers at school; he had been given the key, and it was only as he was about to be initiated that the discovery of his Jewish antecedents led these young "gentlemen" to break their pledge and ask for a return of the key. Needless to say, the young man subsequently left the university.

The present generation of Yalemen, then, is faced with a very different image of the Jew than their fathers' of Sidney Weinberg's generation, who after all probably thought of the few Jews they might have seen around the campus in their day as "greasy grinds" and "meatballs" who were largely "townies" from New Haven who could not have afforded club life anyway. The present conflicts between caste and aristocracy at Yale and on other campuses of the nation, and the gradual disenchantment with the rigidly excluding mores of fraternity row, will eventually be felt in the halls of even the most exclusive clubs as the present generation of Yalemen move on to high positions in our large corporations. Pressures for change, in fact, are already apparent at some of the best clubs in the nation. Before discussing them in the next chapter, however, something should be said about how the courting mores of Eastern Seaboard upper-class females have changed since the war.

The Campus Meritocracy and Upper-Class Courting Mores

In the long run, of course, the family is the basic unit of any class. And the courting mores of the young eventually determine the ethnic composition of a class in the next generation. By and large, the double standard in sexual mores (and the concomitant parental protection of the female) will tend to reinforce racial and ethnic endogamy, while any increase in the freedom of women and the single standard will tend to encourage cross-caste marriages.

The single sexual standard, as far as political rights were concerned, began in this country with the Presidential election of 1920 (the unprecedented Republican plurality at the polls that year was partly due to the fact that upper-class women took advantage of their newly won rights far faster than their lower-class contemporaries). A sexual revolution in social and economic mores followed in the twenties. But within the ranks of the Eastern Seaboard upper class at least, the sexual revolution in education, especially in college attendance, did not take place until the 1940's. In other words, even as late as the 1930's (when parents felt poor anyway), only a minority of upper-class daughters were sent to college. The vast majority remained at home, like their mothers and grandmothers before them, and went through a carefully institutionalized debutante ritual, where their parents made sure that the democratic whims of romantic love were focused on the "right" boys from their own caste backgrounds. The parents were usually successful, and the ritual fulfilled its latent but most important function.

Then the war came, and young men went away to defend their country and the democratic freedom of the whole Western World. For the first time, many of their wives and fiancées found out that it was much easier to get an interesting job if they had been to college. Add to this the frequency of divorce and the general insecurity of the world during and since the war, and even the most tradition-bound parents soon saw the utility of their daughters' having an education in order to support themselves in an emergency.

Today, the debutante ritual is still in full force in most of the major cities in the nation. As a result of our postwar affluence, the ritual is even more elaborate and costly than before the war. Yet, at the same time, it has far less meaning for the debutantes themselves, especially for those with the ability and ambition to go to one of the better Eastern Seaboard colleges for women. They now take their education seriously, and as a result the campus community, on the whole but not entirely, has gradually since the war come to displace the local community with its country clubs and the debutante balls as the major upper-class courting environment.

Campus courting mores are, of course, closely bound to the values of the fraternity system, which are all too often still modeled on the country-club values of parents. On the fraternity-dominated campuses, moreover, the women students are likely to choose their dating partners on the basis of their status in the fraternity hierarchy. This is more often the case among those who have gone to college for the social prestige and campus social life than among those who are seriously committed to some intellectual endeavor.

On the other hand, it is on the campuses of the highest intellectual prestige today that traditional fraternity values are being most vehemently challenged, by both the new generation of students and the administration officials (if not by the professional old grads). Fraternities do not dominate the campus social life at Harvard or Yale (Princeton lags behind in this respect, though no one is entirely satisfied with the club system there) to anywhere near the same extent as, for example, at such less intellectually demanding institutions within the Ivy League as the University of Pennsylvania or Cornell, to say nothing of the fraternity-dominated social life at so many of our large state universities. In addition, of course, one must remember that the very top women's colleges do not have sororities at all. In this connection, it is of interest that, only last year, one of my better women students was rather horrified at the fraternity anti-Semitism at the University of Pennsylvania. For she had spent her first three college years at one of the "Seven Sister" institutions in New England, where, so she said, such attitudes were not only rare but actively spurned by the majority of students. Of Jewish origins herself, she married a Harvard senior (who happened to be a gentile) and is now completing her degree at the University while her husband goes to the Medical School.

What seems to be happening, then, is that a scholastic hierarchy of campus communities governed by the values of admissions committees is gradually supplanting the class hierarchies in local communities which are still governed by the values of parents. And by and large, the higher the scholastic standing of the campus the more the students will be attracted to one another on the basis of intellectual interests as against the traditional affinities of caste and class. This may be especially true among highly intellectual young women. For they are more likely than men, or their less intellectual sisters, to be emotionally attracted by those whom they admire and look up to intellectually. In other words, it is just those proud parents whose daughters have been accepted at the women's colleges of highest prestige who will, in turn, be most often surprised to find their daughters coming home some day to announce their engagement or marriage to a young man outside their (the parents') conception of the permissible endogamous circle. And this is more likely to happen to daughters at places like Radcliffe, Bryn Mawr or Vassar than to those attending second-rate junior colleges or fraternity-dominated institutions of lesser scholastic stature.

Just as the hierarchy of the Church was the main avenue of advancement for the talented and ambitious youth from the lower orders during the medieval period, and just as the business enterprise was responsible for the nineteenth-century rags-to-riches dream (when we were predominantly an Anglo-Saxon country), so the campus community has now become the principal guardian of our traditional opportunitarian ideals. For, since the Second War, there has been a silent but persistent ethnic revolution on our high-

THE PROTESTANT ESTABLISHMENT

prestige campuses along the Eastern Seaboard, where a large proportion of our national leaders in coming generations are now being socialized as peers on the basis of scholastic achievement rather than ancestry. But unfortunately, for some time to come, these campus values of aristocracy will continue to conflict with the caste values which still dominate the local community and corporate leadership in this country. Like the proverbial tail that wags the dog, these values result largely from the caste policies of the admissions committees of the majority of upper-class clubs, which will be discussed in the next chapter.

352

He had a box at the opera and a Stevens-Duryea and nothing to do except go to tailors and visit specialists and occasionally blackball a Jew or a newcomer applying for membership in some club he belonged to.

John Dos Passos

XVI

The
Club

Lacking the communal solidarity which older social structures have inherited from their feudal pasts, American society has always been faced with the dangerous consequences of extreme individualism. Atomized individualism always tends to degenerate into anarchy on the one hand, and more or less extreme forms of centralization on the other. Yet fortunately, up till now, we have avoided both these two extremes through our traditional ability to create a host of mutually excluding, yet interlocking, voluntary associations. "Wherever at the head of some new undertaking," wrote Tocqueville over a hundred years ago, "you see the government in France, or a man of rank in England, in the United States you will be sure to find an association." Following Tocqueville, other commentators on American society have seen that our most stable traditions have been associational and republican rather than individualistic and democratic. "In the past and up to the very present," wrote Max Weber after a visit to this country over half a century ago, "it has been characteristic precisely of the specifically American democracy that it did *not* constitute a formless sand heap of individuals, but rather a buzzing complex of strictly exclusive, yet voluntary associations."

At the upper-class level in America, moreover, the club (a private voluntary association) lies at the very core of the social organization of the accesses to power and authority. Thus Cleveland Amory found that, in familistic and conservative Proper Boston, it was the leading men's clubs rather than the family which were the primary agents of social control. "So severe are Boston's leading clubs that even the blue bloods have to watch their step to gain admission."

It is the anachronistic admissions policies of the leading upper-class clubs in America today, as I will try to show in the present chapter, which lie at the very basis of the decline of upper-class authority, and the resulting confusion in communal and national leadership. The authority structure in this country is indeed in trouble, for instance, when a member of the oldest country club in the nation was able to say, not long before President Kennedy was killed, that he was proud of the fact that his club's admissions policies had not yet descended to the level of accepting any member of the nation's First Family. The absurdity of the statement is more understandable, however, when one takes into account the fact that the vast majority of the distinguished doctors, lawyers and business executives and their families who reside in the Boston suburb where the country club is located (and where John F. Kennedy was born) are categorically unacceptable for membership because of their ethnic origins.

354

Caste and the Country Club

As was seen in an earlier chapter, what Henry James found to be one of the uniquely characteristic American institutions was born with the founding of The Country Club, at Brookline, Massachusetts, in 1882 (the year Herbert Spencer was honored at Delmonico's by the secure and fit Anglo-Saxon establishment). Along with the business and suburban boom which marked the twenties, the country-club movement went through its period of most rapid growth. By 1929, there were some 4,500 clubs in the nation, the highest number ever attained.[1] During the Depression and the Second War, there was a steady decline in private clubs. The trend was not checked until 1956 when, perhaps partly owing to the great popularity of our golf-playing President, new clubs began to mushroom across the suburban landscape. In spite of prohibitive costs of construction and maintenance, new golf courses have been built since 1956 at the rate of about a hundred a year. So important are clubs to the American way of life that their management has now become a recognized profession. The Club Managers Association of America has been formed since the war and now has over two thousand members, with headquarters in Washington, and a professional journal. It is now possible to specialize in this important area of social relations, and some universities are even going so far as to offer a Bachelor of Science degree in club management (the sophistication of this new science was illustrated recently at an annual meeting of the CMAA, when the professional managers were instructed, in the course of a seminar, to use "Chef Recommends" on the menu for items which were either overstocked or unusually profitable). Thus the associational organization of snobbery, like so much else in modern American life, has now been democratized and professionalized.

The boom in suburban clubs since the war has come about for several reasons. Of most importance is the fact that the policies of country-club admissions committees are one of the main ways of perpetuating caste divisions in an age when both the suburbs and elite leadership positions have been greatly democratized. From the time The Country Club, in Brookline, was founded until roughly up to the end of the Second War, the American upper-class suburb was almost entirely the monopoly of Anglo-Saxon Protestants. Country-club membership, then, was largely a reflection of community composition. As the upper classes still lived in large houses with spacious rooms and plenty of servants, moreover, the club was primarily a functional association used for the single purpose of sport (mainly golf, as private tennis courts and swimming pools were the rule).

On the other hand, the country club of today has become a veritable community. Space is at a premium even in the sixty- and seventy-thousand-dollar executive housing developments, while servants are scarce and overdemanding if not unobtainable. Consequently leisure-time and sporting activities have moved to the country club, where restaurants and bars do a thriving business (dues of course can often be written off as a business expense in these days when business and leisure so often interlock). But more than the economic factor is involved. Even the most exclusive suburbs are now no longer the monopoly of Anglo-Saxons, and the club serves to protect one's ethnic purity in increasing heterogeneous neighborhoods. This is especially true as far as elite Jews are concerned, for middle-class Jews are still most likely to settle in predominantly Jewish suburbs. It is the most talented and successful Jewish leaders in the community who of necessity deal on close social terms with gentiles in countless civic and charitable activities, who are also most likely to live in predominantly gentile upper-class neighborhoods. At the same time, as one Jewish civic leader reported: "They'll call on me to lead their Community Chest campaign or help on the Red Cross. But when it comes to the country club, I'm not good enough for them." Catholics are also moving to the suburbs in large numbers. Thus a Democratic political leader who was worried about affluent and suburbanizd Catholics deserting to the Republican Party told Theodore H. White during the last Presidential campaign: "These guys whose grandfathers used to want to be captain of the ward now all want to be president of the country club."[2]

In response to the new suburban heterogeneity as well as to the caste values of the old-stock Protestants who got there first, minority country clubs have multiplied since the war and are now preserving the triple melting pot in the elite suburbs. For example, in the city of Springfield, Massachusetts, there are three leading country clubs: the oldest, the Longmeadow Country Club, has an exclusive membership of some four hundred Protestant families of solid old-stock ancestry (only a few Catholics); the newer and less exclusive Springfield Country Club has three hundred member families, half of whom are Catholic (mostly Irish); and finally, the newest and most lavish club, the Crest View Country Club, has three hundred members, all of them Jewish. In Springfield, according to a student acquaintance of old-stock origins (incidentally, the only one of his clan with the ability and ambition to follow in the long family tradition at Yale), the local upper class has not been at all receptive to the ideals of aristocratic assimilation as far as minority ethnic talent is concerned. Indeed it is no wonder that, according to my student informant, the best people spend quite a lot of time discussing past family accomplishments and criticizing the city's present political leadership, which, of course, is no longer drawn from, or assimilated into, the ranks of the Longmeadow Country Club.

In many ways, then, the caste policies in the modern country club—especially regarding the rigid exclusion of Jews, no matter how prominent they are in the community—are among the sorriest symbols of discrimination in America. By and large, the older generation of Jews have responded to this gentile Babbittry in the suburbs with an opulent Babbittry of their own. Their country-club ritual mirrors that of the gentiles (Jews spend, on the whole, more money on good food and less on alcohol). In the wealthier suburbs, the celebration of Bar Mitzvah rites at the country club at a cost of $10,000 or more is not unheard of. At the same time, the so-called ostentation which gentiles so often give as a reason for excluding Jews from their own more genteel ranks may actually have little existential validity. For few can boast of outdoing, in ostentation, for example, the recent "coming out" party given by Henry Ford II for his daughter at the Detroit Country Club at a cost in the neighborhood of $250,000.

But while this segregated country-club Babbittry may solve the problem for the older generation, it is increasingly inconvenient for their children. For they are now being educated together with their Jewish neighbors in the best private schools, are becoming friends and marrying in some cases, and are absorbing a common set of values and behavior patterns. It is no wonder that they seem to regard the older generation with something less than awe or admiration. Nor is it any accident that some of the best families are now producing offspring who are attracted to the beatnik way of life. For, as several exploratory studies of this postwar movement have shown, the beatniks are appealing to those youths who have dogmatically abdicated from the values of success and snobbery. And, unlike the purposeful, radical youth in the 1930's, who often came from minority backgrounds (often Jewish), the purposefully-purposeless beatniks are more often than might be expected the sons and daughters of solid old-stock Protestant parents.

In teaching at a large Ivy-League university, one finds an increasingly cynical attitude among the students as they face the values of the older generation. Within the past year, for instance, I was having a cup of tea and reading a book in a campus drug store when I was interrupted by an animated conversation in the adjoining booth. A pretty blond senior was bringing her friend up to date on the latest developments in her life. Unconcerned with the desire for solitude on the part of their neighbors, the two young ladies talked in loud tones which were, at the same time, marked by rather overly obvious "preppie" accents, as the younger generation calls them. At any rate, the blonde was discussing her recent engagement to George, a graduate student in economics who also happened to be

358

Jewish. There was, of course, the usual and expected problem with their parents. She was also going against the fraternity mores on the campus. "But you know," the blonde said to her friend, "I finally got bored with the 'tweeds' [fraternity men, I gathered] as a sophomore. . . . And George is the only interesting guy I've met since. . . . For some reason I could talk to him seriously from the very first time we met. . . ." Finally, after listening to her friend's gushing enthusiasms for some time, the other girl asked: "But what will you do with the problem of country clubs and all that sort of stuff after you're married?" "Oh, I've thought of that," the blonde replied. "But you see, George isn't going into business. He's a Democrat and plans to go down to work in the government in Washington, where, he says, all that sort of stuff is much less important."

But there are other less fortunate youths, residents of some of the wealthiest suburbs in the nation, who will not be able to handle "that sort of stuff" so easily. A friend who is an Episcopalian priest is, for example, at the moment counseling two seniors who are planning to marry this June. The girl is of Jewish origins, though not convictions, and her future husband plans not only to go into business but wants also to remain in one of Philadelphia's most exclusive suburbs, where he grew up and knows everybody. This same problem was brought to the attention of the nation and the world when the Rector of St. James the Less, a fashionable Protestant Episcopal Church in Scarsdale, New York, delivered a sermon on the First Sunday after Epiphany, in January 1961. The Rector said, in part, as follows:

This morning I stand before you with a heart overflowing with sorrow and heartache. Something has happened in this community which I feel must be brought to your attention. . . .

My assistants and I, and many in this congregation here present, have the privilege and pleasure of being members of the Scarsdale Golf Club. As I believe you all know, on the Tuesday after Christmas the annual Holly Ball was held at the Scarsdale Golf Club. What has made me sad is that one young man of this parish, of Jewish parentage, whom I baptized at this font . . . was not considered acceptable to be an escort of a young lady of this parish at the Ball. Now, this young lady showed fortitude because, when her friend was not accepted, she withdrew from the Holly Ball—she was not a debutante of this season—she did not "come out" at the Scarsdale Golf Club.

Now I realize that I am dealing with a very complex religious and social issue. I, personally, feel that a member of the Club should be able to take there as his guest anyone who acts with decency, dignity and decorum. . . .

I must, as a priest of this congregation and the pastor of this young man, speak out when a member of my parish, now a Christian, is excluded from the Club. I know the Scarsdale Golf Club is free to work out its own rules and regulations, but I also know that, as a priest of this parish, I must insist that the members of my congregation take a firm stand against a policy which is morally reprehensible. I am not attacking the Club; this is an internal problem of the Club. I am attacking members of my parish, who claim to be Christian, who are not acting as Christians should act in their club.[3]

As everyone knows, of course, the values of Christianity have often been in conflict with those of the country club. Yet most rectors of fashionable parishes have chosen to avoid the issue. Thus the solid parishioners of St. James the Less were probably more shocked at the Rector's public revelation of the issue than at the issue itself. And perhaps they were also shocked when the Rector ended his sermon as follows:

I feel it is my responsibility as your pastor to say that anyone who has in any way, by word or in thought or deed, acquiesced with this position of the Scarsdale Golf Club is no longer welcome to receive Holy Communion at this altar—at God's altar—in this parish until such time as he has worked out his own peace with God in his own way, whether by using the General Confession in Morning or Evening Prayer, or by making his confession to me or any other priest of the Episcopal Church. I say this to those members of this congregation who may have shared directly in this decision, and I say it to anyone here who in his heart and mind agrees with that decision. . . .

I charge you, the members of my congregation, to work and pray with me in this matter, and to see that it shall never happen again in our community.[4]

No doubt similar debutante balls in country clubs across the land are increasingly going to produce embarrassing situations comparable to this one in Scarsdale. At the same time, one suspects that many so-called decent people are only too glad to have someone like the Rector of St. James the Less take a stand against the moral sponginess of the modern suburban way of life. For apparently only one of the 1,800 parishioners of St. James the Less resigned after the sermon. And the young debutante's parents, who after all had gone along with their club's values until this incident, were reported to have said: "We have always been proud of our daughter's stand on this matter."

Finally, it is of interest to observe that the boy, whose father was born of Jewish parents and married to a Roman Catholic, was of far sterner stuff than the protected gentile wife of the Harvard "retread" mentioned in the previous chapter. After all, he had long been conditioned to the country-club values which characterize most suburbs like Scarsdale. "Some of my best friends are members of the Scarsdale Country Club," he said at the time. "I bear no grudges against those club people. I would be discriminating myself if I had any hard feeling. I've learned to live with this kind of thing. Anybody with a Jewish parent does."[5]

Moral conflicts have a way of coming to a head when the conventional mores prove inadequate in new sociological situations. The conflicts between conviction and convention which many leading suburban communities like Scarsdale now face are, of course, important symptoms of the dysfunctional consequences of caste in an age when elite members are coming from diverse ethnic backgrounds. Country-club anti-Semitism is only one aspect of a more general resistance to the need for a representative and authoritative establishment in this country today.

At the same time, it is downtown in the halls of the metropolitan men's club that this same issue is of even more importance. For today, and especially in the years since the end of the Second War, membership in one or two of the leading men's clubs, which lie at the center of communal power in most large cities in the nation, has become a tacit prerequisite for promotion to the top positions in the executive suites of our large national corporations. Insight into the nature of this process may be gained by an examination of the business mores of the industrial city of Pittsburgh.

The Club and the Corporate Elite: The Tail That Wags the Dog

At noon every day in the week, the men at the top of the executive suites in the city of Pittsburgh gather for lunch in a great brownstone pile which has housed the Duquesne Club since 1889. As one old-timer at the club remarked: "The way to tell if a fellow's getting along in any Pittsburgh company is to see if he's yet a member of the Duquesne. As soon as his name goes up for membership, you know he ought to be watched. He's a comer."[6] According to Osborn Elliott, whose book *Men at the Top* is an excellent and intimate study of the mores of modern American business leadership, there are four prerequisites for membership in the Duquesne: "$1,000 initiation fee, $240 annual dues, at least nominal Christianity, and the blessing of your employer, preferably to the extent of his being willing to pay the bills."[7]

The Duquesne Club lies at the very core of the associational organization of leadership in Pittsburgh. In fact, it has been argued by the club's management in the federal courts that income from dues should not be taxable because it is a business organization.

One club member of five years' standing, for instance, "has paid perhaps $30 worth of personal bills himself in that time, while his company has picked up tabs totaling about $6,000."[8] Not only do the large corporations usually support their executives in membership costs; they often have an important say as to whom the club accepts among their younger and rising executives. Thus, if several men from one company are up for membership at the same time, "the corporation usually lets you know who they want to get in first."[9] A major steel company was faced recently with this problem when it had four young executives on the waiting list. A telephone conversation with the president of the firm revealed who ought to be tapped first, and when this fortunate man was elected to membership soon afterward, "all Pittsburgh—including the three men who did not make the grade—became aware of another young man on his way to the top."[10]

Membership in the Duquesne is not only a mark of a man's inclusion within the inner circle of top management. Within this inner circle of executive leadership—and reminiscent of one's days in the Navy during the war, where officers' bars from Norfolk to New Caledonia were differentiated by rank—"a man can be marked by name, rank, serial number (and salary), according to where he eats in the club." By and large, the lieutenants of industry are found lunching on the ground floor, while the higher brass are found upstairs. Thus Osborn Elliott meticulously charts the executive hierarchy in the following paragraphs:

It is when you go upstairs in the Duquesne that you begin to enter the substratosphere of executive power. On the second floor there are no fewer than five dining rooms, including the main one; and in each of these, day after day, the same people sit at the same tables. As you enter the main dining room, the Gulf Oil table is across the way; Gulf's chairman David Proctor sits facing the door, surrounded by his senior vice presidents. In the corner over to the right is the Koppers table, populated by most of the top men in that company, and next to it is the U.S. Steel table, where sales vice presidents break bread together. In another smaller room nearby, Pittsburgh Coke & Chemical's president, chairman and vice presidents gather daily; in still another, Pittsburgh Plate Glass has a central spot, while Alcoa's executive committee chairman, Roy Hunt, holds forth in the corner—next to Jack Heinz's table.

If the Duquesne's second floor feeds the captains of industry, many of the field marshals are to be found on the fourth and fifth floors, where thirty-five suites are rented out by the year (at $12,000 and up) to such companies as U.S. Steel, Gulf Oil, Jones & Laughlin, Blaw-Knox, and Alcoa, to name just a few. These attractively decorated apartments usually have a bedroom, living room and dining room; they are used by the companies' topmost brass for meetings and lunch almost every day, and for dinners perhaps two or three times a week, particularly when a visiting fireman, or rather fire chief, comes to town. . . .

In these company suites new products and mergers are planned, bargaining strategy for labor negotiations is hammered out, multimillion-dollar finacing arrangements are made. Here, and in the public dining rooms below, the professionals of production get together and exchange ideas, day by day. There is a daily exposure of people to people who are all of the same mold or forced into the same mold. This tends, no doubt, to channel their interests and energies toward the mono-purpose goal of productions; and it may well be, as has been said, that Pittsburgh would not be the production marvel it is without the exchange of information, techniques and ideas that take place every noontime at the Duquesne.[11]

Here indeed is a distinctly American institution where close primary relationships are forged between top management men who have the power of decision over transcommunal corporate activities which affect the lives of men and women all over the world, from the Atlantic to the Pacific, from the Monongahela to the Amazon. It is, too, a kind of associational aristocracy-by-ballot which is ideally suited to a dynamic and democratic society's continual need to assimilate new men of talent and power into the top levels of established leadership.

But at the same time this aristocratic function fails, at clubs like the Duquesne, to reach out beyond the boundaries of nominal-Christian affiliations. In the long run, these caste boundaries will inevitably create embarrassing situations which will be downright dysfunctional to the organization and recruitment of leadership. Even today there is in Pittsburgh an executive at the very top level of leadership in one of the nation's major corporations who has never been taken into the Duquesne because of his Jewish origins (even though he has never been associated in any way with the city's Jewish community). But as this executive's high functional position would ordinarily demand Duquesne Club membership, other arrangements have had to be made. In other words, although it may seem absurd, he is *allowed* and *encouraged* to entertain important business associates in his company's private suite on the upper floor of the Duquesne. And he does this in spite of being barred from membership in the club! It may seem hard to believe that such a dehumanizing situation would be tolerated either by this talented executive of Jewish antecedents or by his gentile office colleagues who are also leaders at the Duquesne. But apparently the 1,700 resident and 850 nonresident members of the Duquesne would be contaminated if even one gentleman of Jewish origins were to be made a member of the club. Or perhaps they are all social determinists who have lost faith in their ability to judge men on their individual worth and manners and therefore need the caste line to protect them from the dangerous consequences of exercising their own free will in each individual case. The mistrust of their own moral judgment, moreover, may be hard on the consciences of the non-nominal Christians at the Duquesne. One wonders at the meaning of the so-called religious revival around the Golden Triangle and out at the Pittsburgh Golf Club which was described by the editors of *Fortune* (see above, Chapter II). But perhaps these "Businessmen on Their

Knees" or "Christ Bearers," as *Fortune* so fliply called them, as well as the Protestant Episcopal Bishop who, according to Osborn Elliott, regularly lunched at the table of Admiral Ben Moreel of Jones & Laughlin, have somewhat different interpretations of the teachings of the Church and the nature of human dignity, than did the Rector of St. James the Less in Scarsdale.

More than moral ambiguity is involved here. There is also the question of power and authority. In the city of Pittsburgh since the Second War, for instance, the business community, led by some of the most distinguished members of the Duquesne Club, has produced one of the finest civic and cultural reform movements in the nation. The city has been transformed. At the same time, however, these truly civic-minded gentlemen have not been able to translate their undoubted communal authority into established political power. While the Duquesne is a stronghold of heavy-industry-Republicanism, the majority of the citizens of the city still identify with the leadership of the Democratic Party. And the non-Anglo-Saxon–Protestant Mayor (later Democratic Governor of Pennsylvania), who co-operated with the business community in leading these civic reforms, listed not the Duquesne, but the Pittsburgh Athletic Club as his lone club affiliation in his *Who's Who* biography. In other words, the caste policies followed by the admissions committees of the great metropolitan men's clubs which lie at the core of upper-class authority in every major city in the nation today have contributed more than any other single social force to the anarchy of American leadership. As the onetime Mayor of Boston, John F. Fitzgerald, after participating in the power struggles of his native city for many decades, remarked toward the end of his life: "What this city needs is a lunch club where the blue bloods will eat with the rest of us."

It is not, of course, that the values of the gentile gentlemen who dominate the admissions policies of the Duquesne are out of the ordinary. On the contrary, they mirror the mores of most of the leading metropolitan men's clubs in the nation. In city after city, the admissions policies of the top clubs are increasingly causing our national corporations to bar some of their best-qualified men from top leadership positions. Recently, for example, a leading executive in a nationally prominent corporation was forced to resign because of the caste policies followed by a leading club in Chicago, where the company's head offices are located. This man of Jewish origins was an executive vice president and next in line for the presidency of this famous firm, which was, incidentally, founded and built by Jews. But when the president retired, the executive vice president was informed that he had not been chosen for the presidency because of the so-called "religious" barriers at the leading men's club where top executives meet for lunch. Unlike his counterpart in Pittsburgh, he promptly resigned. Immediately afterward, the board of directors agreed to reconsider his case because of his ability and their need for his leadership. But he refused to consider their new position. Fortunately he had already accepted a high post in the Kennedy Administration, where the criteria for leadership positions were not based on such dysfunctional caste criteria.

One wonders how the younger generation of potential executives now coming out of the leading universities and the graduate schools of business will fit into this pattern of caste exclusion at clubs like the Duquesne. Most of them will, of course, go along with the conventional mores. Or they will choose careers elsewhere; which many sons of present business leaders will surely do for this very reason. And they will presumably be the kind of men who prefer a world where convictions count. A world, for example, where men like Angier Biddle Duke are not afraid to resign from organizations whose policies they consider dysfunctional to the nation's leadership. In this connection, it is important to record the fact that Duke was following the convictions of many men of his generation down in Washington, if not around the Golden Triangle. Thus the Attorney General responded in the same way to the admissions policies of the Metropolitan Club (which incidentally has had a long aristocratic tradition as far as distinguished Jews like the

Lehmans, Schiffs, Warburgs, Strauses and Lippmanns are concerned). And these convictions held by the younger generation in Washington are by no means a monopoly of the Democrats. Robert Kennedy's friend and clubmate at the Metropolitan, George Cabot Lodge, was the first to raise the issue of the club's policies toward Negroes. Perhaps the main point at issue here, is the fact that not only are caste policies dysfunctional as far as the associational organization of leadership within the business community itself is concerned; these policies are also dysfunctional in that they will, in the future, alienate more and more young men of talent and principle from seeking careers in the business world.*

The Club and the Rumblings of Revolt

Although policies of caste exclusion still characterize the vast majority of metropolitan men's clubs in America, there are signs of change, even though the bastions of the business establishment still lag behind. New York City has always been the center of talent and the money-power in America, and its clubs, such as the Union ("the

* Two points about the differing reactions of the political as against the business world to club policies of caste should be made here. In the first place, in contrast to the dominant majority of Anglo-Saxon Protestants who dismiss the matter as a "private and personal problem," the members of minority groups are keenly sensitive to institutionalized exclusion of members of their own groups regardless of their merits and manners. Thus the Negro press featured the prominent resignations from the Metropolitan. The New York Amsterdam News (October 14, 1961), for example, made a thorough survey of the prominent men who belonged to the Metropolitan and headlined the fact that George Lodge, Angier Biddle Duke, Assistant Attorney General Burke Marshall, and Oren Root as well as the Attorney General all resigned from the club. And the paper's readers could understand this kind of behavior far better than many technical political and economic issues they are forced to vote on. And the second point is this: as we live in an age of great moral cynicism where politicians are only supposed to do things which will spawn votes, it is important to record the fact that all the men who resigned from the Metropolitan Club were not men who had run for public office or depended on voter appeal for their jobs. They were men in high appointive positions as well as men of independent wealth who did not depend on their jobs for subsistence.

mother of clubs" in America), Knickerbocker, Brook, Racquet and
Tennis, Union League, Century, Metropolitan and University, have
always been strongholds of our traditional and Anglo-Saxon metropolitan upper class. According to no less an authority than Cleveland Amory, however, "what is happening to the great city clubs of
New York is one of the most extraordinary social changes of our
times."[12]

On the whole, the active club life which marked the masculine
side of upper-class society in New York a generation ago has gone
into a steady decline since the war. While clubmen of Madison
Grant's generation might have belonged to a dozen or more clubs
(as late as 1928, for example, Percy R. Pyne II, of the clan that opposed Woodrow Wilson's attempt to abolish the club system at
Princeton, belonged to some twenty-five of the most prominent
clubs in the city), today few men bother with more than three or
four (Averell Harriman, who listed memberships in ten clubs before
the War, listed only two in the latest Social Register). This steady
decline in club life is, of course, due to many things, among them
the increase in suburban living, the invasion of wives (both into
men's clubs and into men's lives as a whole), the lack of loyal servants and, perhaps most important of all, the democratization of
plutocracy. In discussing these changes in his latest dissection of
upper-class mores, Cleveland Amory arrives at the conclusions that
also lie at the very core of our own thesis. In other words, he finds
that the major and most powerful clubs are still obsessed with
caste exclusion (what he calls the "Society Point of View") and
have simply failed in their aristocratic function. "Generally speaking," he writes, "this country's major clubs, which might have been
expected to provide leadership in the direction of a genuine aristocracy, have instead proved that they have little conception of even
the basic rudiments of the American social process."[13]

And, also in accord with our thesis, Amory sees the decline in
New York's club life as partly a result of the younger generation's
disenchantment with anti-Semitism. "Never have clubs, as clubs,

seemed more forbidding," he writes, "than to the younger generation of the 1960's" and "the blanket anti-Semitism prevailing in so many clubs is an excellent example of this inhibition. . . ."[14]

On the other hand, Amory finds that the most successful social clubs in New York in the 1960's—the Century, the Cosmopolitan, the River, and the Regency, as well as the socio-theatrical and literary clubs like the Lotos, the Players and the Coffee House—all have members who also happen to be of Jewish origins. But above all, the college clubs have been the most successful in the city. Once citadels of snobbery (right after the war, one of my friends was extremely offended that his friend, a Harvard classmate and law partner, was refused membership in the Harvard Club because of his Jewish origins), these clubs are now the most useful in the city because, as one member of the Harvard and Century clubs, who recently resigned from the Union after almost a quarter of a century's membership, put it recently: "I want a club where I can take a couple of friends without producing a birth certificate, a marriage license and a blood test."[15]

It is significant that this gentleman included the Harvard as one of his two remaining clubs, for, in 1958, it quietly elected its first Negro member. And "obviously the time will come," writes Cleveland Amory, "when many clubs will have many Negro members, and when that happens, in the vanguard, of course, will not be the Society clubs but the Aristocratic ones."[16] But in spite of the acceptance of change which marks the policies at the Harvard and Century clubs, such eminent clubs as the Union, Knickerbocker and the Links are still dominated by the Society and bourgeois ideals of caste exclusion.

The differential response to the social changes of our era are reflected in the club system in New York; indeed they reflect the conflicting social forces which lie at the very heart of our whole social system. Sometimes apparently unrelated sociological facts (as, for example, the previously discussed case of the eminent sociologist who supported Nixon) have a way of hanging together to form a pattern. Thus the nature of American leadership at any given time is partly a reflection of its leaders' attitudes toward clubs. It is of interest that Dwight D. Eisenhower, after taking office in 1953, listed some *twenty* club affiliations, in the Washington Social Register; Harry Truman listed none ("I've had so many club snubs I can hardly remember them individually"); President Kennedy listed only one (the aristocratic Brook). And in the same pattern, Eisenhower's Secretary of Defense, the genial and shrewd Charles E. Wilson, lived in the fashionable Grosse Pointe area where he belonged to the Bloomfield Golf and Bloomfield Hunt clubs, as well as the Detroit Club, in the city; President Kennedy's Secretary of Defense, on the other hand, lived in the university community of Ann Arbor and listed no clubs in his *Who's Who* biography, went camping for recreation, and has an abstract and statistical mind with little time for clubby genialities. But by far the most important clue to the difference between the Democratic and Republican leadership in America today is to be found by examining the membership and admission policies of the Links and Century clubs in New York City. If the last election had been decided within the halls of either one of these two clubs, Richard Nixon would have won by a landslide at the Links but he probably would have been beaten at the Century.

Although the Knickerbocker and Union clubs have long been strongholds of the Protestant Anglo-Saxon business establishment in America, centered in the family firm and Wall Street investment banking houses, the Links Club, since the war, has become the New York *rendezvous* of the national corporate establishment. It is of symbolic interest that the Links was founded in 1921, not as a purely business club, but rather "to promote and conserve throughout the U.S. the best interests and true spirit of the game of golf." Its out-of-town membership is almost entirely business and includes such eminent members as a Crocker from San Francisco, a Pillsbury from Minneapolis, a Ford from Detroit, a Field from Chicago, a Humphrey from Cleveland, a Mellon from Pittsburgh, a du Pont from

Wilmington, a Pew from Philadelphia, and a Cabot from Boston. Of course its membership does not include such eminent and public-spirited business leaders as Sidney Weinberg or Meyer Kastenbaum, even though they may be intimate friends of many members. No Jews, and few if any professors or Democrats, belong to the Links.

The Century Association is far older than the Links and was founded for very different purposes by a group of artists and authors, in 1847. But "authors and artists cannot stand apart from the practical world," wrote the founders. "The world of politics and economics and the price of pig iron has a heavy hand in fashioning the artist." And so they invited into their club "gentlemen of any occupation provided their breadth of interest and moral qualities and imagination make them sympathetic, stimulating and congenial companions to the society of authors and artists."[17] This tone set by the founders has stood the test of time. At the Century today, one meets artists, professors, college presidents and distinguished men of affairs from both business and politics. As artists are not likely to be awed by a man's origins, there are Jews among the membership which includes (in rather striking contrast to such business household names as du Pont and Ford) the Boston psychiatrist Carl Binger; Robert K. Merton, one of the nation's most eminent sociologists; artist George Biddle; authors A. M. Schlesinger, Jr., A. A. Berle, Jr., and Walter Lippmann; as well as a host of political and governmental leaders like Adlai Stevenson, Dean Acheson, David Lilienthal and Nelson Rockefeller, to name but a few. It is no wonder that Cleveland Amory finds the Century to be the "most distinguished" and one of the most thriving clubs in the City of New York today (from a Who's Who, if perhaps not from a Social Register, point of view).

In the middle of the twentieth century, then, the contrasting membership and admissions policies at the Links and Century clubs are arresting examples of the forces of caste, on the one hand, and aristocracy, on the other. On the whole, while the Links represents the authority of the business-Republican establishment, the Century's membership reflects the cultural and political leadership of the nation and is far more receptive to the ideals of the Democratic Party. The club affiliations of the Rockefeller family are of interest here. The family is of course Republican, and Nelson is one of the most eminent members of the party. There are eight members of the family listed in the latest edition of *Who's Who in America*, and one or another of them belongs to all the leading clubs in New York City. In spite of their Republican affiliations, and perhaps because of their aristocratic rather than bourgeois values, however, four of them list membership in the Century as against only *three* in the Links: David, the banker, lists membership in both clubs; John D., Jr., John D. III and Nelson list only the Century; James S. and Winthrop, both businessmen, list only the Links; two list no clubs in their *Who's Who* biographies.

The pattern is a revealing one—especially the fact that Nelson lists membership in the aristocratic Century rather than the caste-bound Links. For perhaps Nelson Rockefeller, whose family symbolizes the very essence of established communal authority in this country, may eventually be able to lead his party to a new position of established political authority. But, as the eight Eisenhower years so amply demonstrated, this transformation will not be produced by any single victory or series of victories at the polls; it will not be done through campaign oratory and platforms professing the ideals of civil liberty; it will not be done by putting forth minority candidates for office or by appointing Catholics or Jews to important governmental positions; it will, in the long run, be accomplished only when the established communal leaders who dominate the Republican Party in city after city assimilate within their ranks the most distinguished and talented men in their respective communities, regardless of their ethnic or religious origins. This will not be done until, among other things, the admissions committees of the leading metropolitan men's clubs, in the style of the Century rather than the Links, take seriously their aristocratic role as leaders of assimilating associations in the communal organization of power. Or, as Richard

Nixon put it after his recent defeat, until the Republicans "quit being an exclusive social club."

What is needed, then, is a sociological, rather than a political, revolution within the ranks of the establishment. And this revolution, in accord with the Whig tradition in England rather than the radical tradition in France, needs only to regenerate its original ideals of equality of opportunity. Insight into the origin of the ideals of Lincolnian Republicanism may be obtained by a brief look at the history of Philadelphia's Union League Club.

The Union League
The Rise and Fall of the Lincolnian Ideal

A century ago, at the close of the tragic year of 1862 and not long after the bloody battle of Antietam and Lincoln's announcement of the Emancipation Proclamation, a group of Philadelphia gentlemen founded the Union League.[18] In the traditional American pattern so admired by Tocqueville, this new association was founded in order to support the ideals of the Union cause in the city, and eventually in the nation as a whole.

Pennsylvania had been a Democratic state for some time before the Civil War. Buchanan, the only Pennsylvanian ever to reach the White House, was a Democrat, and General George M. McClellan, who was relieved of his command after Antietam and opposed Lincoln for the Presidency as a Democrat in 1864, was a native Philadelphian. At the time of the League's founding, fully half of the city's population was anti-Lincoln. Many of the city's most distinguished businessmen were Democrats who considered Lincoln a menace to orderly trade with the South (Philadelphia was a textile center). The leaders in Society also tended to be Democrats: according to George Boker—independently wealthy Society leader, poet, clubman, and the "handsomest man in the city"—the best people thought "the President was vulgar, the war was vulgar, and the

374

people who waged it were of the common sort, who would shortly receive a merited castigation from the gentlemen of the South. . . ."[19]

The Union League grew out of violent conflict in principles which split the very heart of Proper Philadelphia into two opposing camps. A group of the city's most cultivated gentlemen had been in the habit of meeting regularly at the famous "Wistar Parties" ever since their founding during the city's Golden Age, in 1789 (a group of cultured and civic-minded businessmen still carry on the tradition today). But the parties were suspended for the first time since their founding because the members finally came to disagree so sharply on the issues of caste and the Civil War. And so, in the autumn of 1862, those Wistar Party regulars who supported Lincoln founded the Union Club. The club was hardly popular among the best people. The distinguished George Boker, one of the club's founders, was even threatened at pistol point on Chestnut Street and was only saved when a friend knocked the pistol out of the assailant's hand. At the club's first meeting, so many members feared to rock the boat of respectability that barely a dozen gentlemen attended. But many distinguished Philadelphians soon followed the lead of men like George Boker. At the Union Club's seventh meeting, on December 27, the members founded the Union League. From its inception, the League was "to be more than a social club which spent pleasant evenings discussing oysters, science and literature," as one of its founders put it. Rather, it was to assume the moral leadership of the Union cause in the city. According to the original Articles of Association, "the primary object of the Association shall be to discountenance and rebuke by moral and social influence all disloyalty to the Federal Government, and to that end the Association will use every proper means in public and private."[20]

The spirit of the League soon spread throughout the city and the nation. Other Union Leagues were founded in New York, Boston, Washington, San Francisco and in many smaller communities in every Northern state. A veritable flood of patriotic pamphlets was distributed from Maine to California urging the support of the party of Abraham Lincoln. In the course of the war, the members of the Philadelphia League organized, equipped and financed at their own expense nine regiments (including one of the first Negro regiments in the nation), two battalions and a troop of cavalry. And even though McClellan was a native Philadelphian, the League led the fight for the successful re-election of Lincoln, in 1864.

But perhaps the most important thing about these early days of the League was the fact that it was founded by men who were true to their convictions and, at the same time, secure leaders of fashionable society and the world of affairs. There was in Philadelphia, in other words, an *authoritative establishment of representative gentlemen who were able to take the lead in an unpopular cause and eventually succeed*. As George Boker put it:

> The moral power which our association exerted upon our members and our guests soon touched the popular heart, and strengthened, consolidated, and organized the patriotic sentiment of our people.... The effects of our meetings had a powerful influence on the social position of disloyal men. They were excluded from our fellowship; they were shut up within their own small coteries.... In vain they complained of social ostracism, or threatened us with reprisal.[21]

At the war's end, then, the leaders of the Union League could look back with pride at a task well done. The members of the Philadelphia League now formed a club and built a great brownstone pile on Broad Street, on the outskirts of center city at that time. Today the mellow and distinguished clubhouse is a reminder of the past, as it sits amidst a sea of sterile skyscraper architecture at the very heart of the city, halfway between City Hall and the famed Academy of Music.

It was at a town meeting at the Academy of Music, in the historic year of 1882 (the year which marked the height, as well as the beginning of the end, of the Republican establishment and the creation of social forces of caste which this book has been engaged in analyzing), that a significant example of the League founders' ideals of freedom as against caste was displayed. For the meeting at the Academy of Music was held in order to publicly protest the expulsion of Jews from the land of the Czars. It was led by some of the League's founders, including George Boker—who had once served as U.S. Minister to Russia—and General H. T. Collis, Civil War hero and Irish-Episcopalian, whose Jewish brother-in-law was one of the city's leading citizens. The League's leadership in this protest meeting was natural enough at that time, for many of its original members— including the president of the city's most fashionable synagogue, the city's leading bibliophile, numerous business and professional leaders, and former officers in the Union Army—were Jews.

But the meeting at the Academy symbolized an era which was gradually drawing to a close. In contrast to the opportunitarian and anticaste ideals held by the club's founding generation, the League soon would come to regard all Jews and all gentlemen of Jewish origins as a pariah caste and categorically ineligible for membership. I was reminded of these lost ideals, while watching a large Republican rally at the Academy of Music during a recent Presidential campaign. As I watched the enthusiastic crowd, which included many affluent members of the Union League, I was struck by the ironic fact that the most forceful speaker on the stage that night was the Senator from New York, Jacob Javits, whose parents, drawn by the American Dream of equal opportunity, had come to this country from Austria and Palestine in the late nineteenth century. Though the respectable Republican crowd at the staid Academy cheered Javits' articulation of their ideals, their local leaders of course would not have accepted him as a member of the League. Nor would they today accept their favorite candidate for the White House, Senator Goldwater, and for the same irrational reasons.

At any rate, though its original ideals have been somewhat dimmed, the Union League gradually came to represent in Philadelphia the essence of established authority. Down through the years, almost every business and financial, professional, civic and

377

political leader of any stature in the city (if of gentile origins) has been a member of the League. This distinguished membership list included every Governor of Pennsylvania until the election of George H. Earle (whose grandfather had been one of the League founders) in the Democratic landslide of 1934. Beginning with the club's hero, Abraham Lincoln, almost every Republican President has been honored and entertained at the club. The most distinguished affair of all was when President McKinley and all his Cabinet, including T. R. Roosevelt, were royally entertained in 1900. Although the League had always been a Republican stronghold, it is of symbolic interest that the first formal restriction of membership to Republicans came during the bigoted and bitter campaign of 1928, when a resolution was formally passed prohibiting admission of Democrats or other "inharmonious elements."[22]

In 1962 the Union League celebrated its hundredth anniversary. "The tensions that beset the United States today are in many ways comparable to those existing when the Union League was formed," said the club's president in opening a year-long series of events which included the awarding of the club's Gold Medal, first given to Abraham Lincoln, to former President Eisenhower, who was also made an honorary member of the club. "The ideals of the Union League," the club's president continued, "still follow closely those set down by its founders. . . ."[23]

But one wonders if these anniversary celebrations did not have somewhat of a hollow ring. For today, in contrast to most of its long history, the League does not symbolize established political authority in the city. Nor do its members seem to be entirely convinced of the ideals for which its founders fought in the generation of Abraham Lincoln; the ideals, for example, which were once so well expressed at a dinner at the club in honor of George Boker, on his appointment by President Grant as Minister to Turkey in 1871. Thus Senator Simon Cameron (former Secretary of War under Lincoln), in the main speech of the evening, recalled the mood of the founding generation:

The Club

Looking backward yet, I remember how this Union League came into existence. In those days it was not considered "genteel" to be a Republican. All who had the terror of social influence—of society, as it is called—had found refuge in a party which had become the champion of caste, and died in the base service of its master. When the war began between caste on the one hand and liberty on the other, a very considerable proportion of those who loved to call themselves "genteel," many gentlemen of fortune, old Federalists always in good society, and a myriad of snobs, who wanted to get into that circle, joined the Democratic Party. It had become a sort of social maxim, when Mr. Buchanan ran for the Presidency, that Democracy and aristocracy, by some occult influence, had become one and the same thing. And it followed that an attempt was made to tramp out everyone who refused to worship the image of slavery and "Democracy."[24]

Indeed, as the League's president said, our problems today are very much like those of Abraham Lincoln's generation. But where are the men like George Boker, at the Union League or in similar clubs across the land in city after city, who are possessed of sufficient convictions to lead a revolution among privileged, but politically powerless, members of clubs like the Union League who refuse to stoop in order to reconquer the leadership their ancestors fought for when they defeated the "champions of caste" of another day? Around the world, the blood-dimmed tide is surely loosed, as Yeats so clearly saw, and the ceremony of innocence will indeed be drowned forever if the best do not regain their traditional convictions. The ancient Anglo-Saxon principles of aristocratic assimilation will, in the long run, be defeated by conventional Anglo-Saxonism, or the Achilles Heel of Caste.

> They are slaves who fear to speak
> For the fallen and the weak. . . .
> They are slaves who dare not be
> In the right with two or three.
>
> *James Russell Lowell*

Conclusion

Essentially this book has been an attempt to analyze the decline of authority in America in the course of the twentieth century. Its central theme has been that authority in any society is always in danger of degenerating into cynical and manipulative power struggles, as Aristotle saw over two thousand years ago, whenever "persons of great ability, and second to none in their merits, are treated dishonorably by those who enjoy the highest honors." While I have concentrated on the dishonorable treatment of distinguished Jews by members of the old-stock establishment, the same problems of caste exclusion and prejudice extend to the members of other minority groups as well.

380

Conclusion

I have, of course, assumed throughout this book that one of the major functions of an upper class is that of creating and perpetuating a set of traditional standards which carry authority and to which the rest of society aspires. James Baldwin recently suggested how this important function was once fulfilled in this country.

> I suppose it can be said that there was a time in this country when an entity existed which could be called a majority, let us say a class, for the lack of a better word, which created the standards by which the country lived or which created the standards to which the country aspired. I am referring or have in mind, perhaps somewhat arbitrarily, the aristocracies of Virginia and New England. These were mainly of Anglo-Saxon stock and they created what Henry James was to refer to, not very much later, as our Anglo-American heritage, or Anglo-American connections. Now at no time did these men ever form anything resembling a popular majority. Their importance was that they kept alive and they bore witness to two elements of a man's life which are not greatly respected among us now: (1) the social forms, called manners, which prevent us from rubbing too abrasively against one another and (2) the interior life, or the life of the mind. These things are important; these things were realities for them and no matter how rough-hewn or dark the country was then, it is important to remember that this was also the time when people sat up in log cabins studying very hard by lamplight or candlelight.[1]

What is honored in a land is usually cultivated there. The traditional standards upon which this country was built and governed down through the years are in danger of losing authority largely because the American upper class, whose White–Anglo-Saxon–Protestant members may still be deferred to and envied because of their privileged status, is no longer honored in the land. For its standards of admission have gradually come to demand the dishonorable treatment of far too many distinguished Americans for it to continue, as a class, to fill its traditional function of moral leadership. Though

381

it still remains an affluent caste, it no longer possesses the qualities of an authoritative aristocracy. Anglo-Saxonism, in other words, is the greatest enemy both of our upper-class institutions and of our valuable Anglo-American traditions of democracy.

This book, of course, has not argued for the abolition of upper-class institutions in the interests of creating a more egalitarian and homogenized society. Quite the contrary. These institutions are vital prerequisites of a secure and organic leadership structure. In an age, moreover, when so many talented Americans are absorbed in success-striving and status-seeking, the institutionalization of a minority community which relieves distinguished men and their families from further status struggles is more important than ever—but only when its membership requirements are based on talent and moral distinction rather than ethnic or racial ancestry. Any vital tradition, Biblical warnings to the contrary, requires the continuous pourings of new wine into old bottles.

Thus I have written with approval, indeed with enthusiasm, of those old-stock aristocrats who, from the days of T. R. Roosevelt and Charles W. Eliot to the present, have attempted to go beyond the caste values of so many of their patrician peers in order to create a more representative establishment in this country. And I have shown how such elite recruiting and producing institutions as the Phillips Exeter Academy and Harvard College have served so well the aristocratic function in this century. But, in the long run, as I have tried to emphasize throughout this book, a truly authoritative and widely honored establishment will be created in this country only when and if the conservative property interests who dominate the clubs, executive suites and fashionable suburbs of this nation, and inevitably support but less often lead the Republican Party, open their hearts and minds and make a concerted effort to attract and welcome distinguished, and temperamentally conservative, American leaders, regardless of race and religion, into their exclusive ranks. When the Union League, Links or Duquesne clubs become as aristocratic as Harvard, Exeter or Groton, we shall have in Amer-

Conclusion

ica an upper class of real distinction and wide authority. Unfortunately, however, the long run may prove to be far too late.

Since I began to write this book just as the New Frontier was coming into power almost three years ago, authority in America has declined to an alarming degree. I refer, of course, to the tragic relationships between the members of our affluent white society—whether Catholic, Protestant or Jew—and the increasingly poverty-stricken, dishonored and dehumanized members of the Negro minority. This is indeed, as President Kennedy announced to the American people several months before his death, the major moral crisis of our time. In the face of it, anti-Semitism may seem to be of minor consequence. There is of course very little similarity between the present position or history of the Jews in this country and that of the Negroes. Yet before closing this book, I should like to suggest how its approach and central theme may have some bearing on the Negro crisis. For this study of how and why Anglo-Saxonism lost authority within our white community during the first half of this century, especially after 1929, should have something to contribute to our understanding of the issue of white supremacy which has surely lost authority, both in America and around the world, in the years since the close of the Second World War.

In the first place, this book has purposely not focused its main attention either on the nature of the Jewish community or on the qualities and personal characteristics of Jews. Rather it has assumed that anti-Semitism and ethnic prejudice in general are largely due to the values and attitudes held by the members of the dominant group. Thus the extreme anti-Semitism of Henry Adams on the one hand, and the more aristocratic attitudes toward Jews held by President Eliot of Harvard on the other, had nothing to do with the characteristics of Jews as such (they were the same for both men). Adams was a distinguished man of privilege without any real power who took refuge in a nostalgic caste pride in ancestry and "race," while Eliot was a gifted leader of men whose affirming and aristocratic values assumed that old-stock Americans should share their

383

institutions and valuable traditions with the hordes of immigrants who came to this country during his reign at Harvard. And it has been the theme of this book that leadership and stability of authority will only be maintained in this country by those who take President Eliot's view as to the nature of American society.

Similarly, I think, the aristocratic view of American society in the second half of the twentieth century demands desegregation. This is the case in spite of the fact that the vast majority of white citizens —whether gentile or Jew, traditional Southerner or professional liberal—still are possessed of deep-seated (if sometimes unconscious and unadmitted) antipathies and prejudices toward the Negro. For prejudices are only overcome, as I think everything in this book implies, after and not before the members of different ethnic and racial groups have lived and worked together over long periods of time, perhaps for several generations. The generation of old-stock gentlemen who followed Franklin Roosevelt into the Democratic Party undoubtedly retained their class-inherited antipathies and condescending attitudes toward Jews and the members of other minorities. Nevertheless, in spite of their prejudices and owing to their aristocratic convictions as to the nature of our society, they saw the need for sharing positions of power and leadership, and working closely, with members of minority groups in the Democratic Party. It was only the second generation of Democrats, having shared a common war experience and having been educated together at Harvard or elsewhere, who were able to look upon their Jewish and other minority-group friends as their social peers. Even they have undoubtedly retained traditional prejudices which may, in turn, be even less prevalent among their children who are growing up in Washington today. The lesson of this analysis of old-stock anti-Semitism, then, points to the fact that the deeply rooted prejudices held by both Southern and Northern whites toward the Negro will never be cured by education or all the good-will propaganda in the world, but only through the participation of Negroes and whites in

Conclusion

an integrated communal life over a long period of time. And the time to begin, whether we like it or not, is now.

But desegregation will only be brought about peacefully through minority leadership and not through popular demand (this is probably true within both the white and Negro communities, though the brave leaders of the latter hate to admit it). Yet where are the white leaders in the South who, in spite of their inherited prejudices (hardly different from our own in the North), still hold an aristocratic view of modern society and are willing to stand up for law and order, the very basis of all authority, and take the lead in the undoubtedly unpopular cause of integration? There are, to be sure, isolated aristocrats who have of necessity been more brave than most Northern liberals. But where are the intellectuals, college presidents and even solid citizens like those who stood up for Wilson's appointment of Brandeis to the Supreme Court or for the unpopular cause of Sacco and Vanzetti? Or have the members of the respectable Southern establishment, like their counterparts in the North during the five years of McCarthyism, abdicated from authoritative leadership in favor of the popular power of the demagogue? In other words, it is misleading and an avoidance of the main issue, I think, to blame the decline of authority in the South today, and the tragic cases of violence which have inevitably resulted, on the values and attitudes of the uneducated and resentful members of mobs, or on the main-chance values of the demagogues who stir up the mobs rather than lead them. For the mob is waiting for a class of aristocratic leaders who, no longer prisoners of a caste nostalgia, are willing and able to set new standards which the average citizen (who always abhors mob violence) can aspire to. My understanding of the problem of authority would be entirely in accord with the following diagnosis of the problem of the Southern mob by James Baldwin:

The most trenchant observers of the scene in the South, those who are embattled there, feel that the Southern mobs are not an

385

expression of the Southern majority will. Their impression is that these mobs fill, so to speak, a moral vacuum and that the people who form these mobs will be very happy to be released from their pain, and their ignorance, if someone arrived to show them the way. I would be inclined to agree with this, simply from what we know of human nature. It is not my impression that people wish to become worse; they really wish to become better but very often do not know how. Most people assume the position, in a way, of the Jews in Egypt, who really wished to get to the Promised Land but were afraid of the rigors of the journey; and, of course, before you embark on a journey the terrors of whatever may overtake you on that journey live in the imagination and paralyze you. It was through Moses, according to legend, that they discovered, by undertaking this journey, how much they could endure.[2]

Now it is only the better part of honesty to admit that all of us today, in the North as well as in the South, are in very much the same position as the ancient Jews. We are paralyzed by imagining the terrors of the journey of desegregation which we must inevitably take. But so must our Puritan ancestors have been before they braved the wild Atlantic on their journey to their Promised Land on New England's stern and rock-bound coast. So it was for all the millions of our ancestors who came here in later generations. And we, in spite of our terrors and fears, must inevitably make good on Abraham Lincoln's promise of freedom to the descendants of those who were so brutally brought here against their will, in what Stanley Elkins has recently shown us to be one of the most inhuman and cruel examples of slavery in the annals of civilization.[3] This long journey to freedom can only be made without violence and communal chaos, however, if a minority of established leaders, with the authority to fill the moral vacuum which now engulfs us all, steps forward above the conforming crowd and, like Moses in ancient Egypt, shows us the way.

Perhaps we shall never succeed. It helps, nevertheless, to place present problems in some kind of historical perspective. Thus our task will seem less hopeless if we remember that the tragic and dehumanizing conditions in the Negro ghettos which exist in every American city today are hardly much worse than the white slums which the young Jane Addams found in the East End of London. Nor are conditions in Harlem now much worse than they were in ghettos on the Lower East Side of New York at the turn of the century.

Finally, and above all, we all need a religious perspective. Racism in all its forms is a direct denial of the teachings of Christianity. It is thus appropriate to recall the advice once given by Frederick Temple, Archbishop of Canterbury in the days when Jane Addams and Beatrice Webb were discovering the horrors of London's East End, when he related the following parable:

In the market-place lay a dead dog. Of the group gathered around it, one said: "This carcass is disgusting." Another said: "The sight of it is torment." Every man spoke in this strain. But Jesus drew near and said, "Pearls are not equal to his teeth. Look not on the failures of others and the merits of thyself; cast thine eye on thine own fault."

Notes

Preface

[1] E. Digby Baltzell, *Philadelphia Gentlemen, The Making of a National Upper Class*. Glencoe, Ill.: The Free Press, 1958, pp. 395–96. See also paperback reprint, *An American Business Aristocracy*, New York: Collier Books, 1962.

Chapter I

[1] Alexis de Tocqueville, *L'Ancien Régime*. Oxford: Basil Blackwell, 1952, p. 105.
[2] See Ruth Painter Randall, *Lincoln's Sons*. Boston: Little, Brown and Company, 1956

388

Notes

3 William Graham Sumner, *The Challenge of Facts and Other Essays.* New Haven: Yale University Press, 1913, p. 25.

4 Arthur S. Link, *Wilson: The Road to the White House.* Princeton: Princeton University Press, 1947, p. 41.

5 Quoted in Henry Cabot Lodge, *Early Memories.* New York: Charles Scribner's Sons, 1913, p. 213.

6 Quoted in Matthew Josephson, *The Robber Barons.* New York: Harcourt, Brace and Company, 1934, p. 374.

7 John R. Dos Passos, *The Anglo-Saxon Century.* New York: G. P. Putnam's Sons, 1903, p. vii.

8 Alexis de Tocqueville, *Democracy in America.* Vol. II. New York: Vintage Books, 1945, p. 141.

9 Walter Lippmann, *A Preface to Morals.* New York: The Macmillan Company, 1929, p. 66.

10 C. Wright Mills, *The Power Elite.* New York: Oxford University Press, 1956. David Riesman, *The Lonely Crowd.* New Haven: Yale University Press, 1950.

11 Andrew Hacker, "Liberal Democracy and Social Control," *American Political Science Review,* 51, No. 4, December 1957, 1015.

12 Quoted in Carl Sandburg, *Abraham Lincoln: The Prairie Years.* New York: Dell Publishing Company, 1960, p. 205.

Chapter II

1 Arthur Mann, *La Guardia: A Fighter Against His Time, 1882–1933.* Philadelphia: J. B. Lippincott Company, 1959, p. 21.

2 *Ibid.,* p. 298

3 *Ibid.,* p. 187.

4 Fiorello H. La Guardia, *The Making of an Insurgent: An Autobiography, 1882–1919.* Philadelphia: J. B. Lippincott Company, 1948, pp. 214–15.

5 Margaret L. Coit, *Mr. Baruch.* Boston: Houghton Mifflin Company, 1957, p. 102.

6 Quoted in T. S. Matthews, *Name and Address.* New York: Simon and Schuster, 1960, p. 244.

7 *Ibid.,* p. 297.

8 *Ibid.,* p. 3.

9 *Ibid.,* pp. 7ff.

10 *Ibid.,* p. 106.

11 *Ibid.,* p. 240.

12 *Ibid.,* p. 298.

Chapter III

[1] *Harper's*, March 1955, p. 81.

[2] Daniel Bell, *The End of Ideology*. Glencoe, Ill.: The Free Press, 1960, p. 128.

[3] Leo Katcher, *The Big Bankroll: The Life and Times of Arnold Rothstein*. New York: Harper & Brothers, 1959, p. 12.

[4] The theory of the triple melting pot in the third generation derives from two main sources: Marcus Lee Hansen, *The Problem of the Third Generation Immigrant*. Rock Island, Ill.: Augustana Historical Society, 1938; and Ruby Jo Reeves Kennedy, "Single or Triple Melting Pot? Intermarriage Trends in New Haven, 1870–1940," *The American Journal of Sociology*, Vol. XLIX, No. 4, January 1944. For a fascinating discussion of this subject, see Will Herberg, *Protestant, Catholic, Jew: An Essay in American Religious Sociology*. New York: Anchor Books, 1960.

[5] Nathan Glazer, *American Judaism*. Chicago: University of Chicago Press, 1957.

[6] Abraham Cahan, *The Rise of David Levinsky*. New York: Harper & Brothers, 1917, p. 3 and p. 528.

[7] Here I am following the historical accounts of American Judaism contained in Nathan Glazer, *op. cit.*, and Oscar Handlin, *Adventure in Freedom: Three Hundred Years of Jewish Life in America*. New York: McGraw-Hill Book Company, Inc., 1954. See also E. Digby Baltzell, *An American Business Aristocracy*, New York: Collier Books, 1962, Chap. 11.

[8] For an excellent study of New York's Jews during this period, see Moses Rischin, *The Promised City: New York's Jews, 1870–1914*. Cambridge, Mass.: Harvard University Press, 1962.

[9] See Cleveland Amory. *Who Killed Society?* New York: Harper & Brothers, 1960, Chap. VIII.

[10] Harvey O'Conner, *The Guggenheims*. New York: Covici-Friede, 1937.

[11] Nathan Glazer, "Social Characteristics of American Jews, 1654–1954," *American Jewish Year Book*, Vol. 56. Philadelphia: The Jewish Publication Society of America, 1955, p. 9.

[12] Handlin, *op. cit.*, p. 144.

[13] *Ibid.*, p. 145.

[14] Myron S. Kaufmann, *Remember Me to God*. New York: Signet Books, 1958.

[15] *Ibid.*, pp. 112–13.

[16] *Ibid.*, p. 180.

[17] Joseph P. Sims, *The Philadelphia Assemblies, 1748–1948*. Privately printed, p. 8.

Notes

18 Lawrence H. Fuchs, "Some Political Aspects of Immigration," *Law and Contemporary Problems*, Vol. XXI, Spring 1956, 271.
19 Philadelphia *Evening Bulletin*, February 29, 1960.
20 San Francisco *Chronicle*, August 1, 1960.
21 *Ibid.* (Emphasis added.)
22 For the career of Douglas Dillon, I have mainly followed Lester Tanzer (ed.), *The Kennedy Circle*. Washington, D.C.: Robert B Luce, Inc., 1961, pp. 139–59
23 *New York Times*, January 16, 1962

Chapter IV

1 Brooks Adams, *The Emancipation of Massachusetts: The Dream and the Reality*. Boston: Houghton Mifflin Company, 1919, p. 99.
2 Edmund Wilson, *A Piece of My Mind*. New York: Anchor Books, 1958, p. 88.
3 *Ibid.*, p. 89.
4 *Ibid.*, p. 91
5 *Ibid.*, pp. 92–95
6 Henry Adams, *The United States in 1800*. Ithaca, N.Y.: Great Seal Books, 1957, p. 115
7 Barbara Miller Solomon, *Ancestors and Immigrants: A Changing New England*. Cambridge, Mass.: Harvard University Press, 1956, p. 38.
8 Harold Dean Cater (ed.), *Henry Adams and His Friends*. Boston: Houghton Mifflin Company, 1947.
9 *Ibid.*, p. 476.
10 *Ibid.*, p. 376.
11 Henry Adams, *Letters of Henry Adams, 1892–1918*. Edited by Worthington Chauncey Ford. Boston: Houghton Mifflin Company, 1938, p. 144.
12 *Ibid.*, p. 145.
13 *Ibid.*
14 *Ibid.*, p. 238.
15 *Ibid.*, p. 234.
16 Cater, *op. cit.*, p. 483. (Emphasis added.)
17 Henry Adams, *Letters*, p. 620.
18 Edmund Wilson, *op. cit.*, p. 96.
19 Richmond B. Hovey, *John Jay Chapman: An American Mind*. New York: Columbia University Press, 1959, pp. 132–33.
20 *Ibid.*, p. 280.
21 *Ibid.*, pp. 285–86.
22 *Ibid.*, p. 288.
23 *Ibid.*, p. 285. (Emphasis added.)

[24] Here I am following the brief biography of Madison Grant found in John Higham, *Strangers in the Land: Patterns of American Nativism, 1860–1925*. New Brunswick, N.J.: Rutgers University Press, 1955, pp. 155–56.

[25] *Ibid.*, p. 156.

[26] Barbara Miller Solomon, *op. cit.*, p. 201.

[27] Harris E. Starr, *William Graham Sumner*. New York: Henry Holt and Company, 1925, p. 346.

[28] Quoted in Richard Hofstadter, *Social Darwinism in American Thought, 1860–1915*. Philadelphia: University of Pennsylvania Press, 1945, p. 20.

[29] *Ibid.*, p. 31.

[30] *Ibid.*

[31] Henry F. May, *Protestant Churches and Industrial America*. New York: Harper & Brothers, 1939, p. 52.

[32] *Ibid.*, p. 52.

[33] *Ibid.*, p. 70.

[34] *Ibid.*, p. 69.

[35] *Ibid.*, p. 94.

[36] *Ibid.*

[37] See Harris E. Starr, *op. cit.*, chapters I and II.

[38] Quoted in Richard Hofstadter, *op. cit.*, p. 44.

[39] Harris E. Starr, *op. cit.*, pp. 300–301.

[40] Quoted in Eric F. Goldman, *Rendezvous with Destiny*. New York: Vintage Books, 1956, p. 69.

[41] Quoted in Ruth Benedict, *Race: Science and Politics*. New York: The Viking Press, 1959, p. 3.

[42] See Richard Hofstadter, *op. cit.*, pp. 138ff.

[43] Edward Alsworth Ross, *The Old World in the New*. New York: The Century Company, 1914, Preface.

[44] *Ibid.*, Chap. VII.

[45] *Ibid.*, pp. 154–55.

[46] Barbara Miller Solomon, *op. cit.*, p. 127.

Chapter V

[1] Here I have followed Richard Hofstadter, *The Age of Reform*. New York: Vintage Books, 1960, Chap. IV.

[2] Charles William Eliot, *American Contributions to Civilization*. New York: The Century Company, 1897, pp. 85–86.

[3] Richard Hofstadter, *op. cit.*, p. 80.

[4] *Ibid.*, p. 137.

Notes

5 Barbara Miller Solomon, *Ancestors and Immigrants: A Changing New England*. Cambridge, Mass.: Harvard University Press, 1956, p. 87.
6 Wallace E. Davies, *Patriotism on Parade: The Story of Veterans' and Heriditary Organizations in America, 1783–1900*. Cambridge, Mass.: Harvard University Press, 1956.
7 *Ibid.*, p. 48.
8 Edward N. Saveth, *American Historians and European Immigrants, 1875–1925*. New York: Columbia University Press, 1948, p. 194.
9 Henry James, *Charles W. Eliot*. Vol. I. Boston: Houghton Mifflin Company, 1940, p. 344.
10 Cleveland Amory, *Last Resorts*. New York: Harper & Brothers, 1952, p. 21.
11 Charles W. Eliot, *op. cit.*, p. 111.
12 Quoted in Carey McWilliams, *A Mask for Privilege*. Boston: Little, Brown & Company, 1948, p. 6.
13 E. Digby Baltzell, *Philadelphia Gentlemen*. Glencoe, Ill.: The Free Press, 1958, p. 285.
14 Edmund Wilson, *A Piece of My Mind*. New York: Doubleday Anchor Books, 1958, p. 97.
15 Cleveland Amory, *op. cit.*, p. 48.
16 *Ibid.*, p. 83.
17 George Birmingham, "The American at Home and in His Club," in *America in Perspective*, edited by Henry Steele Commager. New York: New American Library, 1947, p. 175.
18 John Higham, *Social Discrimination Against Jews in America, 1830–1930*. Publication of the American Jewish Historical Society, Vol. XLVII, No. 1, September 1957, 13.
19 Porter Sargent, *Private Schools*. Boston: Porter Sargent, 1950.
20 *Time*, April 25, 1960
21 E. Digby Baltzell, *op. cit.*, p. 302.
22 Ernest Earnest, *Academic Procession*. New York: Bobbs-Merrill Company, Inc., 1953.
23 *Ibid.*, p. 232.
24 *Ibid.*, p. 208.
25 *Ibid.*, p. 230.
26 Edwin E. Slosson, *Great American Universities*. New York: The Macmillan Company, 1910, p. 105.
27 *Ibid.*, p. 106.
28 Ernest Earnest, *op. cit.*, p. 216.
29 Samuel Eliot Morison, *Three Centuries of Harvard, 1636–1936*. Cambridge, Mass.: Harvard University Press, 1937.
30 *Ibid.*, p. 416.
31 *Ibid.*, p. 422.
32 *Ibid.*, p. 417.

[33] Ernest Earnest, *op. cit.*, p. 207.
[34] Bernard M. Baruch, *Baruch: My Own Story*. New York: Pocket Books, Inc., 1958, p. 54.
[35] Ernest Earnest, *op. cit.*, p. 218.
[36] *Ibid.*, p. 217.
[37] See Hannah Arendt, *The Origins of Totalitarianism*. New York: Harcourt, Brace and Company, 1951, p. 203. And S. Gertude Millin, *Cecil Rhodes*. London: Harper & Brothers, 1933, pp. 99–100.
[38] John P. Marquand, *The Late George Apley*. New York: The Modern Library, 1940, p. 189.
[39] Osborn Elliott, *Men at the Top*. New York: Harper & Brothers, 1959, p. 163.
[40] *Ibid.*, p. 164.
[41] H. G. Wells, *The Future in America*. New York: Harper & Brothers, 1906, p. 134.

Chapter VI

[1] Henry James, *Charles W. Eliot: President of Harvard University 1869–1909*, in Two Volumes. Boston: Houghton Mifflin Company, 1930.
[2] *Ibid.*, Volume II, pp. 238–39.
[3] John Jay Chapman, "President Eliot" in *The Selected Writings of John Jay Chapman*, edited by Jacques Barzun. New York: Anchor Books, 1959, pp. 232–45.
[4] Charles W. Eliot, *American Contributions to Civilization*. New York: The Century Company, 1897, p. 165.
[5] *Ibid.*, p. 136.
[6] Barbara Miller Solomon, *Ancestors and Immigrants: A Changing New England*. Cambridge, Mass.: Harvard University Press, 1956, p. 181.
[7] *Ibid.*, p. 187.
[8] *Ibid.*
[9] *Ibid.*, p. 186.
[10] *Ibid.*
[11] Quoted in Heywood Broun and George Britt, *Christians Only*. New York: The Vanguard Press, 1931, p. 18.
[12] Henry James, *op. cit.*, Vol. II, p. 295.
[13] *Ibid.*, p. 294.
[14] *Ibid.*, p. 159.
[15] Theodore Roosevelt, *The Letters of Theodore Roosevelt*. Vol. III. Edited by Elting Elmore Morison. Cambridge, Mass.: Harvard University Press, 1951, pp. 535–36.
[16] *Ibid.*, Vol. VI, pp. 1042–43.
[17] *Ibid.*, Vol. VI, p. 1359.

18 *Ibid.*, Vol. VIII, p. 1361.
19 *Ibid.*, Vol. VIII, p. 1018.
20 *Ibid.*, Vol. VII, p. 256.
21 *Ibid.*, Vol. VI, p. 1335.
22 Franklin Delano Roosevelt, *F.D.R., His Personal Letters.* Edited by Elliott Roosevelt. New York: Duell, Sloan and Pearce, 1947, pp. 418–19.
23 *Ibid.*, p. 523
24 *Ibid.*, p. 520.
25 Quoted in Arthur M. Schlesinger, Jr., *The Age of Roosevelt: The Crisis of the Old Order, 1919–1923.* Boston: Houghton Mifflin Company, 1957, pp. 323–24.
26 Franklin Delano Roosevelt, *op. cit.*, pp. 502–03.
27 Quoted in Schlesinger, *Crisis of the Old Order*, p. 321.
28 Franklin Delano Roosevelt, *op. cit.*, p. 33.
29 Schlesinger, *op. cit.*, p. 327.
30 *Ibid.*, p. 331.

Chapter VII

1 Jane Addams, *Twenty Years at Hull House.* New York: Harper & Brothers, 1910, p. 3
2 Beatrice Webb, *My Apprenticeship.* London: Longmans, Green and Co., 1926, pp. 209ff.
3 Jane Addams, *op. cit.*, pp. 85–86.
4 Quoted in Garrett Hardin, *Nature and Man's Fate.* New York: Mentor Books, 1961, p. 170.
5 Eric F. Goldman, *Rendezvous with Destiny.* New York: Vintage Books, 1956, pp. 82–85.
6 See E. Digby Baltzell, *Philadelphia Gentlemen.* Glencoe, Illinois: The Free Press, 1958, pp. 230ff.
7 Henry F. May, *Protestant Churches and Industrial America.* New York: Harper & Brothers, 1949.
8 Quoted in Goldman, *op. cit.*, p. 121.
9 See Morton White, *Social Thought in America.* Boston: Beacon Press, 1957.
10 *Ibid.*, p. 39.
11 *Ibid.*, p. 38.
12 See Goldman, *op. cit.*, pp. 116–18.
13 *Ibid.*, p. 118.
14 *Ibid.*, p. 119.
15 Quoted in White, *op. cit.*, p. 115.
16 Quoted in Goldman, *op. cit.*, p. 119.
17 *Ibid.*, p. 120.
18 *Ibid.*, pp. 121–24

[19] For Cooley's life and intellectual background, see *Sociological Theory and Social Research*, introduction and notes by Robert Cooley Angell. New York: Henry Holt, 1930.

[20] C. H. Cooley, "Genius, Fame and the Comparison of Races," *Annals of the American Academy of Political and Social Science*, May 1897, pp. 317–58

[21] *Ibid.*, p. 330.

[22] *Ibid.*

[23] See Robert H. Lowie, *History of Ethnological Theory*. New York: Farrar & Rinehart, 1937; and H. R. Hays, *From Ape to Angel: An Informal History of Social Anthropology*, New York: Alfred A. Knopf, Inc., 1958

[24] Hays, *op. cit.*, p. 57

[25] Quoted in Morton White, *op. cit.*, p. 22.

[26] Hays, *op. cit.*, pp. 119–30.

[27] *Ibid.*, pp. 227ff

[28] Franz Boas, *The Mind of Primitive Man*. New York: The Macmillan Company, 1911, p. 29.

[29] *Ibid.*, p. 272

[30] Quoted in Goldman, *op. cit.*, p. 98.

[31] Quoted in Richard Hofstadter, *Social Darwinism in American Thought, 1860–1915*, Philadelphia: University of Pennsylvania Press, 1945, p. 121

[32] *Ibid.*, p. 143

[33] Oliver Wendell Holmes, Jr., and Frederick Pollack, *Holmes-Pollock Letters: The Correspondence of Mr. Justice Holmes and Sir Frederick Pollock 1874–1932*, edited by Mark DeWolfe Howe. Vol. II, Cambridge, Mass.: Harvard University Press, 1941, p. 8.

[34] *Ibid.*, Vol. II, p. 191.

[35] Quoted in Barbara Miller Solomon, *Ancestors and Immigrants: A Changing New England*. Cambridge, Mass.: Harvard University Press, 1956, p. 185.

[36] White, *op. cit.*, p. 47.

Chapter VIII

[1] Arthur M. Schlesinger, Jr., *The Crisis of the Old Order, 1919–1933*. Boston: Houghton Mifflin Company, 1957, p. 31.

[2] Charles Forcey, *The Crossroads of Liberalism: Croly, Weyl, Lippmann, and the Progressive Era, 1900–1925*. New York: Oxford University Press, 1961.

[3] Arthur S. Link, *Wilson: The Road to the White House*. Princeton: Princeton University Press, 1947, p. 24.

[4] *Ibid.*, p. 32.

Notes

5 Quoted in Henry F. May, *Protestant Churches and Industrial America.* New York: Harper & Brothers, 1949, p. 230.
6 *Ibid.*
7 Alpheus Thomas Mason, *Brandeis: A Free Man's Life.* New York: The Viking Press, 1946, p. 465–66.
8 *Ibid.,* p. 47.
9 *Ibid.,* p. 87.
10 *Ibid.,* p. 687.
11 *Ibid.,* p. 442.
12 *Ibid.,* p. 443.
13 *Ibid.,* p. 470.
14 *Ibid.,* p. 489.
15 *Ibid.,* p. 483
16 *Ibid.,* p. 484.
17 *Ibid.,* p. 481
18 *Ibid.,* p. 664.
19 Francis Biddle, *A Casual Past.* New York: Doubleday & Co., Inc., 1961, p. 219.

Chapter IX

1 John Higham, *Strangers in the Land: Patterns of American Nativism, 1860–1925.* New Brunswick, N.J.: Rutgers University Press, 1955, p. 311.
2 *Ibid.,* p. 309.
3 *Ibid.,* p. 284.
4 Margaret L. Coit, *Mr. Baruch.* Boston: Houghton Mifflin Company, 1957, p. 361.
5 *Ibid.,* p. 362.
6 Adolf A. Berle, Jr., and Gardiner C. Means, *The Modern Corporation and Private Property.* New York: The Macmillan Company, 1932.
7 E. Digby Baltzell, Unpublished Analysis of the Upper Class in San Francisco and Comparison with Philadelphia.
8 See Henry Aaron Yeomans, *Abbott Lawrence Lowell: 1856–1943.* Cambridge, Mass.: Harvard University Press, 1948.
9 Heywood Broun and George Britt, *Christians Only.* New York: Vanguard Press, 1931, p. 74.
10 *Ibid.,* p. 259.
11 *Ibid.,* p. 257.
12 Kenneth Allsop, *The Bootleggers.* London: Hutchinson & Co., 1961, p. 239.
13 *Ibid.,* p. 240.
14 *Ibid.,* p. 236.

[15] *Ibid.*, p. 249.
[16] *Ibid.*, p. 240.
[17] *Ibid.*
[18] F. Scott Fitzgerald, *The Last Tycoon*, together with *The Great Gatsby* and selected stories. New York: Charles Scribner's Sons, 1941, p. 300.
[19] *Ibid.*, p. 180.
[20] *Ibid.*, p. 263
[21] *Ibid.*, p. 281.
[22] Quoted in Broun and Britt, *op. cit.*, p. 276.
[23] H. L. Mencken, *Prejudices: Fourth Series*. New York: Alfred A. Knopf, Inc., 1924, pp. 28–39.
[24] Van Wyck Brooks, *Opinions of Oliver Allston*. New York: E. P. Dutton & Co., Inc., 1949, p. 126.
[25] Edmund Wilson, *The Shores of Light*. New York: Vintage Books, 1961, pp. 498–99

Chapter X

[1] Thomas C. Cochran, *The American Business System: A Historical Perspective, 1900–1955*. Cambridge, Mass.: Harvard University Press, 1957, p. 140
[2] See Arthur M. Schlesinger, Jr., *The Crisis of the Old Order*, Boston: Houghton Mifflin Company, 1957, pp. 76ff.
[3] Samuel Lubell, *The Future of American Politics*. New York: Harper & Brothers, 1951
[4] *Ibid.*, pp. 28–57.
[5] *Ibid.*, pp. 67–69.
[6] *Ibid.*, pp. 78–80.
[7] Ernest Havemann and Patricia Salter West, *They Went to College*. New York: Harcourt, Brace and Company, 1952, pp. 191–95.
[8] See Schlesinger, *op. cit.*, p. 268.
[9] George Wolfskill, *The Revolt of the Conservative: A History of the American Liberty League, 1934–1940*. Boston: Houghton Mifflin Company, 1962, p. 99.
[10] Arthur M. Schlesinger, Jr., *The Politics of Upheaval*. Boston: Houghton Miffin Company, 1960, p. 620.
[11] Quoted in Francis Biddle, *A Casual Past*. New York: Doubleday & Co., Inc., 1961, p. 286.
[12] *Ibid.*, p. 385.
[13] *Ibid.*
[14] Quoted in Arthur M. Schlesinger, Jr., *The Coming of the New Deal*. Boston: Houghton Mifflin Company, 1959, p. 19.
[15] *Ibid.*, pp. 297–301

Notes

16 See *New Yorker*, May 3, 1952, pp. 48–49.
17 For Winant's life, I have used Charles Rumford Walker, "Winant of New Hampshire," *Atlantic Monthly*, April 1941; *Time*, March 9, 1942; and John Gilbert Winant, *Letter from Grosvenor Square*, Boston: Houghton Mifflin Company, 1947.
18 Winant, *Letter from Grosvenor Square*, p. 13.
19 Schlesinger, *Crisis of the Old Order*, p. 397.
20 Schlesinger, *Coming of the New Deal*, p. 21.
21 Quoted in Schlesinger, *The Politics of Upheaval*, p. 325.
22 Quoted in George Wolfskill, *op. cit.*, p. 48.
23 *Ibid.*, p. 152
24 *Ibid.*, p. 158
25 *Ibid.*, p. 102
26 *Ibid.*, pp. 107–108
27 *Ibid.*, p. 83.
28 *Ibid.*, p. 177
29 Schlesinger, *Coming of the New Deal*, p. 568.
30 Quoted in Eric F. Goldman, *Rendezvous with Destiny*. New York: Vintage Books, 1956, p. 289
31 Quoted in George Biddle, *An American Artist's Story*. Boston: Little Brown and Company, 1939, p. 67
32 See cover story, *Time*, June 28, 1937.
33 For an excellent study of the du Pont clan, see John K. Winkler, *The Du Pont Dynasty*. New York: Reynal & Hitchcock, 1935.
34 *Ibid.*, p. 324.
35 Ferdinand Lundberg, *America's 60 Families*. New York: The Vanguard Press, 1937, p. 33.
36 Schlesinger, *Coming of the New Deal*, p. 498.
37 David G. Loth, *Swope of G.E.* New York: Simon and Schuster, 1958.
38 Marquis James, *Biography of a Bank*. New York: Harper & Brothers, 1954, p. 361.
39 *Ibid.*, p. 363.
40 Schlesinger, *Politics of Upheaval*, pp. 620–21.
41 George Wolfskill, *op. cit.*, p. 219.

Chapter XI

1 Edmund Wilson, *The Shores of Light*. New York: Vintage Books, 1952, p. 533.
2 For an excellent analysis of this "Either-or Platonism" of the period, see Arthur M. Schlesinger, Jr., *The Politics of Upheaval*. Boston: Houghton Mifflin Company, 1960, pp. 647–49.
3 Francis Russell, *Tragedy in Dedham*. New York: McGraw-Hill Book Company, Inc., 1962.

[4] *Ibid.*, p. 358.
[5] *Ibid.*, p. 359.
[6] *Ibid.*, p. 306.
[7] *Ibid.*, p. 385.
[8] *Ibid.*
[9] John Dos Passos, "The 42nd Parallel," *U.S.A.* New York: Modern Library, 1937, p. 302.
[10] See Peter Viereck, *Metapolitics: The Roots of the Nazi Mind.* New York: Capricorn Books, 1961.
[11] Edward Alsworth Ross, *Seventy Years of It.* New York: D. Appleton-Century Company, 1936, pp. 277–79.
[12] Frederick Osborn, *Preface to Eugenics.* New York: Harper & Brothers, 1940, pp. 42–43.
[13] Quoted in Schlesinger, *op. cit.*, pp. 648–49.

Chapter XII

[1] See Marguerite Higgins, "Preventive Diplomacy," New York *Herald Tribune*, July 6, 1961.
[2] Eric F. Goldman, *The Crucial Decade—and After: America, 1945–1960.* New York: Vintage Books, 1961, p. 104.
[3] For the McCarthy era, I have used Richard Rovere, *Senator Joe McCarthy.* New York: Meridian Books, Inc., 1960. For an alternate view, see William F. Buckley, Jr., and L. Brent Bozell, *McCarthy and His Enemies.* Chicago: Henry Regnery Company, 1954. The tone of this second view is best expressed in the following line from the "Prologue" by William Schlamm: "He [McCarthy] respects reason so much, in fact, that he clearly overemphasizes its part in the shaping of national policies."
[4] Rovere, *op. cit.*, p. 82.
[5] *Ibid.*, p. 178.
[6] *Ibid.*, p. 23.
[7] S. M. Lipset, "The Sources of the Radical Right," in *The Radical Right*, edited by Daniel Bell. New York: Doubleday & Company, Inc., 1963, pp. 259–312.
[8] Rovere, *op. cit.*, p. 13.
[9] Robert E. Thompson and Hortense Myers, *Robert F. Kennedy: The Brother Within.* New York: Dell Publishing Company, 1962, p. 103.
[10] James MacGregor Burns, *John Kennedy: A Political Profile.* New York: Avon Books, 1960, p. 113.
[11] Daniel J. Boorstin, *The Image, or What Happened to the American Dream.* New York: Atheneum, 1962, p. 58.
[12] Rovere, *op. cit.*, p. 164.

Notes

13 William S. White, *The Taft Story*. New York: Harper & Brothers, 1954.

14 *Ibid.*, p. 85.

15 Quoted in Dean Acheson, *A Democrat Looks at His Party*. New York: Harper & Brothers, 1955, p. 28.

16 White, *op. cit.*, pp. 232–35.

Chapter XIII

1 An interview in *Look*, April 25, 1961.

2 Quoted in Peter Viereck, *Conservatism Revisited*. New York: Collier Books, 1962, p. 156.

3 *Ibid.*

4 Arthur M. Schlesinger, Jr., *The Vital Center: The Politics of Freedom*. Boston: Houghton Mifflin Company, 1949, p. 254.

5 Quoted in Joseph P. McCarthy, *The Remarkable Kennedys*. New York: Popular Library, 1960, p. 68.

6 Quoted in Richard J. Whalen, "Joseph P. Kennedy: A Portrait of the Founder," *Fortune*, January 1963.

7 Lord David Cecil, *Melbourne*. New York: Charter Books, 1962, pp. 17–19.

8 *Time*, November 16, 1962.

9 A useful source for the career of Marietta Tree is Inez Robb, "The Democrats' Golden Girl," *The Saturday Evening Post*, October 22, 1960.

10 *Ibid.*

11 Nathan Glazer and Daniel Patrick Moynihan, *Beyond the Melting Pot*. Cambridge, Mass.: The M.I.T. Press and Harvard University Press, 1963, p. 171.

12 Inez Robb, *op. cit.*

13 *Ibid.*

14 *Ibid.*

15 *Ibid.*

Chapter XIV

1 See John Harmon Burma, "Some Cultural Aspects of Immigration: Its Impact, Especially on Our Arts and Sciences," *Law and Contemporary Problems*, Duke University, Vol. XXI, No. 2, Spring, 1956.

2 Figures cited in an editorial "Our Pool of Scientists," *Philadelphia Evening Bulletin*, December 23, 1962.

3 Thomas C. Cochran, *The American Business System*. Cambridge, Mass.: Harvard University Press, 1957, p. 184.

[4] Adolf A. Berle, Jr., *The 20th Century Capitalist Revolution*. New York: Harcourt, Brace and Company, 1954, pp. 182–83.
[5] W. Lloyd Warner and James C. Abegglen, *Big Business Leaders in America*. New York: Harper and Brothers, 1955.
[6] Unpublished manuscript.
[7] Ralph Lord Roy, *Apostles of Discord*. Boston: Beacon Press, 1953, p. 66.
[8] Fritz Thyssen, *I Paid Hitler*. New York: Farrar & Rinehart, Inc., 1941, pp. 100–101.
[9] *Ibid.*, p. 208.
[10] *Philadelphia Evening Bulletin*, January 11, 1961.
[11] E. J. Kahn, Jr., *The Big Drink*. New York: Random House, 1960, p. 153.

Chapter XV

[1] *Look*, April 25, 1961.
[2] Heywood Broun and George Britt, *Christians Only*. New York: The Vanguard Press, 1931.
[3] W. Lloyd Warner and James C. Abegglen, *Big Business Leaders in America*. New York: Harper & Brothers, 1955, p. 51.
[4] Lawrence Bloomgarden, "Our Changing Elite Colleges," *Commentary*, February 1960.
[5] *The Exonian*, February 22, 1961.
[6] *The Boston Sunday Herald*, February 26, 1961
[7] *Ibid.*, p. 37.
[8] *Alumni Horae*, Autumn 1960.
[9] Paul M. Sweezy, *Power Elite or Ruling Class?* New York: Monthly Review Pamphlet Series, No. 13, p. 29.
[10] *Newsweek*, Vol. LVII, No. 13, March 27, 1961.

Chapter XVI

[1] For an excellent analysis of clubs which I have followed below, see Robert H. Boyle, "Country Clubs," *Sports Illustrated*, February 26 and March 5, 1962.
[2] Theodore H. White, *The Making of the President, 1960*. New York: Atheneum Press, 1962, p. 240.
[3] Benjamin R. Epstein and Arnold Forster, *"Some of My Best Friends . . ."* New York: Farrar, Straus and Cudahy, 1962, p. 2.
[4] *Ibid.*, p. 3.
[5] *Ibid.*, p. 4.
[6] Osborn Elliott, *Men at the Top*. New York: Harper & Brothers, 1959, p. 164.

Notes

7 *Ibid.*
8 *Ibid.*
9 *Ibid.*, p. 171.
10 *Ibid.*
11 *Ibid.*, pp. 166–67.
12 Cleveland Amory, *Who Killed Society?* New York: Harper & Brothers, 1960, p. 227
13 *Ibid.*, p. 226.
14 *Ibid.*
15 *Ibid.*, p. 227.
16 *Ibid.*
17 *Ibid.*, p. 215.
18 See *Chronicle of the Union League of Philadelphia, 1862–1902*, Philadelphia: Wm. F. Fell & Co., 1902; and *Handbook of the Union League of Philadelphia, 1862–1931*, Philadelphia: Wm. F. Fell & Co., 1931.
19 *Chronicle*, p. 37.
20 *Ibid.*, p. 58.
21 *Ibid.*, p. 44.
22 *Handbook of the Union League of Philadelphia*, p. 57.
23 *Philadelphia Evening Bulletin*, January 23, 1962.
24 *Chronicle*, p. 187.

Conclusion

1 James Baldwin, *Nobody Knows My Name.* New York: Delta Books, 1962, p. 129.
2 *Ibid.*, p. 128.
3 Stanley M. Elkins, *Slavery.* Chicago: University of Chicago Press, 1959.

403

Index

Index

Cassatt, Mary, 12
Caste, alienated patrician and, 37–45; anti-Semitism and, 32–34; aristocratic counterattack on, 143–56; campus and, 209–12; closed upper class and, 8; club and, 213–14; conspiracy, McCarthyism and, 282–87; corporate economy and, 206–09; corporation and, 315–34; country club and, 355–62; criminal culture and, 214–18; decline of authority and, 16–21; establishment, see WASP establishment; ideological defense of, 87–108; ideology of, Roosevelt and, 241–52; intellectual counterattack on, 157–78; new immigration and, 21–24; social defense of, 109–42; suburban trend and, 212–14; tendency to, 76–80; theory of the establishment and, 7–10; xenophobia and, 324–25
Cecil, Lord David, 303
Celebrity Register, 288
Census Bureau, U.S., 110
Century Club, New York City, 369, 370, 371, 372–73
Chamberlain, Houston Stewart, 104
Chambers, Whittaker, 282, 283, 286 n.
Chapman, John Jay, 93–96, 120, 145, 148
Chase, Stewart, 13

Chauchoin, Claudette (Claudette Colbert), 47
Chestnut Hill Academy, 124
Cheston, Charles, 36
Chevy Chase Club, Washington, D.C., 86
Chicago School of Sociology, 169
Chilton, Senator, 194
Choate, Joseph H., 192
Choate, William G., 128
Choate School, 81, 128, 272
Christian Anti-Communist Crusade, 326
Christianity and the Social Crisis (Rauschenbasch), 161
Christian Nationalist Crusade, 326
Christian Socialists, 159, 160
Christian Social Union (CSU), 161
Christian Union, 101
Church Association for the Advancement of the Interests of Labor (CAIL), 161
Churchill, Winston S., 62, 240, 293, 309
Civil rights issue, 278–81, 382–86
Civil War, 6, 109–10
Clark, Joseph Sill, 308 n.
Clark University, 171
Class structure, Jewish melting pot and, 53–62
Class system, open, 75
Cleveland, Grover, 181, 186, 201

Counterattack on caste, aristo-
cratic, 143–56; intellectual,
157–78
Country clubs, 27, 62, 123–24,
213–14, 355–62; see also un-
der name of individual club
Country day schools, 122, 124–
25
Courting mores, upper-class,
campus meritocracy and,
349–52
Court-packing plan (1937), 195
Cowley, Malcolm, 13
Coxey, General, 15
Coxey's Army, 114
Creel, George, 255
Crest View Country Club,
Springfield, Mass., 357
Crime, organized, 49, 51
Criminal culture, caste and,
214–18
Criminology, 169
Crisis in Our Immigration
Policy (Ward), 147
Crocetti, Dino (Dean Martin),
47
Crocker, W. H., 256, 257
Croly, Herbert, 182, 183
Cultural relativity, 174
Culture, concept of, New Social
Science and, 164–74
Cummings, E. E., 13
Cummings, Homer, 180
Curley, James M., 79
Cushing, William E., 188
Cutler, Robert, 80
Cutting, Bronson, 237

Danielovitch, Issur (Kirk Doug-
las), 47
Da Re, Aldo (Aldo Ray), 47
Darrow, Clarence, 175
Darwin, Charles, 98, 99, 174
Daughters of the American
Revolution, 114, 115, 237
Daughters of the Cincinnati,
114
Davie, Maurice, 316, 317
Davies, Joseph E., 180
Davies, Wallace Evan, 114
Dearborn (Mich.) Independ-
ent, 95, 205
Debs, Eugene, 15
Declaration of Independence, 7,
25
Deerfield Academy, 128, 347
De Haas, Jacob, 191
Democratic establishment, aris-
tocracy and, 306–13
Democratic Party, xiv, 6, 22, 49,
52, 81, 167, 181, 194–95, 200,
205, 227, 230, 231, 235, 261,
295, 296–301, 309, 310, 313,
316, 317, 329, 331, 366, 373,
379, 384
Democracy, open elite and, 7
Democracy (Adams), 91
Depression, the Great, xiv,
229–30
De Sapio, Carmine, 21
Dewey, Davis R., 108
Dewey, John, 100, 162, 163,
166–67, 181, 196, 264, 267,
268, 269, 273, 297, 298

Index

Morgenthau, Mrs. Henry, Jr., 37, 237
Morison, Elting, 151 n.
Morison, Samuel Eliot, 13, 132–33
Morris, Lloyd, 51
Morris, Newbold, 29
Morristown School, 124
Moynihan, Daniel Patrick, 310
Mullenger, Donna (Donna Reed), 47
Münsterberg, Hugo, 152
Murchie, Guy, 196
Murray, Gilbert, 171
Morrow, Edward R., 311
Mussolini, Benito, 233
Myth of the Twentieth Century (Rosenberg), 274, 328

Nahant, Massachusetts, 123
Nation, 199, 263
National Association for the Advancement of Colored People, 185, 231, 237, 278
National Industrial Recovery Act, 243
National Institute of Social Science, 162
Nationalist magazine, 269
National Science Foundation, 317
Native American Party, 25, 143
Nativism, 111–12, 203, 204
Nazism, 240, 274
Negroes, elite and marginal, 64; in New York City, xi; problems of, xii, 34, 383–87;

Roosevelt and, 231; test scores and, 169; Wilson and, 185
New Deal, the, 22, 52, 178, 180, 195, 229, 231, 235, 237, 238, 242, 243, 252, 253, 254, 260, 262, 265, 266, 271, 283, 290, 298, 300, 312
New England boarding school, the, 127–29
New Freedom, the, 178, 179–96
New Frontier, the, xiv, xvi, 83, 180, 300, 301, 303–05, 314, 383
New Liberalism, the, 181–82, 183, 196
New Nationalism, the, 179, 180, 182
New Republic, 39, 40, 42–43, 181–83, 193, 195, 199, 218, 262, 263, 264, 267
New Social Science movement, 15, 158, 161–63, 174–75, 177, 178, 181, 184, 185; concept of culture and, 164–74; liberal orthodoxy and, 267–76
New York Amsterdam News, 368 n.
New York Bar Association, 166
New York City, xi, 64, 138
New Yorker magazine, 82, 246
New York Herald Tribune, 296
New York Press, 192
New York Sun, 192
New York Times, The, 110, 192, 289
New York World, 30, 192

Index

Schizophrenia, business community and, 252–58; in the establishment, 232–35; Sacco-Vanzetti case and, 262–67

Schlesinger, Arthur M., Jr., 156, 278, 298–99, 311, 339, 372

School and Society, The (Dewey), 163

Schwab, Charles M., 137

Schwartz, Bernie (Tony Curtis), 47

Schwarz, Frederick C., 326

Scotch-Irish Society, 115

Sears, Roebuck & Company, 321

Security and Exchange Act, 242

Sekulovich, Mladen (Karl Malden), 47

Seligman, Henry, 121

Seligman, Joseph, 56, 119, 138

Senate of the United States, 110

Settlement House movement, 159–60, 180

Sevareid, Eric, 311

Seventy Years of It (Ross), 275

Shakespeare, William, quoted, 87

Shaw, George Bernard, 223, 273

Sherman Act, 180

Sherwood, Robert E., 217, 219

Showalter, Max (Casey Adams), 47

Shriver, Sargent, 302

"Significance of the Frontier in American History" (Turner), 163

Sill, Father, 128

Sinclair, Upton, 15

Skikne, Larry (Lawrence Harvey), 47

Sloan, Alfred P., Jr., 254, 255

Slosson, Edwin E., 131, 132

Smart Set magazine, 222, 223

Smith, Adam, 214

Smith, Alfred E., 21, 50, 51, 68, 230–31, 236, 238, 245–46, 262, 290

Smith, Gerald L. K., 326

Smith, Richard Mayo, 108

Social Darwinism, 104, 105, 158, 162, 168, 174, 175, 176, 177, 246; social science and, 98–104

Social defense of caste, 109–42

Social Gospel movement, 159–61, 162, 180, 184–85, 218

Socialism, 4, 180, 246, 262, 268, 271, 276

Socialist Party, 261

Social Organization (Cooley), 163

Social organizations, 70

Social power, 70; legitimation of, 70–72

Social Register, 113, 116, 251, 369, 372

Social sciences, Social Darwinism and, 98–104; value implications of, 174–78; *see also* New Social Science

Social Security program, 239–40

Social status, 70

Society for Italian Immigration, 147

425

CHINA

HaGiang

Lao Cai

CaoBang

Red R.

TuyenQuang

ThaiNguyen

Lang Son

Black R.

SonLa

VinhYen

NaSan

SonTay

Hanoi

1

MocChau

Hoa Binh

6

Haiphong

HungYen

Phu Ly

NamDinh

ThaiBinh

amneua

NinhBinh

BuiChu

PhatDiem

WITHDRAWN FROM STOCK

Thanh Hoa

1

S

VIET

NAM

GULF

Vinh

OF

Nape

HaTinh

12

8

TONKIN

Mu Gia Pass

NaPhao

DongHoi

Thakkek

Mahaxay

D

17°

17°

DongHa

Quang Tri

9

Tchepone

9

Savannaket

Muong Phalane

MuongPhine